LEGAL PATH SERIES®

TORTS

Keyed To

Prosser, Wade and Schwartz's Torts

By Schwartz, Kelly & Partlett
11th Edition

ALSO AVAILABLE IN THIS SERIES:

Civil Procedure keyed to: Friedenthal, 9th Ed
Contracts keyed to: Farnsworth, 6th Ed
Contracts keyed to: Fuller, 7th Ed
Criminal Law keyed to: Johnson, 7th Ed
Criminal Law keyed to: Kadish, 7th Ed
Criminal Law keyed to: Dressler, 3rd Ed
Criminal Procedure keyed to: Kamisar, 11th Ed
Constitutional Law keyed to: Stone, 5th Ed
Constitutional Law keyed to: Sullivan, 15th Ed
Corporations keyed to: Hamilton, 8th Ed
Evidence keyed to: Waltz & Park, 10th Ed
Property keyed to: Dukeminier, 5th Ed
Torts keyed to Epstein, 8th Ed
Torts keyed to Prosser, 11th Ed
Legal Path MBE Bar Review

LEGAL PATH SERIES®

TORTS
First Edition

Jeffrey Bivins, Esq.
Cornell University Law School

Mclaren Legal Publishers LLC
New York

ISBN 0-9768716-4-5
Library of Congress Control Number: 2005933485

Published by
Mclaren Legal Publishers LLC
136 West 21 Street, 8th Floor
New York, NY 10011

www.mclarenpublishing.com
Email: contact@mclarenpublishing.com

Printed in the United States of America

HOW TO USE THIS BOOK

This law school study aid is a "keyed" book. It summarizes all of the major cases in the text book to which it is linked and in the order those cases are printed. Our cases are presented in the IRAC format (Issue, Rule, Analysis and Conclusion). Each case uses a text symbol preceding the Issue, Rule, Analysis and Conclusion of the case referenced. The sentences that follow provide additional factual detail.

"Repetition is the Mother of Learning"

Throughout each case, many of the key Black Letter law and/or Issues are repeated. You may see the same legal conclusion repeated in the Issue, Rule, Analysis and/or Conclusion. This was done intentionally. All too often, the most important concepts in law school are mentioned only once by a law professor in a lecture hall. However, more often than not, what is mentioned the least is what is tested the most. We feel the more you see (and read) exactly what is important, the more likely you will be to remember it. Recalling key legal points quickly is the key to the successful application of those same rules on an exam. This *is* the difference between an "A" and a "C" for the course.

"All of what you need, none of what you don't"

Our law school study guides give you exactly what you need to understand the key principles of the case, including the sometimes elusive Black Letter law. We are not a replacement for an in depth legal analysis of the subject matter covered; however, we do present what is absolutely critical in a very concise format.

"Do it right in the beginning; it'll be easier in the end"

You may notice that the issues for each case are very specific. They are presented to you as accurately as we can print them. However, be mindful that there may be slight variations in their interpretation from lecture hall to lecture hall. With that in mind, our experience has taught us that if you do the labor-intensive, hard work in the beginning of the course and parse out the specific issue(s), rule(s) and conclusion, the analysis will be easier to formulate and write. It is the analysis of a case that separates the A, B and C grades on an exam (trust me).

"Who's the Plaintiff, who's the Defendant?"

You may notice that in some cases, a case title lists the plaintiff v. defendant in one order but the facts list the parties in the opposite order or may refer to the plaintiff/defendant as the petitioner/respondent/appellant/appellee. This is usually seen, for example, when the one party is appealing to a higher court or where various counterclaims and cross-claims are asserted by the parties. When you see the parties change in the facts, keep the procedural history (and the parties) of the case organized in your mind and don't get confused.

Abbreviations used in this book

I   This symbol "I" stands for "Issue" using the IRAC method of case analysis. What follows is the issue of the case.

R   This symbol "R" stands for "Rule" using the IRAC method of case analysis. What follows is the rule or black letter law of the case.

A   This symbol "A" stands for "Analysis" using the IRAC method of case analysis. What follows is the Analysis of the case.

C   This symbol "C" stands for "Conclusion" using the IRAC method of case analysis. What follows is the conclusion of the case.

* Use of the word "his" in this book is gender neutral and is meant to encompass both "his" and "her."

ALPHABETICAL TABLE OF CASES

Anonymous

King's Bench, 1466, Y.B. 5 Edw. IV, folio 7, placitum 18

FACTS

None given.

Is a person liable for the direct results of his actions even if they where performed with the best of intentions and were not unlawful yet still caused injury?

Every man has a duty to perform an act, if he does so at all, such that it does not cause injury or damage to another person or thing.

Every man has a duty to perform an act such that it does not cause injury or damage to another. Similarly, a person is liable for the direct results of his actions even if they where performed with the best of intentions.

Every man has a duty to perform an act such that it does not cause injury or damage to another.

Weaver v. Ward

King's bench, 1616, Hobert 134, 80 Eng.Rep. 284

FACTS

Plaintiff Weaver brought a trespass action against stemming from an accident while the two were engaged in performing military musket practice; Ward's musket accidentally discharged, wounding Weaver. The defendant argued that he could not be held liable because he did not act intentionally and because his musket discharged involuntarily, against his will. Weaver nevertheless claimed that he was entitled to damages because he had a right not to be harmed, despite the fact that he conceded that the act was unintentional.

Can the defendant be held liable for the plaintiff's injury when the harm caused resulted from an unintentional act by the former?

The absence of fault bars liability for trespass.

While the unfortunate harm occurred accidentally and against the defendant's will, the defendant's act did in fact cause the injury suffered by the plaintiff; the direct cause (the defendant's act) did not appear to have been unavoidable. Hence, the court noted that the defendant would be excused from liability only if he were entirely without fault; if the accident was unavoidable; and if he were not negligent. This was not the case here.

The absence of fault bars liability for trespass.

Brown v. Kendall

Supreme Judicial Court of Massachusetts, 1850, 60 Mass. (6 Cush.) 282

FACTS

Defendant Kendall was trying to separate two dogs from fighting, one of which was his own. As he struck the dogs with a stick, he retreated backwards and upon raising the stick to strike once more, accidentally struck the plaintiff, George Brown, who was standing immediately behind him at the time, in the eye causing a severe injury. Subsequently, the plaintiff brought an action of *trespass vi et armis* (a writ for direct harms). The judge refused to instruct the jury, as requested by the defendant, that if 1) both the plaintiff and the defendant were not using ordinary care at the time, or 2) both were using ordinary care, or 3) the defendant was using ordinary care but the plaintiff was not; then the plaintiff could not recover. The court did instruct the jury that if it was not necessary to act, and the defendant was not duty-bound to separate the dogs, then the defendant was responsible for the injury, unless it appeared he was exercising extraordinary care such that the accident was inevitable. Defendant appealed.

Were the jury instructions proper?

The plaintiff holds the burden of proof and must establish that the defendant did not use ordinary care in a suit accusing the defendant of acting unlawfully.

We think as the result of all the authorities, that the rule, as correctly stated, is that the plaintiff must come prepared with evidence to show either that the *intention* was unlawful, or that the defendant was *at fault* (failed to use ordinary care). However, if the injury was unavoidable and the defendant was blameless based on his conduct, then the defendant will not be held liable.

New trial ordered.

Cohen v Petty

Court of Appeals of D.C., 65 F.2d 820 (1933)

FACTS

Plaintiff-appellant Cohen was a passenger in Defendant Petty's car. Four other passengers in the car, including the defendant's wife, indicated that Petty lost consciousness while driving his car and collided with an embankment. The defendant was heard to have said that he "felt sick" to his wife shortly before the accident. Petty claimed that he had no history of losing consciousness, had never fainted before and that as far as he knew, he was in good health. The trial court found in favor of the defendant, stating that e where the act leading to the injury was involuntary and outside of the defendant's control, there can be no negligence. Cohen appealed.

Can a party be held negligently liable for an injury caused by an unforeseeable and involuntary act(s)?

A party can not be held liable under a negligence theory for an injury caused by his unforeseeable and involuntary acts.

A party can not be held liable under a negligence theory for an injury caused by his unforeseeable and involuntary acts. The record clearly shows that defendant lost consciousness right before the collision which gave rise to injury at hand. The record shows that Petty had no history of fainting and had no reason to anticipate it. Thus, under these circumstances, defendant is not chargeable with negligence and the trial court was correct for taking the case from the jury.

Reversed.

Spano v. Perini Corp.
Court of Appeals of New York, 250 N.E.2d 31 (1969)

FACTS

Plaintiff Spano owned a garage in Brooklyn, New York, which was destroyed in a blast when Defendant Perini Corp. (Perini) and another defendant who were engaged in the construction of a tunnel nearby pursuant to a contract with the City of New York. A car owned by Plaintiff Davis, which was in Spano's garage for repairs, was also damaged. Each of the plaintiffs brought suit against the two defendants, as joint venturers. Defendants set off a total of 194 sticks of dynamite at the construction site, which was only 125 feet away from Spano's garage. Spano sued Perini and others, alleging both negligence and strict liability. The two cases were tried together, without a jury, in the Civil Court of the City of New York and judgments were rendered in favor of the plaintiffs. Defendants asked the trial court to dismiss Spano's case because he had failed to prove negligence. The trial court refused and awarded damages of some $4,000 to Spano and $329 to Davis. Both judgments were reversed by the Appellate Term and the Appellate Division affirmed that order, granting leave to appeal to the Court of Appeals (New York's highest state court).

Can a person who sustained property damage caused by the blasting on nearby property maintain an action for damages without showing the blaster was negligent; or stated another way: can a party be held strictly liable for damage to a nearby property when he engages in blasting activities?

A defendant who is engaging in blasting activity is strictly liable for any damage caused to neighboring property.

A showing of negligence is not a prerequisite to recovery when the defendant engaged in blasting activities and that activity damaged some surrounding property. The court's earlier reasoning in *Booth v. Rome* is rejected as its rational has been overwhelmingly rejected in other jurisdictions and fundamentally inconsistent with earlier cases in our own court. A defendant will be held strictly liable for the blasting activity which causes damage to another's property because he does not have the right to interfere with the property owner's use, possession and enjoyment of his (the other property owner's) property, although the defendant still retains the right to engage in the blasting activity itself. However, the right to engage in blasting brings with it the responsibility to bear the cost of any damage resulting from the activity. Moreover, were we to apply the liberal interpretation of *Booth*, thus requiring a plaintiff to prove negligence and not hold the defendant strictly liable, it would be possible for a defendant engaging in blasting to avoid liability by showing that the exercised reasonable care. Since blasting involves a substantial risk, regardless of the degree of care exercised, we see no reason why those engaging in the activity not be held responsible for the damage caused by the blasting.

Reversed.

Garratt v. Dailey

Supreme Court of Washington, 279 P.2d 1091 (1955)

FACTS

Naomi Garratt and Defendant Brian Dailey were in the backyard of the plaintiff, Ruth Garratt. While there, Dailey pulled a chair from underneath the plaintiff before she could sit down on it. As a result, Garratt fell to the ground and suffered a fractured hip and other injuries. Ruth Garratt instituted an action in battery. The trial court dismissed plaintiff's action, indicating that she failed to prove that Dailey had moved the chair for the purpose of bringing about plaintiff's fall to the ground; that he did not have any willful or unlawful purpose for doing so and did not have any intent to harm the plaintiff. Plaintiff Ruth Garratt appealed.

 Can a party be held liable for battery when he is substantially certain that his act will result in a harmful or offensive touching but may not have intended an injury to occur?

 A party is liable for battery when he is substantially certain that his act will result in harmful or offensive touching.

 A party is liable for battery when he is substantially certain that his act will result in harmful or offensive touching. To maintain an action in battery, the defendant must have committed the act intentionally and must know or realize with substantial certainty that his act will bring about a harmful touching or injurious contact. Here, battery would be established if the defendant knew to a substantial certainty that the plaintiff would sit where the chair had been he is liable; the absence of intent to injure the plaintiff does not release the defendant from liability. Thus, the trial court must determine whether or not the defendant possessed such intent coupled with the requisite knowledge that his conduct was substantially sure to lead to the undesired result.

 Remanded for clarification.

Spivey v. Battaglia
Supreme Court of Florida, 258 So.2d 815 (1972)

FACTS

Plaintiff-petitioner Spivey and Defendant-respondent were employees of the Battaglia Fruit Company. While in the lunch room at work, Defendant teasingly put his arms around Plaintiff Spivey in a "friendly unsolicited hug." Immediately after this, Spivey suffered a sharp pain in the back of her neck and ear and into the base of her skull. As a result, petitioner became paralyzed on the left side of her face. She sued the defendant in an action for negligence, and assault and battery. However, the trial court threw out her action for assault and battery on the ground that it was barred by the two-year statute of limitations. The trial court, in a summary judgment motion, dismissed Spivey's action in negligence. The district court affirmed. Spivey appealed the order and brought an action in negligence.

 Can a party who acts with knowledge and substantial certainty that a particular result will follow be held liable for all the consequences flowing from his act regardless of whether or not such consequences are foreseeable or reasonable?

 A party who acts with knowledge and substantial certainty that a particular result will follow is liable for all results flowing from his act even though such consequences may not be foreseeable or reasonable.

 A party who acts with knowledge and substantial certainty that a particular result will follow is liable for all results flowing from his act even though such consequences may not be foreseeable or reasonable. However, knowledge and appreciation of a risk, short of substantial certainty, is not the equivalent of intent. The distinction between the two is one of degree. If one does not fully appreciate the risk, his act qualifies as negligence - but a person who acts with the requisite intent to bring about an act or a consequence, and acts with knowledge and substantial certainty that a particular result will follow, is liable for all consequences of the act, foreseeable or not. Therefore, a person who acts with a lesser degree of intent is liable only for those harms that are reasonably foreseeable. Given all of the above, the distinction between the unsolicited kiss in *McDonald v. Ford* [the district court affirmed on the authority of *McDonald*] and the unsolicited hug in the present case turns on the question of intent and the existence of negligence in each case depends on the circumstances surrounding the case. The trial judge in this case committed an error when he granted summary judgment in favor of the defendant without submitting the case to the jury with appropriate instructions regarding elements of negligence.

 Reversed and Remanded

Ranson v. Kitner

Appellate Court of Illinois, 31 Ill.App. 241 (1889)

FACTS

While hunting for wolves, Defendant-appellant Kitner shot and killed Plaintiff-appellee Ranson's dog under the good faith but mistaken belief that it was a wolf. The trial court returned a verdict in favor of Ranson for $50, the assessed value of his dog. Kitner appeals on the ground that the trial court made an error by not considering his good faith mistake as a defense.

Is good faith mistake a valid defense to an intentional tort when the defendant intended the result of his act?

A good faith mistake is not a valid defense to an intentional tort when the defendant intended the result of his act.

A good faith mistake is not a valid defense to an intentional tort when the defendant intended the result of his act. Thus, the defendant is liable for the plaintiff's damage in spite of the fact that his mistake honest and made in good faith.

A good faith mistake is not a valid defense to an intentional tort when the defendant intended the result of his act.

McGuire v. Almy
Supreme Judicial Court of Massachusetts, 8 N.E.2d 760 (1937)

FACTS

Plaintiff McGuire, a registered nurse, was hired to care for Defendant Almy, who was insane. The plaintiff was on "twenty-four hour duty," slept in the room adjacent to the defendant's, and kept the defendant locked in her bedroom whenever the two were not together. Over the first year or so, the defendant had acted violently on several occasions by breaking dishes and had to be subdued by more than one person on at least two occasions. During one incident, while the defendant was locked alone in her room, the plaintiff heard the crashing of furniture. When she approached the room to investigate, the defendant announced that she would kill anyone who attempted to enter. The defendant was standing near the door with a leg from a low-boy (a piece of furniture), threatening to strike. The defendant's brother-in-law was called and after he arrived, the plaintiff entered the room and attempted to subdue the defendant and remove the broken leg from her hand for her own safety. The attempt was unsuccessful and the plaintiff was subsequently struck on the head by the defendant. The plaintiff sued the defendant for assault and battery. The defendant moved for a directed verdict on an insanity defense, which was denied. Judgment was entered for the plaintiff on the jury's verdict. This appeal followed.

Can an insane person be found liable for the tort of assault and battery?

When an insane person acts intentionally to harm another, she is generally liable for her negligence and intentional torts the same as would a sane person under the same circumstances.

Generally, an insane person is liable for her negligence and intentional torts the same as would a sane person under the same circumstances. Sound public policy requires equal treatment of both groups (the insane and those with normal mental functionality). The rule imposing liability tends to make those watching over an insane person more watchful; tends to place the appropriate burden on the insane person, who must bear the financial liability of her actions just as she bears the financial burden to pay for her care; and tends to avoid the need for a judicial determination of mental capacity in a civil case. Consequently, when an insane person acts intentionally to hurt another or the property of another, she is liable for that damage if she was 1) capable of forming the intent to commit the act; and 2) in fact formed the intent as a defendant of normal mental capacity would have. In the instant case, there was sufficient evidence to permit the jury to conclude that the defendant was capable of entertaining the intent to strike, which she in fact did. Thus, an insane person can be found liable for the tort of assault and battery.

Judgment for the plaintiff.

Talmage v. Smith

Supreme Court of Michigan, 59 N.W. 656 (1894)

FACTS

Six to eight children were playing on one of Defendant Smith's sheds located on his property. After ordering the boys to get down, they left the premises. Plaintiff George Talmage and another boy remained on another shed. Smith ordered the two down but before they succeeded in doing so, Smith threw a stick in the direction of one of the boys. The stick, however, hit the other boy, the plaintiff, in the eye causing him to lose his sight in that eye. In an action for battery and assault, the trial court decided in favor of the plaintiff. Smith appeals on the ground that he did not see Talmage and did not intend to hit him or scare him away. Instead, he argues, was attempting to scare away the other (non-injured) boy.

Can a party be held liable to a 3rd party for an act intended or consequence against a 2nd party but which in fact causes harm to the former (3rd party)?

A party who intends an act or consequence against one but and instead injures a 3rd party will be held liable to the latter for the injuries suffered by him.

A party who intends an act or consequence against one but and instead injures a 3rd party will be held liable to the latter for the injuries suffered by him. Plaintiff's right of recovery depends upon the defendant's intention [to hit somebody], and consequence that follows that intention [injury upon another]. Smith will still be held liable even though he injured someone other than the intended victim. Thus, his liability is predicated on whether he threw the stick with unreasonable force with the intent of hitting one boy, but instead hit another. However, if the defendant threw the stick with the intent to merely frighten the boys, he will not be held liable for the defendant's injury. Similarly, if the throwing of the stick was reasonable under the circumstances, then the plaintiff will be barred from recovering for his injury. Here, the jury reasonably concluded that plaintiff intended to inflict an unjustifiable injury upon one of the boys. Hence, he is liable regardless of whether the boy injured was in fact the intended victim.

Affirmed.

FACTS

No facts given.

Is the intentional touching of another in anger considered battery?

Intentional touching of another in anger is considered battery.

Intentional touching of another in anger is considered battery. If there is no violence or intent to cause harm to another but one touches another person, there is no battery. However, when one uses violence against another, and forces his way in a rude and unwarranted manner, then there is battery.

Intentional touching of another in anger is considered battery.

Wallace v. Rosen

Court of Appeals of Indiana, 765 N.E.2d 192 (2002)

FACTS

Defendant Rosen was a High School teacher at Northwest High School in Indianapolis, Indiana. On April 22, 1994, during a school-wide fire drill, Plaintiff Wallace, who was recovering from foot surgery, was at the school delivering homework to her daughter, Lalaya. Wallace was at the top of a stairway talking with two or three others when the students were led to their designated stairway to exit the school during the drill. Apparently, Rosen claims to have told the group to "move it" but Wallace did not move when told to apparently not hearing Rosen over the noise of the alarm and the other students. At trial, Wallace testified that Rosen pushed her down the stairs. Rosen denied doing so but admitted touching her back. AT the close of trial, the judge refused to give the jury an instruction covering civil battery. The jury found in favor of Rosen and Wallace appealed.

Did the judge's refusal to give the jury instructions on civil battery constitute error? That is, can a person be held liable for a causal touch, which is customary and/or reasonable, without an intent to cause harm?

For battery to be an appropriate instruction, the evidence had to support an inference not only that the defendant intentionally touched the plaintiff, but that she did so in a rude, insolent or angry manner.

Plaintiff first argues that battery is defined as the knowing or intentional touching of another in a rude, insolent or angry manner such that any contact, however slight, may constitute an assault and battery which may be recklessly committed. And while the intent to which tort liability is concerned is not necessarily a hostile intent or a desire to do harm, a certain amount of person contact is inevitable and must be accepted. Absent an expression to the contrary, consent is assumed to all those ordinary contact which are customarily and reasonably necessary to the common every day interaction in life, such as a tap on the shoulder to attract attention or a friendly grasp of the arm. Thus, in the present case, for battery to be an appropriate instruction, the evidence had to support an inference not only that the defendant intentionally touched the plaintiff, but that she did so in a rude, insolent or angry manner. Here, individuals standing in the middle of a stairwell during a fire drill could expect that a certain amount of person contact would be inevitable. Rosen had a responsibility to her students to keep them moving in an orderly fashion down the stairs and out the door. Rosen's touching of Wallace on her shoulder to get her attention cannot be said to be rude or insolent. Wallace has failed to show that the trial court abused its discretion in refusing the battery instruction.

Affirmed.

Fisher v. Carrousel Motor Hotel Inc.

Supreme Court of Texas, 424 S.W.2d 627 (1967)

FACTS

Plaintiff-appellant Fisher, a mathematician employed by NASA, was attending a professional conference at Defendant-appellee Carrousel Motor Hotel. While in line at the buffet of the hotel, he was approached by an employee of Carrousel who snatched the plate from his hand, and shouted that a "Negro could not be served in the club." The employee did not actually make physical contact with Fisher's person and he was in no apprehension of physical injury, but was very embarrassed and offended in front of his associates. At trial, the jury returned a verdict in favor of the plaintiff but the trial judge set aside the jury verdict and decided in favor of Defendant Carrousel. The Court of Appeals affirmed. Fisher appealed.

 Does the seizing or hitting of an object held by or attached to an individual constitute battery even though there was no actual physical contact with the individual's person?

 The seizing or hitting of an object held by or attached to an individual constitutes battery even though there was no actual physical contact with the individual's person.

 The seizing or hitting of an object held by or attached to an individual constitutes battery even though there was no actual physical contact with the individual's person. Here, the intentional grabbing of the plaintiff's plate constitutes battery. It is not necessary that there be contact with the person's body or actual harm to the person. Intentional and offensive touching of anything that is so closely connected to the body of a person is to be customarily viewed as part of that person – a cane, his clothing or anything grasped by the hand which is so intimately connected to the body as to be universally regarded as part of the person. We additionally note that damages for mental suffering are recoverable without a showing of actual physical harm in a case of willful battery.

 Reversed.

I. de S. et ux v. W. de S.
At the Assizes, 1348

FACTS

The defendant W. de S., seeking to purchase wine from the plaintiff's tavern, struck the door with a hatchet. When the Plaintiff I. de S.'s wife stuck her head out the window and ordered him to stop, the defendant swung the hatchet at her, but did not touch her. The plaintiff and his wife sued the defendant for "trespass," a.k.a. assault. The inquest determined that no assault had occurred because there was no damage suffered by the wife.

Where no physical damages are proven, can an action for assault be maintained?

A plaintiff may recover damages for assault even though no physical injuries are shown.

Even though the defendant caused no physical injury to the plaintiff's wife, his actions constitute an assault based on her reasonable apprehension of physical harm. Thus, where no physical damages are proven, an action for assault can still be maintained.

Where no physical damages are proven, an action for assault can still be maintained.

Western Union Telegraph Co. v. Hill

Court of Appeals of Alabama, 150 So. 709 (1933)

FACTS

Plaintiff J. B. Hill went to a Western Union store owned and operated by Defendant Western Union Telegraph Co., in order to have her clock fixed. A Western Union employee, one Sapp, who was behind a desk or counter, made improper advances towards her and told her that he "would fix her clock" if she would come and allow him to pet her and love her. Then, the employee reached over the counter and attempted to touch her. His attempts were unsuccessful because the counter was almost as high as the defendant's shoulders. Thereafter, Hill brought a suit against Western Union for assault and the trial court returned a verdict in her favor. Western Union appeals on the ground that Sapp did not have the present ability to touch Hill from his position.

 Can an action for assault be sustained if the defendant did not have the actual, present ability to cause a harmful or offensive touching?

 An action for assault can be sustained even if the defendant did not have the actual, present ability to cause a harmful or offensive touching.

 An action for assault can be sustained even if the defendant did not have the actual, present ability to cause a harmful or offensive touching. While every battery includes an assault, not every assault includes a battery. To constitute an actionable assault, there must be an intentional, unlawful offer to touch the person in a rude or angry manner so as to create, under the circumstances, a well-founded fear in the mind of the person alleging the assault - even though no actual touching occurred. Here, the defendant presents evidence that the height of the counter was such that Sapp could not have reached Hill even if he wanted to. Still, there was testimony offered that even though the height of the counter was tall, Sapp could have reached beyond it and touched the plaintiff. The evidence as a whole presents a question for the jury and the trial court's instruction to them as such was not erroneous.

 Reversed on the ground that Sapp was not acting within the scope of his employment.

Big Town Nursing Home v. Newman
Court of Civil Appeals of Texas, 461 S.W.2d (1970)

FACTS

Plaintiff Newman, a retired printer 67 years of age, suffered from Parkinson's disease, arthritis, heart problems and other illnesses, was admitted to Big Town Nursing Home (defendant) by his nephew. The admission papers provided that Newman "would not be forced to remain in the nursing home against his will for any length of time." Three days after his admission, Newman decided to leave the nursing home. Newman was caught by the employees of the home and put in a wing with drug addicts and alcoholics. While Newman had been arrested for drunken driving and drunkenness in the past and treated, he had not taken a drink the week prior to admission nor had he used any drugs. Newman attempted to leave the nursing home about six more times, and each time he was caught by the employees and brought back against his will. Additionally, he was prevented from using the phone and he was taped to his bed to prevent him from leaving. As a result, Newman sued Big Town for false imprisonment and the trial court decided in his favor. Defendant appealed on the ground that its employees did not falsely imprison Newman.

Can the defendant be held liable for false imprisonment when it prevented the plaintiff from leaving a confined area without legal justification?

A person is liable for false imprisonment when it imposes a direct restraint on the physical liberty of another or prevented that person, without legal justification, from leaving an area.

A person is liable for false imprisonment when it imposes a direct restraint on the physical liberty of another or prevented that person, without legal justification, from leaving an area. Here, there is ample evidence to show that the plaintiff was falsely imprisoned. First, he was placed in a wing with drug addicts and alcoholics even thought he defendant knowing he did not belong there. Additionally, he was not permitted to use the telephone for 51 days. Defendants, in addition to actual damages, may be liable for exemplary damages if they acted intentionally in depriving the plaintiff from his rights. We hold that they did. Here, the defendants disregarded the plaintiff's rights intentionally so they will be held liable for actual and exemplary damages. However, the amount awarded to the plaintiff in the trial court was excessive.

Affirmed as to judgment and reduced as to amount of recovery.

Parvi v. City of Kingston
Court of Appeals of New York, 394 N.Y.S.2d 161 (1977)

FACTS

In response to a complaint, the police found two brothers fighting behind a building together with Plaintiff Parvi apparently trying to calm them. Parvi, who had apparently consumed alcohol with the other two, told the police that he had no place to go. In response, the police took him to the outskirts of the city and left him at an abandoned golf course there to sober up rather then taken him to jail. Parvi sued the City of Kingston for false imprisonment. Yet at the trial, on cross-examination, Parvi admitted that he did not recollect the events of the night. In response, the trial court dismissed the action on the ground that in order to bring an action in false imprisonment, the individual must be aware of the confinement. The Appellate Court affirmed and Parvi appealed.

Can a defendant be held liable for falsely imprisoning another when the latter was not aware that he was being confined at the time?

A defendant can not be held liable for falsely imprisoning another when the latter was not aware that he was being confined at the time of the alleged imprisonment.

A defendant can not be held liable for falsely imprisoning another when the latter was not aware that he was being confined at the time of the alleged imprisonment. False imprisonment is a "dignitary" tort, and as such it is not suffered unless one is aware of the dignitary invasion – a position shared by the Restatement (Second) of Torts §42. The Appellate Division failed to distinguish between a later recognition of consciousness and the existence of that consciousness at the time of the incident. At his trial, the plaintiff admitted that he had no recollection of what happened on the night in question. Yet, the court failed to determine the key critical issue: whether plaintiff did not recollect due to lapse of memory or whether the plaintiff was not conscious of his confinement at the time that it was occurring. Although the plaintiff was intoxicated at the time of confinement, it is not clear that he unequivocally aware of his confinement. The record suggests that he may have been aware - his response to police commands that he get into the squad car and his conversation with them at the time he was in their car.

Reversed.

17

Hardy v. Labelle's Distributing Co.

Supreme Court of Montana, 661 P.2d 35 (1983)

FACTS

Plaintiff Hardy, a temporary employee assigned duty as a sales clerk in the jewelry department at Defendant Labelle Distributing Co., was falsely accused of stealing a watch. Hardy was approached by the assistant manager of the store, who took her to the manager's office under the pretext of giving her a tour of the store. Hardy denied having stolen the watch and took a lie detector test that verified the same. According to conflicting testimony, the meeting lasted from 20 to 45 minutes. As a result, Hardy brought an action against the defendant for false imprisonment. The trial court found in favor of the defendant on the ground that the plaintiff was not held against her will. Plaintiff appealed.

 Can a person maintain an action for false imprisonment when no threat of force was used to unlawfully restrain a person against his will?

 A person can not maintain an action for false imprisonment when no threat of force was used to unlawfully restrain a person against his will.

 A person can not maintain an action for false imprisonment when no threat of force was used to unlawfully restrain a person against his will. Here, there is evidence supporting the fact that plaintiff was not imprisoned unlawfully. Although plaintiff testified that she felt compelled to stay, she was never told that she could not leave. Moreover, she testified that she would have followed the assistant manager into the office voluntarily even if she was told of the true nature of the meeting. Thus, under these conditions, the jury properly found that plaintiff was *not* falsely imprisoned.

 A person can not maintain an action for false imprisonment when no threat of force was used to unlawfully restrain a person against his will.

Enright v. Groves
Colorado Court of Appeals, 560 P.2d 851 (1977)

FACTS

Defendants Groves, a police officer and the City of Ft. Collins appeal from judgments against them awarding plaintiff $500 actual damages and $1000 exemplary damages on a claim of False imprisonment. Officer Groves, while on duty, noticed a dog running loose, in violation of the City's "dog leash" law, in the direction of a home owned by Plaintiff Enright. Groves then followed the dog which approached a boy who turned out to be the plaintiff's son. The boy, who was ordered to take the dog inside, who told the officer that his mother, the plaintiff, was in the car parked at the curb. Groves then approached Enright and asked her for her license which she refused to hand over to him. She only disclosed her name and address. Groves then grabbed Enright's arm and placed her under arrest for her refusal to present her license. Enright instituted an action against Groves for false imprisonment. The trial court decided in the plaintiff's favor and granted her damages. Groves appealed on the ground that the plaintiff was validly arrested for violation of a city ordinance and as such, her claim for false imprisonment or false arrest was not valid.

Is a police officer liable for false arrest when he arrests a suspect without a warrant or probable cause to believe that an offense has been committed and that the person arrested has committed it?

A police officer is liable for false arrest when he arrests a suspect without a warrant or probable cause to believe that an offense has been committed and that the person arrested has committed it.

A police officer is liable for false arrest when he arrests a suspect without a warrant or probable cause to believe that an offense has been committed and that the person arrested has committed it. The evidence in this case indicates that Groves arrested Enright not for violation of the city's dog leash law, but for her refusal to produce her identification to him. Here, these is not testimony that defendant ever attempted to explain why he was demanding the plaintiff's license. Moreover, there is no law which compels a person to show her identification to a police officer upon demand unless the citizen has committed a punishable offense. Therefore, defendant's demand for the driver's license was not a lawful command, and, as such, Groves was not privileged to use force in arresting Enright.

Affirmed.

Whittaker v. Sandford

Supreme Judicial Court of Maine, 85 A. 399 (1912)

FACTS

Plaintiff was a member of a religious sect of which Defendant was a leader. At some point, plaintiff decided to leave the sect, which had a colony in Jaffa (now Tel Aviv) and in Maine. Defendant offered plaintiff his yacht so that the latter could come back to the United States and was assured she would be allowed to come ashore once they arrive despite her fear to the contrary. However, upon arrival to the United States, defendant refused to provide plaintiff any means of getting to the shore. Ultimately, she was allowed to leave the boat from time to time, but only with a minder present. Eventually, she gained her freedom for herself and her four children with the assistance of the sheriff and a writ of habeas corpus. Consequently, plaintiff sued defendant for false imprisonment. The trial court instructed the jury that for a valid action in false imprisonment a plaintiff must show actual physical restraint but there need not be actual physical force upon the plaintiff herself. In this case, as plaintiff was restrained such that she could not leave the boat, the requirement of physical restraint was satisfied. The trial court, in deciding in favor of plaintiff, dismissed defendant's motion for a new trial. Defendant appealed the trial court's decision on the ground that the court's instructions to the jury regarding the requirements of false imprisonment were erroneous.

 Can the defendant be held liable for false imprisonment when he confines the plaintiff to a bounded area, foreclosing any means of escape, but without exerting any actual physical restraint upon the latter?

 A defendant can be held liable for false imprisonment when he confines the plaintiff to a bounded area, foreclosing any means of escape, even though he did not exert any actual physical restraint upon the latter.

 A defendant can be held liable for false imprisonment when he confines the plaintiff to a bounded area, foreclosing any means of escape, even though he did not exert any actual physical restraint upon the latter. Here, the defendant and owner of the yacht assured the plaintiff that she could leave the boat when they arrived at the American shore. Nevertheless he refused to provide her with a means to disembark from the vessel - a row boat to get her to the coast. The row boat was the only means of getting ashore. As a result, the plaintiff was confined to the yacht, a physical barrier, as though she were actually locked in a room against her will. The defendant had a duty to bring plaintiff to the U.S., as he had promised, *and* also supply her with a means of getting to the shore. Because he did not, he [defendant] will be held liable for false imprisonment.

 Affirmed.

State Rubbish Collectors Ass'n v. Siliznoff
Supreme Court of California, 240 P.2d 282 (1952)

FACTS

The State Rubbish Collectors sued Siliznoff to collect on certain notes; Siliznoff counterclaimed asking that the notes be canceled because of duress and want of consideration. Specifically, the former threatened to beat Siliznoff, destroy his truck and put him out of business completely if he did not pay the note. Consequently, Siliznoff attended a meeting with a member of The State Rubbish Collectors and told him that he [Siliznoff] would pay on the note because he was scared he would be physically injured. Because of this fear, Siliznoff claimed to have gotten ill and vomited several times and was unable to work for several days. The trail court rendered judgment in favor of Siliznoff for $1,250 in general damages and $4,000 in punitive damages. The State Rubbish Collectors arguing that there was no assault because the threats made [to Siliznoff] were not immediate.

 Can the plaintiff be found guilty of a [tortious] assault if he intentionally subjects the defendant to the mental suffering incident to serious threats to his physical well-being?

 A plaintiff may be found guilty of a [tortious] assault if he intentionally subjects the defendant to the mental suffering incident to serious threats to his physical well-being, absent a privilege.

 If the defendant intentionally subjected the plaintiff to such distress and bodily harm resulted, the defendant would be liable for negligently causing the plaintiff bodily harm and is based on the right of one to be free from a negligent interference with one's physical well-being. Therefore, if a cause of action is established, damages for mental suffering ensuing from the acts complained of should be allowed. And while allowing recovery in the absence of physical injury may result in many frivolous claims, the jury is in a better position to determine whether damages should be allowed in each case, even in the absence of physical injury. Here, the State Rubbish Collectors caused Siliznoff extreme fright which resulted in physical injury. Under these circumstances, the liability of the defendant to the plaintiff is clear.

 Affirmed.

Slocum v. Food Fair Stores of Florida

Supreme Court of Florida, 100 So.2d 396 (1958)

FACTS

Plaintiff-appellant Slocum was a customer at Defendant-appellee Food Fair Stores of Florida, when she asked an employee in the store what the price of an item was. The employee responded to her impolitely, or, as she contends, in a malicious or grossly reckless manner. Slocum, who suffered from pre-existing heart disease, suffered a heat attack as a result. Plaintiff thereafter sued the food store to recover money damages for her mental suffering and for her emotional distress. The trial court dismissed the complaint for failure to state a cause of action. This appeal [by Slocum] followed.

 Can a plaintiff recover, based on an independent cause of action, for conduct which causes *mere* emotional distress, as opposed to *severe* emotional distress?

 Conduct that causes mere emotional distress does not rise to a level necessary to allow a plaintiff to recover based on an independent cause of action.

Conduct that causes mere emotional distress does not rise to a level necessary to allow a plaintiff to recover based on an independent cause of action. Were we to draw a line between that conduct likely to cause mere emotional distress and that which causes severe emotional distress, the case before us, based on the facts contained therein, would be excluded. As far as we are able to generalize from caselaw, the rule seems to be that the conduct complained of must be likely to cause severe emotional distress and not mere emotional distress and must exceed all bounds which could be tolerated by the society; the liability for which must be determined based on an objective standard, not a subjective one. Moreover, the act complained of must cause severe emotional distress to a person of ordinary sensibilities. Hence, mere vulgarities and insults do not create severe emotional distress of the type that is legally actionable. An exception to this "rule" exists for innkeepers and common carriers – that is, they are held to a stricter standard with respect to their patrons and may be held liable for mere vulgarities and insults. However, there is no need to extend this rule to the case at bar.

 Affirmed.

Harris v. Jones
Court of Appeals of Maryland, 380 A.2d 611 (1977)

FACTS

Plaintiff-appellant William R. Harris sued Defendant-appellee H. Robert Jones, his supervisor, for intentional infliction of emotional distress. Harris claimed that Jones was aware of Harris speech impediment and Harris sensitivity to it. Despite his knowledge, Jones constantly imitated Harris stuttering and ridiculed him in front of other co-workers at the General Motors plant where they all worked. Additionally, Harris claimed that the defendant's constant ridicule heightened his nervousness and worsened his speech problem. The trial court awarded Harris $3,500 in compensatory damages and $15,000 in punitive damages. The Court of Special Appeals reversed on the ground that a causal connection between the defendant's conduct was missing and because the plaintiff's emotional distress not severe enough to permit him to recover even though it conceded that the defendant's conduct was intentional and/or reckless and extreme and/or outrageous. Plaintiff-appellant Harris appealed.

 Must an individual suffer emotional distress that is *severe* in response to the defendant's conduct in order to recover damages for intentional infliction of emotional distress?

 An individual must suffer emotional distress that is severe in response to the defendant's conduct in order to recover damages for the tort of intentional infliction of emotional distress.

 An individual must suffer emotional distress that is severe in response to the defendant's conduct in order to recover damages for the tort of intentional infliction of emotional distress. Thirty-seven jurisdiction now recognize a right to recover for severe emotional distress brought on by an intentional act; and four elements must be present in order to impose liability under that tort [intentional infliction of emotional distress]: 1) The conduct must be intentional or reckless, and 2) the conduct must be extreme and outrageous, 3) there must be a causal connection between the wrongful conduct and the emotional distress, and 4) the emotional distress must be severe. Section 46 of the Restatement states that conduct that is extreme and outrageous is one that goes beyond ail bounds of decency; to be regarded as atrocious and which is not tolerated in a civilized community. In determining whether conduct is "extreme and outrageous," the nature of the conduct must be determined, not in a vacuum, but rather based on the community standards and on the facts and circumstances of each individual case. Here, the conduct in question was clearly intentional; however, there is not sufficient evidence to prove that there was a causal connection [see 3) above] and that the emotional distress was severe [see 4) above]. While Harris did suffer a vindictive "assault," that humiliation was not, as a matter of law, so brutal as to constitute the "severe" emotional distress.

 Affirmed.

Taylor v. Vallelunga
District Court of Appeal of California, 339 P.2d 910 (1959)

FACTS

Plaintiff Gail G. Taylor's father was beaten and suffered severe bodily injury at the hands of Defendant Vallelunga and others. Unbeknownst to Vallelunga, Taylor was present at the scene and witnessed the beating. Thereafter, Taylor sued Vallelunga for intentional infliction of emotional distress suffered as a result of watching Vallelunga beat her father. However, she suffered no actual physical injury. The trial court dismissed Taylor's action and she appealed.

 May a 3rd party recover damages from a defendant for intentional infliction of emotional distress as the result of witnessing a distressing event involving a close family member when the 3rd party did not suffer any physical injury herself and the defendant was unaware of her presence at the time of the incident?

 A 3rd party may not recover damages for intentional infliction of emotional distress when the defendant was unaware of the 3rd party's presence at the time of the incident and the 3rd party did not suffer any physical injury resulting therefrom.

 A 3rd party may not recover damages for intentional infliction of emotional distress when the defendant was unaware of the 3rd party's presence at the time of the incident and the 3rd party did not suffer any physical injury resulting therefrom. A claim for intentional infliction of emotional distress requires a showing of an intent to cause severe emotional distress. Thus, in order for the 3rd party plaintiff to recover, the defendant must have acted with the intent of causing severe emotional distress to her [the 3rd party] or with knowledge that his conduct is substantially certain to produce such a result. Here, the record indicates that the defendant was unaware of the plaintiff's presence at the scene. Similarly, there is no evidence to suggest that her father was beaten for the purpose of causing *her* severe emotional distress. Lastly, the evidence does not show that the defendant acted in such a way to suggest that such result [her emotional distress] was substantially certain to follow the defendant's conduct.

 Affirmed.

Dougherty v. Stepp
Supreme Court of North Carolina, 18 N.C. 371 (1835)

FACTS

Plaintiff Dougherty sued Defendant Stepp for *trespass quare clausum fregit* (where the defendant unlawfully enters the land of the defendant). The only proof offered by the plaintiff at trial to evidence a trespass was his claim that the defendant entered his (the plaintiff's) unenclosed land with a surveyor, surveyed the land, and claimed it as his own without marking any trees or cutting brush. The trial court instructed the jury that because the defendant did not mark any trees or cut any brush, the claim of trespass failed. The jury thereafter entered judgment for the defendant and the plaintiff appealed.

 Were the trial court's instructions to the jury in error; specifically that the act of entering another's unenclosed land without altering it does not constitute a trespass?

 Trespass is the unauthorized, and therefore unlawful, entry onto the land of another even if no physical damage occurred.

 Every unauthorized, and therefore unlawful, entry onto another's land is a trespass. And while the defendant's acts on the land are relevant to the extent of the injury (damages), it has no bearing on whether such a trespass has in fact occurred. Thus, from the willful entry onto the land of another, the law infers some damage, even if such an injury was as minimal as the treading down of grass or shrubbery, as we see here. The defendant's "pretend ownership" to the land simply aggravates the wrong. The trial court's instructions to the jury were in error.

 Reversed and a new trial granted.

Bradley v. American Smelting and Refining Co.

Supreme Court of Washington, 709 P.2d 782 (1985)

FACTS

Plaintiff Bradley owns property which is four miles away from Defendant American Smelting. Defendant's business involves the smelting of copper, a process which releases various gases, in the form of particulate matter – microscopic, airborne particles of heavy metals, which can not be seen with the human eye. Bradley sued American Smelting in trespass for emitting the gases onto Bradley's property. The case comes before the Supreme Court of Washington on a certification from the U.S. District Court for the Western District of Washington.

 Can a landowner or occupier of land recover in trespass for the deposit of intangible objects or substances on his land?

 A landowner or occupier of land can recover in trespass for the deposit of intangible objects or substances on his land if he shows actual physical damage(s).

 A landowner or occupier of land can recover in trespass for the deposit of intangible objects or substances on his land if he shows actual physical damage(s). Historically, one could recover under a theory of trespass against another where there is a tangible *physical* invasion of the landowner's property. Today, however, this tort theory has been expanded to include *intangibles* as well. *Martin v. Reynolds Metals Co.* was an action in trespass brought against the defendant corporation for causing gasses and fluoride particulates to settle on the plaintiffs' land making it unfit for livestock. *Martin* indicates that in cases of intangible objects may be brought in nuisance or in trespass. While these causes of action are mutually exclusive and distinct - trespass is invasion of the right to exclusive possession, while nuisance is interference with the use and enjoyment of one's property – we hold that the two types of theories may be applied concurrently; and that the injured party may proceed under both theories when the elements of both torts are present. Hence, under the modern law, in order to recover in trespass by intangibles, the following elements must be present: 1) an invasion upsetting an interest in the exclusive possession of the land, 2) an intentional act which results in the invasion, 3) a reasonable probability that the act done could result in the invasion, and 4) significant [not nominal] damages to the property or things thereupon. Here, the plaintiff failed to show any damage to his property and is therefore barred from recovering.

 Plaintiff barred from recovering.

Herrin v. Sutherland

Supreme Court of Montana, 241 P. 328 (1925)

FACTS

Defendant Sutherland, while standing on the land of another hunting ducks and other wild fowl, was repeatedly firing his shotgun at the birds above Plaintiff Herrin's land. Herrin sued Sutherland for trespass requesting damages in the amount of $10. The trial court granted a judgment in favor of Herrin for $1 and Sutherland appealed.

 Does the defendant commit a trespass when he passes over or causes an object to pass over the land of another without ever touching the ground itself?

 One commits a trespass when he passes over or causes an object to pass over the land of another, even if he [or the object] never touches the ground itself.

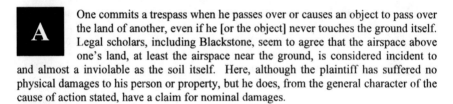 One commits a trespass when he passes over or causes an object to pass over the land of another, even if he [or the object] never touches the ground itself. Legal scholars, including Blackstone, seem to agree that the airspace above one's land, at least the airspace near the ground, is considered incident to and almost a inviolable as the soil itself. Here, although the plaintiff has suffered no physical damages to his person or property, but he does, from the general character of the cause of action stated, have a claim for nominal damages.

 The judgment is affirmed.

Rogers v. Board of Road Com'rs for Kent County

Supreme Court of Michigan, 30 N.W.2d 358 (1947)

FACTS

Plaintiff Rogers sued Defendant, the Board of Road Commissioners for Kent County (the "Board"), to recover damages for the death of her husband, Theodore Rogers, due to the latter's trespass. The Defendant obtained a license to place a snow fence on the Rogers' field parallel to the roadway past decedent's farm. Plaintiff claims that she and her husband allowed the Board to place the fence there upon the understanding that it be removed along with all anchor posts at the end of each winter. The Board failed to do so. One day, while the plaintiff's husband was driving his mowing machine, he struck one of the anchor posts, was thrown to the ground and received serious injuries leading to his death. Rogers brought an action against the Board in trespass. The trial court dismissed her action on the ground that the basis of liability was in negligence and not in trespass. Rogers appealed.

Can a defendant commit a trespass through the continued presence of a structure on land of another, originally put there by the defendant with the former consent of the plaintiff-landowner, after the landowner has effectively terminated his consent or license to allow the defendant to do so?

A defendant commits a trespass by not removing and thus allowing the continued presence of a structure on land of the plaintiff-landowner after the latter has effectively terminated his consent or license to allow the former to do so.

A defendant commits a trespass by not removing and thus allowing the continued presence of a structure on land of the plaintiff-landowner after the latter has effectively terminated his consent or license to allow the former to do so. Here, the failure to remove the anchor posts, as agreed, constituted trespass. This trespass was the proximate cause of Theodore Rogers' death.

Reversed and remanded for further proceedings as shall be found necessary.

Glidden v. Szybiak
Supreme Court of New Hampshire, 63 A.2d 233 (1949)

FACTS

The four-year-old plaintiff, Elaine Glidden, was playing with Defendant Jane Szybiak's dog, Toby, climbing on his back and pulling his ears. Unexpectedly, the dog snapped at her and bit her nose, causing severe injuries. As a result, plaintiff sued Szybiak, and Szybiak defended and motioned for judgment at the end of trial on the ground that since the plaintiff was engaged in the commission of a trespass to chattel at the time the dog bit her, and since her injuries were a result of such a trespass, she could not recover from the defendant for her injuries. The trial court disagreed and found for the plaintiff finding that Glidden was "of such tender years," i.e., she was too young, that she could not be guilty of contributory negligence and as such also too young to be guilty of an intentional tort. Szybiak appealed the trial court's verdict.

Can one sustain an action for trespass to chattel if he has not suffered actual damages as a result of the trespass?

One can not sustain an action for trespass unless he has suffered actual damages as a result of the trespass.

One can not sustain an action for trespass unless he has suffered actual damages as a result of the trespass. A trespass to chattel occurs when one interferes with another's property without the owner's consent. However, a trespass to chattel is not actionable unless there is an actual injury suffered by the owner. This is unlike trespass to land, where no actual injury need be shown. Here, the record does not show that the *dog* was in any way harmed as a result of *plaintiff's actions*. Hence, the plaintiff can recover from the defendant for her injuries.

Affirmed.

CompuServe Inc. v. Cyber Promotions Inc.

U.S. District Court, Southern District of Ohio, 962 F.Supp. 1015 (1997)

FACTS

Defendant Cyber Promotions, Inc. sent hundreds of thousands of unsolicited e-mail advertisements known as "spam" to internet users, many of whom were CompuServe (plaintiff) subscribers. CompuServe is in the business of providing access to the internet and is a major Internet service provider (ISP). As a result, CompuServe requested Cyber Promotions to stop using its computer equipment to process and store the e-mails and terminate its spam. This request prompted Cyber Promotions to send even more e-mails to CompuServe subscribers. Thereafter, CompuServe attempted to screen out the "spam," but Cyber Promotions managed to circumvent CompuServe's attempts. CompuServe received numerous complaints from its subscribers who threatened to discontinue their subscriptions unless the spam was stopped. CompuServe also complains that the mass mailings place a significant burden on its equipment which has finite storage and processing capacity and that it receives no payment from the mass mailers for processing their unsolicited emails. To that end, CompuServe sought a preliminary injunction to bar the practice.

Do unsolicited e-mails sent through an ISP's network constitute trespass to chattels?

A trespass to chattels exists where the value or condition of the chattel is intentionally impaired.

The Restatement (Second) of Torts § 217(b) states that a trespass to chattel may be committed by intentionally using or intermeddling with the chattel of another; where "intermeddling" is defined as intentionally bringing about a physical contact with the chattel. Electronic signals sent by computer have been held to be sufficiently tangible to support a trespass action and it is undisputed that plaintiff has a possessory interest in its computer systems and that the defendant's contact with them [the plaintiff's computer systems] was intentional. Cyber Promotions claims that it did not physically dispossess plaintiff of its equipment or substantially interfere with it and cites Restatement (Second) §221 to support its claim that physical dispossession or substantial interference with the chattel is required for an actionable trespass to occur. We disagree. Restatement (Second) §218 expands the circumstances under which trespass to chattels may be actionable and includes situations where the chattel is impaired as to its condition, quality, and value. Cyber Promotions next argues that there is no "substantial interference" unless the trespasser actually takes physical custody of the property or damages it. Again, we disagree. Both Restatement (Second) §218 and case law indicate the contrary. Cyber Promotion's spam used up CompuServe's disk space and tax its processing power. As a result, these resources are not available to serve CompuServe's own subscribers. Thus, the value of CompuServe's equipment has been diminished even though it has not been physically damaged by the defendant's conduct. Plaintiff also asserts that it has suffered injury apart from the physical impact of

---

30

CompuServe Inc. v. Cyber Promotions Inc.
U.S. District Court, Southern District of Ohio, 962 F.Supp. 1015 (1997)

defendant's emails on its equipment – a so-called intangible injury. To address this concern, Restatement (Second) §218(d) states that recovery can be made for a trespass that harms something in which the possessor has a legally protected interest. Here, Cyber Promotion's e-mails caused some subscribers to cancel their subscriptions, thus hurting CompuServe's reputation. This injury to goodwill and reputation is actionable. Based on the foregoing, CompuServe's Motion for preliminary injunction is granted and Cyber Promotions is enjoined from sending further advertisements to CompuServe e-mail addresses.

Plaintiff's preliminary injunction is granted and defendant is enjoined from sending further advertisements to CompuServe e-mail addresses.

Pearson v. Dodd

U.S. District Court, Dist. Of Columbia Circuit, 410 F.2d 701 (1969)

FACTS

Newspaper columnists Drew Pearson (defendant-appellant) and Jack Anderson (defendant) copied files that had been taken from Senator Thomas Dodd's (plaintiff-appellee) office without his authorization. Later, Pearson printed the contents of the documents which contained information about alleged misdeeds of Dodd. Dodd sued Pearson on the ground that his photocopying of the information constituted conversion. The District Court granted partial summary judgment for Dodd finding liability on a theory of conversion and at the same time denied partial summary judgment on the theory of invasion of privacy. Pearson appealed the U.S. Court of Appeals, D.C. Circuit.

 Can the photocopying of documents constitute conversion?

 The photocopying of documents does not constitute conversion where there is not property right.

 The photocopying of documents here does not constitute conversion. According to the Restatement (Second) of Torts, the tort of conversion requires a *complete* interference with the chattel of another which substantially deprives the other person of possessory rights in the property, not just mere *interference* with it. The measure of damages for conversion is the actual value of the property – and nominal damages will be allowed where there has been no actual damage or injury. We contrast this to trespass to chattels which requires a showing of actual damages and where any recovery is based on the diminution in value of the property. Turing to the facts of the instant case, we find that there was no conversion of the documents at issue. The documents were taken at night, photocopied, and returned the next day before the office opened. Moreover, the information contained on the documents is not protected as a property right - where ideas are formulated and labor expended or where the information is gathered and arranged at some cost and sold as a commodity on the market, a property right exists and the law of conversion will apply [an exception to the rule above]. Here, the documents were not for sale and the Appellee Dodd was not substantially deprived of his use of them. Thus, no action lies on conversion. We affirm the District Court's denial of summary judgment for invasion of privacy and reverse its grant of summary judgment for conversion.

 The District Court's denial of summary judgment for invasion of privacy is affirmed; grant of summary judgment for conversion is reversed.

O'Brien v. Cunard S.S. Co.
Supreme Judicial Court of Massachusetts, 28 N.E. 266 (1891)

FACTS

Plaintiff O'Brien was a steerage passenger aboard the *S.S. Cunard*, a ship going from Queenstown, New Zealand to Boston, owned and operated by Cunard S.S. Co. While in transit to Boston, a surgeon employed by the defendant vaccinated O'Brien pursuant to the laws of Boston which required a certification of a vaccination for small pox. O'Brien held her arm up to be vaccinated and gave no verbal indication to anyone else that she really did not want to be vaccinated. Thereafter, O'Brien sued the defendant for vaccinating her against her will. The trail court directed a verdict in favor of the defendant and O'Brien appealed.

 May a person rely on the other's behavior and overt acts in order to determine whether the latter has consented to the former's conduct, when consent to an act by the former is not clearly expressed?

 A person may rely on the other's behavior and overt acts in order to determine whether the latter has consented to the former's conduct when consent to an act by the former is not clearly expressed.

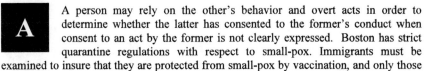 A person may rely on the other's behavior and overt acts in order to determine whether the latter has consented to the former's conduct when consent to an act by the former is not clearly expressed. Boston has strict quarantine regulations with respect to small-pox. Immigrants must be examined to insure that they are protected from small-pox by vaccination, and only those persons who have a certificate of vaccination from the ship's doctor may land without detention in the port of Boston. The record indicates that notices of the vaccination requirement were posted onboard the ship in multiple languages. The ship's doctor could rightly assume that all the passengers read and understood the vaccination requirements, including the plaintiff. Here, the plaintiff held her arm up to the doctor for vaccination and said nothing – she did not indicate that she did not want to be vaccinated. After the vaccination, she took the certificate given to her and used it at the quarantine. The doctor had no way of knowing that she did not wish to be vaccinated. Thus, in light of the above, the doctor's conduct was not unlawful.

 Exceptions overruled.

Hackbart v. Cincinnati Bengals Inc.

U.S. Court of Appeals, 601 F.2d 516 (10th Cir. 1979)

FACTS

Plaintiff Dale Hackbart, a professional football player and defensive back for the Broncos, was injured during a game between the Broncos and the Cincinnati Bengals (defendant) when the latter's player, Charles Clark, an offensive back for the Bengals, stuck Hackbart in the back of his head and his neck. Both players were knocked down by the force of the blow and both got up, without complaining, and returned to their respective sidelines. Thereafter, this suit was filed. At trial, the trial court found that Clark hit Hackbart out of anger and frustration, but without the intent to injure him. Consequently, the trial court ruled that although Clark's act was intentional, the Bengals were not liable as a matter of law because football is a violent game and sanctions and penalties provided by the rules of the game prove relief to those affronted. Hackbart appealed.

 When the rules of a sport bar intentional acts of violence, can a player be held liable for intentionally striking another during an aggressive game?

 When the rules of a sport bar intentional acts of violence, a player can be held liable for intentionally striking another during an aggressive game.

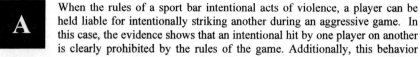 When the rules of a sport bar intentional acts of violence, a player can be held liable for intentionally striking another during an aggressive game. In this case, the evidence shows that an intentional hit by one player on another is clearly prohibited by the rules of the game. Additionally, this behavior [the intentional punching and striking of others] is barred by the general customs of the game which are intended to set up reasonable boundaries so that one player can not intentionally inflict a serious injury to another. Thus, the trial court's ruling as a matter of law was erroneous and the plaintiff was entitled to a review of his rights to determine whether they had been violated.

 Reversed and remanded.

Mohr v. Williams

Supreme Court of Minnesota, 104 N.W. 12 (1905)

FACTS

Plaintiff Mohr was having trouble with her right ear so she contacted Defendant Williams, a physician and surgeon specializing in disorders of the ear, to examine it and make a recommendation. After an examination, Williams determined that she had a perforated eardrum and a large polyp in the middle ear, indicative of disease in the area. Williams also examined Mohr's left ear, but was unable to make a full and complete diagnosis due to a build-up of foreign substances within the ear. After consulting with Mohr's family physician, Williams scheduled her for surgery to remove the polyp in her right ear. After placing Mohr under anesthesia, Williams reexamined both ears, and found that the condition of the left ear was more severe than the right ear. After again consulting with Mohr's family physician, Williams opted to remove part of the eardrum membrane and diseased portions of the left ear. He concluded that the left, and not the right ear, should be operated upon and devoted other treatment to the right ear. No surgery was performed on the right ear. The operation was successful and skillfully performed. However, after surgery Mohr's hearing was impaired so she sued for assault and battery for the non-consensual procedure. A verdict was entered for the plaintiff. After the judge set aside the verdict as excessive and ordered a new trial, both parties appealed.

Can a doctor commit an assault and battery by operating, without negligence, on the plaintiff without her consent?

An unlawful or unauthorized touching of another is an assault and battery, despite the absence of negligence.

The absence of a showing that defendant was guilty of negligence does not relieve the act of the defendant from the charge of an unlawful assault and battery. This is because any unlawful or unauthorized touching of another is an assault and battery. And when the touching is unauthorized, it is inevitably unlawful. In the instant case, the jury concluded that Defendant Williams did not have permission to perform the surgery on the plaintiff's left ear. As a result, his touching was both unauthorized and unlawful, and constituted an assault and battery. Plaintiff's recovery, as a measure of damages for the assault and battery, depends on the character and extent of the injury, the nature of the injury to be corrected, the beneficial nature of the operation, and defendant's showing of good faith. A doctor can commit an assault and battery by operating, without negligence, on the plaintiff without her consent.

Affirmed.

De May v. Roberts

Supreme Court of Michigan, 9 N.W. 146 (1881)

FACTS

Plaintiff Roberts was about to give birth when her physician, Defendant De May, and a stranger, one Scattergood, entered her room. Roberts believed the stranger to be her doctor's assistant, and thus allowed him to be present at the time of the child's birth and allowed him to touch her [hold her hand during delivery]. After it was revealed that the stranger, a young, unmarried man, was not the doctor's assistant and in fact had no knowledge of medicine but was simply accompanying the doctor to carry the necessary equipment for him, she sued. The trial court ruled in favor of the plaintiff and the defendant appealed.

If a person would not have consented but for a mistaken belief concerning a material issue at hand, is that person's consent still valid?

If a person would not have consented but for a mistaken belief concerning a material issue at hand, that person's consent is *not* valid.

If a person would not have consented but for a mistaken belief concerning a material issue at hand, that person's consent is not valid. Here, neither the plaintiff nor her husband was told that the stranger was not the physician's assistant. The labor and birthing experience is an intently private and person one and no person had the right to intrude upon her privacy unless it were absolutely necessary. It is immaterial that Roberts, believing the stranger to be the physician's assistant, gave her consent; she will not be barred from bringing an action against the defendant. The defendant had a duty to disclose the true nature, identity and character of the stranger. He did not.

Judgment for the plaintiff affirmed.

Katko v. Briney
Supreme Court of Iowa, 183 N.W.2d 657 (1971)

FACTS

Defendant Briney posted "no trespass" signs and boarded up the doors and the windows of an old abandoned farm house he inherited from his grandparents to prevent any trespassers from entering. To further protect the abandoned property, Briney set a "shotgun trap" in one of the bedrooms of the house. The gun, a 20-guage spring shotgun, was rigged to the doorknob and would fire if someone attempted to enter the room. There were no warning signs posted anywhere in or around the house and property cautioning trespassers of the presence of the gun. Plaintiff Katko, who was trespassing in the house, was shot in his legs and suffered serious injury to his right leg as a result. Thereafter, Katko sued Briney for damages for injuries that he experienced. The trial court awarded a judgment in favor of the plaintiff for $20,000 in actual damages and for $10,000 in punitive damages. The defendant appealed.

 Is a property owner liable to a trespasser for serious bodily injury or death when the former protects his property from a trespass by the latter via the use of direct or indirect force which causes the injury?

 A property owner will be held liable to a trespasser for serious bodily injury or death if he protects his property from a trespass via the use of direct or indirect force which causes the injury to the latter.

 A property owner will be held liable to a trespasser for serious bodily injury or death if he protects his property from a trespass via the use of direct or indirect force which causes the injury to the latter. Thus, a property owner or occupier may not set a spring gun(s) or other dangerous device, which might injure or kill, for the sole protection of property. In *Allison v. Fiscus*, deadly force was used when the trespasser is committing a felony. There, the plaintiff's right to damages was recognized when he broke into the defendant's warehouse which an intent to steal and was injured when two sticks of dynamite, buried under the doorway which he entered, blew up injuring him. In that case, the *Allison* court held that the question whether a particular trap was justified as a use of reasonable force should have been submitted to the jury. Thus, we hold that no reversible error was committed by the lower court.

 Affirmed.

Hodgeden v. Hubbard

Supreme Court of Vermont, 46 Am.Dec. 167 (1846)

FACTS

Plaintiff Hodgeden bought a stove from Defendant Hubbard's department store on credit and carried it away. Almost at once, Hubbard realized that Hodgeden had misrepresented his credit and financial strength. Hubbard and others immediately set out in pursuit of Hodgeden who by that time was about two miles from the store. When they caught up with him, he [Plaintiff Hodgeden] drew a knife and Defendant Hubbard and the others resorted to force to remove the stove from his [Plaintiff Hodgeden's] possession. Hodgeden brought an action against Hubbard for assault and battery and for trespass to chattel. The trial court ruled in favor of the plaintiff stating that the defendant was not justified in using force to remove the property - his only redress was the legal process. Hubbard thereafter appealed.

May a person recover property from another which was fraudulently obtained from the former via the use reasonable force against the latter?

One may recover property from another which was fraudulently obtained from him [the former] via the use reasonable force against the latter.

One may recover property from another which was fraudulently obtained from him [the former] via the use reasonable force against the latter. Here, the property did not pass to Hodgeden because he [the defendant] obtained possession of it through fraud and misrepresentation. Under such circumstances, the defendant's possession was unlawful. Here, by drawing the knife, the plaintiff became the aggressor, and it was the right of the defendant to hold him by force to remove the stove. As long as he [the defendant] did not use unnecessary force, he [the defendant] was justified.

Judgment reversed.

Bonkowski v. Arlan's Department Store
Court of Appeals of Michigan, 162 N.W.2d 347 (1968)

FACTS

Plaintiff Marion Bonkowski and her husband left Defendant Arlan's Department Store on the night of December 18, 1962 in Saginaw, Michigan when Earl Reinhardt, a private security officer who was hired by the store, followed the two out of the store. He suspected that they had stolen merchandise from the store and in so suspecting ordered couple to stop as they were in the parking lot walking to their car, telling them that someone had seen them steal jewelry from the store and motioned to the plaintiff to return toward the store, which she did. Mrs. Bonkowski denied the allegations but Reinhardt urged her to empty the contents of her purse, which she did into her husband's hands. After producing sales receipts for all the items that she had purchased, and after Reinhardt was satisfied that she had not committed a theft, he returned to the store. Thereafter, Bonkowski brought action for damages against the defendant for slander and false arrest, claiming that she suffered psychosomatic symptoms such as nervousness, headaches, and depression as a result of Reinhardt's action. At the trial the jury returned a verdict in favor of Bonkowski for $43,750 and the trial court dismissed Arlan's motion for a new judgment notwithstanding the verdict [j.n.o.v]. Defendant appealed.

Can a merchant be held liable for false arrest when he reasonably believes that an individual has stolen merchandise from his store and, as a result of that suspicion, detains the individual for a reasonable investigation of the facts?

A merchant may detain the individual for a reasonable investigation of the facts when he reasonably believes that an individual has stolen merchandise from his store and will thus not be held liable for false arrest.

A merchant may detain the individual for a reasonable investigation of the facts when he reasonably believes that an individual has stolen merchandise from his store and will not be held liable for false arrest. This privilege, known as the "shopkeeper's privilege" is a defense to the common law tort of false arrest and is necessary for the protection of a shopkeeper against the dilemma of not being able to arrest shoplifters for fear of liability attached to a possible false arrest. Since the problem of shoplifting has reached serious levels, we believe that the privilege should be recognized in our jurisdiction and extended to those who have left the store and are within the immediate premises of the store. Therefore, on remand, it is the duty of the jury to determine 1) whether or not Reinhardt, acting as an agent of the defendant, reasonably believed that Bonkowski had unlawfully taken goods from the store and 2) whether the investigation that followed was reasonable under the circumstances of the case. If the reasonableness of the arrest and the investigation is lacking, then the defendant can not take advantage of the privilege and it may be liable for false arrest.

Reversed and Remanded.

Surocco v. Geary

Supreme Court of California, 58 Am.Dec. 385 (1853)

FACTS

On December 24, 1849, an infamous fire raged in the City of San Francisco. Defendant Geary, an Alcalde [the Spanish title of the chief administrator of a town] of the City, decided that blowing up Plaintiff Surocco's property would help prevent the spread of the fire. After doing just that, by virtue of the authority granted to him as a city official, the plaintiff brought suit. At the time of the fire, Surocco was removing furnishings and other items that were inside the property and claimed that had his property not been destroyed, he could have removed more, if not all of his goods from the property. The trial court ruled in favor of the plaintiff and the defendant appealed.

 Can a person be held liable for the destruction of another's property when the former's act was performed under the apparent necessity of preventing further harm to the community and executed in good faith?

 A person be held personally liable for the destruction of another's property when the former's act was performed under the apparent necessity of preventing further harm to the community and executed in good faith.

 A person be held personally liable for the destruction of another's property when the former's act was performed under the apparent necessity of preventing further harm to the community and executed in good faith. The right to destroy someone's property to prevent the spread of a raging fire has been traced to the highest law of necessity - "necessity provides a privilege for private rights." The common law provides that necessity may serve as a justification for what would otherwise be a tortious act. Thus, in circumstances such as the one before us, the private rights of individuals yield to the safety and interests of the society as a whole. However, in ever case, the existence of necessity must be clearly shown in order to avoid the imposition of personal liability and an amount of compensation must be given to the owners of the property or structure destroyed, as determined by the legislature. Here, the destruction of the plaintiff's property was clearly a necessity to prevent the spread of the raging fire to the surrounding homes. Thus, Surocco cannot recover for the value of the property lost in the destruction.

 Reversed.

Vincent v. Lake Erie Transportation Co.

Supreme Court of Minnesota, 124 N.W. 221 (1910)

FACTS

Defendant Vincent moored his steamship, the *Reynolds,* to Plaintiff Lake Erie Transportation Co.'s dock to unload its cargo in the port of Duluth. While moored, a violent storm erupted, with strong winds which continued to increase in severity for some time. As a result, navigation was practically suspended in the harbor. No tug boats were available to help take the *Reynolds* back to harbor, so the defendant's ship remained moored to the plaintiff's dock, replacing the mooring lines as they broke. During the storm, the *Reynolds* was continually thrust into the dock by the waves, causing damage. A lawsuit followed and a jury awarded the plaintiff $500 for damage caused by the vessel.

Can the defendant be held liable for damage caused by an act of God?

When a person trespasses upon the land of another by necessity to avoid damage to his own property, the trespasser remains liable for any damage caused to the property of the property owner.

If damage to property is caused by an act of God, without any direct intervention by the defendant, the plaintiff's damages are attributed to the act of God and not the wrongful act of the person sought to be charged. If the defendant had untied the *Reynolds* and permitted it to be thrown about in the harbor by the storm only to be blown into the plaintiff's dock thereafter, the defendant would not be liable for the damage. However, in the instant case, the defendant decided to secure his ship to the plaintiff's dock out of necessity in order to avoid substantial damage to his ship. While the defendant's decision was objectively reasonable, he must be held liable for the damage caused to the plaintiff's property, even in the absence of any negligence on his part. The defendant cannot be permitted to sacrifice the plaintiff's dock in order to spare his own ship at the plaintiff's expense. Thus, a defendant can be held liable for damage caused by an act of God.

Affirmed.

Sindle v. New York City Transit Authority

New York Court of Appeals, 352 N.Y.S.2d 183 (1973)

FACTS

Plaintiff Sindle, a fourteen-year-old boy, along with 65 – 70 of his classmates, boarded a bus owned by Defendant New York City Transit Authority on June 20, 1967, the last day of school. While onboard, the students started vandalizing the bus, breaking windows, and tearing off the advertisements inside of the bus. There was no evidence that the plaintiff partook in this destruction. The bus driver made several stops at his usual appointed stations and admonished the students on at least one occasion, before continuing on. Finally, the bus driver, assessing the damage on the bus, informed the students that he was going directly to the St. George police station, bypassing several of his normal stops. The plaintiff sued the New York City Transit Authority for false imprisonment. The trial court ruling in favor of the plaintiff, and denied the bus company's motion to amend their answer in order to include the defense of justification. The court also excluded all evidence bearing on the justification issue. The defendant, New York City Transit Authority, appealed.

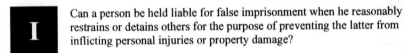 **I** Can a person be held liable for false imprisonment when he reasonably restrains or detains others for the purpose of preventing the latter from inflicting personal injuries or property damage?

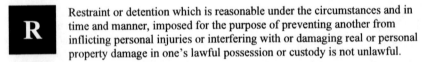 **R** Restraint or detention which is reasonable under the circumstances and in time and manner, imposed for the purpose of preventing another from inflicting personal injuries or interfering with or damaging real or personal property damage in one's lawful possession or custody is not unlawful.

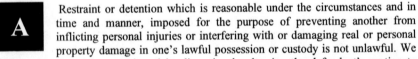 **A** Restraint or detention which is reasonable under the circumstances and in time and manner, imposed for the purpose of preventing another from inflicting personal injuries or interfering with or damaging real or personal property damage in one's lawful possession or custody is not unlawful. We believe that the trial court abused its discretion by denying the defendant's motion to bring evidence of justification. A parent, guardian or teacher entrusted with the care or supervision of a child may use physical force reasonably necessary to maintain discipline or to promote the welfare of the child. Similarly, a school bus driver, entrusted with the care of his student passengers and the custody of public property, has the duty to take reasonable measures for the safety and protection of both. To that end, proof of the reasonableness of the driver's actions under the circumstances should have been allowed into evidence.

 C Reversed and remanded for new trial.

Lubitz v. Wells
Superior Court of Connecticut, 113 A.2d 147 (1955)

FACTS

One day, James Wells Jr., eleven years old at the time, was playing in his backyard with Plaintiff Lubitz, a nine-year-old girl. At some point, he picked up his father's golf club, which had been left there, and proceeded to swing it at a stone on the ground. In doing so, he hit Lubitz in her jaw and her chin with the end of the club and caused her to suffer injuries. Lubitz sues James Wells Sr. in negligence on the ground that he left the golf club in the backyard knowing that children would be playing there. Wells demurred, and challenged the sufficiency of the allegations of the complaint to state a cause of action.

 Can a person be held liable in negligence for those hazards he reasonably "should have known" posed a risk of injury to others?

 A person can not be held liable in negligence for those hazards he reasonably "should have known" posed a risk of injury to others.

 A person can not be held liable in negligence for those hazards he reasonably "should have known" posed a risk of injury to others. The plaintiff argues that James Wells Sr. was negligent because, although he knew the golf club was on the ground in the backyard and that his children play with it, he did not remove the golf club from the backyard. However, it is hardly good sense to hold that the club was so obviously intrinsically dangerous that it is negligence to leave it in the yard. Wells Sr. can not be held liable.

 Demurrer sustained.

Blyth v. Birmingham Waterworks Co.
Court of Exchequer, 156 Eng.Rep. 1047 (1856)

FACTS

Defendant Birmingham Waterworks Co., a not-for-profit company, was legally responsible for laying water mains and fire hydrants throughout the city. The fire hydrants worked properly without incident for twenty-five years. However, one winter, the temperatures fell to a record low freezing one of the water mains causing it to burst, eventually flooding Plaintiff Blyth's house. An engineer for the defendant testified that he thought the ruptured line was caused by ice that formed around the neck of the main caused by the frost. The judge instructed the jury that had the defendant removed the ice earlier, the flooding might have been prevented and challenged the jury to determine whether such act should have been performed by the defendant. The jury returned a verdict for Blythe; the defendant appealed.

Can a defendant be charged with negligence if he failed to take more than reasonable precautions under the circumstances to prevent harm?

In order to avoid negligence, one must act reasonably and prudently, but need not act in an extraordinary fashion nor take unreasonable precautions in order to prevent harm.

In order to avoid negligence, one must act reasonably and prudently, but need not act in an extraordinary fashion nor take unreasonable precautions in order to prevent harm. In the instant case, the defendant took the necessary precautions before installing the fire plugs by taking into consideration the average temperatures during ordinary years in the area and the stress and conditions the laid pipes would have to tolerate. While the precautions the defendants took were reasonable and prudent at the time, they were ultimately inadequate to prevent the damage that occurred. However, such precautions can not be considered negligent, even though they were ineffective. This is because the actual events that caused the frost and flooding were unique and not reasonably foreseeable. Thus, no liability is forced since a reasonable man would not have considered those circumstances. Thus, defendants are not guilty of negligence for failing to take more than reasonable steps to prevent harm.

Reversed.

Gulf Refining Co. v. Williams
Supreme Court of Mississippi, 185 So. 234 (1938)

FACTS

Defendant-appellants Gulf Refining Co. (Gulf) are distributors of gasoline and petroleum products. Gulf sold Plaintiff Willie Williams a drum of gasoline for use in his farm tractor. When Williams attempted to remove the cap of the drum in order to pour the gasoline in his tractor, a spark was produced and caused a fire which burned him severely. It was alleged that the condition of disrepair of the threads in the cap itself caused the fire. Subsequently, Williams brings an action in negligence against Gulf Refining Co. claiming that the defective condition of the cap gave produced a spark and fire which caused his injuries. The jury returned a verdict in favor of Williams and Gulf Refining Co. appealed.

 Can a person or entity be held liable in negligence if his conduct creates a risk of harm which is highly doubtful and unlikely to occur but which does occur, resulting in injury to another?

 A person or entity may be held liable in negligence even if his conduct creates a risk of harm which is highly doubtful and unlikely to occur but which does occur, resulting in injury to another.

 A person or entity may be held liable in negligence even if his conduct creates a risk of harm which is highly doubtful and unlikely to occur but which does occur, resulting in injury to another. Defendant-appellants chief argument is that an explosion of fire due to removing the drum cap is an unusual, extraordinary and improbable occurrence and that there is some case law which bars liability when the occurrence in question is unusual and extraordinary. However, when the inquiry is one of the foreseeability of an event or occurrence under negligence, the question rests not on the probability of the occurrence of the event, but on the whether the occurrence is likely to occur. Therefore, the test for foreseeability is not the balance of probabilities, but the existence of some real likelihood of some damage. Here, if the drum had it been in reasonably good repair, there would have been no liability. However, this was not the case – the evidence indicates that it had been in use for nine years and the threads of the cap were broken, bent and jagged. Hence, the proof is such that a person of ordinary prudence in the defendant's position should have known of the condition of the drum and its cap and should reasonably have anticipated that a sudden fire and explosion would be caused by its condition of disrepair. As such, the defendant is liable for the injuries to plaintiff.

 Affirmed.

Chicago, B. & Q.R. Co. v. Krayenbuhl
Supreme Court of Nebraska, 91 N.W. 880 (1902)

FACTS

A turntable was located between two of Defendant Chicago B & Q.R.'s branch lines [railroad tracks]. Defendant required that its employees lock the turntable when not in use, but they often failed to do just that. One day, when the turntable was unlocked, Plaintiff Krayenbuhl, a child of four years of age at the time, was playing along the tracks and on the turntable with other children when the child's ankle got stuck in between the rails and was severed at the ankle joint. The trial resulted in a verdict in favor of the plaintiff child; the defendant appealed.

 Can an individual or entity be held liable in negligence for not taking reasonable precautions when using an inherently dangerous instrument which benefits the public at large?

 An individual or entity can be held liable in negligence for not taking reasonable precautions to help insure that the risk of injury posed by the use of an inherently dangerous instrument does not outweigh its usefulness and benefit to the public at large.

 An individual or entity can be held liable in negligence for not taking reasonable precautions to help insure that the risk of injury posed by the use of an inherently dangerous instrument does not outweigh its usefulness and benefit to the public at large. The public good demands the use of dangerous machinery, which can not be made absolutely safe and which occasionally results in the death of innocent persons and/or severe injury. When weighed against the benefits to society resulting from the use of such machinery, the so-called utility, the danger from such machinery appears insignificant. However, when the danger outweighs the machine's social utility, the public good demands that restrictions be imposed on its use. Such is the case here. A railroad turntable cannot be rendered absolutely safe, yet the danger it offers may be easily reduced via the use of a simple and inexpensive lock. It is our opinion that the public good requires the use of such a lock. In all cases of negligence, the determination of the question of negligence must be made by taking into consideration the following: 1) the character and location of the premises, 2) the purpose for which they are used, 3) the probability of injury, 4) the precautions necessary to reduce the risk of injury, and 5) the relations between the precautions and their effects on the beneficial use of the premises. Thus, if a defendant does not act in a reasonably prudent manner and omits the precautions which would have been exercised by a man of ordinary care, he [the defendant] will be found guilty of negligence.

 Reversed for error in instructions to the jury.

Davison v. Snohomish County
Supreme Court of Washington, 270 P. 422 (1928)

FACTS

Plaintiff-respondent Edwin F. Davison, while driving his car toward the City of Snohomish (defendant-appellant), crossed a curved bridge, lost control of his car, skidded, struck and broke through a safety railing on the outer edge of the approach. Davison fell to the ground and sustained injuries, as did a passenger who was in the car with him at the time. Davison sued Snohomish County for the negligent construction and maintenance of the bridge and its railings. The trial court decided in favor of Davison and Snohomish County appealed.

 Can township be held liable in negligence for failing to build safety railing to the extent necessary to prevent the respondent's automobile from skidding off the approach when the construction of such a railing would create an excessive financial burden on the county and prevent construction of other roads?

 A township can not be held liable in negligence for failing to build safety railing to the extent necessary to prevent the respondent's automobile from skidding off the approach when the construction of such a railing would create an excessive financial burden on the county and prevent construction of other roads.

 A township is not negligent for failing to build safety railing to the extent necessary to prevent the respondent's automobile from skidding off the approach when the construction of such a railing would create an excessive financial burden on the county and prevent construction of other roads. The use of the automobile as a means of transportation in recent years has caused changes in laws regarding the liability of municipalities with respect to their duty to protect their roads by railings and guards. While railings were very useful in protecting pedestrians, animals and carriages from going off the road, they cannot be required to protect long stretches of roadways and are cannot be expected to prevent an automobile, traveling at a high rate of speed, from leaving the road if the car be in any way deflected as the result of hitting the guard rail. Were municipalities required to install railings along the long stretches of roads to protect vehicles, it would put on them burdens that they cannot bear, and would prevent the construction of additional roads. The evidence of negligence in this case was not sufficient to take the case to the jury.

 Reversed.

United States v. Carroll Towing Co.

U.S. Court of Appeals, 159 F.2d 169 (2nd Cir. 1947)

FACTS

Defendant Carroll Towing, an operator of tugboats and mover of barges in and out of New York Harbor, was moving a barge, the *Anna C*, owned by the Connors Co. on one occasion when it broke from the line of barges being moved and struck a tanker, causing it (the *Anna C*) to leak and sink. The *Anna C* was with a bargee (the operator or captain of the barge) at the time.

 Will negligence be impugned to a defendant when a reasonable precautionary measure could have been taken by the plaintiff but was not, and damage to the latter's property followed?

 The tortfeasor will be held negligent if he failed to take the precautions when the inconvenience to prevent a serious harm was minor.

The tortfeasor will be held negligent if he failed to take the precautions when the inconvenience to prevent a serious harm was minor. Taking steps to avoid breakaway barges requires a consideration of three factors: (1) the probability that the barge will break away; (2) the severity of the injuries a breakaway barge may cause; and (3) the burden on those in a position to prevent the injury. In statistical terms of probability, liability may be imposed if B (the burden of avoiding harm) is less than P (the probability of injury) multiplied by L (the injury). In the instant case, the harbor was busy and filled with activity (a high L; a high P). Had the barge been manned, the accident might not have happened or, at the very least, been minimized. In all probability, the cost associated with keeping the bargee on board would have been insignificant when compared to the damaged caused (a low B). Therefore, B < P x L. Failing to have a bargee on board during a period of time when there was a lot activity in the harbor constituted negligence. Thus, negligence will be impugned to a plaintiff when a reasonable precautionary measure could have been taken by the plaintiff but was not, and damage to the latter's property followed.

 Reversed and remanded.

Vaughan v. Menlove
Court of Common Pleas, 132 Eng.Rep. 490 (1837)

FACTS

Plaintiff Vaughan owned and to cottages to two tenants. Defendant Menlove was a neighbor of Vaughn and placed buildings and a haystack on his property but near the two cottages. Menlove was repeatedly warned of the fire hazard and on one occasion remarked that "he would chance it." In order to mitigate the risk of fire, defendant then placed a chimney in the haystack. In spite of this act, or as a consequence thereof, the hay spontaneously caught fire and spread to Menlove's barn and stables and then to Vaughan's cottages, completely destroying them.

 Is the standard of care required for a finding of negligence based on the best judgment and actual knowledge of the accused (a subjective standard)?

 Negligence is based on the standard of care a reasonable person would use in similar circumstances and determined objectively, not subjectively.

 Historically, the law entitles one to use his property as he wishes so long as he does not injure another's property. If injury to another's land occurs, the occupier of the land must make restitution for the damages caused by his negligence. Here, the jury was instructed to consider whether the fire had started via the defendant's gross negligence and whether he exercised with reasonable caution as would a prudent man under the circumstances. While Menlove did not actually light the fire that caused damage to the plaintiff's property, he did maintain the hay in such a way that it was recognized as a fire hazard by others. Moreover, he was warned and disregarded the warning saying that "he would chance it." And while Menlove argued that he should not be held liable for that which he did not actually know, such a standard is not the standard for imposing negligence. The proper test for negligence is based on the objective standard of what a *prudent man* would have known. To base it on a subjective standard, i.e., what defendant actually knew, would create in severe uncertainties. Thus, the determination of negligence is not made with reference to the defendant's actual knowledge or best judgment.

 Affirmed.

Delair v. McAdoo

Supreme Court of Pennsylvania, 188 A. 181 (1936)

FACTS

As Defendant McAdoo was trying to pass Plaintiff Delair on the same road, traveling in the same direction, his tire blew, causing him to swerve into Delair. The resulting collision caused injury to both plaintiff's car and person. Thereafter, Delair sued McAdoo to recover for damages that he sustained to his person and his property as a result of the accident. There was ample evidence at the trial, indicating that the tires on McAdoo's car were worn out at the time of the accident. The trial jury found in favor of Plaintiff Delair for $7,500. McAdoo appealed. Pennsylvania Appellate Division granted a new trial on the ground that the verdict was excessive, but refused his motion for a j.n.o.v. This ruling is now under review by the Supreme Court of Pennsylvania.

 Can a driver of an automobile be charged with the knowledge that driving with worn tires pose a danger to other drivers on the road?

 A reasonable driver of an automobile be charged with the knowledge that driving with worn tires poses a danger to other drivers on the road and can be held liable in negligence for an injuries that result therefrom.

 A reasonable driver of an automobile be charged with the knowledge that driving with worn tires poses a danger to other drivers on the road and can be held liable in negligence for an injuries that result therefrom. Here, it is clear from the testimony of a witness for the plaintiff that the tires on the defendant's car were worn "pretty well through." The condition of the tires is a question for the jury – that is, whether the tires were worn or not. An ordinary car owner is charged with the knowledge that tires wear with use and that tires that are worn through pose a danger to users of the road. As such, they [the worn tires] should be replaced. An owner or operator cannot escape liability by stating that he did not know of the danger. The law requires owners and drivers of motor vehicles to know of the condition of the parts of their vehicle which are likely to become dangerous if not regularly inspected. Hence, it will be assumed that all such people know of the dangers ascertainable by such an examination.

 Affirmed.

Trimarco v. Klein
Court of Appeals of New York, 451 N.Y.S.2d 52 (1982)

FACTS

Plaintiff Vincent N. Trimarco sued Defendant Klein, his landlord, for injuries that he suffered when the glass shower door in his bathroom broke as he was sliding it open to exit the shower. According to the trial testimony, Trimarco did not know, did haven any reason to know nor was he made aware by his landlord that the shower door was made of ordinary glass, not tempered safety glass. Plaintiff's expert's testimony also produced evidence of custom and usage to show that ordinary glass doors no longer conformed to accepted safety standards and that they were considered dangerous when used as "bathroom enclosures." The jury in the trial court returned a judgment in the plaintiff's favor for $240,000. New York's Appellate Division reversed, dismissed the complaint and reversed on the law holding that no duty was imposed on Klein to replace the shower doors. Plaintiff appealed to the New York Court of Appeals.

 Can custom and usage be used as conclusive evidence of negligence?

 Evidence of custom and usage, although helpful, may not be used as conclusive proof of negligence.

 Evidence of custom and usage, although helpful, may not be used as conclusive proof of negligence; however, it may be used to show that a person who fails to adhere to it may have fallen below the reasonable standard of care. However, no matter how compelling it may be, it is not conclusive evidence of negligence. Before custom and usage can be a compelling indicator of negligence, the jury must be satisfied with its reasonableness. Here, the evidence presented by the plaintiff in this case was enough to send the case to the jury and to sustain the verdict reached. The jury charge on this subject was not in error. The judge was correct to instruct the jury to view evidence of custom and usage with all the other evidence presented to determine the reasonableness of the defendant's conduct under the circumstances. He [the trial judge] also correctly stated to the jury that it was up to them, and them alone, to determine whether or not the custom and usage claimed by the plaintiff did in fact exist. Nevertheless, we reverse and order a new trial because the General Business Law statutes should have been excluded.

 Order reversed, with costs, and new trial ordered.

Cordas v. Peerless Trans. Co.

City Court of New York, New York County, 27 N.Y.S.2d 198 (1941)

FACTS

A chauffeur, who was an employee of Defendant Peerless Transportation, was ordered to drive at gun point by a "hold-up" man. While the car was in motion, the chauffeur, in a desperate attempt to escape, suddenly slammed on his brakes and jumped out of the car. The car which was still in motion hit Plaintiff Cordas, a pedestrian and mother of two, injuring her and her infant children. Cordas sued Peerless in negligence for the injuries that she sustained. The trial court dismissed the complaint and Cordas appealed.

 Is the conduct of the defendant in a crisis situation measured by the standard of care of a reasonable person under normal circumstances?

 The conduct of the defendant in a crisis situation is not measured by the standard of care of a reasonable person under normal circumstances; rather, it is measured by the conduct of a reasonable person in the same or similar situation under like conditions.

 The conduct of the defendant in a crisis situation is not measured by the standard of care of a reasonable person under normal circumstances; rather, it is measured by the conduct of a reasonable person in the same or similar situation under like conditions. Negligence is generally defined as the failure to exercise the sensible care which a reasonable person would ordinarily exercise under a similar circumstance and setting. Thus, negligence is always judged with reference to some relevant time, place, person or situation. As such, an act which may be negligent in one situation, under so-called "normal conditions" may not necessarily be negligent under another - an emergency situation, for example. Here, we can not say the defendant's split-second decision to jump from his car while a loaded gun was pointed at his head was negligent. Nor can we say that his actions must be judged by the reasonable man who was not in such a dangerous and life-threatening situation. Accordingly, we can not hold the defendant liable under the facts presented.

 Reversed.

Roberts v. State of Louisiana
Court of Appeal of Louisiana, 396 So.2d 566 (1981)

FACTS

On September 1, 1977 at about 12:45 p.m., Mike Burson, the blind operator of a concession stand located in the lobby of the U.S. Post Office in Alexandria, Louisiana, left his stand to go to the men's bathroom. While on his way there, Burson bumped into Plaintiff William C. Roberts, causing the latter to fall and injure his hip. Plaintiff sued the State of Louisiana advancing two theories of liability 1) respondeat superior; and 2) in negligence, for the failure of the State to properly supervise and oversee the operation of the concession stand. Specifically that the defendant did not use his cane when he walked to the bathroom thus causing injury to the plaintiff. The trial court dismissed plaintiff's complaint and he appealed.

 In determining the actor's negligence, must the court consider whether the defendant was acting as a reasonable prudent man with same physical characteristics, infirmity and shortcomings of the defendant, under the same or similar circumstances?

 In evaluating the negligence of the defendant, the court must consider whether the defendant was acting as a reasonable prudent man with same physical characteristics, infirmity, limitations and shortcomings of the defendant, under the same or similar circumstances.

 In evaluating the negligence of the defendant, the court must consider whether the defendant was acting as a reasonable prudent man with same physical characteristics, limitations and shortcomings of the defendant, under the same or similar circumstances. Under the theory of respondeat superior, as applied to this case, it is critical that the court find the defendant acted negligently in order to find the state liable. While the standard of care to which the handicapped are expected to perform differs from court to court, one generally recognized modern standard, advanced by Professor William L. Prosser, holds that a man who is blind cannot be held to the same standard of care as one who is not. However, at the same time, the conduct of that individual must be reasonable in light of "his knowledge of his infirmity, which is treated merely as one of the circumstances under which he acts." In this case, Burson, who is totally blind, admits that he did not use his cane on his way to the restroom on the day in question. Rather, he declared that he relied on his facial sense as an adequate technique for short trips in familiar settings. Expert testimony at trial indicated that while the blind often use a cane to navigate unfamiliar surroundings, 9 out of 10 do not use one when moving around in familiar places. Burson testified he worked in the same building for 3 ½ years and was very familiar with his surroundings. In light of the above, we hold that the plaintiff has failed to show that Burson acted negligently – walking too fast, not paying attention or engaged in any acts which may be construed as negligent.

 Affirmed.

Robinson v. Lindsay

Supreme Court of Washington, 598 P.2d 392 (1979)

FACTS

Plaintiff Kelly Robinson, an 11-year-old girl, brings suit against Defendant Lindsay, the owner of a snowmobile driven by Defendant Billy Anderson, a 13-year-old boy. Robinson was a passenger in the snowmobile and lost full use of her thumb in a snowmobile accident. The trial court instructed the jury that a minor must exercise the same reasonable standard of care as a child of like age, intelligence and experience and the jury returned a verdict in favor of the defendant. After a jury verdict in favor of the defendant, a new trial was ordered by the trial court. An Appeal was made by the plaintiff on the ground that the jury instructions were erroneous.

 Should an adult standard of care be applied to a minor child when the child is engaged in adult activities?

 An adult standard of care should be applied to a minor child when that child is engaged in adult activities.

 An adult standard of care should be applied to a minor child when that child is engaged in adult activities. Ordinarily, a child's conduct is compared to the conduct of a reasonable child of the same age, experience, intelligence, maturity, and training. However, an exception exists in many jurisdictions when the child is engaged in an inherently dangerous activity. In such a situation, the child will be held to an adult standard of care. Some courts have couched this exception in terms of a child who is engaged in adult activities. Consequently, the holding of minors to an adult standard of care when they operate mechanized vehicles, an activity normally reserved for adults, has been increasingly accepted and adopted by many courts. And the operation of a snowmobile, a motorized vehicle which requires adult care and competence, is no exception. Accordingly, the defendant-minor in this case, Billy Anderson, should be held to an adult standard of care. The court's instructions to the jury were therefore in error.

C We affirming the order granting a new trial.

Breunig v. American Family Insur. Co.

Supreme Court of Wisconsin, 173 N.W.2d 619 (1970)

FACTS

Defendant Erma Veith was driving home after taking her husband to work when she noticed a white light on the back of a car ahead of her. She followed the light for three or four blocks. The next thing she knew, her car was in a field and then she was at a hospital. Plaintiff Breunig was injured as a result. At trial, a psychiatrist testified that Veith, believing that God was taking ahold of her steering wheel and was directing her car at the time, accelerated into the path of an on-coming truck believing that she might become airborne like Batman. At trial, American Family Insurance Co., Veith's insurance carrier, argued that she was not liable for the plaintiff's injuries because Veith had no way of knowing that she would become delusional at that point in time, resulting in a loss of control of her car. Breunig, on the other hand, argued that Veith had experienced similar episodes in the past. As such, he argued, she had been forewarned, nullifying her "delusional" defense to negligence.

 Is insanity a valid defense to negligence when the accused's history of mental illness was known to her and/or others?

 A sudden, unanticipated event related to a *known* mental illness may not serve as a defense to negligence.

 Mental illness can serve as a defense to negligence only if it affects a person's ability to understand and appreciate her duty (to drive his car with ordinary car, for example) *or* if the insanity does not affect such understanding and appreciation (to operate and control her car in an ordinary prudent manner, for example). Moreover, there must be no history of mental illness that gives rise to a warning of an episode of insanity or sudden incapacity that should have been reasonably foreseen. The policy basis for holding the insane person liable for her tort is: 1) where one of two persons must suffer a loss, it should be borne by the one who caused it; 2) it encourages those responsible for the care and estate afflicted individual to exercise more control over her; and 3) the defense could easily be misused, leading to false claims of insanity to avoid liability. Thus, insanity can not serve as a defense to negligence when the insanity was known and should be anticipated.

 Affirmed.

Heath v. Swift Wings Inc.

Court of Appeals of North Carolina, 252 S.E.2d 526 (1979)

FACTS

Fred Heath, an employee of Defendant Swift Wings Inc. was flying a Piper 180 Arrow airplane which crashed. The pilot, Fred Heath, his wife, son and a family friend, Vance Smathers, were all killed. The administrator (plaintiff) of the son's and the wife's estate brought an action against Swift Wings, Inc. alleging that the husband/father's [Fred Heath's] negligence caused the death of those on board. At the trial, the administrator's expert testified that in his opinion, a reasonably prudent pilot should have made a controlled landing in a nearby cornfield if he were experiencing difficulty attaining flight speed, and had he done so, all aboard would have survived. The trial court instructed the jury that aviation negligence could be defined as failure to exercise the degree and care which an ordinary prudent pilot with the same experience and training as Fred Heath would have used under the same or similar circumstances. The jury returned a verdict in favor of the defendant and the administrator appealed contending that the trial court's jury instructions were erroneous - that the court improperly introduced a subjective standard of care into the definition of negligence by referring to the "ordinary care and caution . . . *having the same training and experience as Fred Heath . . .*"

 Is the negligence of a specialist decided based on the degree of ordinary care and caution exercised by those having the same experience, preparation and education?

 The negligence of a specialist decided based on the degree of ordinary care and caution exercised by those having the same experience, preparation and education – the specialist within the profession may be held to a standard of care greater than that of the general practitioner.

 The negligence of a specialist decided based on the degree of ordinary care and caution exercised by those having the same experience, preparation and education. The trial court erred when it introduced this subjective standard of care into the definition of negligence of professionals; specifically when it charged the jury and defined negligence in this case by referring to the "ordinary care and caution . . . *having the same training and experience as Fred Heath . . .*" We are of the opinion that a greater standard of care should be applied in those situations where persons are shown to possess special skill in a particular endeavor. Consequently, an actor who engages in a business, profession or occupation must exercise the requisite degree of learning, skill, and ability of that calling with reasonable and ordinary care. On the other hand, a specialist in a particular profession may be held to a higher standard of care. In either case, the standard is an objective one. Here, the instructions regarding the pilot's standard of care were erroneous because they allow the jury to consider Fred Heath's own training and experience as a pilot in a formulation of the requisite standard of care, rather than the minimum standard of care that is applicable to all pilots.

 New trial ordered

Hodges v. Carter

Supreme Court of North Carolina, 80 S.E.2d 144 (1954)

FACTS

On June 4, 1948, Plaintiff Hodges's drug store was destroyed in a fire located in Bellhaven, North Carolina. Consequently, he sought to recover for his loss from four insurance carriers who issued polices covering such losses. When the insurances companies refused to compensate Hodges, he hired Defendant-attorneys, H.C. Carter and D.D. Topping, now deceased, to institute separate actions against each carrier. While the defendant-attorneys filed a summons and complaint with the Commissioner of Insurance of the State of North Carolina, defendants did not serve *each* insurance company *separately*. As a result, all four insurance companies filed a motion to dismiss the case for failure of proper service [their reasoning: the Commissioner did not have authority to accept service on behalf of foreign insurance carriers, what amounted to substituted service by mail – there was no statutory authorization for service by mail, only personal delivery]. The trial court denied the motions and on appeal, the Supreme Court of North Carolina reversed and dismissed each action. The plaintiff thereafter sued the defendants in negligence alleging that their failure to properly serve the insurance companies amount to professional carelessness. Defendants defended arguing that they plead in good faith and exercised their best judgment. The trial court ruled in favor of the defendants and the plaintiff appealed.

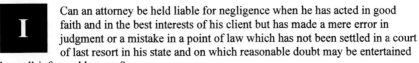

I Can an attorney be held liable for negligence when he has acted in good faith and in the best interests of his client but has made a mere error in judgment or a mistake in a point of law which has not been settled in a court of last resort in his state and on which reasonable doubt may be entertained by well-informed lawyers?

R An attorney will not be held liable for negligence when he has acted in good faith and in the best interests of his client but has made a mere error in judgment or a mistake in a point of law which has not been settled in a court of last resort in his state and on which reasonable doubt may be entertained by well-informed lawyers.

A An attorney will not be held liable for negligence when he has acted in good faith and in the best interests of his client but has made a mere error in judgment or a mistake in a point of law which has not been settled in a court of last resort in his state and on which reasonable doubt may be entertained by well-informed lawyers. Ordinarily, an attorney who engages in the practice of the law and who is acting on behalf of his client impliedly represents that 1) he possesses the requisite learning, skill, and ability necessary to the practice of law; 2) he will use his best judgment in carrying out the action on behalf of his client; and 3) he will exercise reasonable care and diligence in the use of his skill and knowledge in his client's case. Consequently, an attorney acting in good faith and in the best interests of his client is not liable for mere errors in judgment or a mistake in an unsettled point of law but will he held liable for a failure to exercise that degree of knowledge and skill commonly possessed by other attorneys, or for a failure to use diligence and ordinary care, or for a failure to exercise good faith and act in the best interest of his client. Here, the plaintiff has not presented any evidence to show that defendants breached any standard of care or

Hodges v. Carter

Supreme Court of North Carolina, 80 S.E.2d 144 (1954)

duty imposed upon them by the law. When the defendants served the Commissioner on behalf of the four foreign insurance companies, they were merely following a custom which had been followed in the state for more than 20 years and foreign insurance companies have uniformly ratified such procedure by filing their answers or making their defense. The right of the Commissioner to accept service of process on behalf of insurance companies has not yet been tested in the courts. Nevertheless, defendants had obtained the judicial declaration of a judge of our Superior Courts that the acceptance of the service of process by the Commissioner subjected the insurance companies to the jurisdiction of the court. Our earlier decision, granting the insurance companies' motion to dismiss, was not meant to indicate that the defendants in this case were negligent.

Judgment affirmed.

Boyce v. Brown
Supreme Court of Arizona, 77 P.2d 455 (1938)

FACTS

Plaintiff Nannie Boyce and her husband Berlie B. Boyce (hereinafter, the plaintiffs) brought suit against Dr. Edgar H. Brown (defendant) to recover damages for alleged malpractice by the defendant on Nannie Boyce. In September of 1927, Nannie Boyce sought the services of Edgar Brown, a surgeon, to operate on her broken ankle. In doing so, Brown operated on her ankle and repaired the injury using a metal screw to bring together the fragments of broken bone. In November of 1934, Boyce consulted Brown again because of the continued pain in her ankle. Brown treated her again but her condition did not improve. By January of 1936, Boyce sought a second opinion and went to Dr. Kent Mesa, another surgeon, who took an x-ray of Boyce's ankle which evidenced necrosis [the death of cells or tissues through injury or disease, especially in a localized area of the body] of the bone around the screw. Dr. Kent operated on Boyce and removed the screw and Boyce made an uneventful recovery. Her ankle was practical normal after Dr. Kent's operation. Consequently, Boyce sued Brown claiming that his failure to take an x-ray of her ankle constituted negligence. The trial court granted a motion for an instructed verdict in favor of the defendant on the ground that there was no competent testimony presented to suggest that the defendant committed malpractice. Plaintiffs' appealed and argued that the defendant's failure to take an x-ray of Nannie's ankle constituted negligence.

In order to impart liability to the defendant in a medical malpractice case, must the plaintiff prove that the defendant's method of treatment fell below the ordinary standard of medical care set in that medical community?

In order to impart liability to the defendant in a medical malpractice case, the plaintiff must prove that the defendant's method of treatment fell below the ordinary standard of medical care set in that medical community.

In order to impart liability to the defendant in a medical malpractice case, the plaintiff must prove that the defendant's method of treatment fell below the ordinary standard of medical care set in that medical community. A medical practitioner is presumed to possess the degree of skill and learning possessed by the average member of the medical community in which he practices. If he does not possess the requisite skill and learning, he will be held negligent. However, before a physician is held liable in malpractice, the plaintiff must prove: 1) the applicable standard of care in the community by affirmative evidence as established through the testimony of expert witnesses; 2) that the doctor's act or omission deviated from the applicable standard of care; and 3) that the physician was in fact negligent in his acts or omissions. The testimony of other physicians that they would have followed a different course of treatment than that followed by the defendant(s) is not sufficient unless it also appears that the defendants' course of treatment fell below the accepted standard in the community. Here, the only testimony bearing on the medical standards or the proper treatment was that given by Dr. Kent and the defendant himself. The latter testified that he did what was required at the time he examined the plaintiff and the former testified, on

Boyce v. Brown

Supreme Court of Arizona, 77 P.2d 455 (1938)

---

cross-examination, that the method of uniting the bone used by the defendant was a standard one and that the screw was not removed, as a rule, unless it caused trouble. However, Dr. Kent never testified that the method of operation followed by the defendant-doctor deviated from the standard of care in the medical community; nor did he indicate that the defendant's failure to take an x-ray of the plaintiff's ankle was in any way negligent. In many cases, the taking of an x-ray is of no value to the treatment of the patient and may additionally put the patient through unnecessary expense. Thus, in view of Dr. Kent's testimony that plaintiff's arthritis would have been his first thought as to the cause of her pain, this court believes that defendant's failure to take an x-ray of her ankle was not so far a departure from ordinary medical standards as to constitute gross negligence.

 The judgment of the superior court is affirmed.

Morrison v. MacNamara
District of Columbia Court of Appeals, 407 A.2d 555 (1979)

FACTS

Plaintiff-appellant Morrison reported to Defendant-appellee MacNamara, a national board certified medical laboratory located in Washington, D.C., for a urethral smear test screening for tricomonas, a urinary track infection. Plaintiff's test was administered while he was standing. As a result of the test, plaintiff fainted and struck his head on a metal blood pressure stand causing, among other injuries, a permanent loss of his senses of smell and taste. Plaintiff sued defendant on the ground that the latter was negligent in administering plaintiff's test while he was standing. At trial, plaintiff presented evidence that the national standard of care requires that the patient sit or lie down during the smear test. Defendant countered by presenting evidence which showed that in the Washington D.C. metropolitan area, such tests were administered with the patient standing up. The trial court refused to admit plaintiff's "national standard of care" evidence on the ground that plaintiff must present evidence of the standard of care in the same medical community as that of defendant. The plaintiff appealed.

 Must the conduct of health professionals be measured against nationally accepted standards of care when they are certified through a national board certification system?

 The conduct of health professionals must be measured against nationally accepted standards of care when they are certified through a system of national board certification.

 The conduct of health professionals must be measured against nationally accepted standards of care when they are certified through a system of national board certification. Here, plaintiff contends that in view of the national certification of defendant, the latter had to adhere to nationally accepted standards for administering the urethral smear test. Defendant, on the other hand, argues that it should only be held to the standard of care as recognized in the Washington area. Several jurisdictions follow the locality rule, which is particular to medical malpractice and which states that the conduct of members of the medical profession is to be measured only by the standard of conduct expected of the other members of the medical profession in the same locality or the same community. The policy behind the rule was that doctors in rural areas should be protected and should not be held to the same standard of care as their urban counterparts since the former often lacked the same training, education and experience as doctors belonging to the latter group. In this case, however, the rule is irrelevant because Washington, D.C., as the nation's capitol, is not an isolated rural area and because any disparity between the skill and training of urban doctors and rural doctors has for the most part been eliminated due to the standardization of medical education throughout the nation and improvements in transportation and communications. In light of the above, we are of the opinion that at least with respect to *board certified* medical laboratories, staffed by *board certified* medical professionals, the standard of care is to be measured by the national standard.

Morrison v. MacNamara

District of Columbia Court of Appeals, 407 A.2d 555 (1979)

Varying geographical standards of care are no longer valid in view of the uniform standards of proficiency established by national board certification. Here, defendant is a nationally certified medical laboratory, and it holds itself to the public as such. Thus, the trial court's instruction which compares a nationally certified medical professional's conduct with the standard of care in the District of Columbia or a similar locality is erroneous. Judgment in favor of appellees is vacated.

Reversed.

Scott v. Bradford
Supreme Court of Oklahoma, 606 P.2d 554 (1979)

FACTS

Plaintiff Scott's personal physician advised her that she had several fibroid tumors on her uterus and referred her to Defendant Bradford, a surgeon, for their removal. Prior to the surgery, plaintiff signed the usual informed consent form prior to performing a hysterectomy. After the surgery, plaintiff suffered from incontinence [uncontrolled bowel movements] and was referred to a urologist. The urologist corrected the problem after three surgeries. Plaintiff brought a negligence action against defendant on the ground that defendant had failed to inform her of the risks of the surgery and other available alternatives to surgery. She further maintained that had she been so informed, she would not have gone through with the hysterectomy. The trial court instructed the jury on the theory of informed consent; that is, of a physician's duty to disclose to the patient any material risks which might arise and the possibility of alternative treatments. The jury returned a verdict in favor of defendant and the plaintiff appealed.

Can a physician be held negligent if he does not disclose to the patient any material risks of the treatment and/or the possibility of alternative treatments?

A doctor can be held negligent if he does not disclose to the patient any material risks of the treatment and/or the possibility of alternative treatments.

A doctor can be held negligent if he does not disclose to the patient any material risks of the treatment and/or the possibility of alternative treatments. Effective medical treatment consists of the patient's consent [to the medical treatment] based upon his [the patient's] understanding of the treatment, available alternatives, and the collateral risks thereof. This requirement, known as "informed consent," is a duty placed upon the physician by the law. A breach of this duty by the physician may render the patient's consent defective, thereby imparting liability in negligence to the doctor. The "professional standard of care," which is followed by some courts, requires a physician to disclose only that information which is in conformance with the prevailing medical practice in the community. However, one of the most influential informed consent decisions, *Canterbury v. Spence,* holds that the standard measuring performance of the physician's duty to disclose is conduct which is reasonable under the circumstances. We agree with the *Canterbury* Court. A patient's right to decide whether to undergo treatment or not cannot be delegated to the local medical community or its general customs. That is to say that a physician has the duty to inform the patient to the extent necessary for him [the patient] to make an intelligent choice regarding his treatment. When non-disclosure of a particular risk is at issue, an action in negligence [for lack of informed consent] may be brought. The cause of action for lack of informed consent has three elements, and the plaintiff holds the burned of proof. First, is the duty to inform - the plaintiff must prove that the physician has a duty to disclose; and where the risks are known to the patient or where the risks ought to be known by the patient, there is no duty [this may also serve as an affirmative defense raised by the defendant-physician]. Secondly is that of causation [an objective standard]

Scott v. Bradford

Supreme Court of Oklahoma, 606 P.2d 554 (1979)

- the plaintiff must prove that he would not have undergone the treatment had he been properly informed of the risks and alternatives. Here, the court should determine whether a reasonable patient would have undergone the treatment had he been fully informed of the attendant circumstances. The third element is injury - the plaintiff must have suffered actual injury as a result of submitting to the treatment. With proof of injury, there is no cause of action in negligence based on informed consent. In this case, the trial court instructed the jury that defendant should have disclosed the material risks associated with the removal of the tumors and the alternatives available to plaintiff. Thus, these instructions are sufficient.

 Instructions were sufficient.

Moore v. The Regents of the University of California

Supreme Court of California, 793 P.2d 479 (1990)

FACTS

Plaintiff John Moore was treated at the UCLA Medical Center (defendant 1) for hairy-cell leukemia. Dr. Golde (defendant 2) removed Moore's spleen in order to save his life. Before the operation, Defendants Golde and Shirley Quan (defendant 3), a researcher, knew that Moore's blood products could have great research and commercial uses unrelated to his medical care. However, neither defendant informed Moore of their research plan or sought his consent to use his spleen for medical research purposes. Sometime before August 1979, some 3 years after the Moore's first visit to the UCLA Medical Center, Golde established a cell line from Moore's white blood cells, and applied for a patent listing himself and Quan as inventors. Golde later negotiated many lucrative contracts for the commercial use of the cell line and those products derived from it. Moore sued the Medical Center for conversion in that the defendants failed to disclose the medical and commercial value of his cells before obtaining consent the medical procedures by which they were extracted. Plaintiff amended his complaint three times. The superior court sustained all of the defendants' demurrers to the 3rd amended complaint and the Court of Appeal reversed. An appeal was made to the California Supreme Court.

When a doctor removes a patient's body tissue(s) for use in medical research, without the patient's consent or knowledge, may the patient maintain an action for conversion based on an interference with his ownership or right to possession [of his own bodily tissues]?

When a patient's blood and/or tissue is used for medical research, a patient may not sue for conversion; even when his bodily material was used without his knowledge or consent.

We first note that no court has ever reported a decision which imposed conversion liability on another for the use of human cells for medical research. To establish the tort of conversion, a plaintiff must show an actual interference with his ownership or right of possession. In this case, however, there were no ownership rights affected because Moore did not expect to retain possession of his cells after they were removed. Therefore, he cannot later sue for their conversion. There are three reasons why it is inappropriate to impose liability for conversion based on the allegations of Moore's complaint; 1) a fair balancing of the relevant policy considerations cautions against extending the tort. Specifically, and of primary interest is the policy consideration of a competent patient right to make autonomous medical decisions. This policy weighs in favor of providing a remedy to patients when physicians act with undisclosed motives. The second policy consideration is that we not threaten innocent parties who are engaged in socially useful activities, such as researchers, with civil liability. To strike the appropriate balance between the two is essential. 2) Problems in this area are better suited to legislature resolution. The legislature is better suited to decide whether liability should be imposed on the medical and scientific users of human cells who fail to secure the informed consent of the patient from whom the cells were extracted. 3) The tort of conversion is not necessary to protect patients' rights. There is no pressing need for a judicially created rule of strict liability as

Moore v. The Regents of the University of California
Supreme Court of California, 793 P.2d 479 (1990)

a patient's rights are adequately protected by a cause of action based on a physician's duty of disclosure. Were we to do so, strict liability would be imposed on all persons involved; even on those who had no role in the breach of privacy or disclosure obligations. By doing so, the socially useful activities of innocent medical researchers would be affected, creating a possible disincentive to engage in medial research.

Reversed.

Pokora v. Wabash R.y. Co.

U.S. Supreme Court, 292 U.S. 98 (1934)

FACTS

Defendant Wabash Railway operated four tracks running parallel to one another at a level crossing. As Plaintiff Pokora approached the tracks, his vision of the main track was obstructed by boxcars on the first track, so he stopped, looked and listened; however, he did not get out of his truck. At the time, he saw no trains and heard no bells or whistles. Still listening, he crossed the switch, and reaching the main track was struck by a passenger train coming from the north at a speed of twenty-five to thirty miles an hour. At trial, the court directed a verdict for the defendant based on a finding that the plaintiff was contributorily negligent and this judgment was affirmed. The U.S. Supreme Court granted certiorari.

 Should a single uniform rule of law governing the conduct of persons in dangerous situations be applied consistently in all circumstances?

 A jury should be permitted to determine whether the precautions taken by the plaintiff were sufficiently reasonable and prudent to relieve him of contributory negligence.

 Getting out of a vehicle to check for approaching trains is an uncommon precaution as dictated by everyday life; to do so is futile and often more dangerous. As a case-in-point, we take the example of a driver who has left his vehicle to check for an oncoming train. At the time he reaches the tracks on foot, a train may not be approaching. However, by the time he reenters his vehicle and starts to cross the tracks, a train may be upon him. *Baltimore & Ohio R.R. Co. v. Goodman* seemed to require a driver should get out of his vehicle to look for an approaching train at a crossing; however, we find such a requirement unrealistic when presented with the realities of modern day life. In the instant case, because of the line-of-sight obstruction presented by the boxcars, Pokora's could not see the main track or an approaching train. In order to see the main track and thus any moving train, he would have had to leave his truck and walk closer to the tracks until he could see all potential dangers free and clear. By the time he returned to his truck, a train may have appeared, seemingly from out of nowhere, presenting a real and present danger. Thus, the longer it took him to look and return to the driver's seat, the less accurate the information would be since it would afford a moving train more time to approach the crossing and less time for him to see it and react safely. Thus, a single rule governing the conduct of persons in dangerous situations should not be applied consistently to in circumstances as a uniform rule of law. The judgment should be reversed and the cause remanded for further proceedings in accordance with this opinion. It is so ordered.

 Reversed and remanded.

Osborne v. McMasters

Supreme Court of Minnesota, 41 N.W. 534 (1889)

FACTS

Defendant's employee, a clerk in defendant's drugstore, sold the decedent a poison without labeling it "poison," as required by statute. Not knowing the substance was poisonous, she ingested it and died. Plaintiff, the decedent's representative, sued the drug store arguing that the law required the drug store to clearly label all poisonous substances. The defendant defended, arguing that a breach of duty owed could only be supported where a right of action for the alleged negligent conduct existed at common law; and since no such liability existed at common law for selling poison without labeling it, an action for the same can not be maintained under the statute at issue and cited by the plaintiff. The jury found for the plaintiff and the defendant appealed.

 Is an injured plaintiff supplied with a cause of action to recover for damages as the result of the defendant's violation of a statute?

 When a person violates a statute that establishing a duty of care, that person is deemed to have acted negligently, notwithstanding evidence to the contrary.

 When a person violates a statute that establishing a duty of care, that person is deemed to have acted negligently, notwithstanding evidence to the contrary, without the need for other evidence. The common law also provides a remedy for those injures caused proximately by the negligence of others. Here, the legal duty the defendant breached was one imposed by statute. It is immaterial whether the duty was one imposed by a rule of common law or one imposed by statute. In either case, the failure to perform the duty constitutes negligence. Hence, "[t]he only difference is that in the one case the measure of legal duty is to be determined upon common-law principles, while in the other the statute fixes it, so that the violation of the statute constitutes conclusive evidence of negligence."

 Affirmed.

Stachniewicz v. Mar-Cum Corp.
Supreme Court of Oregon, 488 P.2d 436 (1971)

FACTS

A fight erupted in a bar among some of the patrons of American Indian ancestry, who were sitting in a booth. Plaintiff Stachniewicz was seated at a table with some friends. A barroom brawl broke out when one of plaintiff's friends refused to let one of the strangers to dance with the friend's wife because he [the stranger] was intoxicated. Soon after, plaintiff and his friends were involved in the fight. Not long after that, one of plaintiff's friends found the plaintiff lying injured outside the bar. Plaintiff suffered head injuries and could not remember any of the events at the bar. As a result, plaintiff sued Defendant Mar-Cam Corp, the bar operator, for the injuries suffered, contending that defendant was negligent *per se* because it had violated ORS 471.410(3) and Oregon Liquor Control Regulation No. 10-065(2), an Oregon statute and a regulation, respectively; the former prohibited bar owners from selling liquor to patrons who were visibly intoxicated and the latter prohibited bar owners from allowing loud noises and disorderly conduct in their bars. The trial court returned a verdict for defendant, indicating that neither the violation of the statute or the regulation constituted negligence *per se*. Plaintiff appealed.

Does a violation of a statute or regulation constitute negligence *per se* when the violation results in injury to a member of the class of persons protected by the statute or regulation and when the harm is of the kind which the statute or regulation is designed to prevent?

A violation of a statute or regulation constitutes negligence *per se* when the violation results in injury to a member of the class of persons protected by the statute or regulation and when the harm is of the kind which the statute or regulation is designed to prevent.

A violation of a statute or regulation constitutes negligence per se when the violation results in injury to a member of the class of persons protected by the statute or regulation and when the harm is of the kind which the statute or regulation is designed to prevent. However, it is for the court to first examine the appropriateness of the standard of the statute/regulation as a measure of care for civil litigation under the circumstances. Here, the Oregon statute bars the sale of liquor to a person *already visibly intoxicated.* It is a standard which is not appropriate for awarding civil damages because it is very difficult, if not impossible, to determine whether a 3rd party's injuries, as a matter of law, were caused by the already inebriated person. The regulation, however, concerns matters which have a direct relation to physical disturbances in bars, which in turn create the likelihood of injury to customers. Thus, we find it reasonable to assume that the regulation was promulgated to prevent such injuries and to ensure the safety of patrons of bars. Here, the plaintiff was within the class of persons intended to be protected by the *regulation*, and the harm he suffered was the type of injury the regulation was designed to prevent.

Reversed and remanded.

Ney v. Yellow Cab Co.

Illinois Supreme Court, 117 N.E.2d 74 (1954)

FACTS

A thief stole a taxicab owned by Defendant Yellow Cab Co. after an employee left the taxi unattended, with its engine still running. While in fleeing the scene, the thief hit Plaintiff Ney's vehicle and injured him. The act of leaving the taxicab unattended was a violation of section 92 of Article XIV of the Uniform Traffic Act which prohibited individuals from leaving their vehicles unattended without first stopping the engine, locking the Ignition, and removing the key or without setting the parking brake if on an incline. Plaintiff sued the defendant for his injuries arguing that the employee's violation of the statute both constituted negligence and was the proximate cause of his injuries. The trial court held in favor of the plaintiff. The Appellate Court affirmed. Defendant appealed on the ground that the statute in question was not an anti-theft measure but rather a traffic regulation, the violation of which would impose no liability on defendant for the act of a thief.

 Must the plaintiff prove that the violation of the statute at issue is the proximate cause of his injuries when he brings an action in negligence based upon the latter?

 The plaintiff must prove that the violation of the statute at issue is the proximate cause of his injuries when he brings an action in negligence based upon the latter [violation of the statute].

 The plaintiff must prove that the violation of the statute at issue is the proximate cause of his injuries when he brings an action in negligence based upon the latter [violation of the statute]. In this case, the plaintiff takes the position that the statute in question is a safety measure for the benefit of the public and that its violation is prima facie evidence of negligence. Conversely, the defendant argues that the statute is not an anti-theft measure but is a traffic regulation and, as such, its violation does not impose any liability on defendant. Thus, the issue presented [i.e. whether the defendant is liable or not] requires a determination of the following questions: 1) What was the legislative intention? 2) Is the violation of the statute the proximate cause of the injury? 3) Is the act of the thief an intervening, independent, efficient force which breaks the causal connection between the original wrong and the injury sustained? With respect to the first question, we conclude that the entire statute is a public safety measure - the protection of life, limb, and property by prevention of recognized hazards which may result in leaving an unattended vehicle running. While the violation of the statute is in itself is prima facie evidence of negligence, this does not necessarily impart liability to the defendant if the injury sustained by the plaintiff does not have a direct and proximate connection with the violation of the statute. A further problem is presented when an independent agency intervenes and the acts of the agency are illegal or criminal. Wrongful acts of independent third parties, not actually intended by the defendant, are not regarded by the law as the natural consequence of his wrong, and the defendant is not bound to anticipate the general probability of such acts if such acts were not foreseeable. If, however, the intervening criminal act was foreseeable, the causal chain is not broken by the intervention of such act and liability may attach to the original wrongdoer. In this case, there is no compelling reason to hold, as a matter of law, that no actionable negligence can exist. Questions of due care, negligence, and proximate cause, such as those presented in this case, are ordinarily left to the jury to decide. Thus, it is our opinion that the Appellate Court was correct in affirming the judgment of the trial court.

 Affirmed.

Perry v. S.N. and S.N.

Texas Supreme Court, 973 S.W.2d 301 (1998)

FACTS

Plaintiffs Mr. and Mrs. S.N. sued to recover for the injuries sustained by their two children alleging that Defendant Douglas Perry, Janice White and Raul Quintero witnessed child abuse at a daycare and failed to report it to the police or to the proper child welfare authorities. The Texas Family Code requires any person having cause to believe a child is being abused to report the abuse to state authorities; the failure to report any abuse is a misdemeanor under the statute. Plaintiffs allege that Defendant White was told by the wife of the alleged abuser, Francis Keller, that her husband Daniel Keller, had "abusive habits toward children," and that defendant actually witnessed on one occasion Mr. Keller sexually abusing children at the day care center. Defendant did not report the abuse to any authorities. The trial court granted summary judgment for the plaintiffs, but the Court of Appeals reversed and remanded the plaintiff's negligence per se and gross negligence claims for trial. The case now comes before the Texas Supreme Court.

 Does the violation of a child abuse reporting statute impose civil liability under a theory of negligence per se on a defendant who fails to report such abuse?

 A child abuse reporting statute does not create civil liability on a person who fails to report it.

 Preliminarily, we note that plaintiffs' common law negligence claim has not been preserved on appeal; therefore, we will not address this issue and will instead focus only on the negligence per se claim. The threshold questions in every negligence per se case are whether the plaintiff belongs to the class that the statute was intended to protect and whether the plaintiff's injury is the type that the statute as designed to prevent. In this case, plaintiffs' children are clearly within the protected class, and they also suffered the type of injury the statute was intended to prevent - to protect children from abuse. However, this does not end our inquiry. We must also decide if it would be fair and wise to impose civil tort liability for a violation of the statute. The court of appeals in this case listed several factors to consider in deciding whether to apply negligence per se noting that no single factor is determinative. We first consider the fact that, absent a change in the common law, a negligence per se claim against the defendants would impose the element of duty solely from the statute. At common law there is generally no duty to protect another from the criminal acts of a third-party. In contrast, in most negligence per se cases there is a preexisting common law duty to act reasonably under the circumstances, such that the criminal statute role is merely to define more precisely what conduct breaches that duty. As such, applying negligence per se in this case would bring into existence a new type of tort liability that did not exist before. A second factor to consider is whether the criminal statute gives adequate notice by clearly defining what is required. Actually witnessing the abuse, as seen in this case, is clearly enough to cause one to believe abuse is taking place.

However, there are many instances where the abuse is not so clear cut – as in when one becomes aware of abuse through second-hand reports or ambiguous physical signs. Another factor to consider is whether applying negligence per se to the reporting statute would create liability without fault. We agree with the Court of Appeals that it would not because the statute criminalizes only the "knowing" failure to report. This factor weighs in favor of imposing civil liability. The next consideration is whether negligence per se would impose ruinous liability disproportionate to the seriousness of the defendant's conduct. A severe penalty is imposed on the abuser: 5 – 9 years in prison and up to $10,000 in fines. By contrast, a failure to report abuse imposes no more than 6 months in jail and a fine of not more than $2,000. Thus, the fairly severe criminal penalty imposed on the actual abuser compared to the relatively small penalty imposed on the person who fails to report it shows that the legislature intended different legal consequences to attach to each violation and that a failure to report is viewed as a relatively minor, collateral offense, a misdemeanor. Finally, we also look at whether the injury resulted directly or indirectly from the violation of the statute. Here, it was not. Because of the factors discussed here, we conclude that a failure to report child abuse is not negligence per se.

 We reverse the court of appeals' judgment and find that plaintiffs take nothing.

Martin v. Herzog
Court of Appeals of New York, 126 N.E. 814 (1920)

FACTS

The decedent was killed when his buggy collided with the defendant's car. The accident occurred after dark and the deceased was operating his buggy without lights, which was a violation of an applicable statute. At trial, the defendant requested that the court find that the defendant's operation of his buggy without lights was "prima facie evidence of contributory negligence." The request was refused but the jury was instructed that it may consider the absence of lights as some evidence of negligence, but not as conclusive proof of negligence. Plaintiff, the widow of the deceased, was able to get a jury instruction which stated that the failure to drive without a light is not negligence in itself. Stated another way, the failure obey the law was not conclusive evidence of negligence. The jury returned a verdict for the plaintiff-widow, finding the defendant liable and the decedent free from contributory negligence. The appellate division reversed.

 Can an admitted violation of a statute designed to protect the public on the highways constitute negligence when a causal connection between the violation and the injury is weak, cannot be proven or is non-existent?

 Proof of negligence without a causal relationship between the negligence itself and the injury sustained does not support a case for liability, even where a violation of a statute has occurred.

 Proof of negligence without a causal relationship between the negligence itself and the injury sustained does not support a case for liability, even where a violation of a statute has occurred. Defendant should not be required to pay damages if his failure to use lights is the cause of the accident. However, when the trial court charged the jury to decide whether the defendant's failure to have his lights on was negligent, the jury was erroneously granted more authority than it should have been given. This was because jurors determine verdicts based on the facts of a case; but they are not allowed to come to a decision as to whether a statutory duty may be heightened or lessened. We further note that the violation of a statute itself is simply the starting point of the legal analysis, as duty, breach, proximate cause, and damages must also be determined. In this case, the statute clearly established the duty for the benefit of all who travel on the highways; a duty that was admittedly breached by the defendant. The decedent died, so damages are present. However, if causation is missing; that is, if it were determined that the crash was not due to the lack of lights on the buggy, Herzog could only be liable for the decedent's death if the death were caused by some other negligent act of his. Thus, a failure to put on one's lights may have been negligent because by not doing so the applicable statute was breached, but if it did not lead to the accident, *contributory* negligence cannot be imparted to the deceased.

 Affirmed.

Zeni v. Anderson
Supreme Court of Michigan, 243 N.W.2d 270 (1976)

FACTS

On the morning of March 7, 1969, Plaintiff Eleanor Zeni, a nurse, was walking to work on the side of the street with her back to the traffic, in order to get to her work because the sidewalks themselves were covered with snow. While walking on the street, she was hit and severely injured by Defendant Karen Anderson, a college student, who was driving her car in the street within the posted speed limit. Plaintiff sued defendant for the injuries that she suffered and the latter defended on the ground that plaintiff was walking in the street in violation of a statute requiring pedestrians to use sidewalks. At the trial an eyewitness testified that defendant's windows were fogged at the time she hit the plaintiff and that the defendant was traveling too close to the curb. Plaintiff suffered from retrograde amnesia and had no recollection that defendant's car was behind her and could only return to work on a part-time basis. There was testimony at the trial indicating that it was common for nurses to use the roadway instead of the sidewalk during the winter to get to work. The trial court entered a verdict in favor of plaintiff; the court of appeals reversed on other grounds [not discussed here] and the plaintiff appealed.

 Does the violation of a statute create a presumption which can be rebutted by a showing [by the party of the party charged of violating the statute] of an adequate excuse under the facts and circumstances of the case?

 The violation of a statute does create a presumption which can be rebutted by a showing [by the party of the party charged of violating the statute] of an adequate excuse under the facts and circumstances of the case.

 We think the best test of the applicable law can be found in *Lucas v. Carson,* which indicates that evidence required to rebut the presumption of negligence per se should be positive, unequivocal, strong, and credible, *as a matter of law.* Thus, if there is sufficient excuse or justification, there is ordinarily no violation of the statute and the statutory standard is inapplicable. If, however, a violation of a statute is viewed as negligence per se and the defendant held liable despite the due care or reasonable excuses for violation of the statute, then the rule in reality becomes one of strict liability, not negligence. And while a small minority of courts has chosen to view the violation of a statute only as evidence of negligence, we have chosen not to approach his approach. Thus, an accurate statement of law, adopted by this Court, is that when a penal statute is adopted as the standard of care in a civil action for negligence, violation of the statue establishes a prima facie case of negligence. If the factfinder determines such an excuse exists, the appropriate standard of care becomes that established by the common law.

 Reversed.

Goddard v. Boston & Maine R.R. Co.

Supreme Judicial Court of Massachusetts, 60 N.E. 486 (1901)

FACTS

Plaintiff Wilfred H. Goddard slipped and fell on a banana peel that was on the platform when stepping out of a train owned by Defendant Boston & Maine R.R. Co. Plaintiff sued the railroad for the injuries that he sustained as a result of his fall. The trial court directed a verdict in favor of the defendant-railroad and plaintiff appealed.

In order to quash a directed verdict in a negligence action, must the plaintiff offer enough evidence to infer that the defendant was engaged in negligent conduct and that that conduct caused the plaintiff's injury?

In order to quash a directed verdict in a negligence action, the plaintiff must offer enough evidence to infer that the defendant was engaged in negligent conduct and that that conduct caused the plaintiff's injury.

In order to quash a directed verdict in a negligence action, the plaintiff must offer enough evidence to infer that the defendant was engaged in negligent conduct and that that conduct caused the plaintiff's injury. In this case, the banana skin upon which the plaintiff slipped may have been dropped within a minute by one of the passengers who was leaving the train.

Exceptions overruled; affirmed.

Anjou v. Boston Elevated Railroad Co.

Supreme Judicial Court of Massachusetts, 94 N.E. 386 (1911)

FACTS

Plaintiff Helen G. Anjou was a passenger who had just disembarked from on of Defendant Boston Elevated Railways Co.'s cars. After exiting the car, she asked one of the railroad employees for directions to another car. While following the employee on a narrow platform toward the stairway he indicated, plaintiff slipped and fell on a banana peel and was injured. She sued the defendant claiming negligence. The banana peel was described by several people as dry, black and dirty, as if "trampled over a good deal." It was one of the duties of the employees at the train station to remove anything on the platform that would interfere with the safety of the passengers. The trial court directed a verdict in favor of defendant and the plaintiff appealed.

Is a directed verdict for the defendant proper when the plaintiff has proffered evidence sufficient to support an inference of the former's negligence?

A directed verdict for the defendant is not proper when the plaintiff has offered evidence sufficient to support an inference of the former's negligence.

A directed verdict for the defendant is not proper when the plaintiff has offered evidence sufficient to support an inference of the former's negligence. In this case, the inference might have been drawn from the appearance and condition of the banana peel that it had been on the platform for a long time, where it could have been seen and removed by a reasonably careful employee of the railroad performing his duty. Accordingly, one can reasonably argue that it was not dropped on the platform a moment before the passenger fell on it. The defendant had an obligation to ensure the reasonable safety of its passengers. This was not the case, so one can conclude that there was evidence of negligence on the part of the defendant and that that evidence should have been submitted to the jury.

Judgment for plaintiff.

Joye v. Great Atlantic and Pacific Tea Co.
U.S. Court of Appeals, 405 F.2d 464 (4th Cir. 1968)

FACTS

Plaintiff Willard Joye slipped and fell on a banana in a supermarket owned by Defendant Great Atlantic and Pacific Tea Co. (A&P). At trial plaintiff offered no direct evidence as to how long the banana had been on the floor before the accident, but the circumstantial evidence showed that the floor may not have been swept for as long as 35 minutes. Apparently no one saw the banana until after Joye fell, at which time it was described as dark brown and dirty. The district court found that A&P had *constructive* notice that the banana was on the floor and that it was negligent in leaving the banana on floor. A verdict was reached in favor of plaintiff and the court denied A&P's motion for a j.n.o.v. [directed verdict]. Defendant appealed.

 In order to prove the defendant's negligence, must a plaintiff present evidence of the defendant's knowledge of a dangerous condition?

 Actual or constructive knowledge of a dangerous condition must be proven to impose liability on a defendant for injuries caused by the condition and may be established through direct or circumstantial evidence.

 Actual or constructive knowledge of a dangerous condition must be proven to impose liability on a defendant for injuries caused by the condition and may be established through direct or circumstantial evidence. Here, plaintiff presented no direct evidence as to how long the banana had been on the floor. No one saw the banana until after Joye fell on it. There was no evidence that defendant put the banana on the floor or had actual notice of its presence. Thus, plaintiff's case turns on the sufficiency of the evidence to establish constructive notice. However, the circumstantial evidence was insufficient to allow a jury to determine whether the banana had been on the floor for 30 seconds or 3 days. Based on these uncertain facts, the jury could not have imposed constructive notice on defendant. Judgment of the district court is reversed and we remand to that court with instructions to enter judgment in favor of the defendant.

 Judgment reversed.

Ortega v. Kmart Corp.
Supreme Court of California, 36 P.3d 11 (2001)

FACTS

Plaintiff Richard M. Ortega was shopping at Defendant Kmart's Torrance, California store when he slipped on a puddle of milk on the floor adjacent to a refrigerator and suffered severe knee injuries. At trial, plaintiff testified that he did not notice whether the puddle milk was fresh, stale, cold or odorous. He could not present evidence showing how long the milk was on the floor. He did, however, claim that because the evidence showed Kmart had not inspected the premises in a reasonable period of time before his fall, a jury could infer the milk was on the floor long enough for the employees to discover its presence and clean it up. The jury returned a verdict in plaintiff's favor and awarded him $47,200; Kmart appealed.

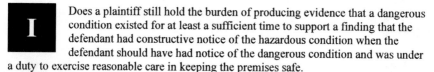

I Does a plaintiff still hold the burden of producing evidence that a dangerous condition existed for at least a sufficient time to support a finding that the defendant had constructive notice of the hazardous condition when the defendant should have had notice of the dangerous condition and was under a duty to exercise reasonable care in keeping the premises safe.

R The burden of proof is not shifted to the defendant; a plaintiff still holds the burden of producing evidence that a dangerous condition existed for at least a sufficient time to support a finding that the defendant had constructive notice of the hazardous condition even when the defendant should have had notice of the dangerous condition and was under a duty to exercise reasonable care in keeping the premises safe.

A The burden of proof is not shifted to the defendant; a plaintiff still holds the burden of producing evidence that a dangerous condition existed for at least a sufficient time to support a finding that the defendant had constructive notice of the hazardous condition even when the defendant should have had notice of the dangerous condition and was under a duty to exercise reasonable care in keeping the premises safe. The plaintiff need not show actual knowledge – knowledge may be shown by circumstantial evidence "which is nothing more than one or more inferences which may be said to arise reasonably from a series of proven facts." Whether the dangerous condition existed before the accident; long enough for a reasonably prudent person to have discovered it is a question of fact to be decided by a jury. Each accident must be evaluated in light of the unique circumstances of each individual case. Thus, we conclude that the plaintiffs still have the burden of providing producing evidence of the dangerous condition existed for at least a sufficient time to support a finding that the defendant had constructive notice of the hazard and similarly conclude that plaintiffs may demonstrate constructive notice on the part of the defendants if they can show that the site had not been inspected within a reasonable period such that a person exercising due care would have noticed it. For these reasons, we affirm the court of appeal's judgment.

C Judgment of the Court of Appeals is affirmed.

Jasko v. F.W. Woolworth Co.

Supreme Court of Colorado, 494 P.2d 839 (1972)

FACTS

Plaintiff Jasko was injured when she slipped on a piece of pizza that was on the floor near the "pizza-hoagie counter" of Defendant F.W. Woolworth Co.'s store. Thereafter, plaintiff brought a negligent suit against defendant to recover for her injuries. The trial court entered a judgment in favor of defendant holding that the plaintiff failed to show that defendant had actual or constructive notice of the pizza on the floor. Plaintiff appealed contending that it was the defendant's method of sale which created a dangerous situation, such that she [plaintiff] was not required to prove that defendant was on notice of the specific item on the floor.

 Must a plaintiff prove that the defendant had notice of the dangerous condition which caused her injury when such a condition is of a type that is continuous and/or easily foreseeable?

 A plaintiff need not prove that the defendant had notice of the dangerous condition which caused her injury when such a condition is of a type that is continuous and/or easily foreseeable.

 A plaintiff need not prove that the defendant had notice of the dangerous condition which caused her injury when such a condition is of a type that is continuous and/or easily foreseeable. Here, the dangerous condition was created by the defendant's method of sale itself, and the fact that the floors were constantly cleaned shows that the defendant knew of the condition. The practice of selling pizza on wax paper created the reasonable probability that food will inevitably drop to the floor, thus creating a safety hazard. Consequently, in such a situation, the plaintiff need not prove that the defendant was on notice of the condition. The notice requirement is necessary where the dangerous condition is out of the ordinary. In such a situation, the store owner is allowed reasonable time to discover and correct the condition. However, that was not the case here as the dangerous conditions were continuous and easily foreseeable. Hence, notice requirement disappears. Ruling of the Court of Appeals is reversed and the cause remanded to it for further remand to the trial court and new trial.

 Reversed and a new trial is granted.

H.E. Butt Groc. Co. v. Resendez

Supreme Court of Texas, 988 S.W.2d 218 (1999)

FACTS

While shopping at one of defendant's H.E. Butt Grocery Stores (HEB), Plaintiff Maria Resendez slipped and fell near two grape displays. She brought suit against the defendant in negligence, alleging the customer display sampling stand posed an unreasonable risk of harm that caused her injuries. The trial court rendered a judgment on a jury verdict in favor of the plaintiff and the Court of Appeals affirmed concluding that the HEB sampling stand posed an unreasonable risk of harm to store customers. Defendant appealed to the Supreme Court of Texas.

Can a mere display of produce for customer sampling constitute an unreasonable risk of harm to customers?

The mere display of produce for customer sampling does not constitute an unreasonable risk of harm to customers.

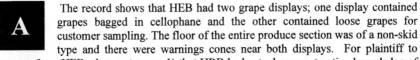

The record shows that HEB had two grape displays; one display contained grapes bagged in cellophane and the other contained loose grapes for customer sampling. The floor of the entire produce section was of a non-skid type and there were warnings cones near both displays. For plaintiff to recover from HEB, she must prove 1) that HRB had actual or constructive knowledge of a condition on the site; 2) that the condition posed an unreasonable risk of harm; 3) that HRB did not exercise reasonable care to reduce or eliminate the risk; and 4) HEB's failure to use such care was the proximate cause of the plaintiff's injuries. Plaintiff presented no evidence to suggest that the display created an unreasonable risk to customers falling on grapes. The mere *existence* of the display is not enough – some more must be offered. In Corbin v. Safeway Stores Inc. it was the manner in which the defendant-store displayed the grapes – in a slanted bin over a linoleum tile floor with no protected floor mat – that created an unreasonable risk of harm [i.e., customers falling on grapes falling from the display onto the floor]. Here, there is no evidence that the manner of the display created such a risk. HEB's petition for review granted, Court of Appeals judgment reversed.

Judgment of the Court of Appeals is reversed.

Byrne v. Boadle

Court of Exchequer, 159 Eng.Rep. 299 (1863)

FACTS

The plaintiff was passing along a highway in front of the defendant's place of business when he was struck by a barrel of flour the defendant was allegedly lowering from a window above. Several eyewitnesses testified that the barrel fell and indeed struck the plaintiff. At trial and in its own defense, the defendant argued that the plaintiff had offered no evidence of his allegations of negligence to merit sending the case to the jury. The jury assessed damages in the amount of £50 for the plaintiff but the court nonetheless entered a nonsuit against the plaintiff and in favor of the defendant. The plaintiff appealed.

When it is more likely than not that an injury is due to the defendant's negligence, must the plaintiff still prove the defendant's negligence?

The doctrine of res ipsa loquitur (literally "the thing speaks for itself") requires the defendant to produce contrary evidence or be found liable for negligence when it is more likely than not that an injury is due to the defendant's negligence and the instrument which caused the injury was within the defendant's control.

This case rests on the presumption that the defendant's servants were involved moving the barrel or in lowering the barrel from the upper window. Were this not the case, the defendant is charged to prove otherwise by submitting evidence to the contrary. A plaintiff is typically obliged to submit proof of negligence when he alleges it; however, in some cases, such as this one, the mere fact that an accident has occurred is evidence of the negligence itself. Since a barrel would not ordinarily roll out of the window of a warehouse unless someone was negligent, to require an injured plaintiff to call witnesses to establish such negligence seems to me to be preposterous. A better, alternative approach to the issue of negligence under the aforementioned conditions would be that where a particular accident presupposes the existence of negligence, it is up to the defendant to prove otherwise. This is the doctrine of res ipsa loquitur. Thus, when it is more likely than not that an injury is due to the defendant's negligence, and the instrument causing the injury is within the defendant's control, the plaintiff does not need prove negligence unless the defendant produces evidence to the contrary.

Affirmed.

McDougald v. Perry
Supreme Court of Florida, 716 So. 2d 783 (1998)

FACTS

Plaintiff-appellant Lawrence McDougald was driving behind a tractor-trailer driven by Defendant-respondent Henry Perry and his employer, C&S Chemical Co., after a large, 130 lb. spare tire came out of the cradle underneath the trailer and fell to the ground as the defendant drove over some railroad tracks. As the trailer's rear wheels drove over it, the tire bounced up and into the windshield of the plaintiff's Jeep. The spare tire was held in place in its cradle by its own weight and additionally secured by a 6 ft. long chain wrapped around it. The chain was attached to the body of the trailer by a latch device. Defendant testified at trial that he performed a pre-trip inspection which included an inspection of the chain, but admitted he did not check every link in the chain. The jury subsequently returned a verdict in favor of the plaintiff. On appeal, the district court reversed with instruction that the trial court direct a verdict in respondent's favor concluding that the trial court erred by instructing the jury on res ipsa loquitur.

Can an injured plaintiff be permitted the benefit of an inference of negligence on the part of the defendant; that is, assert that a particular accident could not have occurred in the absence of some negligent act on the part of the defendant?

Res ipsa loquitur provides an inference of negligence when the accident is the type that does not occur without negligence and when the defendant is in exclusive control of the circumstances.

An injured plaintiff may be permitted the benefit of an inference of negligence on the part of the defendant. That is, assert that a particular accident could not have occurred in the absence of some negligent act on the part of the defendant. The trial court correctly instructed the jury on the doctrine of res ipsa loquitur [Latin for "the thing speaks for itself"]. It is a rule of evidence that permits, but does not require, an inference of negligence in certain circumstances. It can provide an injured plaintiff with an inference of negligence where there is no direct proof of negligence. Here, plaintiff must show that the instrumentality causing the injury was under defendant's exclusive control and that the accident is one that would not ordinarily occur without negligence on the part of the one in control. The plaintiff need not proffer expert testimony to raise such an inference of negligence; and is furthermore not required to eradicate all other possible causes of the accident. All that is required is a showing that on the whole it is more likely than not that there was negligence associated with the cause of the accident. However, to prevail at trial, the plaintiff must still present sufficient evidence, beyond the accident itself, from which the jury could infer that the accident would not have occurred but for the defendant's breach of due care. In light of the above, we conclude that the spare tire escaping from the trailer is the type of accident, as a matter of general knowledge, that would not occur but for the lack of reasonable care by the person who had control of the spare tire.

Reversed and remanded with directions to reinstate the jury's verdict in favor of plaintiff.

Larson v. St. Francis Hotel

District Court of Appeal of California, 188 P.2d 513 (1948)

FACTS

Plaintiff Larson, while walking past Defendant St. Francis Hotel, was struck by a heavy armchair and was injured. Thereafter, she sued the owners of St. Francis Hotel. No one saw the chair before it hit Larson and there was no identification on the chair as belonging to the defendant. Plaintiff presented the foregoing facts at trial, the extent of her injuries and rested her case, relying upon the doctrine of res ipsa loquitur. On defendant's motion, the trial court entered a nonsuit verdict [in favor of the defendant] and the plaintiff appealed.

 Can the doctrine of res ipsa loquitur be applied to a situation where the plaintiff's injury is caused by an instrumentality which may not have been within the exclusive control of the defendant and where the accident might have happened despite the fact that the defendant exercised due care?

 The doctrine of res ipsa loquitur does not apply to a situation where the plaintiff's injury could be attributable to more than one cause, some of which are not within the exclusive control of the defendant or where the accident might have still happened despite the fact that the defendant exercised due care.

 The doctrine of res ipsa loquitur does not apply to a situation where the plaintiff's injury could be attributable to more than one cause, some of which are not within the exclusive control of the defendant or where the accident might still have happened despite the fact that the defendant exercised due care. *Gerhart v. Southern California Gas Co.*, as cited by the plaintiff, provides that in order to rely on the doctrine of res ipsa loquitur the plaintiff must prove 1) that there was an accident; 2) that the instrumentality causing the accident was under the exclusive control and management of the defendant; 3) that the accident was such that it would not happen absent negligence on the part of the defendant. The doctrine of res ipsa only applies where the cause of injury is under the exclusive control of the defendant, not where the accident may have been attributable to one of several causes, for some of which the defendant is not responsible. Where it appears that the accident resulting in the injury was caused by one of two causes for which the defendant is responsible for one but not for the other, the plaintiff must fail, if the evidence does not show that the injury was the result of the former cause. Applying the rule above to the fact of the instant case, we conclude the doctrine does not apply here. A hotel does not have exclusive control, actual or potential, over its furniture - guests of the hotel have at least partial control. Moreover, one cannot conclude that the accident would not have occurred absent negligence on the part of the defendant since the chair could have been thrown from the window of the hotel by a hotel guest.

 Judgment affirmed.

Ybarra v. Spangard
Supreme Court of California, 154 P.2d 687 (1944)

FACTS

Plaintiff Ybarra entered the hospital with appendicitis and his physician arranged for Defendant Dr. Spangard to perform an appendectomy. Once in the operating room, Co-defendant Dr. Reser, an anesthetist, pulled Ybarra's body to the head of the operating table to correctly place him for surgery. Ybarra then received the anesthetic and the surgery commenced. When Ybarra awoke in a hospital room surrounded by two nurses, he noticed pain in his right shoulder which he did not have prior to entering the operating room. Although he was treated for the pain during his stay, it worsened. After his discharge from the hospital, Ybarra developed paralysis in his shoulder muscles. After consulting with two separate physicians, he was told him that his pain was the result of trauma or injury. Subsequently, Ybarra sued the anesthetist and the other named defendants for his injuries under the theory of res ipsa loquitur. The trial entered judgments of nonsuit as to all defendants and plaintiff appealed.

 Can res ipsa loquitur be used to both prove and allocate liability for an injury; even when a plaintiff is unable to determine individual guilt among more than on defendant?

 When a plaintiff receives unusual injuries while unconscious while unconscious and in the course of medical treatment, all those defendants who had any control over the defendant's body or the instrumentalities which might have caused the injuries may be properly called upon to meet the inference of negligence (res ipsa loquitur) by giving an explanation of their conduct.

 The goal of res ipsa loquitur is to provide a plaintiff without access to the facts a basis upon which to recover for his injuries. In the instant case, the plaintiff was rendered unconscious during surgery and did not and could not possible know what had happened during that time. After he awoke, he noticed pain that was not present before he was rendered unconscious and during the operation. He identified the cause of his injury as best he could but could not explain in detail what happened to him while he was anesthetized. However, the defendants could and thus should be required to tell him. Hence, res ipsa loquitur can be used to both prove and allocate liability for an injury; even when a plaintiff is unable to determine individual guilt among more than on defendant.

 Reversed.

Sullivan v. Crabtree

Court of Appeals of Tennessee, 258 S.W.2d 782 (1953)

FACTS

The Sullivans (plaintiffs) brought an action against Defendant Crabtree for the death of their son, Robert, a passenger in defendant's tractor-trailer truck. Robert was killed when the truck swerved off the highway and overturned. The evidence at trial suggested that defendant's truck suddenly swerved when it was overtaken and passed by another truck. As a result, it overturned down a steep cliff, and crushed the decedent to death. Defendant testified that there was some loose gravel on the road and that he may have lost control when his brakes grabbed or gave way. The jury entered a verdict in defendant's favor. The Sullivans appealed claiming that the defendant's negligence was, as a matter of law, the cause of the decedent's death and that there was no evidence supporting a verdict for defendant relying on the doctrine of res ipsa loquitur.

 Is a court compelled to enter a verdict for the plaintiff, as a matter of law, if the latter successfully establishes a prima facie case of negligence against the defendant based on the theory of res ipsa loquitur?

 A court is not compelled to enter a verdict for the plaintiff, as a matter of law, if the latter successfully establishes a prima facie case of negligence against the defendant based on the theory of res ipsa loquitur.

 In the instant case, plaintiffs insist that the facts of this case brought it within the rule of res ipsa loquitur requiring a finding of negligence in the absence of an explanation disproving negligence. We disagree. While the evidence presented made a case for res ipsa loquitur, this court is not of the opinion that the jury was required to make an inference of negligence. The application of res ipsa loquitur could give rise to three different prospects: 1) It warrants an *inference* of negligence which the jury may or may not choose to draw [as their judgment dictates]; or 2) it raises a presumption of negligence which requires the jury to find negligence if the defendant does not produce evidence sufficient to rebut the presumption; or 3) it raises a presumption of negligence and shifts the burden of proof to the defendant, requiring him to prove by a preponderance of evidence that the injury was not caused by his negligence. The effect of the doctrine varies depending on the facts and evidence in each individual cause of action. Sometimes, in rare cases, the inference of negligence may be so strong as to *require* a verdict for the plaintiff. However, in ordinary cases such as the one before us, the doctrine simply makes a case for the jury to choose the inference of defendant's negligence in preference over other permissible inferences. Here, the jury could reasonably conclude that the cause of the accident was from the brakes of the truck giving away and not the result of negligence on the part of the defendant.

 Affirmed.

Perkins v. Texas and New Orleans Ry. Co.
Supreme Court of Louisiana, 147 So.2d 646 (1962)

FACTS

Plaintiff Perkins, the 67-year-old widow of the decedent, Tanner Perkins, sought damages for the death of her husband, caused when Defendant Texas and New Orleans Railroad Co.'s train crashed into the car in which the decedent was riding, at a railroad crossing, killing him. At trial, evidence was offered to show that the railroad company had installed a swinging red light and a bell at the crossing in order to warn of an approaching train and that at the time of the accident, this signal was operating. The evidence at trail also suggested that the speed of the train at the time of the accident was 37 miles per hour; 12 miles in excess of the permitted speed limit, and that this violation was, standing alone, evidence of negligence. The trial court ruled in favor of plaintiff and awarded damages and the Court of Appeals affirmed. The defendant railroad appealed and the Supreme Court of Texas granted certiorari to review the judgment of the Court of Appeals.

If one's negligence is a substantial factor in causing harm to another, is it [the negligence] also a cause-in-fact of the injury?

When one's negligence is a substantial factor in causing harm to another, is it also the cause-in-fact of the injury.

The prime issue in the case is whether the excessive speed of the train was the cause in fact of the fatal collision. Under the instant circumstances, if the excessive speed was obviously a substantial factor in bringing about the collision and would not have occurred without it. If, however, the collision would have occurred regardless of the speed of the train, then it would not be considered a substantial factor. Here, the train engineer testified that even if the train was moving at 25 m.p.h., which was the permitted speed, he would not have been able to stop the train in time to avoid the accident. This evidence, however, does not fully resolve the issue; it does not fully determine whether the collision would have been averted at the slower speed. Therefore, we must determine the speed of the car and the distance that it would have had to travel to pass safely over the tracks to avoid a collision. The witness testimony is in conflict as to the speed of the automobile. Despite this, the plaintiff argues that had the train been traveling at its proper speed, the driver of the automobile "might have" had more time to take measures to avert the collision. Thus, she reasons, the collision "might not" have occurred. We disagree. While remotely probable, it is devoid of evidentiary support. It is, in essence, pure conjecture. Therefore, the speed of the train was not a substantial factor in bringing about the death of the decedent.

Reversed.

Reynolds v. Texas & Pac. Ry. Co.

Court of Appeals of Louisiana, 37 La.Ann. 694 (1885)

FACTS

Plaintiffs, Mr. and Mrs. Reynolds, bring suit to recover for the injuries sustained by Mrs. Reynolds after she fell down the unlit steps at Defendant Texas & Pac. Ry. Co.'s station while rushing to get to the train, suffering serious injuries. At the non-jury trial, the court granted a verdict in favor of the plaintiffs and awarded them $2,000. The defendant appealed arguing that while the unlit steps constituted negligent conduct, plaintiff might have fallen anyway despite the negligence of the railroad.

Where the negligence of a defendant greatly adds to the chances of an accident resulting in the plaintiff's injury, does the mere possibility that the accident might have occurred without the defendant's negligence break the chain of causation between the negligence and the injury?

Where the negligence of a defendant greatly adds to the chances of an accident resulting in the plaintiff's injury, the mere possibility that the accident might have occurred without the defendant's negligence does not break the chain of causation between the negligence and the injury.

Where the negligence of a defendant greatly adds to the chances of an accident resulting in the plaintiff's injury, the mere possibility that the accident might have occurred without the defendant's negligence does not break the chain of causation between the negligence and the injury. It is possible that plaintiff could have fallen, even had the stairwell been well lit, without any negligence on the part of the defendant railroad. However, where, as in this case, the negligence of the defendant greatly multiplies the chances of accident to the plaintiff, the mere possibility that it might have happened without the negligence is not sufficient to break the chain of causation between the negligence and the injury. Courts in such matters consider the natural and ordinary course of events, and do not indulge in imaginary suppositions. The evidence here connects the injury with the defendant's negligence.

Judgment affirmed.

Gentry v. Douglas Hereford Ranch Inc.
Supreme Court of Montana, 962 P.2d 1205 (1998)

FACTS

Plaintiff Gentry, the widower of Barbara Gentry, the deceased, brought a wrongful death and survival action against Defendants Bacon and Douglas Hereford Ranch, Inc. after his wife was shot during a hunting accident. Barbara Gentry was accidentally shot and killed by Defendant Bacon who was planning to hunt deer on his wife's grandmother's ranch, the defendant-corporation here. As he was returning to a house on the property with his rifle in hand, he stumbled near some wooden stairs and the rifle discharged hitting Barbara Gentry in the head. She died several weeks later. Plaintiff argued Defendant Bacon was negligent in handling the rifle and that Defendant Ranch was negligent in maintaining the stairs in a dangerous condition that caused the accident. Bacon filed bankruptcy and was dismissed from the case leaving only the Ranch as defendant. Ranch moved for summary judgment, which was granted, and plaintiff appealed.

Will an action in negligence fail if the plaintiff fails to offer sufficient proof that the defendant's conduct was a cause in fact of the accident?

Evidence that defendant's conduct was a cause in fact of the accident must be offered to successfully prosecute a case for negligence [note: this is just one element of four that needs to be proven – see below].

A negligence action requires proof of four elements: 1) a duty; 2) a breach of that duty; 3) causation; and 4) damages. The causation element requires proof of both *cause in fact* and *proximate cause*. A party's conduct is a cause in fact of an event if the event would not have occurred *but for* that conduct. If a plaintiff fails to offer proof of one of these elements, the action in negligence fails. Plaintiff alleges that Ranch failed to maintain the stairs in a reasonably safe condition; that the bottom stair was unstable and that the area was cluttered with debris. At trial, however, Bacon testified that he did not remember what caused him to stumble but that he thought it was a step. Plaintiff seized upon this testimony to argue that it alone is enough to allow the trier of fact to infer that the step caused the defendant to stumble and discharge his rifle. Yet, on several other occasions, Bacon testified that he did not remember what caused him to stumble. Thus Bacon's "smoking gun testimony" at best can raise only a suspicion. Either way, as a matter of law, neither assumption nor conjecture is enough to defeat a motion for summary judgment. No substantial evidence that any condition on the property caused Bacon to stumble and fall was submitted by the plaintiff. We therefore conclude the following: 1) that the negligence element of cause in fact was not proven as a matter of law; 2) that Ranch is not vicariously liable for Bacon's negligence because Bacon was not an employee or agent of Ranch; and that 3) the District Court did not err when it held that defendants were not negligent in the manner that contributed to the injury and death of Barbara Gentry.

Affirmed.

Kramer Service. v. Wilkins

Supreme Court of Mississippi, 186 So. 625 (1939)

FACTS

Plaintiff-appellee Wilkins, a guest at a hotel operated by Defendant-appellant Kramer Service Inc., was injured when a piece of glass fell from a broken transom [a horizontal crosspiece over a door or between a door and a window above it or a small hinged window above a door or another window.] onto his temple as he was opening a door at defendant's hotel. There was evidence that the transom was in disrepair for a time long before the accident. Two years after the injury, the injury still had not healed. As a result, plaintiff went to a skin specialist and was informed thereafter by him that he, the plaintiff, had developed skin cancer in the injured area. At trial, the testimony of two medical experts was introduced, one of whom stated under oath that the probability of plaintiff's injury resulting in skin cancel was about 1 in 100 or 1%; while the other expert testified that there was no causal connection whatsoever between the injury and the cancer. The jury entered a verdict in favor of plaintiff and defendant appealed.

 Is proof that a past event possibly happened or that a certain result was possibly caused by a past event sufficient, in probative force, to take the question of the defendant's negligence to the jury?

 Proof that a past event possibly happened or that a certain result was possibly caused by a past event is not sufficient, in probative force, to take the question of the defendant's negligence to the jury in order to impose liability on him.

 Proof that a past event possibly happened or that a certain result was possibly caused by a past event is not sufficient, in probative force, to take the question of the defendant's negligence to the jury in order to impose liability on him. It is not sufficient, in terms of the imposition of liability, to show that the negligence of one person and injury suffered by the other merely co-existed. Proof that the injury was caused by the negligence is what is required. Moreover, it is not sufficient for the plaintiff to show *a possibility* that the injury complained of was caused by the negligence. Possibilities are not enough to sustain a verdict. The expert medical testimony in this case shows that there is a *possibility* that skin cancer could be caused by the instant injury but the probability of such a result is practically nonexistent. According to the uncontested testimony proffered at trial, the cause of cancer still remains unknown.

 Affirmed as to liability; reversed and remanded on the amount of damages.

Herskovits v. Group Health Coop. of Puget Sound
Supreme Court of Washington, 664 P.2d 474 (1983)

FACTS

Decedent Herskovits received medical attention from Defendant Group Health Cooperative's medical personnel for respiratory problems. About a year afterward, another doctor diagnosed him with lung cancer and Herskovits died just less than 2 years later. The decedent's estate filed suit, alleging that the failure to make a timely diagnosis reduced the chance of the decedent's survival from 39% to 25%; a 14% reduction. Defendant made a motion for summary judgment which was granted by the trial judge because the plaintiff failed to show that absent negligence of the part of the defendant, the decedent had at least a 51% chance of surviving.

Can an estate maintain a professional medical negligence action as a result of a failure to timely diagnose a disease which caused a probable reduction in the chance for survival, but where the state cannot show/prove that a timely diagnosis would have allowed the decedent to live to normal life expectancy; specifically, can the estate of the deceased maintain an action against the defendant hospital and its employees if they were negligent in diagnosing a lung cancer which reduces his chances of survival by 14%?

Evidence of a reduction in the chance of survival was sufficient for a jury to determine whether the death was proximately caused by defendant's negligence in failing to timely diagnose the condition at issue.

The estate of the defendant need not show that the probability of survival was 51% as evidence of a *reduced chance* of survival is sufficient for a jury to determine that the failure to timely diagnose was a proximate cause of the decedent's death. The medical testimony of a reduced chance of survival by 14% is sufficient to allow the issue to go to the jury, even though decedent's overall chance of survival was less than 50%.

We reverse the trial court and reinstate the cause of action.

Daubert v. Merrell Dow Pharmaceuticals Inc.

U.S. Court of Appeals, 43 F.3d 1311 (9th Cir. 1995)

FACTS

Plaintiff-petitioners Jason Daubert and Eric Schuller were two minors born with serious birth defects. They and their parents sued Defendant-respondent Merrell Dow Pharmaceuticals Inc., alleging that an anti-nausea drug, Bendectin, marketed by the latter caused the aforementioned afflictions. After extensive discovery, respondent moved for summary judgment arguing, among other things, that Bendectin does not cause birth defects *in humans*. In support of its motion, defendant introduced an affidavit of a renowned physician epidemiologist, Dr. Steven H. Lamm, who stated he reviewed all the literature on Bendectin, more than 30 published studies involving over 130,000 patients and that in no study had the drug caused birth defects when ingested by pregnant women. In response, plaintiffs introduced testimony of eight experts of their own who concluded that the drug caused birth defects. These experts based their conclusions on tests which were performed in test tubes and on live animals and on the "re-analysis" of previously published studies. The trial court granted respondent's motion for summary judgment on the ground that the evidence presented by the plaintiff-petitioners did not constitute scientific evidence because such evidence is admissible only if the principle of on which it is based is "sufficiently established to have general acceptance in the field to which it belongs." The Court of Appeals for the 9th Circuit affirmed the lower court's decision, citing *Frye v. United States*, and holding that expert testimony based on a scientific technique is inadmissible unless the technique is "generally accepted" as reliable in the relevant scientific community. The Supreme Court of the United States granted certiorari, held that "General acceptance" is not a necessary precondition to admissibility of scientific evidence under FRE 702, and remanded the case back to the 9th Circuit.

Must scientific evidence be "general accepted" in the scientific community before it is admitted into evidence?

"General acceptance" is not a necessary precondition to admissibility of scientific evidence [under FRE 702]; however, the expert's testimony must still be both reliable [capable of repetition] and relevant.

On remand from the U.S. Supreme Court, we undertake the task of "ensuring that an expert's testimony both rests on a reliable foundation and is relevant to the task at hand." The Federal Rules of Evidence do not require "general acceptance" of a scientific technique in the scientific community as an absolute prerequisite to admissibility of expert witness testimony. The standard for admissibility of evidence pre-*Daubert* was the so-called *Frye* test gleaned from *Frye v. United States*, whereby scientific testimony was admissible if it was based on a scientific technique generally accepted within the scientific community to which it belongs. This test was specifically overruled by the U.S. Supreme Court which held that the Federal Rules of Evidence, specifically Rule 702, superseded the *Frye* test and that nothing in the text of the 702 rule mandates "general acceptance" as an absolute prerequisite to admission of expert testimony. Even so, the trial judge still is charged with the duty, under the Federal Rules, to ensure that all scientific testimony or evidence admitted is both reliable and relevant. Thus, "general acceptance" may be a factor, but it is not a necessary precondition to the admissibility of scientific evidence under the Federal Rules of Evidence.

"General acceptance" is not a necessary precondition to admissibility of scientific evidence [under FRE 702]; however, the expert's testimony must still be both reliable [capable of repetition] and relevant.

Hill v. Edmonds

Supreme Court of New York, 270 N.Y.S.2d 1020 (1966)

FACTS

This is an action in negligence to recover damages for personal injuries sustained by Plaintiff-appellant Hill, a passenger in Defendant-appellee Edmonds' car, when the latter collided with a truck driven by one Bragoli, also a defendant. Bragoli had parked his truck, on a stormy night, in the middle of the road without any lights on whereupon Edwards collided with it from the rear. However, at trial testimony was offered which showed that Edmonds saw the truck when it was four car lengths ahead of her and could have swerved in time to avoid it. At other points during the trial, however, she [Defendant Edmonds] indicated that she did not know exactly what happened at the time of the crash. Based upon Edmonds' testimony, the trial court dismissed the complaint against Bragoli and the plaintiff appealed.

Where separate acts of negligence come together to produce a single injury, can each tortfeasor be held liable for the whole [concept of joint and several liability] even though his individual act alone may not have caused the result?

Where separate acts of negligence merge to produce a single injury, each tortfeasor can be held liable for the whole even though his individual act alone may not have caused the result.

Where separate acts of negligence merge to produce a single injury, each tortfeasor can be held liable for the whole even though his individual act alone may not have caused the result. In this case, based on Edmonds' proffered testimony, the accident would not have occurred had the truck driver not left his truck in the middle of the road without lights on [this assumes that Edmonds was negligent]. Accordingly, the complaint against the truck owner must be reinstated.

New trial ordered.

Anderson v. Minneapolis, St. P. & S. St. M. R.R. Co.
Supreme Court of Minnesota, 179 N.W. 45 (1920)

FACTS

A forest fire, which originated in a bog, was started by the negligent conduct of Defendant Minneapolis, St. P. & S. ST. M. R.R. Co. ("Railroad") Co. and spread over a large area causing destruction. It subsequently merged with a fire from another independent source and burned over Plaintiff Anderson's property. Thereafter, plaintiff brought suit against the defendant to recover for the damage to his property. At trial, the court instructed the jury that if it found that the fire caused by Defendant Railroad was a material and substantial factor in damaging the plaintiff's property, then the Railroad was liable. The jury returned a verdict in favor of the plaintiff, rejecting the Railroad's motion for a j.n.o.v, or in the alternative, a motion for a new trial. The Railroad appealed on the ground that since both fires could have independently destroyed the property, it should not be found liable.

 When the negligent conduct of more than one tortfeasor causes injury to the plaintiff, can each individual tortfeasor be held independently liable?

 When the negligent conduct of more than one tortfeasor causes injury to the plaintiff, each individual tortfeasor can be held independently liable if each was a substantial factor in bringing about the plaintiff's injury.

 When the negligent conduct of more than one tortfeasor causes injury to the plaintiff, each individual tortfeasor can be held independently liable if each was a substantial factor in bringing about the plaintiff's injury. Defendant argues that it should not be held liable if the plaintiff's property was damaged by more than one fire, each combining with the other, some of which were caused by the defendant's negligent conduct and others which were not. The defendant's proposition is based on *Cook v. Minneapolis, St. P. & S.S.M. Ry. Co.,* where two fires merged and the court refused to hold one defendant liable where the other fire was of innocent origin. We refuse to adopt the *Cook* doctrine. We do not believe that defendant should be relieved of liability regardless of whether its negligent conduct was a substantial and material factor in causing the plaintiff's injury. There should be liability in such a case. Thus, to conclude, we hold that if a fire set by the defendant's negligence unites with a fire of an independent origin, there is joint and several liability, even though either fire would have independently destroyed the property.

 Affirmed.

Summers v. Tice

Supreme Court of California, 199 P.2d 1 (1948)

FACTS

Plaintiff Summers, Defendants Tice, and Simonson went hunting quail on the open range together. Both defendants armed with twelve-gauge shotguns and the same size and kind of shells. Prior to entering the field, Summers discussed the hunting procedure with the defendants, especially when shooting and to "keep in line." During the course of the hunt the three men proceeded up a hit at different points along the base, thus forming a "triangle." Tice and Simonson had summers in their line of sight and both knew his location. Tice then flushed out a quail which rose to a height of 10 feet between the defendants and the plaintiff. Both defendants shot at the quail, shooting in the plaintiff's direction. As a result, Summers was shot in the eye and in the upper lip. It was not possible to determine which shot caused which injury or who actually fired the shot that hit the plaintiff.

 Can two defendants both be found negligent when only one of them actually injured the plaintiff, but it cannot be determined which of the two's negligent behavior was the actual cause of the injury sustained by the plaintiff?

 When two or more parties acted negligently in causing an injury but it cannot be determined which tortfeasor actually caused the injury, both parties will be held liable (joint and several liability).

 Joint and several liability imposes liability on two or more defendants when it is not possible to determine which defendant factually caused the injury. The defendants argue that they are not joint tortfeasors because they were not acting in concert and that they should not be jointly and severally liable because there is not sufficient evidence to show which defendant was guilty of the negligence which caused the injuries. We disagree. The lower court was correct in finding that the negligence of both of the defendants caused the injury because they were both responsible for the harm sustained and thus must be held jointly and severally liable. If this were not the case, both defendants would escape liability and the injured party could not recover because the plaintiff would have to prove which defendant caused the harm; a near impossible task. We feel this is a burden better carried by the defendants as they are in a better position to prove otherwise. We therefore uphold the lower court finding that the defendants were negligent and that plaintiff was not contributorily negligent.

 Judgment affirmed.

Sindell v. Abbott Laboratories
Supreme Court of California, 26 Cal.3d 588 (1988)

FACTS

Plaintiff Sindell alleged that she developed cancer as a result of a drug administered to her mother during pregnancy, prior to her [the plaintiff's birth]. The drug, Diethylstilbestrol (DES), was a form of synthetic estrogen given to pregnant mothers to prevent miscarriage. It was manufactured by Defendant Abbott Laboratories and marketed by approximately 195 companies, not joined as defendants. Plaintiff sued Defendant Abbott Laboratories along with four other manufacturers who together produced 90% of the total DES manufactured in the U.S. because she could not identify the specific manufacturer of the DES lot ingested by her mother. The trial court dismissed the action, and declined to apply the theory of liability set forth in *Summers v. Tice,* [where both defendants were held responsible when only one was negligent because the defendants there acted concurrently], because not all of the potential defendants in the instant case were joined in the plaintiff's suit and because there was no "concert of action" on their part. Plaintiff appealed.

Can a plaintiff who has been injured as the result of a drug ingested by her mother during pregnancy recover from a defendant manufacturer of that drug when she knows the type of drug involved but cannot identify the precise manufacturer among those many drug makers who produced the drug from identical formulas?

Where more than two defendants negligently produced a drug which caused an injury to a plaintiff, the plaintiff may recover from the defendants even though the plaintiff cannot prove which specific defendant produced the drug that was the direct cause of the her injury.

Where more than two defendants negligently produced a drug which caused an injury to a plaintiff, the plaintiff may recover from the defendants even though the plaintiff cannot prove which specific defendant produced the drug that was the direct cause of the her injury. Plaintiff relies on the theory of enterprise liability suggested in *Hall v. E.I. Du Pont de Nemours & Co., Inc.* In that case, the court used the enterprise liability theory to allow recovery where the defendants, acting independently, had adhered to an industry-wide standard with regard to safety features [of blasting caps], that they had delegated some functions of safety investigation and design, thereby jointly controlling the risk to the plaintiff. Thus, if the plaintiffs in that case could establish that the blasting caps were manufactured by one of the defendants, the burden of proof as to causation would shift to the defendants. The court in that case determined that the theory of liability applied to industries composed of a small number of units. We reject the application of this theory to the instant facts of this case. Here, at least 200 companies manufactured DES, so the drug manufacturing industry cannot be said to be "composed of small numbers of units." Additionally, the *Hall* court held that the defendant companies in that case "controlled the risk to the plaintiff." No such conclusions apply in this case. Were we to apply *Hall* to this case, the plaintiff would be barred from any recovery. Thus, the most persuasive argument for finding for the plaintiff is advanced in *Summers v. Tice,* which held that as between an innocent plaintiff and negligent defendants, the latter should bear the cost of injury. However, *Summers* cannot apply here directly because not all the manufacturers of DES are named

Sindell v. Abbott Laboratories

Supreme Court of California, 26 Cal.3d 588 (1988)

as defendants and it is impossible for the plaintiff to join all the manufacturers of DES, especially since many of the manufacturers are not in business any more. Yet the rationale in *Summers* should be extended. To that end, a substantial share of the appropriate market provides a ready means to apportion damages seams fair; which is to say that each manufacturer's liability would approximate its responsibility for the injuries caused by its own products in proportion to its own market share of the amount of DES sold. In that way, the plaintiff's damages can be apportioned based on the total contribution of each manufacturer to the DES market.

 Reversed.

Atlantic Coast Line R. Co. v. Daniels

Court of Appeals of Georgia, 70 S.E. 203 (1911)

FACTS

Facts not given.

In defining proximate cause as a basis of liability, should courts set absolute limits in an attempt to trace the connection between a given cause and a given effect?

In defining proximate cause as a basis of liability, courts should not set absolute limits in an attempt to trace the connection between a given cause and a given effect.

In defining proximate cause as a basis of liability, courts should not set absolute limits in an attempt to trace the connection between a given cause and a given effect. Courts do not attempt to deal with cause and effect in any absolute degree, but only in a way that is within the scope of human understanding. Hence, qualifying words such as "proximate" and "natural" have come into use as setting limits between a cause and its effect beyond which courts will not look. Thus, the standard for legal liability cannot be shown by a plaintiff who shows only that a defendant's act was the cause of his injury and that without such an act there would be no injury. Were we to accept this reasoning as a basis for legal responsibility, a ridiculous conclusion would follow: if the plaintiff had not been born, there would be no injury. Instead, courts should ask: was the defendant's wrongful act the proximate cause of the plaintiff's injury?

In defining proximate cause as a basis of liability, courts should not set absolute limits in an attempt to trace the connection between a given cause and a given effect.

Ryan v. New York Central R.R. Co.

Court of Appeals of New York, 35 N.Y. 210 (1866)

FACTS

On July 15, 1854, in Syracuse, New York, one of Defendant New York Central Rail Road's engines started a fire that spread to their woodshed which contained a large quantity of wood, which, also burned. Plaintiff Ryan's house was 130 feet from the woodshed and caught fire from the heat and sparks. Plaintiff's house was completely destroyed as were several other homes in the vicinity. Plaintiff brought suit but the defendant was granted a nonsuit and the judgment was affirmed by the General Term. Plaintiff appealed.

 Should a defendant still be held liable when the damage suffered by the plaintiff was remote but still the result of a defendant's negligence?

 Liability will not be imparted to a defendant when the resulting harm is too remote to be an ordinary and natural result of the defendant's negligent act.

 If an unexpected fire occurs, the immediate and expected result is that the building on which cinders and sparks fall will burn and be damaged or destroyed. However, it is neither ordinary nor expected that if the fire moves to house A, and then to house B, and so on, it will eventually burn house Z. If the fire does indeed reach house Z and burn it, should the defendant liable for the damage to house Z, or for all of the house burned to get to it? We say no. At some point, the liability becomes too attenuated to be foreseeable as the natural and probable consequence of the first event, i.e., the burning of house A. In the instant case, the immediate result of the fire was the destruction of the defendant's own woodshed; any destruction beyond is considered remote. To require an owner to guaranty the security of his neighbors on both sides, and to an unlimited extent, would create a liability which would hinder all of society. No community could exist, let alone function. Thus, in a commercial setting such as that which exists in our own country, where people live close together, every man runs the risk that his neighbor's conduct may visit a hazard upon himself. The remoteness of the damage in this case prohibits recovery in this case.

 The judgment should be affirmed.

Bartolone v. Jeckovich

Supreme Court of New York, 481 N.Y.S.2d 545 (1984)

FACTS

Plaintiff Bartolone, a 48-year-old male who lived alone and worked out of a Union Hall as a carpenter, was injured in a four-car automobile collision in Niagara Falls with Defendant Jeckovich and others for which the defendants were found liable. Plaintiff suffered whiplash and minor injury to his lower back as a result of the accident but did not require hospitalization. Prior to the accident, plaintiff worked out about 4 hours a day at the YMCA as a bodybuilder. On weekends, he pursued nonphysical interests such as painting, singing, playing the guitar and creating sculptures. Since the accident, however, he became delusional, withdrawn, hostile, and refused to participate in his prior interests. Three psychiatrists and one neurosurgeon testified on his behalf at trial. Plaintiff's psychiatrists testified to plaintiff's fear of doctors because of his mother's death due to cancer and that he engaged in body building to ward off cancer and cope with his emotional problems. His bodily fitness was extremely important to him because, as they put it, it provide him a sense of control over his life such that he was able to functionally normally in society. It was the experts' opinion that the accident with defendant rendered plaintiff incapable of his former physical feats, depriving him of the mechanism with which plaintiff coped with his emotional problems. As a result, he deteriorated both mentally and physically. The jury returned a verdict of $500,000 in favor of plaintiff, but he trial court set aside the judgment on the ground that there was no basis for the jury to conclude that plaintiff's mental breakdown could be attributed to the accident. Plaintiff appealed.

Can a defendant be held liable to the plaintiff for an aggravation of a pre-existing condition made worst by the former's negligent conduct?

A defendant can be held liable to the plaintiff for an aggravation of a pre-existing condition made worst by the former's negligent conduct.

A defendant can be held liable to the plaintiff for an aggravation of a pre-existing condition made worst by the former's negligent conduct. In both *Steinhauser v. Hertz Corp.* and *Bonner v. United States* the issue of aggravating the plaintiffs' injury via their own [the respective defendants] negligence was submitted to the jury. In *Bonner,* the plaintiff's auto accident with the defendant aggravated her pre-existing psychotic illness with which she was able to cope prior to the accident. In *Steinhauser,* the plaintiff, a four year old girl, was struck by another car. And within minutes after the accident she began to exhibit bizarre behavior. There, the Second Circuit Court found that the plaintiff had a predisposition to abnormal behavior which activated into schizophrenia by the emotional trauma of the accident connected with the accident. In both cases, the courts determined that the issue of aggravation of a pre-existing illness was one which should be considered by the jury. The instant case is no different as there is more than enough evidence to suggest that

Bartolone v. Jeckovich

Supreme Court of New York, 481 N.Y.S.2d 545 (1984)

---

plaintiff was able to function in a normal manner prior to the accident, despite suffering from a pre-existing condition, but that the accident provoked his condition rendering his situation more severe than before the accident.

  Reversed; jury verdict reinstated.

In Re Arbitration between Polemis and Furness, Withy & Co., Ltd.

Court of Appeal, 3 K.B. 560 (1921)

FACTS

Plaintiff-respondent Polemis and his partner chartered their ship to Defendant-appellants Furness, Withy & Co., to carry cargo to Casablanca, Morocco, and included benzine or petrol in cases. While discharging cargo in Casablanca, a heavy plank fell into the hold where the petrol was stored and caused an explosion. The resulting fire consumed the ship and all of the remaining cargo. The owners of the vessel brought suit against the defendants for the value of the ship. The claim was referred to arbitration and the arbitrators stated a special case for the opinion of the court. The findings of fact stated, in pertinent part, that the local dockworkers were acting as agents of the defendants at the time of the explosion; that they caused a plank to fall into the hold causing a spark which ignited vapors in the hold creating the explosion; that the causing of the spark could not reasonably have been anticipated; and that there was no evidence that the dockworkers chosen for the job were known or likely to be negligent. Damages were stated in the amount of £196.165.

When a negligent act causes an unforeseeable harm, can the tortfeasor still be held liable?

A tortfeasor will be held liable for damages when his *act* can be reasonably foreseen to possibly cause harm even though the specific type or scope of *damages* may not (be reasonably foreseen).

The arbitrators found as fact that the falling of the plank was due to the negligence of the defendant's servants. The resulting fire appears to have been caused as a direct result of the falling of the plank. Under these circumstances I consider it immaterial that the causing of the spark by the falling plank could not have been reasonably foreseeable. The anticipations of the one who is negligent is irrelevant. Here the act was negligent and the negligent act caused the damage. At any rate, the extent and type of harm caused by a negligent act is similarly irrelevant; it is still a negligent act and the tortfeasor is responsible for any and all damages which flow from it. Hence, it is immaterial that this type of *damage*, an explosion and resulting fire caused by a spark, was not reasonably foreseeable because the negligent act of dropping of a plank into the hold was the direct cause of the injury. The damages claimed for the loss of the ship are not too remote.

The arbitrator's decision should be affirmed.

Overseas Tankship (U.K.) Ltd. v. Morts Dock & Engineering Co. Ltd. "Wagon Mound No. 1"

Privy Counsel, A.C. 388 (1961)

FACTS

Defendant-appellants negligently discharged oil into Syndey Harbor while their ship was berthed. After their ship set sail, the oil was carried by the wind and tide to the plaintiff-respondent's wharf, which was used to repair other ships in the harbor; plaintiff often utilized welding equipment to carry out its daily activities. The plaintiff's supervisor was concerned that the oil that drifted near the wharf would be ignited by the sparks from the welding equipment so he ordered the workmen to stop welding or burning. To allay his concerns, he spoke with the manager of the CalTex Oil Company, who told him that the oil was not flammable. The plaintiff's workmen were ordered to continue their welding work, but to be diligent in not allowing any flammable materials to fall off the wharf. Less than 3 days later, a fire broke out and severely damaged the wharf. Apparently, there was a rag or piece of waste cotton floating in the oil underneath the wharf and when molten metal fell from the wharf it caught on fire. The floating oil fire then ignited, either directly or indirectly, a pile of wood in the water. The resulting fire then spread to the rest of the oil in the water eventually causing the damage to the wharf. The trial judge held that the defendant could not have possibly known and could not reasonably been expected to have known that the oil was capable of being set afire when it spread to the water.

 Can a defendant be held liable for all unforeseeable consequences that flow directly from its negligent act, even if the act the set in motion the series of events was insignificant, trivial or minor?

 A negligent tortfeasor will be held responsible for only those reasonably foreseeable consequences of its negligent act.

 A negligent party will not be held responsible for any and all damage attributable to its negligent act; rather, it will be held liable for only those injuries that are *reasonably foreseeable*. The decision of the Court of Appeal in *Polemis* should longer be regarded as good law. The rule of *Polemis* plainly asserted that if the defendant is guilty of negligence, he will be held liable for all the consequences that flow from his act, reasonable or *not*. Thus, the actor will be held liable for all consequences so long as they are said to be "direct" and even though they may be unforeseeable. Prior to *Polemis*, courts have hinged the responsibility of a negligent tortfeasor on whether 1) the injury brought about by the act was reasonably foreseeable; and (2) if the consequence was natural, necessary or probable. *Polemis* erroneously substituted the test of "foreseeability" with a "direct consequences" test. In doing so, *Polemis* also abandoned the reasonable person standard upon which the concept of foreseeability is based. The two are not the same or interchangeable. Thus, utilizing the "direct consequences" test, a negligent party could be held liable for substantial losses even though its negligent act was minor; however, this is an unjust and unfair result. A

Overseas Tankship (U.K.) Ltd. v. Morts Dock & Engineering Co. Ltd. "Wagon Mound No. 1"

Privy Counsel, A.C. 388 (1961)

person must be held responsible for the *probable consequences* of his or her act, to require anything more would impart injustice.

Appeal allowed.

Overseas Tankship (U.K.) Ltd. v. Miller Steamship Co. "Wagon Mound No. 2"

Privy Council, 1 A.C. 617 (1966)

FACTS

Defendant-appellant Overseas Tankship negligently discharged oil in a dock where Plaintiff Miller Steamship's two ships were moored. After defendant's ship set sail, the oil was carried by the wind and tide to the wharf, which was used to repair other ships in the harbor and where welding equipment was used. Apparently, there was a rag or piece of waste cotton floating in the oil underneath the wharf and when molten metal fell from the wharf it caught on fire. The floating oil fire then ignited, either directly or indirectly, a pile of wood in the water. The resulting fire then spread to the rest of the oil in the water eventually causing the damage to the wharf and to plaintiff's property. The trial judge held that the defendant could not have possibly known and could not reasonably been expected to have known that the oil was capable of being set afire when it spread to the water. The Supreme Court of New South Wales affirmed. Plaintiff appealed to the Privy Council.

 Does foreseeability depend on a balancing between possible risk and the magnitude of the potential damage that may result from such a risk?

 Whether a defendant's acts will produce foreseeable consequence depends upon a balancing of the risks involved and the magnitude of damages that may flow from that risk.

 Whether a defendant's acts will produce foreseeable consequence depends upon a balancing of the risks involved and the magnitude of damages that may flow from that risk. Here, some risk of fire would have been present to a reasonable man in the position of the ship's engineer and such a reasonable man would have appreciated the risk that serious damage to the ship and other property could occur [it was foreseeable]. A risk should only be neglected where there is valid reason for doing so. Here, there was no justification for discharging the oil in the water; and it would have been reasonable for the engineer to stop the discharge because he should have known that it was possible to ignite oil on water. Additionally, he should have known that such ignition would occur only under exceptional circumstances. Even though the risk is minimal it should not have dismissed if it could have been easily prevented. If it is clear that a reasonable man would have realized the risk and prevented it, then it must follow that the defendant-appellants are liable in damages.

 Plaintiff's appeal allowed.

Palsgraf v. Long Island R.R. Co.
Court of Appeals of New York, 162 N.E. 99 (1928)

FACTS

Plaintiff-respondent Helen Palsgraf was standing on the Defendant-appellant Long Island Railroad Co.'s platform waiting for a train after buying a ticket to go to Rockaway Beach. Another train pulled into the station and two men ran to catch it. The first man jumped aboard as the train was moving, but the second man, who was carrying a package, look as if as if he were about to fall so an employee of the defendant on the train reached out to help him board. Contemporaneously, another employee of the defendant on the platform pushed him from behind. In the process, the man dropped his package which fell under the train and exploded. The package contained fireworks; yet there was nothing in the appearance of the package to give notice that it contained explosives. The resulting explosion created a shock wave which knocked over scales at the other end of the platform where the plaintiff was standing. She was hit by the scales and thereby injured. A judgment was rendered in favor of the plaintiff entered upon a verdict. The Appellate Division affirmed and this appeal follows.

Can a defendant be held liable for damages when the act that caused the injury was not a reasonably foreseeable result of the act?

A defendant will be liable for damages when his act was negligent; an act is negligent when a reasonable person could anticipate and appreciate the resulting risk of harm as the result of the act.

Negligence is not actionable unless there is an invasion of a legally protected interest or a violation of a right, but when there is no reasonable apprehension that an act creates a risk of harm to anyone, that act is not negligent. In the instant case, there was nothing in the appearance of the package to give notice that it contained explosives. Thus, we may assume that negligence, in relation to the plaintiff, would entail liability for any and all consequences, however novel or extraordinary.

Reversed.

Yun v. Ford Motor Co.

Superior Court of New Jersey, Appellate Div., 647 A.2d 841 (1994)

FACTS

On November 27, 1988, Plaintiff Yun Cho was driving her van on the Garden State Parkway in New Jersey when the spare tire on her van loosened, fell off, and rolled across two lanes of traffic, ultimately coming to rest against the median guardrail. The spare tire assembly on the van had earlier been bent as a result of an accident she had been involved in. Plaintiff had instructed her mechanic not to fix it, as she was waiting for the other driver's insurance company to handle the repairs. After the spare tire fell off the van, plaintiff safely drove the van to the right side of the freeway and stopped. Thereafter, Chang, her 65 year old passenger and father, got out of the van and ran across two lanes of the freeway to retrieve the spare tire and some other parts. On his way back to the car while crossing the freeway, Chang was struck and killed by another vehicle. Plaintiff sued a number of defendants, including Defendant Ford Motor Company.

 May the issue of proximate cause, usually reserved for the jury's determination, be treated as a matter of law for the court to determine when the injury was not caused by the defendant?

 The issue of proximate cause, usually reserved for the jury's determination, may be treated as a matter of law for the court to determine when the injury was not one that was reasonably or foreseeability caused by the defendant.

 The alleged defect in the spare tire carrier assembly was not the proximate cause of Chang's injury because his dangerous act of crossing a busy freeway at night and in violation of the law constituted highly extraordinary conduct, thereby breaking the chain of causation. At most, the presence of the spare tire created a condition upon which the subsequent intervening force acted and, as such, there is no proximate cause relationship between the defective product and the injury. Liability should not extend to injuries received as a result of Chang's senseless decision to cross the freeway under such dangerous conditions. To hold otherwise would be illogical and unfair. Common sense should have persuaded Chang to wait for assistance or abandon the bald tire. Proximate cause is usually an issue reserved for the jury's determination. But in certain cases, it has been held so intertwined with issues of policy as to be treated as a matter of law for the court to determine. This is especially true where the manner and type of harm caused to the plaintiff is unexpected. It was not reasonably foreseeable that if the spare wheel assembly was defective, that Chang would violate the law by twice crossing the freeway to go to the median to retrieve the parts and be killed by a passing car. Furthermore, reasonable people could not differ that the continued driving for 30 days with knowledge of the defect and the senseless and illegal crossing of the Parkway were intervening superseding causes of the accident which broke the chain of causation.

 Affirmed.

Derdirian v. Felix Contracting Corp.

New York Court of Appeals, 434 N.Y.S.2d 166 (1980)

FACTS

Plaintiff Derdiarian was working at an excavation worksite sealing a gas main as the employee of the subcontractor hired by Defendant Felix Contracting Corp. Plaintiff was hit and severely injured when an automobile driven by James Dickens hit him after the driver suffered an epileptic seizure and lost control of his car. As a result of the impact, plaintiff was thrown in the air and suffered severe injuries and severe burns to his body. Thereafter, plaintiff sued defendant claiming that the latter had negligently failed to take measures to insure the safety of workers at the excavation site. At trial, plaintiff's traffic safely expert, Lawrence Lawton, testified that the usual method of safeguarding workers is to erect a barrier around the excavation site and to have two flagmen around the site instead of the one provided by the defendant. Defendant defended on the ground that plaintiff's injury was caused by freakish accident caused by the automobile driver's negligence and that, as a matter of law, there was no causal connection between its alleged breach of duty [negligent conduct] and plaintiff's injury.

Where the act of a 3rd party intervenes between the defendant's negligent conduct and the plaintiff's injury, is the causal connection automatically severed?

Where the act of a 3rd party intervenes between the defendant's negligent conduct and the plaintiff's injury, the causal connection *is not* severed if the intervening act is a normal and foreseeable consequence of the risk created by the defendant's negligence.

Where the act of a 3rd party intervenes between the defendant's negligent conduct and the plaintiff's injury, the causal connection is not severed if the intervening act is a normal and foreseeable consequence of the risk created by the defendant's negligence. If the intervening act is extraordinary under the circumstances, not foreseeable in the normal course of events, or independent or far removed from the defendant's conduct, then it may well be a superseding act which breaks the causal connection. Issues of foreseeability are for the trier of fact to decide. However, there are cases where only one conclusion may be drawn from the facts and where the issue of legal cause may be decided as a matter of law. Specifically, where the independent intervening act operates but does not flow from the original negligence of the defendant, as a matter of law there is not causal link between the defendant's negligence and the plaintiff's injury. In the case before us, the automobile driver's negligence, does not, as a matter of law, sever the causal link. From the record, the jury could have found that defendant negligently failed to safeguard the excavation site. A key risk of defendant's failure to erect barriers around the excavation site is the possibility that a driver will negligently enter the work site and cause injury to the workers. The driver's negligence does not relieve defendant from liability. The jury could have concluded that the foreseeable and normal result of the risk created by defendant was injury of a worker by a car entering the improperly protected area. Moreover, the fact that defendant could not anticipate the precise manner of the accident or the extent of

Derdirian v. Felix Contracting Corp.
New York Court of Appeals, 434 N.Y.S.2d 166 (1980)

plaintiff's injury does not relieve it from liability where the general risk of injury is foreseeable.

 Affirmed.

Watson v. Kentucky & Indiana Bridge & R.R. Co.
Court of Appeals of Kentucky, 126 S.W. 146 (1910)

FACTS

A tank car owned by Defendant Kentucky and Indiana Bridge & R.R. Co. (the "railroad") derailed and its valve broken negligently spilling gasoline onto the street. A bystander, one Duerr, struck a match which caused an explosion injuring Plaintiff Watson. At trial, Duerr testified that he dropped his matches in the gasoline after lighting a cigar. Other witnesses, however, testified that Duerr deliberately lit a match and threw it in the gasoline after saying to a companion, "Let's go set the damn thing on fire." The trial court directed a verdict in favor of the defendant-railroad, finding that Duerr's act was malicious and intentional. Plaintiff appealed.

Is a defendant who commits a negligent act liable for the additional intentional intervening malicious acts of a third party; malicious acts which are not reasonably foreseeable?

A defendant who commits a negligent act is not liable to the plaintiff for the additional intentional intervening malicious acts of a third party if those malicious acts are not reasonably foreseeable.

A defendant who commits a negligent act is not liable to the plaintiff for the additional intentional intervening malicious acts of a third party if those malicious acts are not reasonably foreseeable. As a preliminary matter, the question of proximate cause is one which should be decided by the jury. Thus, in holding that Duerr in lighting or throwing the match acted maliciously or with intent to cause the explosion, the trial court invaded the province of the jury. Turning to the crux of the case, we agree with the trial court that if the action of Duerr in lighting the match was malicious and intentional, then the defendant is relieved of liability. The railroad could not have reasonably foreseen that a person would maliciously light a match for the evil purpose of producing an explosion. Hence, if the intervening agency is so unexpected or extraordinary as that the defendant could not or ought not to have anticipated it, the defendant will not be held liable. To be sure, a defendant is not bound to anticipate the criminal acts of others and is not liable for them.

Reversed and remanded.

Fuller v. Preis

New York Court of Appeals, 363 N.Y.S.2d 568 (1974)

FACTS

Plaintiff-executor Fuller, in a wrongful death action, recovered a jury verdict for $200,000 for the death of the decedent, Dr. Lewis, against Defendant Preis, the driver of the car with whom the decedent was involved in a car accident. Seven months after getting in to an accident, the decedent, Dr. Lewis, committed suicide. While he walked away from the accident apparently unharmed, he had in fact suffered head injuries which later produced seizures which had not existed prior to the accident. On the day of his suicide, the decedent had had three seizures. Plaintiff Fuller, executor of the decedent's estate, claimed in his suit that defendant's negligence in the automobile accident was the proximate cause of the decedent's suicide. The appellate division set aside the verdict and dismissed the complaint and the plaintiff-executor appealed.

Is an act of suicide, as a matter of law, a superseding cause in negligence law which precludes liability of the original tortfeasor?

An act of suicide is not, as a matter of law, a superseding cause in negligence law which precludes liability of the original tortfeasor, the initial tortfeasor may be held liable for the wrongful acts of the 3rd party if foreseeable.

An act of suicide is not, as a matter of law, a superseding cause in negligence law which precludes liability of the original tortfeasor, the initial tortfeasor may be held liable for the wrongful acts of the 3rd party if foreseeable. Thus, there is no public policy or precedent limiting recovery for suicide of a tortiously injured person driven "insane" by the consequence of the tortious act. Dr. Lewis was mentally healthy immediately prior to the accident. After the accident, however, he suffered from seizures – no fewer than 38 for the seven months between the accident and his death. On the day of the suicide, the decedent suffered from three seizures, and his wife testified that he had locked himself in the bathroom, and was heard muttering, "I must do it, I must do it," and then a gunshot rang out. In this case, the jury found that the decedent knew what he was doing, and intended to do what he did, and yet, he was incapable of controlling the "irresistible impulse" to destroy himself. When a suicide is preceded by a history of trauma, brain damage, epileptic seizures, depression, and despair, the issue of whether the suicide was a rational act of a sound mind or a result of an irresistible impulse, the theory of the trial as seen here, is a question of fact for the jury.

Order of the Appellate Division should be reversed and a new trial ordered.

McCoy v. American Suzuki Motor Corp.

Supreme Court of Washington, 961 P.2d 952 (1998)

FACTS

On a cold November evening while driving on I-90 outside Spokane, Washington, Plaintiff James McCoy, a Suzuki Samurai, driving in front of him swerved off the road and overturned. The driver of that car was seriously injured and plaintiff stopped to render him assistance. A state trooper arrived on the scene and asked plaintiff to place flares on the interstate to warn approaching vehicles, which he did. Plaintiff, concerned that the stationary flares were inadequate, walked further down the interstate from the accident scene, with lit flares in each hand, to manually direct traffic to the inside [free and safe] lane. About two hours later, the accident scene was cleared, leaving only the trooper and plaintiff on the roadway. Plaintiff began walking back on the shoulder of the road to his car with a lit flare in the hand closest to the road. When he was 3 or 4 car lengths from the trooper, the trooper drove away without any comment to plaintiff. Moments later, plaintiff was struck from behind by a hit-and-run vehicle. Plaintiff sued Defendant American Suzuki Motor Corp., the manufacturer of the car, among others, for its allegedly defective Samurai which allegedly caused the wreck in the first place. The defendant moved for summary judgment asserting: 1) the rescue doctrine does not apply; and 2) even if it does, plaintiff must still, but cannot, prove that it [the defendant] proximately caused his [the plaintiff's] injuries. The trial court found that the rescue doctrine did apply but that the alleged defect was not the proximate cause of the plaintiff's injuries and granted summary judgment of dismissal. Plaintiff appealed and the Court of Appeals reversed finding the Doctrine applied and that the rescuer [the plaintiff] need not prove the defendant proximately caused the his injuries. An appeal was made to the Supreme Court of Washington.

 1) Does the rescue doctrine apply in product liability actions? 2) If the Doctrine can be applied, must the plaintiff show proximate causation?

 The rescue doctrine may be invoked in product liability actions and the rescuer is required to show that the defendant proximately caused his injuries if it so invoked.

 The rescue doctrine may be invoked in product liability actions and the rescuer is required to show that the defendant proximately caused his injuries if it so invoked. The rescue doctrine allows an injured rescuer to sue the party which caused the danger requiring the rescue in the first place. This doctrine serves to inform tortfeasors that it is foreseeable a rescuer will come to aid the person imperiled by the tortfeasor's actions, and therefore the tortfeasor owes the rescuer a duty similar to the duty he owes the person he imperils. Additionally, the rescue doctrine negates the presumption that the rescuer assumed the risk of injury when he knowingly undertook the dangerous rescue, so long as he does not act rashly or recklessly. To successfully invoke the Doctrine, the rescuer must demonstrate: 1) the defendant was negligent to the person rescued and that negligence caused the peril or appearance of peril to the person rescued; 2) the peril or appearance of peril was imminent; 3) a reasonably prudent person would have concluded such peril or appearance

McCoy v. American Suzuki Motor Corp.

Supreme Court of Washington, 961 P.2d 952 (1998)

---

of peril existed; and 4) the rescuer acted with reasonable care in effectuating the rescue. The Court of Appeals found that plaintiff demonstrated sufficient facts to put the issue of whether plaintiff is entitled to rescuer status to the jury and that the plaintiff did need not to prove that the defendant proximately caused his injuries. We do not question the fist part of the Appeals Court's finding but disagree with the second conclusion. The Doctrine is applicable to the instant case and the defendant's argument that the rescue doctrine may not be invoked in product liability actions is erroneous. The rescue doctrine is a reflection of a societal value judgment that rescuers should not be barred from bringing suit for knowingly placing themselves in danger to undertake a rescue. We conceive of no reason why this doctrine should not apply with equal force when a product manufacturer causes the danger. However, the rescuer, like any other plaintiff, still must show the defendant proximately caused his injuries. Concluding that the rescue doctrine applies to a product liability suit and that a rescuer must still show the defendant proximately caused his injuries, we question whether the plaintiff in this case has demonstrated that the defendant here proximately caused his injuries. Thus, if the Suzuki Samurai is found to be defective the jury could find it foreseeable that the vehicle would roll and that an approaching car would cause injury to either those in the Suzuki Samurai or to a rescuer, depending on the specific facts to be proved. Here, we do not find that the alleged fault of defendant, if proved, is so remote from the injuries that its liability should be cut off as a matter of law. Accordingly, we will not dismiss this case for lack of legal causation and instead remand the case for trial consistent with this opinion.

 Remanded.

114

Kelly v. Gwinnell
Supreme Court of New Jersey, 476 A.2d 1219 (1984)

FACTS

Defendant Gwinnell had a few drinks of scotch at Defendant Zak's home, left plaintiff's home, and while driving was involved in a head-on collision with Plaintiff Marie Kelly, who was seriously injured as a result. Gwinnell was visibly drunk when he departed Zak's home. In fact, Zak walked Gwinnell to his car, chatted with him and watched as he drove off. Plaintiff sued Defendant Gwinnell, who in turn joined Defendant Zak as a co-defendant. At trial, the court granted Defendant Zak's motion for summary judgment, holding that a host, as a matter of law, is not liable for the negligence of an adult social guest who has become intoxicated at his [the host's] home. The Appellate Court affirmed and Defendant Gwinnell appealed.

Is a host liable to the victim of an automobile accident for the negligence of an adult social guest who has become visibly intoxicated at his [the host's] home and where the risk of harm to others, including the plaintiff-victim, is reasonably foreseeable?

A host is liable to the victim of an automobile accident for the negligence of an adult social guest who has become visibly intoxicated at his [the host's] home poses a risk of harm to others, including the plaintiff-victim, which is reasonably foreseeable.

A host is liable to the victim of an automobile accident for the negligence of an adult social guest who has become visibly intoxicated at his [the host's] home poses a risk of harm to others, including the plaintiff-victim, which is reasonably foreseeable. The test for negligence is an objective test, such that when the negligent conduct of a party creates a risk of harm or danger to others, setting off foreseeable consequences that lead to the plaintiff's injury, the negligent conduct is deemed the proximate cause of the injury. Here, the facts suggest that Gwinnell was served liquor at Zak's home and that Zak knew that Gwinnell was visibly intoxicated when he [Gwinnell] left to get into his car. A reasonable person in Zak's position could foresee that the providing of alcohol to Gwinnell would make it more likely that Gwinnell would not be able to operate his car carefully. As a result, it is reasonable and foreseeable that Gwinnell was likely to injure someone as a result of negligent operation of his vehicle. Thousands of deaths occur due to consumption of alcohol and drunk driving. We therefore now allow for the imposition of liability on a host who serves liquor to an adult guest, knowing the guest is intoxicated and that he will thereafter operate a motor vehicle and expand our prior decisions that before today only limited liability to 1) licensees who served liquor for profit or 2) social guests who served liquor to minors to now include. Our decision to extend liability is supported by public policy considerations.

Reversed and remanded.

Enright v. Eli Lily & Co.

Court of Appeals of New York, 568 N.Y.S.2d 550 (1991)

FACTS

Plaintiff Karen Enright's grandmother ingested the DES, a drug designed to reduce the probability of a miscarriage, during her pregnancy which resulted in the premature birth of Patricia, plaintiff's mother, in 1960. Plaintiff alleges that the drug caused reproductive abnormalities in her mother, which in turn led to her [the plaintiff's] premature birth, abnormalities of her reproductive system, cerebral palsy and other disabilities attributable to her *in utero* exposure to the drug. Between 1947 and 1971, DES, a synthetic estrogen-like substance, was manufactured by about 300 companies including Defendant Eli Lily & Co., to prevent miscarriages and taken by millions of women. The trial court dismissed plaintiff's claims and the Appellate Division affirmed, but reinstated plaintiff's cause of action based on strict products liability holding that he strong public policy in favor of providing a remedy to victims justified the recognition of the strict liability claim(s).

 Can a daughter recover against a tortfeasor(s) for an injury sustained by her mother, which then results in injuries to her [the plaintiff] as a later conceived child in a DES drug-related case?

 A daughter can not recover against the original tortfeasor(s) for an injury sustained by her mother, which then results in injuries to her [the plaintiff] as a later conceived child in a DES drug-related case.

 Recently, we have held that liability could be imposed on a DES manufacturer in accordance with their share of the national DES market, even though the plaintiff is unable to identify the specific manufacturer at fault for her injuries. In *Albala v. City of New York,* the court rejected the extension of cause of action in favor of a child for injuries suffered as a result of a preconception tort committed against the child's mother. The plaintiff now before us argues that the cause of action should be extended as a matter of policy in DES cases. We disagree. Here, the plaintiff has not identified any special features of DES litigation that justify the recognition of such a cause of action. The fact that this is a DEA case alone does not justify a departure from the *Albala* rule. First, the nature of the plaintiff's injuries both here and in *Albala* – birth defects – and their cause – harm to the respective mothers bodies – are indistinguishable. That is, both causes of action, here and in *Albala*, could not be confined without the drawing of arbitrary and artificial boundaries. Yet it is our judicial duty to confine liability within manageable limits. Hence, limiting liability to those who ingested DES and those who were exposed to it *in utero* will serve this purpose. Such limitation will not deter manufacturers from improving their products because the manufacturer is still subject to liability for all of those who were injured. For these reasons, we decline to recognize a cause of action on behalf of the plaintiff.

 Cause of action not recognized.

Bierczynski v. Rogers
Supreme Court of Delaware, 239 A.2d 218 (1968)

FACTS

Defendants Robert C. Race and Ronald Bierczynski, ages 18 and 17 respectively, were racing their cars against one another at twice the speed limit and in violation of various speed statutes when Race lost control of his car collided with Plaintiff Rogers' car, injuring the latter. However, Bierczynski was at all time in the proper lane and in control of his car and brought the vehicle to a stop 35 feet from the scene of the accident. At no time before, during or after the race did Bierczynski's car come in contact with the car driven by the plaintiff. At the trial, the jury found both defendants negligent and entered a verdict in favor of plaintiff against both defendants jointly. Defendant Bierczynski appealed; Defendant Race joins with the plaintiffs in upholding the judgment below.

Can two parties who engage in an activity that causes an injury to a 3rd person be held liable to the victim even though only of the two tortfeasors directly inflicted the injury?

Where two tortfeasors engage in an activity that causes an injury to a 3rd person, both can be held jointly liable to the victim even though only of the two tortfeasors directly inflicted the injury.

Where two tortfeasors engage in an activity that causes an injury to a 3rd person, both can be held jointly liable to the victim even though only of the two tortfeasors directly inflicted the injury. In many states, car racing on public roads is prohibited by statute, the violation of which constitutes negligence per se; however, our jurisdiction has no such statute. Nevertheless, such speed competition constitutes negligence in our State [of Delaware] because a reasonable, prudent person would not engage in such conduct. Consequently, those parties involved in the race are wrongdoers and *each* participant is liable for harm to a third person arising from the tortuous conduct of the other because he has induced and encouraged the tort. Hence, if both defendants in this case were involved in a car race, each is liable to plaintiff even though one of them, Bierczynski, was not directly involved in the collision itself. Since the jury found that both defendants were racing, Bierczynski, as one of the racers, is still liable.

See Rule above.

Coney v. J.L.G Industries Inc.

Supreme Court of Illinois, 454 N.E.2d 197 (1983)

FACTS

This is an action based on strict products liability in a wrongful death action brought by Plaintiff Coney, the administrator of the estate of Clifford M. Jasper, after the latter died while operating a hydraulic aerial work platform manufactured by Defendant J.L.G. Industries Inc. ("JLG"). Defendant defends on the ground that Jasper committed contributory negligence in operating the machine and that Jasper's employer, V. Jobst & Sons, also committed contributory negligence by failing to provide a "groundman" and for failing instruct and train Jasper on the safe operation of the platform. Plaintiff contends that defendant is responsible for the full amount of damages regardless of any other person's negligence. Illinois has adopted the doctrine of corporate negligence.

 Does the doctrine of comparative negligence eliminate joint and several liability?

 The doctrine of comparative negligence does not eliminate joint and several liability.

 Prior to *Alvis v. Ribar*, where Illinois adopted pure comparative negligence, a plaintiff who was found guilty of even the slightest negligence is barred from recovery [a/k/a contributory negligence]. Having said that, Defendant argues that with the adoption of the doctrine of comparative negligence, where damages are apportioned according to each party's fault, it is no longer rational to hold the defendant liable for more than his share of the damages. We disagree. The majority of courts adopting comparative negligence still retain joint and several liability. There are general four reasons for retaining joint and several liability: 1) Apportionment of fault under comparative negligence does not make an indivisible injury divisible; a concurrent tortfeasor is liable for all damages to the plaintiff, and in many instances that tortfeasor's negligence alone is sufficient for causing the plaintiff's entire injury. 2) Where plaintiff is not negligent, without joint and several liability the plaintiff would be forced to bear the portion of the loss for those defendants who are unable to pay. 3) Even where the plaintiff is negligent, he is not as culpable as the defendant because his negligence is lack of due care for himself and not for others. 4) If joint and several liability is eliminated, a plaintiff may not be able to recover adequate damages for his injuries. In *Alvis* we adopted the doctrine of comparative negligence [not *contributory* negligence]. Under this doctrine, a plaintiff who is contributorily negligent is allowed to recover damages which are reduced according to the percentage of fault attributable to him [the plaintiff]. Were we to eliminate joint and several liability as the defendant urges, the burden of the insolvent or immune defendant would fall on the plaintiff.

 Affirmed and remanded.

Bartlett v. New Mexico Welding Supply Inc.

Court of Appeals of New Mexico, 646 P.2d 579 (1982)

FACTS

This case involves an automobile accident involving three vehicles. Plaintiff Jane Bartlett slammed on her brakes to avoid hitting an unknown driver who suddenly backed out of a service station, the so-called "lead car." An employee of Defendant New Mexico Welding Supply, driving behind the plaintiff, could not brake in time and rear-ended the plaintiff. Thereafter, plaintiff sued defendant in negligence and defendant defended on the ground that the driver of the lead car, who remained unknown, caused or contributed to the accident. At trial, the jury at the trial court determined that plaintiff's injury was $100,000 and that defendant's negligence contributed to plaintiff's accident and damages to the extent of 30%, while the negligence attributable to the unknown driver was 70%. Plaintiff moved to recover the entire $100,000 from defendant, however the motion was denied and a new trial was granted. Defendant requests interlocutory appeal and the Court of Appeals of New Mexico so granted the request.

 Is a concurrent tortfeasor jointly and severally liable for the entire amount of the plaintiff's judgment in a comparative negligence jurisdiction?

 A concurrent tortfeasor is not jointly and severally liable for the entire amount of the plaintiff's judgment in a comparative negligence jurisdiction.

 Prior to the case of *Scott v. Rizzo*, which adopted pure comparative negligence in our state, either the defendant or the unknown driver could be held liable for the full amount of damage caused by their combined negligence under the common law rule. We acknowledge that joint and several liability for concurrent tortfeasors has been retained by judicial decision in pure comparative negligence states. However, its retention rests on two grounds; neither of which is defensible. The first ground in based on the concept that the plaintiff's injury is "indivisible" for purposes of joint and several liability. That is, just because the percentage of each party's negligence can be defined, it does not mean that the plaintiff's injury is divisible. Following this reasoning to its logical conclusion, one can find that a tortfeasor who is 1% at fault could be liable for 100% of the plaintiff's damages. The concept of "one indivisible harm" based on the common law is obsolete. The second ground for retaining joint and several liability is to favor plaintiffs and protect them against insolvent defendants. While this reason might appear to make sense, it is not defensible when there is more than one defendant in the case. Thus, we reject the concept of joint and several liability in cases of comparative negligence and hold that in this case the defendant is not liable for only for 30% of the damages, not for the entire amount.

 Order for New Trial Reversed.

Bundt v. Embro

Supreme Court of New York, Queens County, 265 N.Y.S.2d 872 (1965)

FACTS

Five plaintiffs, including Plaintiff Bundt bring a suit in negligence against a number of defendants, including Defendant Embro for injuries received in an automobile collision involving two vehicles. Plaintiffs also sued a city contractor alleging that the latter had negligently obstructed the view of a stop sign at the intersection during some repair work on a highway. Defendants seek leave to amend their answers on the ground that plaintiffs had already recovered a judgment and satisfaction against the State of New York in the Court of Claims for the same injuries and that the judgment was thus satisfied.

 Is a party entitled to more than one satisfaction for the same harm when he has suffered a harm not capable of partition via the negligence of more than one tortfeasor?

 A party is not entitled to more than one satisfaction for the same harm when he has suffered a harm not capable of partition via the negligence of more than one tortfeasor.

 A party is not entitled to more than one satisfaction for the same harm when he has suffered a harm not capable of partition via the negligence of more than one tortfeasor. A party injured by joint tortfeasors may recover damages against either or all and although there may be several lawsuits and multiple recoveries, there may only be one, single satisfaction. We reject plaintiff's argument that the rule of satisfaction of the judgment has no application to the Court of Claims judgment because that rule, that the satisfaction of the judgment against one joint tortfeasor which discharges the other defendant-tortfeasors, also applies to the State of New York. Proof of this can be found under Section 8 of the Court of Claims Act, where it states that the State of New York holds the same position as a private defendant. Thus, if the trial court determines that the State is a joint tortfeasor with defendants, the satisfaction of the judgment against the State would thus discharge the defendants.

 Leave to amend is granted to the defendants.

Cox v. Pearl Investment Co.
Supreme Court of Colorado, 450 P.2d 60 (1969)

FACTS

Plaintiff Cox and her husband sought recovery from Defendant Pearl Investment Co. for injuries sustained when plaintiff fell on property owned by the defendant. Defendant's tenant, Goodwill Industries, had previously paid plaintiff $2,500 in consideration for her signing a contract called "Covenant Not to Proceed with Suit." The contract expressly reserved to plaintiff the right to sue any other persons against whom she may have a claim arising out of the accident. The trial court granted defendant's summary judgment on the ground that it viewed the covenant as a release, having given no effect to the operative words "reserving to plaintiff the right to sue any other persons." The trial court therefore ruled that the document barred any further action against defendant as a joint tortfeasor. Plaintiff appealed.

Is one joint tortfeasor released from liability by a covenant [contract] not to sue, signed by and between the other joint tortfeasor and the plaintiff, where the parties to the contract intend that the plaintiff not be barred from suing that tortfeasor not a party to the covenant?

A covenant not to sue, signed by and between one joint tortfeasor and the plaintiff, where the parties to the contract intend that the plaintiff not be barred from suing the other joint tortfeasor [not a party to the covenant] does not release the non-covenanting co-tortfeasor from liability.

In granting defendant's motion for summary judgment, the trial court relied on *Price v. Baker* which held that the release of one joint tortfeasor is the release of all. While we confirm this to be still the rule in Colorado, we now state that the instrument involved in Prince, was erroneously interpreted to be an absolute and full release of all joint tortfeasors. It is not. In its place, the manifest intent of the parties to the contract should be taken onto consideration. This is a fundamental tenet of contract law. Where a contract expressly releases one joint tortfeasor, but reserves to the plaintiff the right to sue the other tortfeasors who may be liable, the contract should not be treated otherwise. Here, the restriction in the contract clearly shows that the plaintiff has not received full compensation and that her right to sue any other potential defendant is not barred. No non-settling joint tortfeasor is prejudiced by such a reading of the contract since the amount of the judgment against them will be reduced by the amount paid by his co-tortfeasor. We follow and apply the holding of *Matheson v. O'Kane,* which stated that where it is evident that the consideration paid to the plaintiff was not intended as full compensation for the plaintiff's injury and was intended to preserve liability of other tortfeasors, effect should be given to the intent of the parties even though the agreement signed by the plaintiff was in the form of a release. Restatement of Torts, Section 885, which is modeled on caselaw like *Matheson* provides that a release will be construed as a covenant not to sue where the right to sue other tortfeasors is expressly reserved.

Reversed and Remanded.

121

Elbaor v. Smith

Supreme Court of Texas, 845 S.W.2d 240 (1992)

FACTS

Plaintiff Smith was involved in an automobile accident, suffered series injuries, including a compound fracture of her left ankle. Consequently, she sought treatment from the Dallas/Fort Worth Medical Center on the night of the accident and was subsequently transferred to Arlington Community Hospital where she was treated by Drs. Elbaor, Stephens, Gatmaitan, and Syrquin. She received treatment over the next few years but ultimately, her ankle joint became fused. Plaintiff filed malpractice action against all the named medical professionals and facilities but prior to the trial, she entered into a settlement agreement with the Dallas/Fort Worth Medical Center, Arlington Community Hospital and later into a "Mary Carter" agreement for $405,010 with all the remaining doctors, except Dr. Elbaor. The Mary Carter agreement provided that the settling doctors would remain as defendants and participate in the trial against Elbaor, after which the doctors would be paid back all or part of the settlement amount from plaintiff's judgment against Elbaor. Dr. Elbaor requested that the Mary Carter Agreement be voided as against public policy. The trial court denied this request and the case proceeded to trial. While the Agreements were not entered into evidence, the trial judge was troubled by them and took remedial measures to mitigate their harmful effects: allowed counsel to explain the Agreements to the jury and instructed the jury regarding them. The jury allocated 88% of the liability in the case to Elbaor and 22% to the other defendant-doctors. The trial court, deducting credits for settlement, entered judgment against Elbaor for $1,872,818 and the Court of Appeals affirmed. Dr. Elbaor appealed.

Do "Mary Carter" agreements, which create a tremendous incentive for the settling defendant to ensure that the plaintiff succeeds in obtaining a sizable recovery, violative of public policy?

"Mary Carter" agreements, which create a tremendous incentive for the settling defendant to ensure that the plaintiff succeeds in obtaining a sizable recovery [thus motivating the defendant to assist greatly in the plaintiff's presentation of her case], are violative of public policy.

"Mary Carter" agreements, which create a tremendous incentive for the settling defendant to ensure that the plaintiff succeeds in obtaining a sizable recovery [thus motivating the defendant to assist greatly in the plaintiff's presentation of her case], are violative of public policy. A Mary Carter agreement is one where the plaintiff enters into a settlement agreement with a defendant and goes to trial against other defendant(s). The settling defendant guarantees a minimum payment to the plaintiff which may be offset in whole or in part by an excess judgment recovered against other non-settling defendants at trial. Such agreements provide great incentive for settling defendants to help ensure that the plaintiff receives a large recovery and thus, motivate such defendants to help the plaintiff in the presentation of his case. While such agreements are characterized as promoting settlement and compromise, their effect is just the opposite - they act to ensure a trial against the non-settling defendant. Judge Spears in *Smithwick* noted the falsity of the premise of the Mary Carter agreement when he stated that it presents to the jury a sham of adversity between the plaintiff and the non-settling defendants, while the settling defendants are actually assisting the plaintiff to secure a large judgment and exonerate the settling defendants. Mary Carter agreements allow a plaintiff to enlist the help of the settling defendants and encourage the more blameworthy defendants to "cut a deal" with the plaintiff to pay modest damages or no damages at all. The public policy favoring fair trials outweighs the policy favoring the partial settlement of cases that encourage rather than discourage future litigation.

Reversed and Remanded.

Knell v. Feltman

U.S. Court of Appeals, D.C., 174 F.2d 662 (1949)

FACTS

Plaintiff Evelyn Langland and her husband, passengers in an automobile owned and operated by Kenneth E. Knell (cross-defendant), sued Defendant Ralph L. Feltman, the owner of a taxicab which collided with Knell's car for injuries sustained as a result of the collision. Defendant then filed a third-party complaint against Knell on the ground that the accident was caused by the contributing or sole negligence of Knell. At trial, the jury entered judgment against defendant for $11,500 and against Knell in favor of defendant for $5,750, finding both negligent and the negligence of each contributed to the accident. Cross-defendant Knell appeals arguing that the defendant did not have a right to contribution because the plaintiffs did not bring action against Knell, he did.

 Does the right to contribution exist only between tortfeasors liable in common to the plaintiff and against whom the plaintiff has obtained a judgment?

 The right to contribution does not exist only between tortfeasors liable in common to the plaintiff and against whom the plaintiff has obtained a judgment.

 The right to contribution does not exist only between tortfeasors liable in common to the plaintiff and against whom the plaintiff has obtained a judgment. Cross-defendant Knell's argument is untenable on two grounds.

First, Federal Rule of Civil Procedure 14(a) specifically provides that a defendant may bring into the action another person who may be liable to the defendant for all or any part of the damages, even if the plaintiff does not seek a judgment against him. Secondly, the right to seek contribution belongs to the tortfeasor who has been forced to pay and the existence of the right cannot depend on the selection of defendants made by the plaintiff. Were this the case, a plaintiff could choose arbitrarily or intentionally to deliberately attach liability to one defendant alone, or collude with one tortfeasor against whom the plaintiff has a cause of action, to impose liability solely on another against whom he has a cause of action for the same wrong. The "no contribution rule," denying contribution to joint tortfeasors, is typically said to begin with *Merryweather v. Nixan.* In *Merryweather,* the plaintiff and defendant intentionally damaged a mill and the plaintiff, having satisfied the judgment of the mill owner sued for contribution. The *Merryweather* case has often been cited in support of the sweeping proposition that no contribution can be had between joint tortfeasors. Yet it is important to note that the ruling in that case is limited to the denial of contribution between willful or intentional wrongdoers. Thus, we conclude that where a tort is committed by the concurrent negligence of two or more persons, *who are not intentional wrongdoers*, contribution should be allowed.

 Affirmed.

Yellow Cab Co. of D.C. Inc. v. Dreslin
U.S. Court of Appeals, 181 F.2d 626 (D.C. Cir. 1950)

FACTS

Plaintiff-appellees Mr. Dreslin and his wife (the "Dreslins") were driving was involved in an automobile accident with a taxicab owned by Defendant-appellant Yellow Cab Company of D.C., Inc and driven by one of its agents. Mrs. Dreslin and other passengers in her car sued the defendant and Mr. Dreslin joined them claiming loss of consortium, medical expenses and damages relating to the automobile itself. Defendant asserted as an affirmative defense that Mr. Dreslin was contributorily negligent and also cross-claimed against Mr. Dreslin for damages to the taxicab and for contribution for any sums recovered by Mrs. Dreslin against it. The jury found that both Mr. Dreslin and defendant were negligent. The court disallowed a judgment against Mr. Dreslin by Mrs. Dreslin; that is, no contribution was required by Mr. Dreslin for the payment from defendant to Mrs. Dreslin. In disallowing the judgment, the court held that "the right of contribution arises from a joint liability," and as Mr. Dreslin could not be liable in tort to his wife, there was no joint liability and therefore no right of contribution. Defendant appealed.

May an injured party compel contribution from a tortfeasor who has no liability to the former?

Before contribution can be compelled against a party, the injured party must have a cause of action against the party from whom contribution is sought – that is, joint liability must exist.

Before contribution can be compelled, joint liability must exist. Because Mr. Dreslin and Mrs. Dreslin were married, the rule of immunity between husband and wife precludes Mr. Dreslin from having any liability to his wife for her injuries. The rights of common obligation arise out of a common liability such that in the case of a common obligation, the discharge of the obligation by one obligor without payment from the other gives the latter an unfair advantage to which he is not equitably entitled. However, there must be a common obligation for contribution to be obtained. Stated another way, in order to be entitled to contribution, the injured party must have had a cause of action against the party from whom contribution is sought. Here, Mr. Dreslin had no such cause of action against Mrs. Dreslin; as a validly married couple under the protection of the applicable immunity rule, he cannot be jointly liable with defendant for her injuries. The argument that Mr. Dreslin escapes any of the applicable burdens associated with his negligence fails to appreciate the sound public policy of the preservation of domestic peace and felicity, upon which the rule of immunity between husband and wife is based.

Affirmed.

Slocum v. Donahue

Court of Appeals of Massachusetts, 693 N.E.2d 179 (1998)

FACTS

Defendant Robert Donahue plead guilty to motor vehicle homicide in the death of the plaintiffs' (the "Slocums") eighteen month old son, Todd Slocum. Plaintiffs thereafter filed a civil action against defendant alleging negligence and gross negligence. At trial, plaintiffs' allege that defendant inadvertently pushed the door mat on the driver's side under the throttle, racing the engine such that when he started backing out of his driveway, his car continued to accelerate across the street, hitting the curb and becoming airborne. The infant was found under the car after it crashed through a fence across the street. Defendant alleged that he repeatedly stepped on the brakes, but the car continued to accelerate until it hit Todd Slocum and that defendant had been drinking at the time. Defendant then filed a third-party complaint against Ford Motor Company seeking contribution and indemnity. Defendant's expert testified that the floor mat in the car manufactured by Ford was defective in that it interfered with the operation of his brakes causing them to fail. Before trial, however, Ford agreed to pay plaintiffs $150,000 in exchange for a release of any claim. Ford then moved for summary judgment on defendant's claim against it, which was granted. Defendant appealed from the final judgment dismissing their 3rd party complaint against Ford

 Is a joint tortfeasor entitled to indemnification or contribution from a co-tortfeasor who obtained a release from the plaintiff?

 A joint tortfeasor is not entitled to indemnification from a fellow tortfeasor where the would-be indemnitee is *not* held derivatively or vicariously liable for the wrongful act of another.

 Under G.L. 231B, §4, our state's statute regarding the right to contribution, when a release is given in good faith to one of two or more persons who are liable for the same injury, it will discharge the tortfeasor to whom it is given from all liability for contribution to any other tortfeasor. In this case, defendant argues that the settlement between Ford and plaintiff was not made in good faith because 1) it was for less than the value of the case and 2) because Ford allegedly was going to allow plaintiff to use its [Ford's] experts at trial so that the defendant's attempt to impugn liability to Ford at trial would be unsuccessful. We are unmoved by the defendant's arguments. In view of the fact that defendant pleaded guilty in the criminal case and that he admitted that he had been drinking vodka at the time of the accident, it would not be unreasonable for a jury to conclude that Ford was *not* liable. Next, we similarly reject defendant contention that plaintiff's use of Ford's expert witnesses is evidence of collusion. It is merely speculation to argue that the plaintiff settled with Ford because they believed Ford was not responsible for the death of their son and not because Ford was a "deep-pocket defendant." Nothing in the evidence suggests otherwise and mere speculation alone is not enough to require a further hearing on the issue of good faith. As to defendant's contribution and indemnity claims against Ford, Massachusetts statute G.L. c. 231B, the Right to Indemnity, provides that contribution is allowed between joint tortfeasors who cause injury to another. Here, contribution is not allowed because plaintiff released Ford in good faith and according to the statute, this release discharges Ford from liability for contribution to defendant. Defendant is also not entitled to indemnification from Ford because indemnity is allowed only when the indemnitee did not join in the wrongful act where the would-be indemnitee (here the defendant) is derivatively or vicariously liable for the wrongful act of another (here Ford). It would be simply impossible for the jury here to have found that the defendant was vicariously liable for the conduct of Ford. Summary judgment in favor of Ford was appropriate.

 Judgment affirmed.

Bruckman v. Pena

Colorado Court of Appeals, 487 P.2d 566 (1971)

FACTS

Plaintiff William Pena was injured when his car collided with the truck driven by Defendant Bruckman and owned by Defendant Armored Motors Service. Plaintiff's injuries were aggravated when he got into a second collision approximately one year later. Plaintiff sued both defendants for all the injuries suffered and the court instructed the jury that it must attempt to apportion the amount of disability between the first and second accidents if possible but if it could not, then the defendants named in the action [owner and driver] would be liable for the entire injury. The jury returned a verdict in favor of plaintiff. Defendants appeal and seek reversal of the verdict asserting that the court's instructions to the jury were made in error.

 Can a defendant be held liable to a plaintiff for the full extent of his injuries after the plaintiff is subsequently injured again and when the plaintiff is unable to apportion the damages between the causes of the first and second injuries?

 A defendant can not be held liable to a plaintiff for the full extent of his [the plaintiff's] injuries after the plaintiff is subsequently injured again and when the plaintiff is unable to apportion the damages between the causes of the first and second injuries.

 A defendant can not be held liable to a plaintiff for the full extent of his [the plaintiff's] injuries after the plaintiff is subsequently injured again and when the plaintiff is unable to apportion the damages between the causes of the first and second injuries. The general rule in negligence cases is that the plaintiff has the burden of proof to show that his damages were proximately caused by the negligence of the defendant. Here, the trial judge's instruction is erroneous because it allows the plaintiff to recover damages against the defendant for injuries received subsequent to the negligent conduct of the defendant. In effect, the instruction relieves the plaintiff of his burden of proof and shifts the burden on the defendant to prove that the plaintiff's damages can be apportioned between the two accidents. Plaintiff's argues *Newbury v. Vogel* applies to the instant facts. We disagree. Under *Newbury,* a tortfeasor who injures one suffering from a pre-existing condition is liable for the entire *damage* to the plaintiff where no apportionment is possible. Here, however, plaintiff advocates not only that the first tortfeasor [i.e., the defendant] should be held liable not only for damage that he caused, but that he should also be responsible for the injuries he subsequently suffered as a result of negligence of another party.

 Reversed and remanded.

Michie v. Great Lakes Steel Div., Nat'l Steel Corp.

U.S. Court of Appeals, 495 F.2d 213 (4th Cir. 1974)

FACTS

Plaintiff-appellees Michie and 36 other individuals in Canada sued Defendant-appellants Great Lakes Steel Division ("Great Lakes"), National Steel Corporation and one other corporation in the United States, jointly and severally, alleging that noxious pollutants emitted by the defendants' plants were carried into Canada, across the Detroit river, creating a nuisance and damaging persons and properties. The action was filed based on diversity, each individual claimed damages ranging between $11,000 and $35,000 from all three defendants jointly and severally. Defendant Great Lakes and the other corporations moved to dismiss the complaint claiming that *each* plaintiff individually did not meet the minimum amount in controversy for diversity jurisdiction as set forth in 28 U.S.C. §1332 (1970). The District Court denied the motion. The three defendant-corporations filed an interlocutory appeal from the District judge's denial of their motion to dismiss.

May a court hold all the defendants jointly and severally liable when the independent but concurrent acts of the defendants caused an indivisible harm to the plaintiff and no reasonable means of dividing up the damages is apparent?

A court can hold all the defendants jointly and severally liable when the independent but concurrent acts of the defendants caused an indivisible harm to the plaintiff and no reasonable means of allocating damages is apparent.

We follow *Maddux* wherein it was said that it is unfair to impose the burden of proving specific shares of harm done by the defendant on the injured party. Hence, where the injury to the plaintiff is separable and liability for the injury or damages may be apportioned to the defendant with reasonable certainty, then the defendants will not be held jointly and severally liable. If, however, the division of liability is not possible, not clear-cut solution readily presents itself as the authorities are divided. Some courts hold that the case is over and simply dismiss the entire claim. We reject such a position because under that scenario, the tortfeasors will be relieved from all liability and thus escape punishment even though their conduct was negligent and injurious. We hold instead that where division of liability is unattainable, the injury itself is indivisible and the tortfeasors will be held jointly and severally liable. The best summary of the rational for the rule is found in *Harper and James* where joint and several liability is imposed in four different situations: 1) where the actors knowingly join in the tortious conduct; 2) where the tortfeasors fail to perform a common duty owed to the plaintiff; 3) where there is a special relationship between the parties; and 4) where, although no concerted action between the tortfeasors exist, the harm produced by their actions is indivisible. The case before us falls into category four. Therefore, where the harm is indivisible, the court shifts the burden from the plaintiff to the wrongdoers.

As modified in regard to punitive damages, the judgment of the District Court is affirmed.

Dillon v. Twin State Gas & Electric Co.

Supreme Court of New Hampshire, 163 A. 111 (1932)

FACTS

This is an action by Plaintiff Henry Dillon, administrator of the estate of the deceased, a 14 year old boy, against Defendant Twin States Gas & Electric Co., a company which maintained electric wires which carried electric current across a public bridge spanning the Androscoggin River in Berlin, New Hampshire. The wires ran through the vertical and horizontal girders above the bridge, where insulated for weather protection but not against contact. No current passed through the wires during the daytime except by chance. The 14-year-old victim lost his balance while sitting on top of the bridge girders, grabbed one of the wires to keep from falling, was electrocuted and died. At trial, defendant's motion for directed verdict was dismissed and it subsequently appealed arguing that the victim would have fallen to his death anyway regardless of defendant's negligence.

 Where a plaintiff would suffer injury in spite of the defendant's negligence, will the plaintiff's damages be measured based on the plaintiff's actual injury?

 Where a plaintiff would suffer injury in spite of the defendant's negligence, the plaintiff's damages will be measured based on the plaintiff's actual injury.

 Where a plaintiff would suffer injury in spite of the defendant's negligence, the plaintiff's damages will be measured based on the plaintiff's actual injury. Here, the defendant's only liability to the decedent was exposing him to the danger of live wires; the deceased was not entitled to any protection from the defendant to keep from falling. Therefore, if it is found that the boy would have fallen to his death regardless of the electrocution, the defendant is not liable, except for that injury attributable to him from the electric shock. In that situation, however, the boy's life or his earning capacity has no value, and no damages could be sustained against the defendant. If, however, it is found that the boy's fall would have resulted in injury only but not death, then the loss of life or earning capacity would be measured by its value in this injured condition.

 Exceptions overruled.

Winterbottom v. Wright
Exchequer of Pleas, 152 Eng.Rep 402 (1842)

FACTS

Defendant Wright contracted with the Postmaster–General to supply mail coaches, provide for their complete maintenance and assume sole responsibility for their upkeep. Atkinson, knowing of the contract, independently contracted with the Postmaster-General to provide horses and drivers for the coaches. Plaintiff Winterbottom, one of the drivers for Atkinson, was hurt when a latent defect caused the coach he was driving (and serviced by the defendant) to break down, throwing him to the ground and injuring him. The defendant demurred (a request made to a court, asking it to dismiss a lawsuit on the grounds that no legal claim is asserted) to the defendant's action.

 Can a plaintiff sue a defendant for injuries he suffered as the result of defects in a product provided by the latter, when there is no privity of contract between the two?

 The plaintiff, or any injured consumer, bystander, or user of a defective product, cannot bring an action on the contract against another where there was no contractual relationship (privity of contract) between the two; however, he is permitted to sue the immediate vendor of the product.

 There was no contractual relationship between plaintiff, the injured party and the defendant, the provider of the coaches. Absent such a relationship, the plaintiff is precluded from recovering for his injuries. Were we to allow such an action to proceed, every bystander who was injured by the defective coach might bring an action against the coach supplier. This would lead to absurd and outrageous consequences, without limit. However, when a party has undertaken a public duty, he becomes responsible to the public and thus will be held liable for any injury caused by him or his servant's negligence. In the instant case, Wright did not breach his contract with the Postmaster-General and executed all of his contractual responsibilities to the latter's satisfaction. Plaintiff was not in privity of contract with either Wright or the Postmaster-General. Plaintiff is simply an injured 3rd party and defendant should not now be liable in tort to 3rd parties absent a legal duty. No such duty exists here between the two parties to the instant action.

 See Rule above.

MacPherson v. Buick Motor Co.
Court of Appeals of New York, 111 N.E. 1050 (1916)

FACTS

Defendant Buick Motor Co., an automobile manufacturer, sold an automobile to a retail dealer, who then resold the car to Plaintiff MacPherson. MacPherson was injured after being thrown out of the car following a wheel collapse. Apparently, the wooden wheel contained a defect and crumbled into fragments which on the car. The wheel was bought by Buick from another manufacturer. Evidence was submitted, however, that the defects in the wheel could have been discovered through reasonable inspection, but such an inspection was not made. There is no claim that Buick knew of the defect and willfully concealed it.

 Does a manufacturer owe a duty of care to all potential, foreseeable plaintiffs of its product?

 Manufacturers owe a duty of care, and thus will be held liable to ultimate purchasers, when the product they create is inherently dangerous, capable of loss of life or limb, known to be dangerous in ordinary use if defectively made and is likely to be used by person other than the initial purchaser.

 When the nature of a thing is such that it is reasonably certain to place life and limb in peril when negligently made, liability will attach if there is knowledge of the danger, and not a mere possibility of it, and where danger is capable of being foreseen. Under such circumstances, the manufacturer will be held liable to all users of his product, not just the initial purchasers. The duty to insure safety in the fact of foreseeable negligence should not be based solely on the existence of a contract between the injured person and the manufacturer. This is because when it is known that a product will be used by those other than the original purchaser in the normal course of business, then the manufacturer's duty is not limited to those he is in privity of contract with. Under these circumstances, the manufacturer of the product is under a duty to these users to manufacture the product with care, non-negligently and without defects. Here, we note that the nature of an automobile creates an inherent danger if manufactured defectively. Defendant clearly knew of the dangerous propensities of a car and is also charged with the knowledge that persons other than the original purchaser, the dealer, would be using the car as end-users. Since the dealer buys cars from the manufacturer to resell to the public, it would be ridiculous to appoint the dealer as the only entity to whom the manufacturer owes a legal duty. Moreover, the manufacturer cannot shirk its duty to inspect the component parts by claiming that it did not manufacture those specific parts itself, it owes not duty to inspect for defects. As a manufacturer, Buick was responsible for the final, finished product. This responsibility includes subjecting the component parts to ordinary "quality control" tests.

 Judgment for the plaintiff, affirmed with costs.

H.R. Moch Co. v. Rensselaer Water Co.
Court of Appeals of New York, 159 N.E. 896 (1928)

FACTS

Defendant Rensselaer Water Co. contracted with the City of Rensselaer to supply water for city sewer flushing, street sprinkling, schools and public buildings and fire hydrants. Water also was to be furnished to private customers within the city, at specific rates set forth in a schedule. While this contract was in effect, a building caught fire, and the flames spread to a warehouse owned by Plaintiff Moch Co., destroying the building and its contents. Rensselaer Water was promptly notified of the fire, "but omitted and neglected after such notice" to supply an adequate quantity of water, with adequate water pressure on tap, to fight the fire, although it was able to do so and even though its contract required it "to furnish enough water . . . to prevent the spread of fire."

 Can a defendant be held liable for a failure to supply enough water to fight a fire when no contractual or special relationship exists between the *injured* party and the defendant which would compel the latter to aid the former?

 When the non-performance of a contract results only in the denial of a benefit, as opposed to active harm, no liability will be imparted to the defendant.

 When the non-performance of a contract results only in the denial of a benefit, as opposed to active harm, no liability will be imparted to the defendant. Inaction by one which results in actively causing harm to another will impart liability on the offending party. If we were to expand liability any further, an indefinite number of potential beneficiaries of the performance would be created and an involuntary assumption of new relations would follow. This would create unacceptable results. We think the action is not maintainable as one for breach of contract. Here, the plaintiff is not a beneficiary of the Rensselaer Water-City of Rensselaer contract because the City was not under any legal duty to supply its inhabitants with protection against fire. We note that the overwhelming authority in this area treats the benefit to the public under these types of contracts as incidental and secondary. We do not think the action is maintainable as one for a common law tort either as there is no evidence of an intention that Rensselaer Water be answerable to individual residents and, in the words of the U.S. Supreme Court, "[t]he law does not spread its protection so far." We also do not think the action maintainable as one for a breach of a statutory duty; as there was no statute in place that imposed liability for failure to supply water. Hence, Rensselaer Water cannot be held liable under this cause of action.

 Affirmed.

Clagett v. Dacy

Court of Special Appeals of Maryland, 420 A.2d 1285 (1980)

FACTS

Plaintiff-appellant Clagett and others were the high bidders at a foreclosure sale but failed to acquire the property because Defendant Dacy, one of the attorneys for the creditors, twice failed to follow proper procedure for the sale. As a result, the debtor redeemed his land by discharging the loan and the plaintiff lost the opportunity to buy the property and resell it at a profit. Plaintiffs sued defendant to recover the loss, alleging that defendant owed plaintiffs a duty to conduct the sale with due diligence both "properly and carefully." The Circuit Court sustained defendant's demurrer without leave to amend and the plaintiff appealed.

May an attorney be held liable to a person who he is not in privity of contract with and who is not the intended to beneficiary of his legal services?

An attorney will not be held liable to a person who he is not in privity of contract with and who is not the intended to beneficiary of his legal services [re: the attorney's performance].

An attorney will not be held liable to a person who he is not in privity of contract with and who is not the intended to beneficiary of his legal services. The general rule is that a third party beneficiary may any defaulting party to a contract, attorney or otherwise, made for the 3rd party beneficiary's benefit. And while *Prescott v. Coppage* seems to suggest a modest relaxation of the strict privity requirement, the court made it clear that this rule does not permit third parties to sue attorneys on pure negligence theory, that is, for a violation of some general duty arising in the absence of an underlying contractual attorney-client relationship. In *Donald v. Garry*, a 3rd party action was supported against an attorney where damage resulted from the attorney's negligence to a person intended to be benefited by his [the attorney's] performance irrespective of any lack of privity of contract between the attorney and the party to be benefited. In light of the above, the plaintiff's declaration fails to state a cause of action. Here, the defendant attorney was representing the creditor (mortgagee), not the plaintiff-bidders. Moreover, the respective interests of the parties [bidder v. mortgagee] interests were diametrically opposed: The mortgagee's goal is to extract the highest bid possible from the sale while the bidder's goal is to pay the lowest price achievable. Thus, given the opposing interests at work here, the defendant's attorneys could not lawfully represent the two groups.

Judgment affirmed; appellants to pay costs.

Hegel v. Langsam
Court of Common Pleas of Ohio, 273 N.E.2d 351 (1971)

FACTS

Plaintiffs, the Hegels, the parents of a 17 year old minor student from Chicago, Illinois and who was a enrolled at the University, sued Defendant Langsam, a university official, for allowing the student to associate with criminals, to become a drug user, and for failing to return the student to plaintiff's custody on demand.

Can a university be held liable to the parents of a minor for breaching an alleged duty by *not* supervising and monitoring the private lives of its students?

A university does not have the duty to manage the private lives of its students, and, as such, can not be held liable to the parents of a minor for not controlling the comings and goings and for not supervising and monitoring the student's associations.

A university does not have the duty to manage the private lives of its students, and, as such, can not be held liable to the parents of a minor for not controlling the comings and goings and for not supervising and monitoring the student's associations. A university is not a nursing home, a boarding school or a prison. Persons who meet the qualifications of the university are presumed to have sufficient maturity to conduct their own personal affairs. There is no requirement of law which imposes on the university the duty to regulate the private lives of its students, or to control their associations.

Affirmed.

L.S. Ayres & Co. v. Hicks

Supreme Court of Indiana, 40 N.E.2d 334 (1942)

FACTS

Plaintiff Hicks, a six-year-old boy, was accompanying his mother when he fell in Defendant L.S. Ayres & Co.'s store and got his fingers stuck in the escalator. Defendant's employees unreasonably delayed stopping the escalator, thus aggravating plaintiff's injury. Plaintiff sued defendant to recover for injuries sustained. The trial court entered a judgment for plaintiff and denied a new trial; defendant appealed.

 When the instrumentality which caused injury to the plaintiff is under the defendant's control, is the latter under a duty to rescue the former when that person is still in danger of further injury?

 The defendant, [a store owner or an invitor, for example], has a duty to rescue the plaintiff, the person in peril, if the instrumentality that caused the latter's injury is in control of the defendant.

 The defendant has a duty to rescue the plaintiff, the person in peril, if the instrumentality that caused the latter's injury is in control of the defendant. Generally, the law recognizes no duty to rescue a person who is in danger. However, where there is a special relationship between the parties involved, a duty exists, and the failure to render assistance may amount to negligence. This is especially true when failure to render assistance aggravates the injury even though the initial injury may have been caused by the negligence of the injured party himself – the defendant may still be negligent. Moreover, this duty is not annulled when the person in control of the instrumentality did not cause of the initial injury. Here, the plaintiff was an invitee, and received his injuries in using an instrumentality offered by defendant and under its control. Therefore, the duty to rescue plaintiff existed. However, since this duty arose *after* the initial in jury to plaintiff, the defendant cannot be charged with anticipation or prevention of the injury; only with failure to exercise reasonable care to prevent the aggravation of the injury. Therefore, defendant-appellant is only liable for damages which were proximately resulted from aggravation of the injuries.

C Reversed.

J.S. and M.S. v. R.T.H.
Supreme Court of New Jersey, 714 A.2d 924 (1998)

FACTS

Plaintiffs J.S. and M.S., two young girls ages 12 and 15, spent a great deal of time with their 65 year-old neighbor, called "R.T.H." for purposes of this litigation, at his horse barn, riding and caring for his horses. After he established relationship with them and they trusted him, he began to sexually abuse both plaintiffs, abuse which continued for more than a year. Following his conviction and imprisonment, the girls and their parents brought this action against R.T.H. and his wife, R.G.H. for damages, arguing that the wife's negligence both her and R.T.H., her husband, liable for the plaintiffs injuries. The husband conceded liability for both intentional and negligent injuries inflicted, however his wife denied that she could be found negligent for the same. The defendant-Wife also filed a cross claim for contribution and indemnification against her husband, alleging that even if the plaintiffs' allegations were proven true, her husband was the sole and primary cause of any injuries to them. The trial judge entered summary judgment on behalf of the defendant-wife and on appeal, the Appellate Division reversed and remanded an order granting the plaintiffs extended discovery. The Supreme Court of New Jersey granted the defendant-wife's petition for certiorari.

Is a spouse under a duty of care to prevent the sexual abuse of a child when he/she spouse suspects his/her partner of actual abuse or the possibility of abuse and, if such a duty does exist, does a breach of that duty constitute a proximate cause of the harm suffered?

When a spouse has actual knowledge or special reason to know of the likelihood of his or her spouse engaging in sexually abusive behavior against a particular person or persons, a spouse has a duty of care to take reasonable steps to prevent or warn of the harm; and a breach of that duty constitutes a proximate cause of the injury suffered.

When a spouse has actual knowledge or special reason to know of the likelihood of his or her spouse engaging in sexually abusive behavior against a particular person or persons, a spouse has a duty of care to take reasonable steps to prevent or warn of the harm; and a breach of that duty constitutes a proximate cause of the injury suffered. The concept of foreseeability of the risk of harm is the key component in the determination of whether a duty exists, and it is based on the defendant's knowledge of the risk of injury, as measured by an objective standard. Knowledge may be an actual or constructive: actual knowledge is an actual awareness of the risk while constructive knowledge is where the defendant is charged with being "in a position" to "discover the risk of harm." The scope of the duty imposed is determined via a review of the totality of the circumstances. In this case, the defendant-wife's husband sexually assaulted young girls who he lured into a trusted relationship. The abuse occurred on her property over the course of amount a year. Although conduct involving sexual abuse is often secretive, clandestine, and furtive, there are a number of factors that are relevant in a determination as to whether or not it is foreseeable to a spouse that her/his partner would sexually abuse a child. They are: whether such abuse has occurred before; the number, date and nature of those prior offenses; where and when those offenses occurred; and whether the offense was against a stranger or a victim known to the abuser, to name a few. There exists a strong public policy to protect

J.S. and M.S. v. R.T.H.

Supreme Court of New Jersey, 714 A.2d 924 (1998)

children from sexual abuse, however there is also an interest in protecting the marital relationship. However, society's interest in preserving the marital relationship cannot outweigh the interest in protecting children from sexual abuse. Therefore, the issues foreseeability, the interests of the parties, and public policy concerns support the imposition of a duty of care. This leads us at last to the issue of proximate causation, which must be addressed in any determination imposing liability for a breach of a duty. In this case, it does not seem highly extraordinary that a wife's failure to prevent or warn of her husband's sexual abuse or his propensity for sexual abuse would result in the occurrence or the continuation of such abuse. Nor can it be said that the injuries suffered by the plaintiffs constituted an extraordinary result of the husband's abuse or an extraordinary consequence of the defendant-wife's own negligence. Thus, the defendant-wife's negligence could be found to be a proximate cause of the plaintiffs' injuries.

 Accordingly, we affirm the judgment of the Appellate Division.

Tarasoff v. Regents of the University of California
Supreme Court of California, 131 Cal.Rptr. 14 (1976)

FACTS

Prosenjit Poddar was a patient treated by psychotherapists employed by the Cowell Memorial Hospital at the University of California (defendant). While undergoing treatment, he confided to his therapist, Dr. Lawrence Moore that he intended to kill Plaintiff Tarasoff's daughter. It was alleged that on Moore's request, the campus police briefly detained Poddar, but that they released him when he appeared rational. It was further claimed that Dr. Harvey Powelson, Moore's superior, then directed that no further action against Poddar be taken. The therapists did not warn Tarasoff or his daughter, Tatiana Tarasoff, of the plot. Two months after Poddar admitted to his therapists that he killed Tarasoff's daughter in her home by shooting her first with a pellet gun and then stabbing her 17 times with a kitchen knife. Plaintiff predicates liability on two grounds: 1) defendant's failure to warn plaintiff of the danger and their failure to confine Poddar. Defendants, in turn, assert they owed no duty of reasonable care to the victim and that they are immune from suit under California law. The superior court sustained defendants' demurrers to plaintiffs' second amended complaints without leave to amend. This appeal followed.

 Is a therapist under a duty to warn 3rd parties of a danger posed by his patient?

 Where a patient poses a serious likelihood of committing violence against another, his therapist is under a duty to warn foreseeable victims against the possibility of such a danger.

 A therapist has a duty to warn likely victims of potential harm to them by a patient if the therapist diagnoses the patient as presenting a serious likelihood of violence. Defendants assert that no special relation between the victim and defendant therapists exists to impart liability on them. We disagree. The doctor-patient relationship is significant and sufficient enough to create a special duty to exercise reasonable care to protect others; with a duty to 3rd parties established by the foreseeability of harm. Defendant counter by arguing that the imposition of duty to exercise reasonable care to protect 3rd parties is unworkable because therapists cannot accurate predict violent behavior. However, we do not mandate perfect performance and accuracy with respect to the diagnosis of the patient by the therapist; however, a therapist need exercise only *reasonable care* in making the diagnosis. We recognize the public interest in supporting effective treatment of mental illness and in protecting the confidentiality rights of patients, however, the need to protect the public outweighs the need for confidentiality and the danger posed by unnecessary warnings.

 Reversed.

State of Louisiana ex rel. Guste v. M/V Testbank

U.S. Court of Appeals, 752 F.2d 1019 (5th Cir. 1985)

FACTS

In the early evening of July 22, 1980, the outbound container ship, the M/V Testbank (defendant) collided with the M/V Sea Daniel, an inbound bulk carrier, causing 12 tons of pentachlorophenol, PCP, to fall over board. It was the largest spill in U.S. history [at the time]. Consequently, the U.S. Coast Guard closed the water for navigation and temporarily suspended fishing and all other related activities, including approximately 400 sq. miles of the surrounding marsh and adjacent waterways. Various parties filed numerous lawsuits representing many types of interests which were consolidated before the same judge in the Eastern District of Louisiana. Defendant moved for summary judgment as to all claims for economic loss unaccompanied by actual physical damage to property and the District Court granted defendant's motion for summary judgment for all the claimants except commercial oyster men, shrimpers, and fishermen who utilized the damaged waterways for commercial use. The Fifth Circuit Court affirmed and the case is re-examined en banc by the United States court of Appeals for the 5th circuit.

 May a plaintiff recover for solely for economic loss if the loss resulted from physical damage to property in which the plaintiff had no proprietary interest?

 A plaintiff may not recover for pure economic loss if the loss resulted from physical damage to property in which the plaintiff had no interest.

 A plaintiff may not recover for pure economic loss if the loss resulted from physical damage to property in which the plaintiff had no interest. In *Robins Dry Dock v. Flint,* the Supreme Court of the United States held that a tort to the person or property of one man does not make the tortfeasor liable to another merely because the injured person has a contract with the other person. Here, the instant plaintiffs argue that *Robins* should be limited to losses suffered for inability to perform contracts between the plaintiff and others; that is to say, plaintiffs argue that *Robins* applies only to the negligent interference of contract rights. We disagree. When viewed in its historical context, *Robins* represents more that a limit on the recovery for interference of contractual rights, it is a pragmatic limitation imposed by the Supreme Court based upon the tort doctrine of foreseeability. Plaintiffs next argue that the prerequisite of a physical injury is arbitrary, and that the question of remoteness and foreseeability should be left to the trier of fact. Yet those who advocate the elimination of the requirement of physical damage [i.e., the instant plaintiffs] offer not viable substitute in its place. Without a bright line rule of damage to a proprietary interest, no reliable determinable measure of the limit of foreseeability could exist and such a lack of predictability would create unfair and unjust results. Lastly, in an effort to circumvent the *Robins* rule, plaintiffs attempt to categorize their losses as a public nuisance, suggesting that when a defendant unreasonably interferes with public rights by obstructing navigation, he creates a public nuisance for which recovery is available to all who have sustained "particular damages." We find this position unavailing since the damages at issue are so great as to justify distinguishing losses suffered by the general

State of Louisiana ex rel. Guste v. M/V Testbank

U.S. Court of Appeals, 752 F.2d 1019 (5th Cir. 1985)

public from those commercially affected. Thus, the task at hand is to determine who has suffered pecuniary loss so great as to distinguish his losses from similar losses suffered by others. In this court's opinion, there is no advantage in allowing this difficult task to skirt the *Robins* rule.

Affirmed.

Daley v. LaCroix

Supreme Court of Michigan, 179 N.W.2d 390 (1970)

FACTS

At about 10 p.m. on July 16, 1963, Defendant LaCroix's car went off the road, traveled 63 feet in the air and 209 feet beyond the edge of the road, struck a utility pole, sheared off a number of high power electric lines leading to Plaintiff Timothy Daley's property and causing a massive explosion and considerable property damage as a result. Plaintiffs Timothy and Estelle Daley sued defendant for property damage and emotional disturbance caused as a result of the explosion and surrounding circumstances. The trial court directed a verdict in defendants' favor, and the Court of Appeals affirmed on the ground that Michigan law denies recovery of damages for negligent infliction of emotional distress in the absence of physical impact [there was physical damage to property, but the plaintiffs were not physically injured themselves].

Can a plaintiff recover damages in the absence of any physical impact upon his/her person, but where he/she has suffered physical injury as a result of emotional distress caused by a defendant's negligence?

A plaintiff who has suffered physical injury as a result of emotional distress caused by a defendant's negligence may recover damages, even in the absence of any physical impact upon the plaintiff.

Generally, courts will deny recovery for mental disturbance in the absence of physical injury [Exceptions: injuries involving telegraphic companies and the negligent mishandling of corpses]. Compensation for purely a mental component of damages where the defendant negligently inflicts *immediate physical injury* has always been awarded as "parasitic damages." The rational behind the general rule is one of protection against fraudulent or imaginary claims and to stem the flood of litigation which may result therefrom. Thus, where there is no personal injury to the plaintiff due to the defendant's negligence, courts have generally precluded any recovery. We, however, hold otherwise. Based on precedence and the scientific and factual information available, we conclude that the impact rule should be overruled. Therefore, where there is definite and objective physical injury to the plaintiff, as a result of emotional distress caused by the defendant's negligence, the plaintiff may recover damages for such injuries even in the absence of physical impact with the plaintiff's person. A plaintiff's recovery, however, is limited to those reactions to be expected of a normal person, except where the defendant has specific knowledge of the plaintiff's hypersensitivity. Turning to the case before us and applying the foregoing, we hold that the record presents insufficient facts from which a jury could reasonably find or infer a causal relationship between the fright occasioned by the defendant's negligence and the injuries allegedly sustained by the plaintiffs.

The order of the trial court granting directed verdicts against the plaintiffs and the affirmance by the Court of Appeals are reversed and remanded for new trials.

Thing v. La Chusa
Supreme Court of California, 771 P.2d 814 (1989)

FACTS

Defendant James V. LaChusa, an automobile driver, struck and injured John Thing, a minor child. Plaintiff Maria Thing, his mother, who was nearby but who nether saw nor heard the accident, sued defendant alleging great emotional distress and shock brought on when she arrived at the scene of the accident and saw her bloody, unconscious child, who she believed was dead, lying on the ground. The trial court granted defendant's motion for summary judgment on the ground that plaintiff could not establish a claim for negligent infliction of emotional distress because she did not actually witness or hear [i.e. perceive] the accident. Plaintiff appealed.

May a parent whose child was injured by a negligent driver but who did not actually witness or hear the accident recover damages for emotional distress?

A parent whose child was injured by a negligent driver but who did not actually witness or hear the accident can not recover damages for emotional distress.

A parent whose child was injured by a negligent driver but who did not actually witness or hear the accident can not recover damages for emotional distress. Traditionally in California the right to recover damages for negligent infliction of emotional distress was limited to cases where 1) the victim himself was physically injured and damages for emotional distress were awarded as parasitic damages, or 2) to cases where the plaintiff was within the "zone of danger," did not suffer injury as a result of physical impact, but did suffer physical injury as a result of emotional trauma. With the advent of *Dillon v. Legg,* however, the "zone of danger" requirement was abandoned and recovery was allowed for emotional distress by a mother who witnessed her child being run over by a negligent automobile driver. Yet even in *Dillon,* recovery was limited only to reasonable foreseeable plaintiffs whose injuries were reasonably foreseeable. In *Molien v. Kaiser Foundation Hospitals,* both the physical harm and accident or sudden occurrence elements were eliminated in favor of recovery based on a plaintiff's status as a "direct victim" of the defendant's negligence. A "direct victim" is a person whose emotional distress is a reasonably foreseeable consequence of the defendant's negligent conduct. In *Molien,* the court held that the husband of a patient who was erroneously diagnosed as having syphilis was a reasonably foreseeable victim and that the tortious conduct of the defendants [hospital and doctor] was directed at him [the husband] as well as the patient. In light of the foregoing, we hold that in order for a plaintiff to recover for damages for emotional distress caused by observing the negligently inflicted injury of a 3rd party, only if: 1) the plaintiff is closely related by blood or by marriage to the injured 3rd party, since it is more likely that they will suffer a greater degree of emotional distress than a disinterested witness to negligently caused pain and suffering or death; 2) is present at the scene of the injury-causing event and is aware that the injury is causing injury to the victim; and 3) as a result of serious emotion distress, the plaintiff suffers an emotional impact beyond the impact that can be anticipated whenever he learns that a relative is injured. Recovery is

Thing v. La Chusa

Supreme Court of California, 771 P.2d 814 (1989)

---

barred in this case because the plaintiff was not present at the scene of the accident and did no observe the injury-causing event giving rise to any injury to her child. The order granting summary judgment was proper.

Judgment of the Court of Appeal is reversed.

Endresz v. Friedberg
New York Court of Appeals, 248 N.E.2d 901 (1969)

FACTS

Plaintiff Janice Endresz, seven months pregnant at the time with twins, was struck by Defendant Friedberg's automobile in the winter of 1965 and delivered stillborn twins two days later. Plaintiff and her husband, Steve Endresz, sued defendant in negligence and for the wrongful death of the twins. Additionally, the plaintiff couple brought action for the loss of the babies on their own [the deceased children's] behalf. The New York Special Term [trial court] dismissed the wrongful death claims holding that such a claim may not be maintained for the death of an unborn child [or children]. Plaintiffs appealed and the case now comes before the New York Court of Appeals.

May the parents of a stillborn child/children maintain a wrongful death action for the death of the unborn child/children?

The parents of a stillborn child/children may not maintain a wrongful death action for the death of the unborn child/children.

In New York, the parents of a stillborn child may not maintain a wrongful death action for the death of the unborn child. The personal representative of a decedent may maintain an action to recover damages for a wrongful act which caused the death of the decedent. However, before there may be a "decedent," there must be a birth, that is, a person born alive and while the statute is silent on the subject, we are fairly certain that the Legislature did not intent to include "unborn" fetus within the term "decedent." That said, the plaintiffs are not without recourse: the mother of a stillborn child may sue for injury which she may have suffered personally, and the father may sue for loss of consortium and the mother's services. Were we to allow the type of recovery plaintiffs' advocate, such an award would give the parents a windfall and would not constitute compensation to the injured party, but punishment to the wrongdoer. In light of these considerations, we do not feel that as a matter of public policy, a cause of action for a pecuniary loss should accrue to the plaintiff as of a stillborn fetus by way of the negligence of the defendant.

The order appealed from should be affirmed.

Procanik by Procanik v. Cillo
Supreme Court of New Jersey, 478 A.2d 755 (1984)

FACTS

Plaintiff-patient Rosemary Procanik was diagnosed by Defendant Dr. Cillo as having measles during the first trimester of her pregnancy. Defendant Dr. Cillo ordered tests for German measles [a/k/a Rubella Titer Test] which were indicative of past infection of Rubella. However, he ordered no further tests to conclusive determine the presence of German measles and instead told the plaintiff-patient that she had "nothing to worry about because she had become immune to German measles as a child." Upon his advice, Rosemary allowed her pregnancy to continue and gave birth to infant-plaintiff Peter Procanik, who was suffered from congenital rubella syndrome and multiple birth defects. Peter's parents brought a wrongful life action against defendant on behalf of their son, claiming that defendant was negligent in failing to diagnose Rosemary with German measles and for depriving Peter's parents of the choice of terminating the pregnancy. Infant-plaintiff Peter sought damages for pain and suffering for his "impaired childhood" and also sought special damages for the expenses that he would incur as an adult for medical, nursing and other health-related services. The Law Division granted defendant's motion to dismiss the complaint for failure to state a cause of action and the Appellate Division denied affirmed. Plaintiffs appealed to the Supreme Court of New Jersey.

May an infant file a "wrongful life" claim [causes of action that describe the causes of actions of parents and children when the negligent treatment deprives parents of the option to terminate a pregnancy to avoid the birth of a defective child] to recover general damages for impaired childhood and pain and suffering?

An infant may not file a "wrongful life" claim to recover general damages for an impaired childhood and/or pain and suffering.

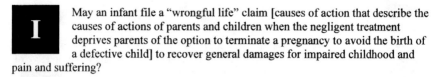

An infant may not file a "wrongful life" claim to recover general damages for an impaired childhood and/or pain and suffering but may recover the extraordinary medical expenses attributable to his affliction as special damages. In the present context, "wrongful life" refers to a cause of action brought by on behalf of a defective child who claims that but for the defendant-doctor's negligent advice to or treatment of its parents, the child would not have been born. "Wrongful birth" applies to the cause of action of parents who claim that the negligent advice or treatment deprived them of the choice of avoiding conception or, as here, of terminating the pregnancy. In *Gleitman v. Cosgrove,* if a doctor negligently diagnosed or treated a pregnant woman who was suffering from a condition that might cause her to give birth to a defective child, neither the parents nor the child could maintain a cause of action against the negligent doctor; the rational being that the measurement of "the value of life with impairments against the value of the nonexistence of life itself" was a logical impossibility. In *Berman v. Allan,* the parents of a child with Down's Syndrome sought to recover for their emotional distress and for the expenses of raising the child. In that case, the court allowed the recovery for the parents' emotional distress because the availability of abortions supported the right of a woman to choose to terminate her pregnancy. That

Procanik by Procanik v. Cillo
Supreme Court of New Jersey, 478 A.2d 755 (1984)

court, however, rejected any cause of the parents' claim for "medical and other expenses that will be incurred in order to properly raise , educate and supervise the child" and similarly rejected a cause of action in an infant born with birth defects reasoning that a "life born with serious defects is more valuable than nonexistence. . ." In the instant case, the parents are not claiming that the *negligence* of the doctor caused the infant's birth defects; they claim that had it not been for the *negligent advice* of the defendant-doctor, the infant's birth would have been terminated. While we acknowledge a duty owed to the infant on the part of the defendant which the latter breached, policy considerations have led us to reject a cause of action by an infant for his "wrongful life." The problem, faced by a number of jurisdictions, and as illuminated in both *Berman* and *Gleitman*, is that there is both an absence of cognizable damages and a difficulty in ascertaining the proper measure of damages. The crux of the problem is that there is no rational way to measure the nonexistence or to compare the nonexistence with the pain and suffering of an impaired existence. As such, it is simply too speculative to permit an infant plaintiff to recover for emotional distress because of birth defects when the plaintiff claims he would be better off if he hadn't been born. We will, however, allow damages for extraordinary medical expenses needed to treat and care for such children. We allow recovery of those costs, either by the parents or the child, but not both.

Judgment reversed in part, and remanded.

Taylor v. Olsen

Supreme Court of Oregon, 578 P.2d 779 (1978)

FACTS

While driving on a windy January evening, Plaintiff Taylor's car hit a tree which had shortly before splintered and fallen across the road on which he was traveling. Plaintiff sued the defendant, Marion Olson, the owner of the property on which the tree had been located, for injuries sustained. The trial court directed a verdict in favor of defendant and the plaintiff appealed.

 Can a landowner be held liable for a dangerous condition on his property if he failed to recognize and prevent a reasonable risk of harm to others as a result of such a condition?

 A landowner is under the duty to use common and ordinary methods to examine conditions on his/her property and to take reasonable care to prevent an unreasonable risk of harm to others.

 A landowner is under the duty to use common and ordinary methods to examine conditions on his/her property and to take reasonable care to prevent an unreasonable risk of harm to others. The extent of the landowner's responsibility, either to inspect his trees or only to act on actual knowledge of a danger can not be defined by categorizing the land as urban or rural. Here, there was testimony that the defendant had bought the land for logging purposes and had, during the 5 – 6 weeks prior to the accident, logged half of the timber on his land, including the trees next to the road where the accident had occurred. The evidence tends to show that only by chopping or boring into the trunk of the tree could one discover possible decay of the kind that caused the fall of the tree at issue. Thus, the question of the defendant's responsibility is not *whether* he had some responsibility to give attention to the safety of the tree but rather how far such responsibility should extend. Here, there is no evidence to suggest that chopping through the bark or drilling into the trunk would have been the normal method to examine a standing tree for decay. Nor is there any evidence that the defendant was on notice or should have been on notice of such a danger. Barring such evidence, the defendant is not liable.

 Affirmed.

Salevan v. Wilmington Park Inc.
Superior Court of Delaware, 72 A.2d 239 (1950)

FACTS

Plaintiff Salevan suffered injuries when a baseball struck him in the head as he was walking past by a ballpark. Defendant Wilmington Park Inc owned the land upon which the facility was located and was additionally charged with the maintenance and renting of the park. At trial, the evidence showed that during the course of an average game, 16-18 foul balls would come from inside the park and land beyond the park's field but within the fenced enclosure; of that amount, 2 to 3 foul balls make it past the fence surrounding the park and into the adjacent street. Plaintiff sued defendant claiming that the defendant was on notice of the fly-away balls onto the street and beyond the fence and that its failure to take reasonable precautions against the possibility of injury to others constituted negligence.

Is a landowner under a duty to take reasonable precautions to prevent injury to others using roadways adjacent to his land when knows or should know of dangerous conditions on his property the breach of which may constitute negligence?

A landowner is under a duty to take reasonable precautions to prevent injury to others using roadways adjacent to his land when knows or should know of dangerous conditions on his property the breach of which may constitute negligence.

A landowner is under a duty to take reasonable precautions to prevent injury to others using roadways adjacent to his land when knows or should know of dangerous conditions on his property the breach of which may constitute negligence. The question of what precautions are reasonable must depend on the facts and circumstances of each individual case. Here, the required precautions are those necessary based on the nature of the game and its past history in the particular location in question. While the defendant has taken some precautions [the protection of the public via the fence] these precautions were not enough. The evidence is uncontradicted that the defendant knew or should have known that the baseballs flew out of the park and some of them even flew beyond the fence. Additionally, the defendant knew or should have known that its present precautions were insufficient because the balls were *still* flying out of the park and beyond the fenced-in enclosure and onto the adjacent street.

Judgment for the plaintiff.

Sheehan v. St. Paul & Duluth Ry. Co.

U.S. Court of Appeals, 76 Fed. 201 (7th Cir. 1896)

FACTS

Plaintiff Sheehan while walking on Defendant St. Paul & Duluth Ry. Co.'s tracks without permission, caught his foot between the rail and cattle guard on the tracks, and was injured. A train, owned by the defendant-railroad ran over plaintiff's foot. The train's crew had no notice of plaintiff until the train had already reached him. Plaintiff brought suit against the defendant-railroad for his injuries. The trial court directed a verdict in favor of the defendant on the ground that there was no wrongful act on the part of the railroad defendant. Plaintiff appealed.

 Does a landowner owe a duty of care to a trespasser when the landowner had no actual or constructive notice of his presence?

 A landowner does not owe a duty of care to a trespasser when the landowner had no actual or constructive notice of his presence.

 A landowner does not owe a duty of care to a trespasser when the landowner had no actual or constructive notice of his presence. Here, the plaintiff was not a passenger, at a public cross walk, at a place where the public was licensed to travel; he was simply a trespasser on the defendant's property. While some courts have held that a trespasser is owed some duty exists on the part of the railroad to exercise some degree of care towards the trespasser, most courts cases have held that a trespasser who enters in such an area assumes all risks of dangerous conditions which may be found there. This is contrasted with the positive duty of care absolutely owed by the railroad at street crossings or other public places at which it is presumed that people will pass. Thus, in the absence of notice, the case of a trespasser in an area which is *not open to the public* is evident. In such situations, since there is no constructive notice of trespassers [there is no obligation to be on a constant lookout for trespassers], the obligation of the railroad arises at the moment of discovery of the trespasser. At that point, unless the trainmen acted unreasonably in avoiding the injury to the plaintiff, there will be no liability on the part of the railroad. Thus, an obligation is placed upon the company to exercise some degree of care when the danger becomes apparent.

 Affirmed.

Barmore v. Elmore
Appellate Court of Illinois, 2nd District, 403 N.E.2d 1355 (1980)

FACTS

Plaintiff Leon Barmore was a guest at Defendant Thomas Elmore Sr.'s home, when the latter's 47-year-old son, Thomas Elmore Jr., attacked the plaintiff with a steak knife, eventually stabbing the plaintiff in the chest several times. Plaintiff and defendant were both officers of a Masonic lodge, and plaintiff's visit was for the purpose of discussing lodge business. The defendant attempted to restrain his son prior to the incident, but he was unsuccessful, and the son followed plaintiff outside the house and stabbing him. Plaintiff sued defendant and his wife for injuries he suffered, claiming that defendant was negligent in failing to warn plaintiff of the dangerous condition on the property – namely their son who had a history of mental illness. The trial court directed a verdict in favor of defendant and the plaintiff appealed.

Does the owner or occupier of land have the duty to warn a licensee [social guest] of hidden dangers unknown to the licensee/social guest?

The owner or occupier of land has the duty to warn a licensee [social guest] of hidden dangers unknown to the licensee [social guest].

An invitee is one who enters upon the property of another in furtherance of the owner's business. A licensee or a social guest is one who enters the premises by the owner's permission for the purpose of companionship, diversion, or entertainment. Whether a land owner/occupier will be liable to another and how far that liability will extend is based on the status of the injured party; that is, whether the defendant-victim party was an invitee or a licensee at time he was on the owner's property and was injured. The licensee generally takes the owner's property as he finds it - the owner only owes him the duty to warn of hidden dangers which are unknown to the licensee, but known to the owner. With regard to an invitee, the owner owes a duty to exercise reasonable care in keeping the premises reasonably safe. In the instant case, the plaintiff asserts that there is sufficient evidence to establish his status as an invitee, thereby raising the duty of care owed to him by the defendant. We disagree; plaintiff is properly regarded as a licensee. While the plaintiff was at the home of the defendant to pay his dues to the Masonic lodge and discuss Lodge business, the benefit of his service went to the organization, not to the defendant himself. Even though the defendant failed to warn the plaintiff of the danger on the premises, the evidence shows that the defendant did not know or have reason to know of his son's tendency to commit violence against the plaintiff. Defendant knew that his son had mental problems and that he had been involved in at least three violent incidents ten years prior; however, some length of time had passed since then without incident, such that the defendant any reason to know or believe that the son would behave in a violent manner on the day in question.

Affirmed.

Campbell v. Weathers

Supreme Court of Kansas, 111 P.2d 72 (1941)

FACTS

Plaintiff-appellant Campbell entered Defendant-appellee Weathers' lunch counter and cigar store, loitered for twenty minutes with making a purchase and then went to the back of the store to use the restroom. There, plaintiff stepped on an open trap door in a dark hallway and was injured. Plaintiff sued defendant for the injuries he suffered. At trial, the evidence showed that plaintiff had been a frequent customer of defendant over the course of a number of years, had stopped at the defendant's store a number of times, used the restroom on numerous occasions and was never informed that the toilet was not intended for public use. The trial court sustained defendant's demurrer to the evidence and the plaintiff appealed.

In order to be considered an invitee, must a person entering a place of business open to the public make a purchase?

A person entering a place of business open to the public need not make a purchase therein in order to be considered an invitee.

A person entering a place of business open to the public need not make a purchase therein in order to be considered an invitee. The threshold question before us is the relationship between the plaintiff and the defendant. Specifically, was the plaintiff an invitee, licensee or trespasser? We start our inquiry with the following: Defendant's business was open to the public and was engaged in the business of selling cigars and lunches to the public. Plaintiff had been a customer there for many years, had stopped at the defendant's store a number of times and had used the restroom on numerous occasions. Moreover, defendant's employees conceded that the restroom was not regarded as private and was used by other customers as well. We cannot accept the theory that because a regular customer had not actually made a purchase, but rather used the restroom only, he is not considered invitee. A customer entering a store may not have intended to make a purchase at the time but may nevertheless become interested, for example, upon seeing something new in a display or on some future occasion. An invitee is one who is either expressly or impliedly invited onto the premises of another to further the economic interest of the owner/occupier. Therefore, if one goes into a place of business with an intention of presently or in the future becoming a customer and making a purchase, he will be considered an invitee. Here, the plaintiff may rightly be regarded as an invitee for purposes of this litigation.

Reversed.

Whelan v. Van Natta
Court of Appeals of Kentucky, 382 S.W.2d 205 (1964)

FACTS

Plaintiff-appellant Whelan entered Defendant-appellee Van Natta's grocery store and purchased cigarettes. Plaintiff then asked defendant about a box for his son, and the defendant, who was busy at the time told him to go to the backroom. Plaintiff went to the rear of the store and opened the door to the storage room, which was dark. Hunting around for a box, plaintiff fell into an unseen staircase and was injured. At trail, defendant testified that he did not warn plaintiff of the staircase and that the light had been on in the morning but did not know if it was still on at the time of the accident. The trial court entered judgment in favor of defendant-appellant, holding that he was a licensee at the time of his fall, such that the plaintiff-appellee owed him no duty to provide a safe place, except for those intentional or willful acts which might endanger his safety. The plaintiff-appellee appealed.

When does an invitee cease to be an invitee?

An invitee ceases to be an invitee after the expiration of a reasonable time within which to accomplish the purpose for which he is invited to enter or remain.

An invitee ceases to be an invitee after the expiration of a reasonable time within which to accomplish the purpose for which he is invited to enter or remain. Here, plaintiff argues he entered the store on business and therefore holds the status of an invitee up to an including his fall. However, according to the Restatement of Torts (second), the possessor of land is only subject to liability to the invitee for harm sustained while he is on the land within the scope and area of his invitation. Upon the expiration of this status the invitee becomes a trespasser or a licensee depending on whether he is there with consent or without. Therefore, when the invitee goes outside of the area of his invitation, he becomes a trespasser or licensee, depending upon whether he goes there with or without the permission of the possessor of land. Here, plaintiff entered the shop as an invitee and he remained as such while within the area and scope of the invitation. However, when he when to the stockroom, he became a licensee. The same would hold true for invitee who is permitted by the shopkeeper to go to the bathroom or to make a call – the invitee would become a licensee.

Affirmed.

Rowland v. Christian

Supreme Court of California, 443 P.2d 561 (1968)

FACTS

Plaintiff James Rowland was an invited guest in Defendant Nancy Christian's apartment. While Rowland was using the bathroom, a porcelain handle on one of the faucets broke, severing the nerves and tendon of his right hand. Christian knew that the handle was cracked, and asked her landlord to repair it two weeks prior, but did not warn Rowland about it. It was not obvious that the handle was cracked or that Rowland knew or should have known about the defect. The defendant moved for summary judgment on grounds that that the plaintiff was a social guest and that the defenses of contributory negligence and assumption of the risk barred the action. The court granted the motion and summary judgment was entered for Defendant Christian.

By failing to warn the plaintiff of the potentially hazardous condition in the apartment, did the defendant breach a duty owed to the plaintiff?

A guest should reasonably be entitled to rely upon a warning of a dangerous condition by his host so that he, like the host, will be in a position to take special precautions when he comes in contact with the dangerous condition; stated another way, the occupier of land has the duty to warn guests on his property of known dangers and act as a reasonable person would act in view of the probability that injuries may occur to others on the property.

By failing to warn the plaintiff of the potentially hazardous condition in the apartment, the defendant breach a duty owed to the plaintiff. A possessor of land has the duty to act as a reasonable person in view of the likelihood of injuries to others might occur on his property. We depart from the common law rules of liability for negligence classifying the plaintiff as a licensee, invitee, or trespasser and hold that while such classifications no longer determine liability, they are still relevant in determining the duty of care owed. Thus immunity form tort liability should not be predicated on whether a person is a licensee, invitee, or trespasser, but rather on factors such as the closeness of the connection between the injury and the conduct of the defendant, the policy of preventing future harm, and the prevalence and availability of insurance.

Judgment is reversed.

Borders v. Roseberry
Supreme Court of Kansas, 532 P.2d 1366 (1975)

FACTS

Plaintiff-appellant Gary D. Borders was a social guest at Defendant-appellee Roseberry's tenant's apartment when he fell on the icy steps and was injured. Plaintiff sued defendant, the landlord, for the injuries suffered. The trial court held in favor of defendant and plaintiff appeals on the ground that the trial court committed reversible error in holding that the landlord, as a matter of law, owed no duty to him [as a social guest of a tenant] for known conditions on the tenant's property.

 Does a landlord, as a matter of law, owe a duty of care to the social guest of his tenant to remedy known dangerous conditions on the property?

 A landlord does not, as a matter of law, owe a duty of care to the social guest of his tenant to remedy known dangerous conditions on the property.

 A landlord does not, as a matter of law, owe a duty of care to the social guest of his tenant to remedy known dangerous conditions on the property. The relationship of landlord-tenant is not, by itself, sufficient to make the landlord liable for the tortuous acts of his tenant. Usually, it is the tenant's duty, as the person in possession of the property, to keep the premises in reasonably safe condition. This general rule of non-liability, however, has a number of exceptions which have been created as a matter of social policy. They are: A landlord and/or lessor is liable 1) for undisclosed dangerous conditions known to the landlord/lessor, and unknown to the lessee; 2) for conditions dangerous to persons outside of the premises (such as those traveling on public roads adjacent to the premises); 3) when the premises are leased for the admission of the public; 4) where parts of the premises are retained in the lessor's control which the lessee is entitled to use [these areas may include common passageways which do not belong to the tenant and are under the control and possession of the landlord]; 5) where he/she contracts to repair; and 6) where he/she has been negligent in making repairs [this exception applies where the tenant does not know that the purported repairs have not been made or that they have been made negligently]. Here, the tenant was fully aware that the steps were in an icy condition such that the landlord could easily assume that the tenant would warn the guests about it. We have additionally concluded that the facts of the case do not establish liability on the part of the landlord based on negligent repairs made by him. We do not believe that the evidence of this case justifies a departure from the established rule of law [that a landlord is not liable for dangerous conditions which are known to the tenant notwithstanding the exceptions noted] and the plaintiff does not cite any authority to suggest otherwise.

 Judgment of the district court is affirmed.

Pagelsdorf v. Safeco Ins. Co. of America

Supreme Court of Wisconsin, 284 N.W.2d 55 (1979)

FACTS

Plaintiff Pagelsdorf was helping Blattner, the tenant of landlord Mahnke, move some furniture. During this time, the plaintiff leaned against a defective second-floor balcony railing which collapsed, causing him to fall to the ground below. Consequently, plaintiff sued Defendant Safeco Insurance Co. of America, the landlord's insurance company, for the injuries he sustained from the fall. The trial court classified the plaintiff as the licensee of Mahnke, and the jury found in it the landlord had no knowledge of the defective condition of the railing. Judgment was entered dismissing plaintiff's complaint and he appealed arguing that the landlord owed him [the plaintiff] a duty to exercise ordinary care in maintaining the premises.

 Does a landlord owe a tenant and anyone on the premises with the tenant's consent, a duty to exercise ordinary care in maintaining the premises in safe condition?

 A landlord owes a tenant and anyone on the premises with the tenant's consent, a duty to exercise ordinary care in maintaining the premises in safe condition.

 A landlord owes a tenant and anyone on the premises with the tenant's consent, a duty to exercise ordinary care in maintaining the premises in safe condition. Traditionally, when property was leased, the landlord was not liable for injuries to his tenants and their visitors as a result of defective conditions on the property. Exceptions to this rule exist, but none are applicable to the instant facts [see *Borders v. Roseberry*, supra]. We feel, however, that a better policy would be to abandon the general rule of non-liability of landlords and instead hold them to a duty to exercise reasonable care in the maintenance of the premises. In *Antoniewicz v. Reszcynski*, we abolished the common law distinctions between licensees and invitees. Thus, hold today in favor of a different rule: When the property is leased, a landlord owes a tenant and anyone on the premises with the tenant's consent, a duty to exercise ordinary care in maintaining the premises in safe condition. Our position is supported by tort law policies which dictate that one is liable for injuries which result from the creation of a foreseeable risk of injury to others; and the public policy *limitations* on the application of this principle are retreating. Today, the contemporary apartment lease is regarded as a contract and not a conveyance of property which releases the landlord of all liability. This rule should be applied retrospectively.

 Reversed and Remanded.

Kline v. 1500 Massachusetts Ave. Apartment Corp.

U.S. Court of Appeals, 439 F.2d 477 (D.C. Cir. 1970)

FACTS

Plaintiff-appellant Sarah B. Kline lived in an apartment building owned by Defendant-appellee 1500 Massachusetts Avenue Apartment Corp. When she first moved into her apartment in 1959, defendant provided security at all entrances. By the mid-1966, however, the main entrance had no doorman and an alternate entrance was generally left unguarded and was often unlocked at night. Shortly after 10:00 p.m. on November 17, 1966, Kline was injured after being assaulted and robbed in a common hallway in the building. The landlord was on notice of a similar crime in the same hallway as Leona Sullivan, another female tenant, had been assaulted only two months prior, but the defendant did not take any steps to provide security nonetheless. The District Court held as a matter of law that no such duty existed which should be placed on a landlord to protect tenants. Plaintiff appealed.

Is a landlord under an affirmative duty to protect its tenants from the criminal acts of 3rd parties?

A landlord is under an affirmative duty to protect tenants from those criminal acts of 3rd parties which are foreseeable.

A landlord is under an affirmative duty to protect tenants from those criminal acts of 3rd parties which are foreseeable. The *common areas* of the building were under the exclusive control of the defendant. Hence, the tenants were not in any position to make those common areas safer. The crime was foreseeable, as the defendant-appellee was put on notice by the attack on another tenant two months before the attack on the plaintiff. Moreover, the defendant was repeatedly warned about the lax security but did nothing. Plaintiff Kline was led to believe she could expect the same level of protection as that which existed in 1959, the year she first moved in. The liability of defendant is clear on the record. Reversed and remanded for the determination of damages. We find that a duty by the landlord to its tenants exists to protect the latter from foreseeable criminal acts committed by 3rd parties and that the applicable standard of care was breached by the defendant. We therefore reverse and remand the District Court's judgment for a determination of damages for the plaintiff-appellant.

Reversed and remanded.

Anderson v. Sears, Roebuck & Co.

U.S. District Court, Eastern Dist. Of Louisiana, 377 F.Supp. 136 (1974)

FACTS

Infant-plaintiff Helen Britain, a young child, was severely burned when plaintiff's house caught on fire as the result of a defective heater manufactured by Defendant Sears, Roebuck & Co. Plaintiff suffered third degree burns on over 40% of her body and had to undergo numerous operations and blood transfusions, including a skin graft. The evidence showed, not unexpectedly, that the plaintiff also suffered great physical, mental and emotional trauma and that she will continue to suffer from physical and mental pain in the future, incurring future expensive medical expenses in the process. The jury awarded a sum of $2,000,000 to plaintiff, finding the defendant negligent in the manufacture of the heater. Defendant moved for a remittitur [in the context of a jury verdict, remittitur refers to a judge's order reducing a judgment awarded by a jury when it exceeds the amount asked for by the plaintiff. In the context of appellate procedure it refers to an appellate court sending a case back to the trial court so that the case can be retried, or so that trial court can enter an order that conforms to the findings of the appellate court] of the verdict.

May a trial court review a jury's award of damages to determine whether it exceeds the maximum amount which the jury could reasonably award?

The legal standard on which to gauge a jury verdict for remittitur purposes is the "maximum recovery rule" which directs a trial judge to review a jury's award of damages and determine whether it exceeds the maximum amount which the jury could reasonably award.

For remittitur purposes, under the so-called ""maximum recovery rule," a trial court may review a jury's award of damages to determine whether it exceeds the maximum amount which the jury could reasonably award. For the purposes of this case, there are five cardinal elements of damages: 1) past physical and mental pain; 2) future physical and mental pain; 3) future medical expenses; 4) loss of earning capacity; and 5) permanent disability and disfigurement. The record indicates that the plaintiff suffered third degree burns all over her body, and that she underwent several operations, was hospitalized many time and endured painful skin grafts to reduce her deformities and scarring. The undisputed testimony shows one of the most tragic aspects of this ordeal is the mental and emotional trauma that accompanies the physical pain and suffering as evidenced by her bedwetting, nightmares, speech impediments, withdrawal and refusing to sleep alone. As such, the jury's award of $600,000 is not unreasonable for *past* physical and mental pain. In terms of *future* physical and mental pain, the record shows that the scarring and pulling of the skin, during the growth of plaintiff will cause severe pain and will cripple her emotions in varying degrees. The evidence also points out that she is recommended to undergo 27 future operations, extending over her adult life. In terms of future medical expenses, the evidence suggests that plaintiff will continue to need medical guidance, treatments, surgery, counseling, recommended operations, and other necessary medical help. Finally, in light of plaintiff's physical, mental, and emotional disability, a jury could reasonably conclude that she will not be able to earn a living for herself for the rest of her life. Totaling the maximum jury award supported by the evidence for each of the foregoing indicates that a monetary award of $2,980.000 would not have been unreasonable. Obviously, the jury's actual award of $2,000,000 is well within this range.

Motion for remittitur denied.

Richardson v. Chapman

Supreme Court of Illinois, 676 N.E.2d 621 (1997)

FACTS

Plaintiff Keva Richardson was a 23 year old driver of an automobile in which Plaintiff Ann McGregor was a passenger. Plaintiffs were stopped at a red traffic light when they were hit from behind by a semi-truck driven by Defendant Chapman. Plaintiff Richardson suffered a fracture of the fifth cervical vertebra, which severely damaged her spinal cord and resulted in incomplete but permanent quadriplegia. She also received many facial injuries, not all of which were able to be repaired. As a result of her physical condition, Richardson is at risk for several serious health complications and had a life expectancy of 54.5 years at the time of trial. Richardson was awarded $22,358,814 as follows: $258,814 for past medical care, $11,000,000 for future medical care, $900,000 for past and future lost earnings, $3,500,000 for disability, $2,100,000 for disfigurement, and $4,600,000 for pain and suffering. Plaintiff McGregor, on the other hand, received a laceration on her forehead, which eventually healed with minimal scarring, missed about two weeks of work after being treated and released from the hospital that same day. Plaintiff McGregor testified that she suffers from nightmares about the accident. She was awarded a total of $102,215 as follows: $1,615 for past medical expenses, $600 for lost earnings, and $100,000 for pain and suffering.

When there is a wide disparity between the expert testimony at trial and the jury's ultimate award for damages, should the jury award be considered excessive and thus reduced?

An award of damages will be deemed excessive if 1) it falls outside the range of fair and reasonable compensation; 2) results from the passion or prejudice of the jury unsupported by the evidence; or 3) if it is so large that it shocks the judicial conscience.

An award of damages will be deemed excessive if 1) it falls outside the range of fair and reasonable compensation; 2) results from the passion or prejudice of the jury unsupported by the evidence; or 3) if it is so large that it shocks the judicial conscience. In the instant case, defendant first challenges the method of calculation that plaintiff's expert and economist, Professor Charles Linke, used to determine the present value of Plaintiff Richardson's future economic losses. Professor Linke calculated both an upper threshold dollar amount and lower threshold dollar amount basing the difference between the two on different assumptions concerning future growth rates and interest rates. This approach was a reasonable one since the expert did not adopt a method which would either under-compensate or over-compensate Richardson. Defendant next contends that the damages awarded to both plaintiffs are excessive. Richardson was awarded nearly $1.5 million more than the larger of the two figures supplied by Professor Linke; however, we note that the trier of fact enjoys a certain decree of leeway in awarding compensation for future medical costs. However given the disparity between the trial testimony and the jury's ultimate award, we will not attribute the entire difference between those sums simply to miscellaneous costs Richardson is likely to incur in the future. Thus, we conclude that it is appropriate, by way of remittitur, to reduce by $1,000,000 the difference between the award for Richardson's future medical expenses and the higher figure presented at trial; the remainder of the award will stand as not duplicative or excessive, contrary to the defendant's argument. The record shows that Richardson suffered devastating, disabling injuries as a consequence of the accident. We cannot say that the present award to Richardson is the result of passion or prejudice, or that it shocks conscience. Turning to Plaintiff McGregor's award, we believe that the sum of $100,000 awarded for pain and suffering was excessive as McGregor was not seriously injured in the accident receiving only a minor abrasion to her forehead. A more appropriate figure for pain and suffering would be $50,000 and, by way of remittitur, and we accordingly reduce the judgment entered to $52.215.

 Judgment of the appellate court is affirmed in part, reversed in part, and vacated in part, and the judgment of the circuit court is affirmed in part, reversed in part, and vacated in part.

Montgomery Ward & Co. v. Anderson

Supreme Court of Arkansas, 976 S.W.2d 382 (1988)

FACTS

Plaintiff-appellee Shirley Anderson was badly injured in a fall while shopping at Defendant Montgomery Ward & Co. Inc.'s retail store in Little Rock, Arkansas. The personnel at the defendant's store sent plaintiff to the hospital to be treated where she underwent surgery and other medical services totaling $24,512.45. Thereafter, and the hospital reached an agreement to discount her medical bill by 50%. Defendant moved *in limine* [a request submitted to the court before trial in an attempt to exclude <u>evidence</u> from the proceedings] to prohibit plaintiff from presenting the *total* amount billed by the hospital, and asked that plaintiff's evidence be limited only to the *actual* amount she was responsible for paying. In response, plaintiff asserted that the collateral-source rule prohibited defendant from introducing evidence of the discount. The trial court excluded the evidence.

 Is the reduction or forgiveness of a debt for medical services a collateral source to be sheltered by the collateral-source rule?

 Free or discounted medical services are a collateral source under the collateral source rule and may not to be considered in assessing the damages due a plaintiff for her personal injuries.

 The collateral-source rule applies unless the evidence of the benefits from the collateral source is relevant for a purpose other than the mitigation of damages. The "collateral source rule" is a statement of court-made public policy which holds that a tortfeasor should be obligated to pay the *entirety* of the loss caused by tortious conduct *without regard* to the availability of public or private sources of benefits available to ameliorate the economic impact of the loss. Even though the plaintiff receives a windfall in the form of a double recovery [for example, if the hospital fee totaled $100,000 and an agreement was made to reduce that amount by half, the plaintiff would only be required to pay $50,000; however in a suit against the defendant, the jury, without knowing of the collateral source, the 50% reduction agreement, might award the plaintiff the full $100,000. Thus, the plaintiff gets a double recovery: $100,000 when she only paid $50,000], the rationale behind the rule is that the claimant should benefit from the collateral source recovery rather than the tortfeasor. However, a collateral source of recovery may be introduced 1) to rebut the plaintiff's testimony that he was compelled by financial necessity to return to work prematurely or to forego additional medical care; 2) to show that the plaintiff had attributed his condition to some other cause, such as sickness; 3) to impeach the plaintiff's testimony that he had paid his medical expenses himself; 4) to show that the plaintiff had actually continued to work instead of being out of worked, as claimed. In this case, we find that none of the foregoing exceptions apply to the facts at hand and thus hold that gratuitous and discounted medical services fall under the collateral-source rule. Accordingly, such services are not to be considered in assessing the damages due a plaintiff in a personal injury cause of action. Accordingly, we hold that the Trial Court did not err by excluding evidence of the hospital's discount as a collateral source.

Affirmed.

Zimmerman v. Ausland

Supreme Court of Oregon, 513 P.2d 1167 (1973)

FACTS

Plaintiff-appellee Zimmerman suffered a torn semilunar cartilage in her knee as the result of an automobile accident caused by the negligence of Defendant-appellant Ausland. At the trial, defendant's expert testified that had the torn cartilage been "surgically excised," the injury would not have been permanent. Plaintiff, however, had not undergone the operation and did not indicate she would do so in the future. The jury awarded plaintiff $7,500 in damages, which included damages for "permanent injury" to the knee in that she could no longer engage in strenuous physical activities as she had done so prior to the accident. Defendant appealed, arguing that the trial court erred in instructing the jury on whether the plaintiff sustained permanent injury and on the plaintiff's life expectancy.

 Can a plaintiff recover damages for a permanent injury sustained as the result of the defendant's negligence if the permanent injury could have been rendered temporary by treatment and a reasonable person in the same situation and under similar circumstances would have done so?

 A plaintiff can not recover damages for a permanent injury sustained as the result of the defendant's negligence if the now permanent injury could have been rendered a temporary injury with the proper treatment and a reasonable person in the same situation and under similar circumstances would have done so.

 As a preliminary matter, we note that defendant did not request instructions on the mitigation of damages. Thus, that question was not submitted to the jury. Nevertheless, if the court finds that *as a matter of law* the plaintiff *unreasonably* failed to mitigate damages, damages for permanent injury will be barred. Conversely, if the plaintiff's failure to obtain the surgery [to make the injury non-permanent] is not unreasonable, in light of the "reasonable person standard," recover damages for such an injury will be allowed. The general test applied in determining whether the plaintiff has unreasonably failed or refused to mitigate damages by submitting to a particular operation is whether, under the circumstances of the particular case, an ordinary prudent person would do so [i.e. , the duty to exercise reasonable care under the circumstances]. The factors which determine whether the plaintiff was reasonable in failing to mitigate include: 1) the risk involved in the treatment, 2) the probability of success, 3) the money or effort required and 4) the pain involved. No case holds that a plaintiff with a torn cartilage in her knee must submit to surgery or be barred, as a matter of law, from recovery of damages for permanent injury. Moreover, the instant facts do not definitively show that the plaintiff must submit to surgery or be barred, as a matter of law. Nevertheless, the defendant was entitled to introduce evidence of these questions and submit them to the jury with suitable instructions. After examining the record in this case, we conclude that testimony offered by the plaintiff, if believed by the jury, could lead the jury to find that the plaintiff did suffer permanent injury.

 Affirmed.

Cheatham v. Pohle
Supreme Court of Indiana, 5789 N.E.2d 467 (2003)

FACTS

Plaintiff Doris Cheatham and Defendant Michael Pohle divorced in 1994 before which the latter had taken photographs of the two in the nude and engaging in various consensual sexual acts. In early 1998, defendant made copies of these photographs and added plaintiff's name, her work location, her new husbands name and her attorney's name and distributed at lease 60 copies in and around the small town where both the plaintiff and the defendant still lived and worked. Plaintiff sued alleging invasion of privacy and intentional infliction of emotional distress as causes of action. The jury awarded her $100,000 in compensatory damages and $100,000 in punitive damages. Plaintiff appealed and argued that the new statute, Indiana Code 34-51-3-6, enacted in 1995, violated the Takings Clause found in the Indiana Constitution and the Fifth Amendment of the U.S. Constitution because it provided, in part, that 75% of the punitive award be paid to the treasurer of the state.

Is a state statute which provides, in part, that 75% of the punitive award be paid to the treasurer of the state violative of both the state's Constitution and the Fifth Amendment of the U.S. Constitution?

A state statute which provides, in part, that 75% of the punitive award be paid to the treasurer of the state is not violative of either the state's Constitution and the Fifth Amendment of the U.S. Constitution

To the extent that punitive damages are recoverable, they are a creature of the common law. As a result, the General Assembly [of the state] is free to eliminate it completely and also has wide discretion in modifying this "quasi-criminal" sanction. Some jurisdictions have eliminated it while others recognize punitive damages as an acceptable award in any form. Indiana, like several other states has taken the middle ground – permitting juries to award punitive damages and thereby inflict punishment on the defendant, but placing restriction on the amount the plaintiff may recover, as we see here with state statute at issue, Indiana Code 34-51-3-6. Turning to the state and federal Takings Clause issues, we note that any interest the plaintiff may have in a punitive damage award is a creation of state law. The plaintiff has no property to be taken except to the extent state law creates such a property right. The Indiana legislature has chosen to define the plaintiff's interest in the award as only 25% of any award, and the remainder is to go the Violent Crime Victims' Fund by way of the state treasurer. The award to the plaintiff is not the property of the plaintiff nor is her prejudgment claim a property interest. Accordingly, neither the Takings Clauses of the federal or state Constitutions nor the other provisions of the Indiana Constitution were violated by the statute at issue.

The judgment of the trial court is affirmed.

State Farm Mutual Auto. Ins. Co. v. Campbell

U.S. Supreme Court, 538 U.S. 408 (2003)

FACTS

In 1981, Plaintiff-respondent Curtis Campbell, while traveling with his wife in Utah, decided to pass six vans traveling in front of him on a two-lane highway. Todd Ospital was operating his vehicle in the oncoming lane and saw Campbell heading towards him traveling on the same road and traveling in the wrong direction. To avoid hitting Campbell, Ospital swerved onto the shoulder of the road, loosing control of his vehicle and colliding with a vehicle driven by Robert G. Slusher. Ospital was killed and Slusher was rendered permanently disabled, the Campbells were unharmed. An early investigation by investigators found that Campbell's unsafe attempted pass of the six vans had caused the accident. Campbell's insurance company, Defendant-petitioner State Farm, rejected settlement offers from Ospital's estate ($50,000) and Slusher ($25,000) for the policy limits, ignoring advice from their own investigators and took the case to trial. A verdict was returned against Campbell for $185,849. By 1989, the Utah Supreme Court declined Campbell's appeal in the wrongful death and tort actions. Thereafter, even though State Farm paid the entire judgment, Campbell sued State Farm for bad faith, fraud and intentional infliction of emotional distress in its treatment of the claim against him. At trial, Campbell received an award of $2.6 million in compensatory damages and $145 million in punitive damages; the judge reduced those amounts to $1 million and $25 million, respectively. The Utah Supreme Court affirmed the $1 million amount and reinstated the $145 million award. State Farm appealed.

Was the Due Process Clause of the 14th Amendment violated by the award of $145 million in punitive damages on $1 million compensatory judgment?

The Due process Clause of the Fourteenth Amendment prohibits the imposition of grossly excessive or arbitrary punishments on a tortfeasor.

A The Due Process Clause of the Fourteenth Amendment prohibits the imposition of grossly excessive or arbitrary punishments on a tortfeasor. Compensatory damages are intended to redress a plaintiff's concrete loss, while punitive damages are aimed at the different purposes of deterrence and retribution. The Due Process Clause prohibits the imposition of grossly excessive or arbitrary punishments on a tortfeaser. Punitive damages awards serve the same purpose as criminal penalties. However, because civil defendants are not accorded the protections afforded criminal defendants, punitive damages pose an acute danger of arbitrary deprivation of property, which is heightened when the decisionmaker is presented with evidence having little bearing on the amount that should be awarded. Thus, this Court has instructed courts reviewing punitive damages to consider (1) the degree of reprehensibility of the defendant's misconduct, (2) the disparity between the actual or potential harm suffered by the plaintiff and the punitive damages award, and (3) the difference between the punitive damages awarded by the jury and the civil penalties authorized or imposed in comparable cases. To determine a defendant's reprehensibility-- the most important indicium of a punitive damages award's reasonableness--a court must

State Farm Mutual Auto. Ins. Co. v. Campbell

U.S. Supreme Court, 538 U.S. 408 (2003)

consider whether: the harm was physical rather than economic; the tortious conduct evinced an indifference to or a reckless disregard of the health or safety of others; the conduct involved repeated actions or was an isolated incident; and the harm resulted from intentional malice, trickery, or deceit, or mere accident. It should be presumed that a plaintiff has been made whole by compensatory damages, so punitive damages should be awarded only if the defendant's culpability is so reprehensible to warrant the imposition of further sanctions to achieve punishment or deterrence. In this case, State Farm's handling of the claims against the Campbells merits no praise, but a more modest punishment could have satisfied the State's legitimate objectives. Instead, this case was used as a platform to expose, and punish, the perceived deficiencies of State Farm's operations throughout the country. However, a State cannot punish a defendant for conduct that may have been lawful where it occurred. Nor does the State have a legitimate concern in imposing punitive damages to punish a defendant for unlawful acts committed outside of its jurisdiction. The Campbells argue that such evidence was used merely to demonstrate, generally, State Farm's motives against its insured. Lawful out-of-state conduct may be probative when it demonstrates the deliberateness and culpability of the defendant's action in the State where it is tortious, but that conduct must have a nexus to the specific harm suffered by the plaintiff. More fundamentally, in relying on such evidence, the Utah courts awarded punitive damages to punish and deter conduct that bore no relation to the Campbells' harm. Due process does not permit courts to adjudicate the merits of other parties' hypothetical claims under the guise of the reprehensibility analysis. Punishment on these bases creates the possibility of multiple punitive damages awards for the same conduct, for nonparties are not normally bound by another plaintiff's judgment. For the same reasons, the Utah Supreme Court's decision cannot be justified on the grounds that State Farm was a recidivist. To justify punishment based upon recidivism, courts must ensure the conduct in question replicates the prior transgressions. There is scant evidence of repeated misconduct of the sort that injured the Campbells, and a review of the decisions below does not convince this Court that State Farm was only punished for its actions toward the Campbells. Because the Campbells have shown no conduct similar to that which harmed them, the only relevant conduct to the reprehensibility analysis is that which harmed them.

Reversed and remanded.

Moragne v. States Marine Lines Inc.

U.S. Supreme Court, 398 U.S. 375 (1970)

FACTS

The complaint sets forth that Edward Moragne, a longshoreman, was killed while working aboard the vessel Palmetto State in navigable waters within the State of Florida. Plaintiff-petitioner Moragne, as his widow and representative of his estate, brought this suit in a state court against Defendant-respondent States Marine Lines, Inc., the owner of the vessel, to recover damages for wrongful death and for the pain and suffering experienced by the decedent prior to his death. The claims were predicated upon both negligence and the unseaworthiness of the vessel. States Marine removed the case to the Federal District Court on the basis of diversity of citizenship and there filed a third-party complaint against respondent Gulf Florida Terminal Company, the decedent's employer, asserting that Gulf had contracted to perform stevedoring services on the vessel in a workmanlike manner and that any negligence or unseaworthiness causing the accident resulted from Gulf's operations. Both States Marine and Gulf sought dismissal of the portion of petitioner's complaint that requested damages for wrongful death on the basis of unseaworthiness. They contended that maritime law provided no recovery for wrongful death within a State's territorial waters, and that the statutory right of action for death under Florida law, Fla. Stat. 768.01 (1965), did not encompass unseaworthiness as a basis of liability. The District Court dismissed the challenged portion of the complaint on this ground, citing this Court's decision in The *Tungus v. Skovgaard*. The Court of Appeals certified to the Florida Supreme Court the question whether the state wrongful-death statute allowed recovery for unseaworthiness. After reviewing the history of the Florida Act, the state supreme court answered this question in the negative. On return of the case to the Court of Appeals, that court affirmed the District Court's order, rejecting petitioner's argument that she was entitled to reversal under federal maritime law without regard to the scope of the state statute. The court stated that its disposition was compelled by our decision in *The Tungus*. The U.S. Supreme Court granted certiorari.

Should maritime law allow a cause of action for wrongful death?

Maritime law should allow a cause of action for wrongful death.

We brought this case here to consider whether *The Harrisburg*, in which this Court held in 1886 that maritime law does not afford a cause of action for wrongful death, should any longer be regarded as acceptable law. We hold that a cause of action should exist and petitioner is not foreclosed from bringing this action under federal maritime law, based on unseaworthiness, for the wrongful death within state territorial waters of her husband, a longshoreman, as a wrongful-death action under such law is maintainable for breach of maritime duties. *The Harrisburg* is overruled. The law in *The Harrisburg* is based in the common law doctrine of felony-merger in England. Under that doctrine, the common law did not allow civil recovery for an act which constituted a tort and a felony. Yet the historical justification

Moragne v. States Marine Lines Inc.

U.S. Supreme Court, 398 U.S. 375 (1970)

for the rule in England never existed here. In our country, punishment for felonies does not include forfeiture of property; therefore there was nothing to bar a subsequent civil suit. Despite all of the above, most American courts adopted the English rule. Today, however, every state in the country has a wrongful death statute. Thus, taken as a whole, it appears that there is no public policy against allowing recovery for wrongful death. In this case Congress did not intend to prevent recovery in this area and the doctrine of stare decisis does not preclude a change in the law. Both the Death on the High Seas Act and the numerous state statutes can be of guidance on this issue.

 Reversed and Remanded.

Selders v. Armentrout

Supreme Court of Nebraska, 207 N.W.2d 686 (1973)

FACTS

Plaintiff Selders and other plaintiff brought a wrongful death action against Defendant Armentrout and other defendants for the wrongful death of their three minor children aged 9, 13, and 15. At trial, the court instructed the jury limited on the measure of damages for medical and funeral expenses and the monetary value of the contributions and services which the plaintiff could have reasonably expected to receive from the children, less the reasonable cost to the parents for supporting the children. Defendants contend that the measure of damages, as instructed, was appropriate and should and was be limited only to pecuniary losses. Plaintiff appealed. Plaintiffs, however, argue that the loss of society, comfort and companionship are proper and compensable elements of damage and that evidence of the amounts invested or expended for nurture, education and maintenance of the children before death is proper. The foregoing was not included in the jury instruction and the plaintiff's appealed.

Should the measure of damages for the wrongful death of a minor child be limited to pecuniary losses alone or should it also include loss of society, comfort, and companionship of the child?

The measure of damages for the wrongful death of a minor child is not limited to pecuniary losses alone and thus should include loss of society, comfort and companionship of the child.

Defendant's position comports with the common law. That is, recovery for the death of a minor child was limited to the loss of pecuniary benefits only; the justification for which was the fact that historically, children were viewed as economic assets to the parents, before the advent of child labor laws. Hence, a child's earnings and services could be established, and the pecuniary loss was the measure of damages for the parents. In modern society, however, evidence of damages reflect the future life of the decedent had he lived. As such, the very nature of any future recovery is deemed speculative as it can not be quantified with any degree of precision. Limiting the measure of damages to the child's economic value less the expenses spent for educating and raising the child would render the child worthless in the eyes of the law because such a value would be negative value, monetarily and arithmetically speaking. Only in rare cases will the death of a child result in monetary gain. We have allowed recovery for the loss of society, comfort and companionship for the wrongful death of a spouse. Hence, there is no reason for treating damages for the wrongful death of a child more any differently; that is, more harshly. We thus hold that the measure of damages for the wrongful death of a minor child should be extended to include the loss of society, comfort and companionship of the child. This holding overrules prior decisions of this and other lower courts which are in conflict with it.

Judgment as to damages reversed and remanded.

Murphy v. Martin Oil Co.
Supreme Court of Illinois, 308 N.E.2d 583 (1974)

FACTS

Plaintiff Murphy brought a suit in negligence against Defendant Martin Oil Co. after the deceased, plaintiff's husband, was injured due to a fire on defendant's property which ultimately resulted in his death nine days after he sustained life-threatening injuries. Plaintiff's cause of action consisted of two counts: Count 1 was based on the state's Wrongful Death Statute and Count 2 was brought under the state's Survival Statute. Plaintiff requested recovery of damages for the decedent's mental and physical suffering; for loss of wages during the nine-day period; and for the loss of his clothing worn at the time of the injury. The trial court dismissed Count 2, while the appellate court affirmed it in part, but rejecting plaintiff's action for the pain and suffering of the decedent. Both plaintiff and defendant appeal.

Can the spouse of a decedent recover for the loss of property [destruction of decedent's clothes], wages, and pain and the suffering of the decedent during the period between the injury and his eventual death?

The spouse of a decedent can recover for the loss of property, wages, and pain and the suffering of the decedent during the period between the injury and his eventual death.

The spouse of a decedent can recover for the loss of property [destruction of decedent's clothes], wages, and pain and the suffering of the decedent during the period between the injury and his eventual death. The Survival Statute provides that actions for replevin, actions to recover damages for an injury to the person [excluding libel and slander] and actions for recovery of damages to personal and real property survive a decedent. In 1882 case of *Holton v. Daly,* the court held that Wrongful Death Act was the sole remedy when a tortious injury resulted in death and that the Survival Statute allowed survival of a cause of action only when the injured party died from a cause other than that which caused the injuries which created the cause of action. Thus, an action for personal injuries could not survive if the death of the party resulted from the conduct which caused the injury. This construction of the two statues persisted for 70 years. Today, however, the modern trend in most jurisdictions is to allow a cause of action for personal injuries and a wrongful death claim even though the decedent's death resulted from the tortious conduct which caused the decedent's injury as well as recovery for the decedent's pain and suffering. It is our opinion that remedies available under *Holton* are woefully deficient. To that end, we declare *Holton* and those cases that followed it overruled.

Judgment affirmed in part, reversed in part.

Butterfield v. Forrester

King's Bench, 102 Eng.Rep. 926 (1809)

FACTS

This is a case involving the obstruction of a highway. Defendant Forrester was making repairs on his home and placed a pole across part of the road nearby. Plaintiff Butterfield was riding his horse down the same road at around 8:00 p.m., at a time when candles were just beginning to be lit along the road, enough to allow visibility up to 100 yards. A witness observed the plaintiff riding violently down the road, hit the pole, and thrown down to the ground with his horse and injured. The witness opined that had the plaintiff not been riding so hard, he might have observed and avoided the obstruction.

If a plaintiff fails to exercise ordinary care, can he be barred from recovering for injuries he sustained?

A plaintiff may not recover for the injuries he suffered if he failed to exercise ordinary care and that failure was a cause of his injuries.

A plaintiff may not recover for his own injuries if he failed to exercise ordinary care and that failure was a cause of his injuries. Plaintiff may not look to another's negligence when assessing blame in order to avoid blame for his own imprudent actions. The plaintiff was riding his horse as fast as it could go through the streets of Derby. Had he used ordinary car and rode slower, he may have seen the obstruction and avoided the accident. Hence, because he failed to exercise ordinary care, he is barred from recovering for injuries he sustained.

A plaintiff may not recover for the injuries he suffered if he failed to exercise ordinary care and that failure was a cause of his injuries.

Davies v. Mann
Exchequer, 152 Eng.Rep. 588 (1842)

FACTS

Plaintiff Davies allowed his mule to graze on the side of a public road; the animal was tied in such a way as to prevent its movements beyond a certain range. Meanwhile, Defendant Mann's wagon sped down the road, ran over the mule and killed it. Plaintiff sued defendant for the loss of his animal. At trial, the court instructed the jury 1) that even if the plaintiff's act of tying the mule to the road was illegal or negligent, the defendant can still be held liable if his negligence was the proximate cause of the mule's death and 2) to find for plaintiff if defendant could have avoided the accident by the exercise of ordinary care on the part of the driver. The jury found for plaintiff. Defendant moved for a new trial claiming that the instructions to the jury were erroneous.

May a defendant escape the consequences of his negligence if he claims contributory negligence on the part of the plaintiff even though the injury may have been avoided had he [defendant] acted reasonably?

A defendant may not escape the consequences of his negligence buy claiming contributory negligence on the part of the plaintiff when the injury may have been avoided had he [defendant] acted reasonably.

A defendant may not escape the consequences of his negligence buy claiming contributory negligence on the part of the plaintiff when the injury may have been avoided had he [defendant] acted reasonably. Here, the plaintiff's negligence, or lack thereof, in tying the mule to the road is of no consequence because the injury may have been avoided had the defendant acted reasonably. He did not, so he [the defendant] will be held liable for the death of the mule even though the mule may have been there illegally.

See Rule above.

McIntyre v. Balentine

Supreme Court of Tennessee, 833 S.W.2d 52 (1992)

FACTS

In the early evening on November 2, 1986, Plaintiff Harry Douglas McIntyre and Defendant Clifford Balentine were involved in an accident while driving their respective vehicles. Plaintiff sued defendant for his personal injuries and defendant defended on the ground that plaintiff was contributorily negligent - he was of driving while intoxicated and had a blood-alcohol level of 0.17% at the time. However, evidence at trial also suggested that defendant was driving at an excessive speed and also consumed alcohol that evening. Finding both equally at fault, the jury nonetheless ruled in favor of the defendant. Plaintiff appealed on the grounds that the trial court erred in failing to instruct the jury on the doctrine of comparative negligence. The Court of Appeals affirmed, holding that comparative negligence was not the law in Tennessee. Plaintiff appealed and requested that the court adopt a system of comparative fault in Tennessee.

 Should Tennessee adopt the principle of comparative fault thus replacing the existing rule of contributory negligence?

 Tennessee should replace the doctrine of contributory negligence with the rule comparative fault which allows the plaintiff to recover damages, reduced in proportion to the plaintiff's percentage of fault, when the plaintiff's negligence is less than the defendant's.

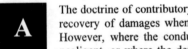 The doctrine of contributory negligence completely bars a plaintiff from the recovery of damages when he [the plaintiff] is even the least bit at fault. However, where the conduct of the defendant was intentional or grossly negligent, or where the defendant had the last clear chance to prevent the injury, or where the plaintiff's negligence was "remote," the plaintiff may recover. The doctrine of comparative fault, on the other hand, allows the plaintiff to recover damages in an amount reduced in proportion to the plaintiff's percentage of fault. Comparative fault can be "pure" or "modified." Under pure comparative negligence, the plaintiff's damages are reduced in proportion to the percentage of negligence attributed to him. Under modified comparative negligence, however, the plaintiff may recover damages, but only if the plaintiff's negligence either: 1) does not exceed 50% (called "50% jurisdictions") or 2) is less than the defendant's negligence (called "49% jurisdictions"). Today, we adopt the modified version because we think it inappropriate that a party should be able to recover in tort even though he may be 90% at fault, for example, which is allowed under the so-called "pure" version. Thus, in all trials where the issue of comparative fault is before the jury, the latter should be instructed on the effect of its finding on both the plaintiff and the defendant. In the case before us, because the jury found made a gratuitous apportionment of fault without the benefit of proper instructions of the trial court, we find that their "equal" apportionment is not sufficiently trustworthy to form basis for final determination of the case.

 Reversed in part and remanded.

Seigneur v. National Fitness Institute Inc.
Court of Special Appeals of Maryland, 752 A.2d 631 (2000)

FACTS

Plaintiff Gerilynne Seigneur was injured while undergoing an initial evaluation at a fitness club owned and operated by Defendant National Fitness Institute Inc. ("NFI"). Plaintiff decided to join NFI to begin a weight loss and fitness program on a one-month trial basis on the recommendation of her chiropractor. When she signed her membership contract, she disclosed that she had a history of serious lower back problems and that her general physical condition was poor. As part of the application process, she signed a Participation Agreement which, in essence, stated that NFI would not be liable for any claims, injuries, damages, actions or courses of action arising out of or in connection with the use of its services and facilities and that all exercises shall be the undertaken by her at her sole risk. During her initial evaluation on the weight machines, she received a serious injury to her shoulder. She and her husband filed a negligence suit and defendant defended on the ground that it was not liable by virtue of the Participation Agreement she signed; that it was valid and enforceable and that defendant was entitled to judgment as a matter of law. Plaintiffs responded that the exculpatory clause was void as against public policy. Judgment was rendered in the defendant's favor.

Can an exculpatory clause signed by the plaintiff bar a suit in negligence against the defendant for injuries sustained by the former or is the clause void as against public policy precluding its enforcement?

An exculpatory clause will be considered valid and enforceable if: 1) is plain and unambiguous; 2) it is not the product of fraud, mistake, undue influence, overreaching or the like; 3) where no legislation exists to the contrary; 4) where the party protected by the clause does not engage in acts of recklessness, wanton or gross negligence; 5) when the bargaining power of one party to the contract is not so grossly unequal so as to put that party at the mercy of the other's negligence; and 6) when the transaction does not involve the public interest.

In Maryland, an exculpatory clause will be considered valid and enforceable if: 1) is plain and unambiguous; 2) it is not the product of fraud, mistake, undue influence, overreaching or the like; 3) where no legislation exists to the contrary; 4) where the party protected by the clause does not engage in acts of recklessness, wanton or gross negligence; 5) when the bargaining power of one party to the contract is not so grossly unequal so as to put that party at the mercy of the other's negligence; and 6) when the transaction does not involve the public interest. In the instant case, there is no suggestion that the agreement between NFI and the plaintiff was the product of fraud, mistake, undue influence, overreaching. The exculpatory clause unambiguously provided for the release and discharge of NFI from liability with respect to the active or passive negligence of the latter, its servants, agents or employees. Plaintiff has not alleged that NFI engage in acts of recklessness, wanton or gross negligence. And while she does allege that 5) and 6) above are applicable, the clause was both prominently displayed in the Participation Agreement and plaintiff makes no claim that she was unaware of this provision prior to her injury. Moreover, there were numerous other health clubs providing the same services as NFI. Hence, we can not say that the bargaining power of one party to the contract is not so grossly unequal so as to

Seigneur v. National Fitness Institute Inc.
Court of Special Appeals of Maryland, 752 A.2d 631 (2000)

put that party at the mercy of the other's negligence. In a determination as to whether the clause would be against public policy, we note that there was no special legal relationship and no overriding public interest which demand that this contract provision, entered into voluntarily by two private parties, should be rendered ineffectual. NFI does not provide an essential public service so as to render it "patently offensive" to the citizens of Maryland; the services of a health club are not of great importance or of practical necessity to the public as a whole. Nor is it nearly as important as institutions or businesses such as innkeepers, public utilities, common carriers or schools.

 Judgment affirmed.

Rush v. Commercial Realty Co.

Supreme Court of New Jersey, 145 A. 476 (1929)

FACTS

Plaintiff Mrs. Rush was a tenant of one of two houses controlled by Defendant Commercial Realty Co. Defendant provided a detached privy [an outdoor toilet; an outhouse] for the use of both houses. It was the only privy available to the two houses. Plaintiff used the privy and fell through the floor or through a trap door in the floor. She descended nine feet into the pit at the bottom and had to be extricated with a ladder. Plaintiff sued for her injuries and the defendant moved for nonsuit and a directed verdict on the grounds that plaintiff assumed the risk of injury. The trial court denied the motions, and defendant appealed arguing that that the trial court erred in doing so.

Where a plaintiff has no meaningful choice but to encounter a known risk, can that person be said to have voluntary assumed the risk of possible injury?

Under the doctrine of implied assumption of the risk, a person does not voluntarily accept a risk when no reasonable alternatives exist.

Under the doctrine of implied assumption of the risk, a person does not voluntarily accept a risk when no reasonable alternatives exist. Here, defendant had the duty to maintain the privy such that they will be held liable for the defective condition of the floor which caused the injury. Plaintiff had no choice, she was compelled by nature to use the privy and she did so. She was not required to leave the premises and go elsewhere so she did not voluntarily assume a known risk. Whether she was n contributorily negligent is another matter, one which we, as a court, can not decide [a question for the jury to answer].

Affirmed.

Blackburn v. Dorta
Supreme Court of Florida, 348 So.2d 287 (1977)

FACTS

No facts provided.

Is the doctrine of implied assumption of risk still viable as an absolute bar to recovery subsequent to the adoption of the rule of comparative negligence in *Hoffman v. Jones*?

The affirmative defense of implied assumption of risk is merged into the defense of contributory negligence and the principles of comparative negligence enunciated in *Hoffman v. Jones* shall apply in all cases where the defense is asserted.

Since our decision in *Hoffman v. Jones*, contributory negligence no longer serves as a complete bar to plaintiff's recovery but is to be considered in apportioning damages according to the principles of comparative negligence. Thus, the doctrine of implied assumption of risk is not still viable as an absolute bar to recovery following the adoption of the rule of comparative negligence. Assumption of the risk is divided into categories of Primary and Secondary. Primary assumption of the risk is simply another way of saying that the defendant was not negligent, either because he owed no duty to the plaintiff or because he did not breach a duty owed [to the plaintiff]. Secondary assumption of the risk is an affirmative defense to an established breach of duty owed by the defendant to the plaintiff. The key threshold question to dispose of this issue is the following: Is liability equated with fault under a doctrine which would totally bar recovery by one who voluntarily, but reasonably, assumes a known risk while one whose conduct is unreasonable but termed "contributory negligence" is permitted to recover a proportionate amount of his damages for injury? We answer in the negative. There is no sound rationale for retaining this subset of assumption of risk in light of our modern doctrine of comparative negligence as it is more equitable to allow one partial recovery based on comparative negligence than to deny recovery based on assumption of risk. Therefore, the affirmative defense of implied assumption of risk is merged into the defense of contributory negligence and the principles of comparative negligence enunciated in *Hoffman v. Jones* shall apply in all cases where the defense is asserted.

See Rule above.

Teeters v. Currey
Supreme Court of Tennessee, 518 S.W.2d 512 (1974)

FACTS

Plaintiff Teeters gave birth to a child on June 5, 1970. Following delivery, medical complications Defendant Currey, her attending physician, recommended that he perform a bilateral tubal ligation on her in order to avoid future pregnancies. On December 6, 1972, plaintiff was hospitalized and the doctor that treated her discovered that she was pregnant. On March 9, 1973, plaintiff gave birth to a premature child with severe complications and, pursuant to medical advice another tubal ligation was performed on her. Thereafter, plaintiff sued defendant for malpractice alleging that he was negligent in performing the original tubal ligation. Defendant defended based upon the one-year statute of limitations for malpractice suits. The trial court granted a verdict for defendant and plaintiff appealed, arguing that her cause of action accrued when she actually discovered the malpractice.

 For the purposes of Tennessee's statute of limitation, when does the cause of action accrue [when the actual injury occurred or when the injury was, or should have been, discovered]?

 In cases where medical malpractice is asserted to have occurred through the negligent performance of surgical procedures, the cause of action accrues and the statute of limitations commences to run when the patient discovers or should have discovered in the exercise of due diligence and reasonable care for his own welfare, the resulting injury.

 The statute of limitations for malpractice begins to run after the negligent injury was, or should have been discovered, and not before. Tennessee's statute applicable to an action for malpractice must be brought within one year of accrual. Historically, our courts have held that a cause of action accrues immediately upon the infliction or occurrence of an injury such that the mere ignorance or failure of a plaintiff to discover the cause of action or subsequent injury does not toll the statute. In order to mitigate the harsh effects of a such a rule, the majority of jurisdictions have adopted the " discovery doctrine" which states that the statute does not begin to run until the negligent injury was, or should have been, discovered. Today, we adopt this rule in those cases where medical malpractice is alleged to have occurred through the negligent performance of surgical procedures. Here, plaintiff's cause of action accrued when she discovered that she was pregnant, i.e., in December 1972. Her action was brought 11 months later. Thus, her action was timely.

 Reversed and remanded.

Freehe v. Freehe

Supreme Court of Washington, 500 P.2d 771 (1972)

FACTS

Plaintiff Clifford Freehe sued his wife for injuries allegedly sustained by him because of her negligent maintenance of a tractor that she owned and for the alleged failure to warn him of the tractor's unsafe condition. The injuries occurred on a farm that was the separate property of defendant. Plaintiff had no interest in the farm and was not an employee of defendant. The trial court granted defendant's motion for summary judgment based on the doctrine of interspousal tort immunity. Plaintiff appealed.

 Can one spouse be held liable for a tort committed against the other spouse?

 Spouses are not immune from liability in personal injury cases.

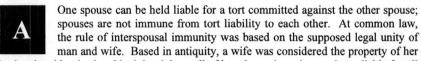 One spouse can be held liable for a tort committed against the other spouse; spouses are not immune from tort liability to each other. At common law, the rule of interspousal immunity was based on the supposed legal unity of man and wife. Based in antiquity, a wife was considered the property of her husband and her husband had the right to all of her choses in action, and was liable for all the torts of his wife. In modern times the justification for the common law rule based on the foregoing fall apart. Nonetheless, several arguments are nevertheless asserted for maintaining interspousal immunity today. First, it is argued that allowing a married person to sue his spouse would destroy the peace and tranquility of the home. We disagree. If a peaceful home environment exists, spouses will likely not sue each other and risk the consequences. Second, it is argued that an injured spouse already has an adequate remedy through criminal and divorce laws. We again disagree. Criminal and divorce laws do not actually compensate the injured spouse for the damage done. Third, proponents argue that permitting litigation between spouses would flood the courts with trivial matrimonial disputes. This has not occurred in other jurisdictions, and courts could apply typical doctrines like consent and assumption of risk to weed out these cases. Finally, proponents suggest that permitting suits between spouses would encourage collusion and fraud where one or both spouses are insured. Courts must address this problem, when and if it occurs, and depend upon the efficacy of the judicial process to ferret out the meritorious claim from the fraudulent one. Absent an express statutory provision or a compelling policy, tortfeasors should not be immunized from liability in a whole class of cases because of the *possibility* of fraud or for any other reason in support of interspousal immunity.

 Reversed and remanded.

Renko v. McLean
Court of Appeals of Maryland, 697 A.2d 468 (1997)

FACTS

When Plaintiff Natasha Renko, [a minor at the time] was 17 years old, she suffered serious injuries when her biological mother, Defendant Teresa McLean, negligently drove their car into the rear of another vehicle. Following her 18th birthday, plaintiff filed suit against her mother, the defendant, alleging negligence in the operation of the motor vehicle. Defendant defended by filing a motion to dismiss based on parent-child immunity. Plaintiff responded by requesting that the court recognize an exception to the rule for motor tort cases. The court refused and entered judgment for defendant; plaintiff appealed.

Is there an exception to the parent-child immunity doctrine for motor tort cases occurring when the plaintiff was a minor at the time and suffered injuries in connection therewith?

Maryland does not recognize an exception to the parent-child immunity doctrine for injuries sustained in motor tort cases occurring during the child's minority.

The rational behind the parent-child immunity doctrine serves to prevent fraud and collusion among family members to the detriment of 3rd parties and the threat that intra-familial litigation will deplete family resources. It is a relationship recognized both at common law and by the General Assembly [Maryland's Legislature]. While some exceptional circumstances may sever the doctrine from its rationale and reason, this in no way detracts from our fundamental belief that the parent-child immunity rule is still essential to the maintenance of discipline and to the stability of family harmony. We have thus continued to hold that today's parent-child relationship, as recognized by this court and the Legislature, furnishes no compelling reason to abrogate the rule. Plaintiff nonetheless mounts a three-pronged attack upon the parent-child immunity doctrine. She asserts that 1) adult children should be allowed to maintain actions against their parents for injuries occurring during their minority; 2) no contemporary justification exists to apply the doctrine to the facts of the case sub judice in light of compulsory motor vehicle liability insurance; and 3) any such application is violative of the Maryland Declaration of Rights and of the Fourteenth Amendment of the Constitution. We have permitted suits between parents and their minor children in limited circumstances: when a child has suffered cruel or unusually malicious conduct at the hands of a parent and when the child's parent's business partner has committed negligence in the operation of the partnership. However, we refuse to create an exception that would effectively nullify the rule and open the floodgates to every conceivable dispute between parent and child. Other Jurisdictions have been moved by arguments calling for the abolition of the parent-child immunity doctrine in motor tort cases; however we have not been so persuaded. In a normal case, liability insurance becomes relevant only after an insured's liability is fixed in an appropriate legal proceeding. As between a parent and child, it becomes the reason for the cause of action; the purpose that justifies the suit's existence. Thus, unlike a true adversarial proceeding, an insurer if forced into the unenviable position of attempting to defend a suit that is insured has every

Renko v. McLean

Court of Appeals of Maryland, 697 A.2d 468 (1997)

incentive to lose. Furthermore, many families carry medical insurance which would necessarily compensate the child for injuries and related expenses. Allowing children to recover for pain and suffering and other non-economic damages might potentially weigh down a family with a judgment it cannot afford to pay because the amount exceeds the policy limit. Lastly, as to the argument that the doctrine's as applied in motor vehicle torts is violative of the Maryland Declaration of Rights and of the Fourteenth Amendment, we find these assertions to be without merit.

Judgment affirmed, with costs.

Abernathy v. Sisters of St. Mary's

Supreme Court of Missouri, 446 S.W.2d 599 (1969)

FACTS

Plaintiff Abernathy, a patient at a hospital operated by the Defendant Sisters of St. Mary's, alleged that a hospital employee negligently failed to assist him as he moved from his hospital bed to the bathroom. As a result, plaintiff fell and suffered injuries. He brought suit against the defendant for $35,000 in damages. Defendant moved for summary judgment, arguing that the hospital was a religious, nonprofit corporation and charitable institution and, therefore, is immune from tort liability. The trial court sustained the motion, judgment was entered for the defendant and the plaintiff appealed.

Are non-governmental charitable institutions insulated from negligence liability?

Non-governmental charitable institutions can be held liable for their own negligence and negligence of their agents.

A non-governmental charitable institution is not immune from liability for negligence. The doctrine of charitable immunity, which held that charitable institutions were immune from tort liability, was adopted by this state in 1907 in the case of *Adams v. University Hospital*. At that time, *Adams* held that it was better that an individual suffer injury without compensation than risk the probability that the public would be deprived of the benefits of the charity. In essence, the interest of the latter was deemed to be so great that the former's interest was considered secondary to it. The rationale was justifiable at that time in order to encourage and protect charities. Today, however, charity is big business, often comprising big corporations who receive huge tax deductions for their donations. Modern corporations should pay their own way and most do carry liability insurance. The old rational for the doctrine fades in light of modern considerations. Yet two main arguments remain in support of charitable immunity. We find them both unconvincing. The "implied waiver" theory states that persons who accept the benefits of a charity implicitly agree that they will not sue the charity for torts. This is a mere fiction; the theory is unsound at best. It is impossible to say, for example, that a conscious, unconscious, gravely ill or insane person brought to the hospital and treated implicitly agrees he will not assert a claim against it for a wrong done to him. The "trust fund" theory states that funds given to charities for charitable purposes cannot be used to pay judgments. This theory confuses a right to sue with the right to satisfaction of a judgment. Thus, we hold that in this case and all future cases, a non-governmental charitable institution is liable for its own negligence and for the negligence of its agents and employees acting within the scope of their employment.

Reversed and remanded.

Ayala v. Philadelphia Board of Public Education

Supreme Court of Pennsylvania, 305 A.2d 877 (1973)

FACTS

Plaintiff-appellant William Ayala, Jr. was injured when his arm was caught in a shredding machine in the upholstery class of a Philadelphia public school. Plaintiff's arm had to be amputated, and he sued for his injuries. Plaintiff alleged that the school district was negligent in failing to supervise the upholstery class, in supplying the machinery without a proper safety device, in maintaining the machine in a dangerous condition, and in failing to warn the children of the dangerous condition. Defendant-appellee Philadelphia Board of Public Education ("school district") interposed preliminary objections, asserting the defense of governmental immunity. The objections were sustained and an order in the defendant's favor was entered; plaintiff appeals.

Are state and local governments immune from tort liability?

State and local governments are not immune from tort liability.

State and local governments are not immune from tort liability. The historical roots of the governmental immunity doctrine are rooted 1788 English case of *Russell v. Men of Devon*, where the court expressed the fear that without governmental immunity there would be multiplicity of lawsuits without end. The rational being that it was better that an individual sustain an injury than that the public should suffer an inconvenience. The justification for the doctrine, as well as the rule itself, can longer be supported in modern, American society. We reject the medieval absolutist notion that the entire burden of damages should be imposed against an individual who suffers injuries. Notions of fairness and equity, however, dictate that damages should be distributed among the society as a whole. We similarly find no merit in the so-called justification that excessive litigation would result, as this theory lacks empirical support. Equally unpersuasive is the argument that governments lack funds from which claims could be paid. As many writers have pointed out, the fallacy in the "no-fund theory" is that it assumes the very point which is sought to be proved – that payment of damage claims is not a proper purpose. The availability of public insurance is available to spread the losses throughout society. Exposure of the government to liability will have the effect of increasing governmental care and concern for the welfare of those who might be injured by its actions.

Reversed and remanded.

Riss v. New York
New York Court of Appeals, 293 N.Y.S.2d 897 (1968)

FACTS

Plaintiff Linda Riss was terrorized for more than six months by a man, Burton Pugach, whom she had rebuffed romantically. Pugach threatened to have plaintiff killed or maimed if she did not yield to him. Plaintiff went to the police, but her pleas for aid were ignored. Plaintiff became engaged to another man, and during her engagement party Pugach telephoned and warned her that it was her last chance. Plaintiff again begged the police for help, but she was again refused assistance. The next day, a thug hired by Pugach threw lye in plaintiff face. Plaintiff was blinded and her face was permanently scarred as a result. Plaintiff sued the City of New York as the defendant for its negligent failure to provide adequate police protection. The trial court dismissed the complaint, the appellate division affirmed, and plaintiff appealed.

When a victim is injured as the results of another intentional tort, can a city be liable for the negligent failure to provide police protection?

When a victim is injured as the results of another intentional tort, a city can not be held liable for its negligent failure to provide police protection.

A city is immune from liability for the negligent failure to provide police protection. The amount of police projection available to individuals is limited by community resources and is a legislative-executive decision. For the courts to proclaim a new general duty to protect specific individuals would be an unauthorized determination of how the limited police resources should be deployed without predictable limits. Putting in place municipal liability by this court would be an improper assumption of and encroachment into our state's legislative authority. In absence of legislation indicating otherwise, we will not carve out an area of tort liability for police protection to members of the public.

Affirmed.

Delong v. Erie County

New York Supreme Court, 455 N.Y.S.2d 887 (1982)

FACTS

Plaintiff Amalia DeLong and her family lived in a suburb of Buffalo in Erie County that was served by the 911 emergency telephone system which was operated by the Central Police Services, an agency of Erie County, the defendant in this case. One morning, plaintiff called 911 and told the complaint writer that a burglar was breaking into her house. The response was that help would be sent right away. However, the dispatcher wrote down the incorrect address and failed to follow proper procedures by not asking the name of the caller, determining the exact location of the call, and by not following up on the call when he received a report of "no such address." Consequently, plaintiff's call was treated as a fraudulent one. Plaintiff was found stabbed to death in her home as the result of a savage attack. Plaintiffs, representing the estate of the deceased, sued Defendant-municipality Erie County for negligence. The jury awarded $200,000 for pain and suffering, and defendant appealed.

Where a municipality has assumed a duty to a particular person which it must perform in a non-negligent manner, can it successfully raise the defense of governmental immunity?

Municipalities are not immune from liability when they voluntarily assume a duty and hold themselves out to those in need of help as the entity to be called when one is in need of assistance.

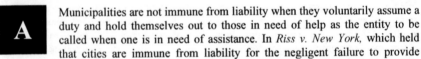

Municipalities are not immune from liability when they voluntarily assume a duty and hold themselves out to those in need of help as the entity to be called when one is in need of assistance. In *Riss v. New York*, which held that cities are immune from liability for the negligent failure to provide adequate police protection, there was no special relationship between the police and the victim which would have given rise to a special duty. However, the court was clear to point out that where the police undertake responsibilities to particular members of the public, the municipality may lose its immunity. Here, the plaintiff waited for the response to her 911 call, and was led to believe that she could do so with confidence. Because the defendant held itself as the one to call when one is in need of assistance, the defendant voluntarily assumed a duty and was thus required to perform this duty in a non-negligent manner, which it failed to do. We find the defendant's argument that it could not be held liable unless the police conduct in some way increased plaintiff's risk to be unavailing. Quite the contrary, we find that her reliance on the complaint writer's assurance did increase her risk by causing her to remain defenseless in the home rather than fleeing outside to safety.

Judgment affirmed with costs.

Deuser v. Vecera
U.S. Court of Appeals, 139 F.3d 1190 (8th Cir. 1998)

FACTS

Plaintiff Deuser attended the Veiled Prophet Fair on a Fourth of July weekend in St. Louis, Missouri. The Fair was held on the National Expansion Memorial, a national park, and a special use permit was issued to the City of St. Louis by the U.S. Secretary of the Interior. Plaintiff was observed grabbing women's buttocks and was given a warning by Park Rangers David Vecera and Edward Bridges, defendants in this action. Identified as a troublemaker, they continued to watch him. After defendants observed plaintiff urinating in public, he was arrested. Still aroused, plaintiff argued with defendants and continued making rude comments to female visitors. The chief ranger decided to turn Deuser over to the city police; however, they were unable or unwilling to process him due to an overwhelming workload created by the fair itself. Defendants and police decided to release plaintiff away from the park so he would not return to the fair that evening. He was freed in a parking lot somewhere in St. Louis, alone, with no money and no transportation. Plaintiff then wandered onto an interstate highway and was struck and killed by a car. His blood alcohol level was 0.214% at the time of his death, well above the legal limit for intoxication. Defendant's survivors brought various state and federal claims against defendants; including a wrongful death action against the United States under the Federal Tort Claims Act ("FTCA") based on the allegedly negligent acts of the park rangers. The case was dismissed by the trial court judge and the survivors appealed.

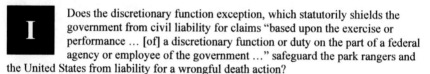

I   Does the discretionary function exception, which statutorily shields the government from civil liability for claims "based upon the exercise or performance ... [of] a discretionary function or duty on the part of a federal agency or employee of the government ..." safeguard the park rangers and the United States from liability for a wrongful death action?

R   The discretionary function exception to the Federal Torts Claims Act which protects the discretionary conduct of government agents acting within the scope of their authority safeguards the park rangers and the United States from liability for a wrongful death action.

A   The Federal Tort Claims Act (FTCA) was enacted by Congress to waive sovereign immunity on behalf of the United States. The discretionary function exception to the FTCA is statutory and shields the government from civil liability for claims based upon the exercise or performance of a discretionary function or duty on the part of a federal agency or an employee of the Government, whether or not the discretion involved is abused. To determine whether the discretionary function exception applies here to protect defendants and the United States from suit, we must first consider whether the actions taken by the defendant-rangers were discretionary, that is, "a matter of choice." If defendants had a policy they were to follow in releasing plaintiff, then there is no discretion in the conduct for the exception to protect. Two guides exist for law enforcement to follow: the Standard Operating Procedures for an arrest and the Veiled Prophet Fair Operations Handbook. Both provide rules and guidance for the enforcement of laws: the former, arrest procedures; the latter, traffic control, liquor law violations, city ordinances in effect and a variety of crimes against persons from simple assault to murder. The Handbook does not, however, provide procedures to be followed in the event an arrest is made. These guidelines should

Deuser v. Vecera

U.S. Court of Appeals, 139 F.3d 1190 (8th Cir. 1998)

not be considered a substitute for sound judgment and discretionary action on the part of the defendant-rangers. The rangers still retained discretion to decide when and whether to make an arrest. Here, plaintiff was not charged with a crime, so there was no reason to follow the procedures for incarceration [plaintiff was *arrested* but he was not *charged*]. We thus hold that releasing him without charging him with a crime [terminating the arrest] was a discretionary function reserved to the judgment of the rangers. Notwithstanding the foregoing, we next must decide whether the kind of judgment exercised by the defendant-rangers in terminating the arrest was the type of conduct the discretionary function exception was designed to protect. To be protected, the defendant's conduct must be grounded in the social, economic, or political goals of the handbook's discretionary enforcement guidelines. We believe that all three conditions were satisfied by the defendants, and as such, their conduct was a classic example of a permissible exercise of policy judgment. An important function of the rangers during the Fair, according to the Handbook, was to serve and protect visitors; so the decision to remove plaintiff from the park served the social goals of protecting the many patrons of the Fair and ensuring that their enjoyment of the festivities was not diminished by the obnoxious and offensive behavior of a fellow attendee. The economic goal served by releasing plaintiff without charging him was to preserve already scarce law enforcement resources, and the political goal was that of having all law enforcement agencies involved working together. When the police opted not to process plaintiff's arrest, the defendant-rangers appropriately did not override the decision of the lead agency for law enforcement, according to the Handbook. Thus, the rangers acted properly to preserve that cooperation by releasing plaintiff as the local police requested. Consequently, we hold that the discretionary conduct of the park rangers is a permissible exercise of policy judgment which is protected by the discretionary function exception.

 The judgment of the District Court is affirmed.

Bussard v. Minimed Inc.
California Court of Appeals, 105 Cal.App.4th (2003)

FACTS

Defendant Minimed Inc. hired a pest control company to spray to eliminate fleas at its facility during non-working hours. The following morning, Irma Hernandez, a clerical employee, arrived at work and noticed a funny smell similar to "Raid." By noon, she told two supervisors she did not feel well; one of the supervisors asked if she wanted to see the company doctor, the other asked if she was well enough to drive home. She declined to see the doctor and said she felt well enough to drive home. Nine other employees of defendant who went home early feeling sick. Thereafter, while driving, Hernandez rear-ended a car stopped at a red traffic light driven by Plaintiff Barbara Bussard. Plaintiff filed this action against defendant in vicarious liability under the doctrine of respondeat superior, alleging Hernandez was acting within the scope of her employment when she drove home ill. Defendant-respondent moved for summary judgment, arguing that the "going-and-coming" rule meant that Hernandez was not with the scope of her employment during the commute home and that, as a result, it should not be held vicariously liable under the doctrine. The trail court agreed and entered summary judgment. Plaintiff-appellant appealed to the California Court of Appeal.

 Is a plaintiff-employee's daily commute, for the purposes of vicarious liability under the doctrine of respondeat superior, considered within the scope of employment such that a defendant-employer may be held liable for injuries sustained and/or caused by the plaintiff-employee during that time period?

 An employee's daily commute, for the purposes of vicarious liability under the doctrine of respondeat superior, is generally not considered within the scope of employment such that an employer may be held liable for injuries sustained and/or caused by the employee during that time period; however, the rule does not apply in a situation where the employer contributed to the injury.

 Under the doctrine of respondeat superior, an employer is ordinary liable for the injuries its employees cause to others in the course of their work. The doctrine imposes liability whether or not the employer was negligent, and whether or not the employer had control of the employee. The doctrine's underlying principle is that a business should absorb the costs its underlings impose on others. Despite the doctrine's broad applicability, courts have not defined it so broadly as to include an employer's daily commute. Thus, a general rule was established that an employee is outside the scope of employment which engaged in his ordinary commute to and from his place of work; the so-called "going-and-coming" rule. However, this rule has its exceptions. One such exception is where an employee endangers others with a risk arising out of or related to work. The test for determining whether such a danger arises from or related to work is a foreseeability test. This type of foreseeability, however, is different than the foreseeability of negligence. This type of foreseeability merely means that in the context of the particular enterprise, an employee's conduct is neither unusual nor startling. In this case, Hernandez suffered pesticide exposure at work which caused her to be light-headed at the time of the accident. That an employee might not be fit to drive for several hours is not such a "startling or unusual event" that we find a car accident unforeseeable. Hence, the trial court erred in finding that the going-and-

Bussard v. Minimed Inc.

California Court of Appeals, 105 Cal.App.4th (2003)

---

coming rule barred plaintiff-appellant's claim of respondeat superior. That rule was a distraction since the trust of appellant's claim was that Hernandez was an "instrumentality of danger" because of what had happened to her at work. Thus, the rule did not apply because Hernandez's decision to drive was an opportunity to raise the rule and should not obscure the fact that her job had contributed to the accident. Thus, summary judgment was improper. Judgment reversed and the court is directed to enter a new and different order denying defendant-respondent Minimed Inc.'s motion for summary judgment.

 Motion for summary judgment denied.

O'Shea v. Welch
U.S. Court of Appeals, 350 F.3d 1101 (10th Cir. 2003)

FACTS

Defendant Welch, an Osco store manager, was driving from his store to the Osco District Office to deliver football tickets that had been obtained from a vendor for distribution among Osco managers. During his drive, he made a spur of the moment decision to pull into a service station striking Plaintiff O'Shea's car in the process. Plaintiff filed suit against defendant for negligence in failing to yield and against Osco in vicarious liability. On cross-motions for summary judgment, the district court held that no reasonable jury could conclude that defendant was acting within the scope of his employment. This appeal followed.

 Does liability attach to an employer when an injury occurred to another while the employee was on deviation for personal business during official business and, if so, does such a deviation take him outside the scope of his employment?

 The analysis as to whether liability attaches to an employer when the employee deviated for personal business is based on a determination of whether the employee was on a frolic or a detour.

 Pursuant to Kansas law, an employer is only liable for injuries caused by an employee acting within the scope of his employment. An employee is acting within the scope of his employment when he is performing services for which he has been employed, or when he is doing anything which is reasonable incidental to his employment. The test is not whether specific conduct was expressly authorized or forbidden by the employer, but whether such conduct should have been foreseen from the nature of the employment or the duties related to it. Appellant urges us to adopt the slight deviation rule which is already followed in worker's compensation cases. Pursuant to this analysis, it must be determined whether the employee was on a frolic or a detour; the latter is a deviation that is sufficiently related to the employment to fall within its scope thereby impugning liability to the employer, while the former is the pursuit of the employee's personal business as a substantial deviation from or an abandonment of the employment, foreclosing any liability claimed by the injured against the employer. Applying the [slight deviation] analysis to the present case, we think that the question of whether the detour to the service station was with the scope of defendant's employment is for the jury to decide. The following factors help determine whether the employee has embarked on a slight or substantial deviation: 1) the employee's intent; 2) the nature, time and place of the deviation; 3) the time consumed in the deviation; 4) the work for which the employee was hired; 5) the incidental acts reasonably expected by the employer; and 6) the freedom allowed the employee in performing his job. We thus conclude that a reasonable jury could conclude that he was acting with that scope of employment.

 Remanded.

Murrell v. Goertz

Court of Appeals of Oklahoma, 597 P.2d 1223 (1979)

FACTS

Russell Westbrook, not a party to this action, was an independent newspaper distributor for Defendant-appellee Oklahoma Publishing. Westbrook employed Co-Defendant Bruce Goertz as his employee to deliver newspapers. However, Oklahoma Publishing had no knowledge of Goertz's employment in this capacity. On August 26, 1976, when Goertz delivered the morning newspaper to Plaintiff-appellant Murrell, an argument erupted culminating in plaintiff slapping Goertz. Goertz retaliated by striking plaintiff, resulting in injuries requiring a hospital stay. Appellant filed suit in the District Court of Oklahoma County, seeking a total of $52,500 for past and future medical expenses, pain and suffering and exemplary damages. An order sustaining the defendant's motion for summary judgment in favor of co-defendant-appellee Oklahoma Publishing was granted at the trial level and plaintiff-appellant appealed.

 Can an employer be held liable for the torts of an independent contractor?

 An employer is not liable for the torts of his independent contractor.

 It is well settled that a company is not liable for the torts of his independent contractor. However, the line of demarcation between the independent contractor and an employee is no clearly drawn. An independent contractor is one who is engaged to perform a certain service for another according to his own methods and manner, free from the control and direction of an employer in all manners connected with the performance of the service except as to the result. The employee, by contrast, is under the direction of the employer and has limited to no control over the methods and manners connected to the performance of his work. Hence, if a company does not have the right to control the physical details of the work of a worker, the worker is an independent contractor and not an employee. Here, Oklahoma Publishing did not have the right to control the work of Goertz because he was an employee of Westbrook. In fact, Oklahoma Publishing did not even know of Goertz's existence. Therefore, Goertz was an independent contractor and could not be considered an employee of Oklahoma Publishing. Consequently, Oklahoma Publishing is not liable for his tort.

 Judgment affirmed.

Maloney v. Rath
Supreme Court of California, 445 P.2d 513 (1968)

FACTS

Defendant Rath's automobile collided with a car driven by plaintiff after she hired Peter Evanchik, a mechanic, to repair her brakes. He did so negligently. Three months later, her brakes failed and defendant was involved in an auto accident with plaintiff. Plaintiff seeks to hold defendant liable for Evanchik's negligence under a theory of respondeat superior. The trial court determined that Evanchik's negligent repair of the brakes caused the accident and rendered a judgment in favor of the defendant. Plaintiff appealed.

 Is the duty to keep a motorist's brakes in working order a non-delegable duty or can such a duty be delegated to an independent contractor?

 A motorist may not delegate her duty to keep her brakes in working order to an independent contractor.

 Some duties of care may not be delegated to third parties and some may not. If a third party is injured because of the negligence of an independent contractor, that third party may hold the "employer" directly liable if that duty of care was non-delegable to an independent contractor. Thus, the question becomes: what duties are non-delegable? The list includes, but is not limited to: 1) the duty of a general contractor to construct a building safely; 2) the duty of landowners to maintain their lands in a safe condition; and 3) the duty of employers and suppliers to comply with the Labor Code. The Restatement (Second) of Torts §423 provides that one who carries on an activity that presents a grave risk of serious bodily harm or death may not delegate his duty of care to an independent contractor and §424 provides that one who is under duty by statute to provide safeguards for the safety of others may not delegate his duty of care to an independent contractor. Here, defendant was driving an automobile, which certainly presents a grave risk of serious bodily harm such that she was required by the Vehicle Code to keep her car brakes in good working order. Hence, her duty to keep her brakes in good working order was non-delegable to Evanchik.

 Judgment reversed.

Popejoy v. Steinle

Supreme Court of Wyoming, 820 P.2d 545 (1991)

FACTS

While Connie Steinle was taking her daughter and niece to town to purchase a calf to be raised on her ranch, she negligently collided with Plaintiff-appellant Ronald Popejoy's vehicle. Connie died as a result of the accident and plaintiff was diagnosed with injuries initially described as "muscle strain." Fifteen months after the accident, plaintiff began experiencing serious pain in his back and required surgery. After plaintiff unsuccessfully attempted to reopen Connie Steinle's estate, which had been closed more than a year earlier, he filed a creditor's claim against the representative (defendant-appellee) of the estate of William Steinle, her husband, who had died in the interim following Connie's death of an illness unrelated to the accident. Plaintiff seeks to impute Connie Steinle's negligence to William Steinle, arguing that he is vicariously liable for her negligence because her "business trip" to pick up the calf was part of a joint venture between Connie and her husband, William Steinle. The trail court granted the Estate's motion for summary judgment holding that Mr. Steinle had no financial or other interest in the purpose of the trip to town such that vicarious liability could be imposed upon him. This appeal followed.

 Can a defendant be held vicariously liable for the negligence of another under a theory of joint venture if there was no common interest in the venture by the parties; no common purpose shared; no equal right of control in the direction of the enterprise or no shared profit-making, pecuniary or financial interest or motive?

 A defendant is not vicariously liable for the negligence of another under a theory of joint venture unless the joint venture had a distinct business or pecuniary motive and purpose.

 Preliminarily, given the facts of this case, we note that there is no relevant distinction between a joint enterprise and a joint venture. Although the Restatement (Second) of Torts §491 comment c des not define the elements of a joint venture, it does list four elements of joint enterprise: 1) an agreement among the members of the group; 2) a common purpose; 3) a community of pecuniary interest; and 4) an equal right of control of the enterprise. In *Holiday v. Bannister,* where a father was held liable under a joint enterprise theory for negligence of his son during a hunting trip when the latter accidentally shot and killed another hunter, we emphasized the importance of the profit motive. We did so because we though it inappropriate to import the commercial concept of joint venture into non-commercial situations, social settings or situations which are more often matters of friendly or family cooperation and accommodation. Here, it is evident that Connie Steinle was not in a joint venture or enterprise with William Steinle. The record clearly shows that Connie Steinle was going into town to purchase the calf for her daughter and that the daughter was the sole intended recipient of the animal. Affidavits also indicated that her father did not ordinarily have any ownership interest in the cattle that she, her sisters or her mother raised. And while it was true that the daughter's calves and other pets were often sold, the proceeds from such sale did not go to the account of Connie Steinle and William Steinle, but to the account of the daughter. All in all, Connie Steinle and William Steinle were not joint venturists because there was no profit motive to their actions. Thus, William Steinle cannot be held vicariously liable for the negligence of Connie Steinle.

 The decision of the trial court is affirmed.

Shuck v. Means

Supreme Court of Minnesota, 226 N.W.2d 285 (1974)

FACTS

Defendant Hertz, a car rental agency, leased a rental car to George A. Codling. Codling permitted Defendant Means to drive this car, who in turn negligently collided with and injured Plaintiff Shuck, a passenger in the other car. Means was uninsured at the time of the accident. The trial court concluded that Means was operating the vehicle with the implied consent of Hertz, finding the defendant liable under the Minnesota Safety Responsibility Act, the applicable statute at issue. Defendant appealed.

 Is a car rental agency liable in negligence when it leased its vehicle to one person but the car was subsequently operated by another person who negligently caused injury to a fourth party in violation of the rental agreement?

 A car rental agency is liable for the negligence of an individual who drives its rental car, even though it did not rent the car to that individual.

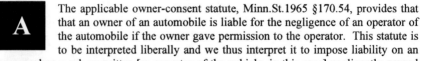

 The applicable owner-consent statute, Minn.St.1965 §170.54, provides that that an owner of an automobile is liable for the negligence of an operator of the automobile if the owner gave permission to the operator. This statute is to be interpreted liberally and we thus interpret it to impose liability on an owner when a sub-permittee [or operator of the vehicle, in this case] negligently caused injury to another. This interpretation is based on the belief that permission, as used by statute, refers to permission given by the owner for use of its car *being driven* and not use of the car by a specific *driver*. In addition, we hold that an owner is liable for a sub-permittee's negligence even if the owner explicitly forbade the operation by the sub-permittee, as was evident in *Granley v. Crandall*. Here, Defendant Hertz gave permission for the use of its vehicle, and that is all that is required to hold it liable for Means' negligence.

 Judgment affirmed.

Smalich v. Westfall

Supreme Court of Pennsylvania, 269 A.2d 476 (1970)

FACTS

Plaintiff Julia Smalich was killed while riding as a passenger in her own car after Defendant Felix Rush Westfall, the driver at the time, negligently collided with a car driven by Defendant Stephanna Blank. The estate of Julia Smalich (plaintiff) sought damages against both defendants for both wrongful death and a survival action. Both defendants defended on the ground that the estate (plaintiff) was barred from recovery because Julia Smalich was the owner of the negligently driven automobile such that Defendant Westfall's negligence was imputed to her [Julia Smalich]. A trial jury found that Defendant Westfall's negligence was the proximate cause of the collision. After trial, the court en banc ruled that, under the facts, the contributory negligence of Westfall must be impugned to the owner of the automobile as a matter of law and precluded recovery by the Estate against Defendant Blank. The Estate of Smalich appealed.

 Can the contributory negligence of a driver be passed along to a passenger riding in her own automobile in a suit for wrongful death and a survival action?

 Contributory negligence may not be imputed to a passenger riding in her own automobile without a finding of either a master-servant relationship or the existence of a joint enterprise.

 Generally, a driver's negligence will not be imputed to a passenger unless a relationship exists between the two making the passenger vicariously liable for the driver's negligence. To that end, a passenger will only be vicariously liable for the negligence of a driver when there is either a master-servant relationship or a finding of joint enterprise. Under the facts of the instant case and under an ordinary situation such as the one we have here, we doubt that the owner-passenger, Julia Smalich, had the right and ability to control the actions of the negligent driver, Defendant Felix Rush Westfall. What is likely is that there was a reasonable mutual understanding between the two: that Defendant-driver Westfall was to exercise reasonable care and retain control over the car subject to the duty of obedience to owner-passenger Julia Smalich as to such things as destination. No master-servant relationship existed nor was there a joint enterprise between the two. Hence, negligence could not have been imputed to her and therefore she cannot be barred from recovery by imputed contributory negligence.

 Judgment reversed.

Rylands v. Fletcher

Exchequer, 159 Eng.Rep. 737 (1865)

FACTS

Defendant John Rylands, a textile mill owner, needed an additional source of water for his steam-powered mill, so he hired some workers to create a reservoir by excavating a portion of his land. Unfortunately, the land surrounding the reservoir contained a latent defect and the water burst through an abandoned coal-mining shaft which connected to active coal mines owned by Plaintiff Thomas Fletcher. The flooding caused severe damage to the plaintiff's active mines and he had to stop mining permanently. Defendant did not know of the latent defect in his topsoil, or that the old coal mine shafts connected to the active ones, or that Fletcher was working in the active mines, and thus could not have known that the reservoir filled with water posed a dander to person and property if it escaped.

Can the defendant be held liable for the damage to the plaintiff's land?

A lawful act done on one's own land, performed non-negligently, precludes liability for the injurious consequences to another's land which may result from such an act.

In the instant case, there was no trespass. The act of doing damage was not immediate. Similarly, the record does not support negligence on the defendant's part. To hold the defendant liable without negligence would make him an insurer against the consequence of a lawful act upon his own land when he had no reason to suspect that any damage was likely to ensue. Therefore, I am of the belief that there must be negligence in order to invoke liability.

Defendant is not liable.

Miller v. Civil Constructors Inc.
Illinois Court of Appeal, 651 N.E.2d 239 (1995)

FACTS

Plaintiff Gerald Miller was injured when a stray bullet ricocheted during some firearm practice in a nearby gravel pit. Plaintiff brought suit against Defendant Civil Constructors Inc. in strict liability arising from their alleged "ultrahazardous" activity for which plaintiff claims they were legally responsible either because of their control of the premises or their discharge of the firearms. The circuit court dismissed the strict liability counts of his complaint against the defendants and plaintiff appeals from those orders.

 Should the use of firearms be classified as an "ultrahazardous" activity so as to subject the defendants to claims based on a theory of strict liability?

 The use of firearms should not be classified as an "ultrahazardous" activity so as to subject the defendants to claims based on a theory of strict liability.

The concept of strict liability comes from the English rule in *Rylands v. Fletcher* (1868) which states that under the theory, "the defendant will be liable when he damages another by a thing or activity unduly dangerous and inappropriate to the place where it is maintained, in light of the character of that place and its surroundings." Most jurisdictions have adopted it to impose strict liability on owners and users of land for harm resulting from abnormally dangerous activities and conditions. Our review of the relevant authority discloses that the discharge of firearms resulting in injury presents a question of negligence and that the standard of care is ordinary care – not the high degree of care associated with strict liability. Nonetheless, we review §520 of the Restatement which list several factors which we will consider in determining whether an activity is abnormally dangerous [ultrahazardous]: 1) the existence of a high degree of risk of some harm to persons, land or the chattels of others; 2) the likelihood that the harm that results will be great; 3) the inability to eliminate the risk via the exercise of reasonable care; 4) the extent to which the activity to the place where it is carried on; and 5) the extent to which its value to the community is outweighed by its dangerous attributes. In this case, we note that the essential question is whether the risk created is so unusual, either because of its magnitude of because of the circumstances surrounding it, as to justify the imposition of strict liability. We feel it is not. The risk of harm to person or property, even thought great, can be virtually eliminated by the exercise of reasonable care. Second, the use of firearms is a matter of common usage and the harm posed comes from their misuse rather than from their inherent nature alone. Third, the activity in this case was carried on at a firing range in a quarry; we assume that the location was appropriate for such activity. Thus, we conclude that plaintiff's allegations are legally insufficient to show the activity should be considered ultrahazardous.

 Judgment affirmed.

Indiana Harbor Belt R.R. Co. v. American Cyanamid

U.S. Court of Appeals, 916 F.2d 1174 (7th Cir. 1990)

FACTS

Defendant American Cyanamid, a chemical manufacturer, loaded 20,000 gallons of liquid acrylonitrile, a highly flammable and toxic chemical used in large quantities to make acrylic fibers, plastics, dyes and other goods, onto a railroad tank car for shipment to New Jersey from its manufacturing plant in Louisiana. The railroad tank car was leased by the defendant from North American Car Corporation. A Missouri Pacific Railroad train picked up the tank car and carried it to the Blue Island railroad yard, which was owned by Plaintiff Indiana Harbor Belt Railroad, a small switching line located in the Chicago metropolitan area. Several hours after the tank car arrived at the yard, employees of the switching line noticed fluid gushing from the bottom of the car. By the time the leak was stopped, all 4,000 gallons of acrylonitrile contaminated the surrounding area. Because liquid acrylonitrile is both highly toxic and flammable, homes around the railroad yard had to be evacuated. The Illinois EPA order Indiana Harbor Belt Railroad to take extensive decontamination measures ultimately costing the line $981,022.75. Consequently, Indiana Harbor Belt Railroad sued American Cyanamid to recover its losses under a theory of strict liability for shipping a hazardous chemical. After the district judge denied the defendant's motion to dismiss the strict liability count, the plaintiff moved for summary judgment on that count, which was granted.

 Can a shipper be held strictly liable for shipping a hazardous chemical through a metropolitan area?

 Strict liability does not attach to a shipper of hazardous chemicals through a metropolitan area because such an activity is not an abnormally dangerous activity.

 The relevant activity is transportation, not manufacturing and shipping. This essential distinction the plaintiff ignores. As such, strict liability does not attach to a transporter of hazardous chemicals through a metropolitan area because such an activity is not an abnormally dangerous activity. Negligence, not strict liability, is the proper way to redress the harm caused by that activity when the danger can be avoid by using due care and due diligence. However, even with respect to the instant facts, the leak was not caused by the acrylonitrile itself. Rather, it was caused by carelessness; whether that of the North American Car Corporation in failing to maintain or inspect the car properly, the defendant in doing the same, Missouri Pacific when it had custody of the car and failed to notice the ruptured lid, or some combination of the three. And although the acrylonitrile is flammable even at relatively low temperatures, it is not so corrosive or otherwise destructive that it would eat through or otherwise damage or weaken a tank car's valves although they are maintained with due care.

 Reversed and remanded.

Foster v. Preston Mill Co.
Supreme Court of Washington, 268 P.2d 645 (1954)

FACTS

Defendant Preston Mill Company was conducting blasting operations. These operations frightened a mother mink owned by Plaintiff B.W. Foster. Consequently, the mother mink killed her kittens, causing damages to the plaintiff. At trial without a jury, judgment was rendered for plaintiff in the amount of $1,953.68. The theory adopted by the court was that after the defendant received notice of the effect which its blasting operations were having on the mink, it was absolutely liable for all damages of that nature sustained afterwards. Defendant appealed.

 Is a person carrying on an abnormally dangerous activity strictly liable for any and all damage caused?

 A person carrying on an abnormally dangerous activity is not strictly liable for damage which is not within the range of danger created by the ultrahazardous activity; that is, the individual is liable for that harm caused within reasonable limits.

 Restatement §519 states, in pertinent part, that a person carrying on an abnormally dangerous activity is strictly liable for any damages of the type *which make the activity ultrahazardous.* We are in agreement with this position. Some reasonable bounds to the liability imposed by strict liability must exist. Applying the foregoing to the instant case, we find no liability. What makes blasting an abnormally dangerous activity is the possibility of injury and damage caused by direct contact with high-velocity flying debris, not the vibration and noise which might cause a mink to kill her kittens.

 Judgment reversed.

Golden v. Amory

Supreme Judicial Court of Mass., 109 N.E.2d 131 (1952)

FACTS

Defendants owned and operated a dike and a hydroelectric plant. As a result of the hurricane of September 21, 1938, the Chicopee River overflowed caused damage to several plaintiffs' property. The judge directed verdicts for the defendants and the plaintiffs appealed.

Is a defendant, carrying on an abnormally dangerous activity, absolutely liable if damage caused by that activity was brought on by an intervening act of God?

A defendant, carrying on an abnormally dangerous activity, is not absolutely liable if damage caused by that activity was brought on by an intervening act of God.

The rule of *Rylands v. Fletcher* holds that a defendant is liable for damages caused by an abnormally dangerous activity that he brings onto his land or collects and keeps on his land that may cause damage to others. However, the rule does not apply when an intervening act of God brings about the injury. In this case, even though defendants were engaged in abnormally dangerous activities, the operation of a dike and a hydroelectric plant, there is no liability because a hurricane, which is an act of God, brought on the damage.

Exceptions overruled; judgment affirmed.

Sandy v. Bushey
Supreme Judicial Court of Maine, 128 A. 513 (1925)

FACTS

Plaintiff Sandy's horse was let out to pasture on Defendant Bushey's property. Defendant had his own horse on his property, which was known to him to be vicious. When plaintiff went to feed his horse, defendant's horse approached in a threatening manner. Plaintiff drove the defendant's horse away, but it returned and kicked him, causing plaintiff to sustain injuries.

1) Can the owner of an animal be held strictly liable for damage caused by it when the owner has knowledge of its dangerous propensities? 2) Is contributory negligence a defense to strict liability?

The owner of an animal is strictly liable for damage caused by it if the animal's dangerous, vicious or evil propensities are known to the owner; Contributory negligence is not a defense to strict liability.

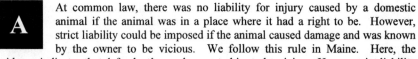

At common law, there was no liability for injury caused by a domestic animal if the animal was in a place where it had a right to be. However, strict liability could be imposed if the animal caused damage and was known by the owner to be vicious. We follow this rule in Maine. Here, the evidence indicates that defendant's was known to him to be vicious. Hence, strict liability attaches. With respect to the issue of contributory negligence, defendant attempts to evade liability by arguing that he should not be liable because plaintiff was contributorily negligent. This argument is unfounded. States which bar recovery when the plaintiff has been contributorily negligent do so under a theory of *negligence* for cases involving animals. Here, we use strict liability for cases involving animals. Thus, in our jurisdiction, to escape liability the defendant must show that the plaintiff, with full knowledge of the evil propensities of the animal, wantonly excited him or voluntarily and unnecessary put himself in the way of such an animal. In such a case, the plaintiff will be adjudged to have brought the injury upon himself and his recovery will be barred. That was not the case here. In fact, plaintiff attempted to drive defendant's horse away. The defendant knew that the horse was vicious, thus he is strictly liable for the damage caused to plaintiff.

Motion overruled; judgment affirmed.

MacPherson v. Buick Motor Co.

Court of Appeals of New York, 217 N.Y. 382 (1916)

FACTS

Defendant Buick Motor Co., an automobile manufacturer, sold an automobile to a retail dealer, who then resold the car to Plaintiff MacPherson. MacPherson was injured after being thrown out of the car following a wheel collapse. Apparently, the wooden wheel contained a defect and crumbled into fragments which on the car. The wheel was bought by Buick from another manufacturer. Evidence was submitted, however, that the defects in the wheel could have been discovered through reasonable inspection, but such an inspection was not made. There is no claim that Buick knew of the defect and willfully concealed it.

 Does a manufacturer owe a duty of care to all potential, foreseeable plaintiffs of its product?

 Manufacturers owe a duty of care, and thus will be held liable to ultimate purchasers, when the product they create is inherently dangerous, capable of loss of life or limb, known to be dangerous in ordinary use if defectively made and is likely to be used by person other than the initial purchaser.

 When the nature of a thing is such that it is reasonably certain to place life and limb in peril when negligently made, liability will attach if there is knowledge of the danger, and not a mere possibility of it, and where danger is capable of being foreseen. Under such circumstances, the manufacturer will be held liable to all users of his product, not just the initial purchasers. The duty to insure safety in the fact of foreseeable negligence should not be based solely on the existence of a contract between the injured person and the manufacturer. This is because when it is known that a product will be used by those other than the original purchaser in the normal course of business, then the manufacturer's duty is not limited to those he is in privity of contract with. Under these circumstances, the manufacturer of the product is under a duty to these users to manufacture the product with care, non-negligently and without defects. Here, we note that the nature of an automobile creates an inherent danger if manufactured defectively. It its wheels are unsafe, the likelihood of injury is great. Defendant clearly knew of the dangerous propensities of a car and is also charged with the knowledge that persons other than the original purchaser, the dealer, would be using the car as end-users. Since the dealer buys cars from the manufacturer to resell to the public, it would be ridiculous to appoint the dealer as the only entity to whom the manufacturer owes a legal duty. Moreover, the manufacturer cannot shirk its duty to inspect the component parts by claiming that it did not manufacture those specific parts itself. As a manufacturer, Buick was responsible for the final, finished product. This responsibility includes subjecting the component parts to ordinary "quality control" testing.

 Judgment for the plaintiff, affirmed with costs.

Baxter v. Ford Motor Co.
Supreme Court of Washington, 12 P.2d 409 (1932)

FACTS

During the Month of May, 1930, Plaintiff-appellant Baxter purchased a Model A Ford from Defendant St. John Motors, a Ford dealer, who had acquired the automobile from Co-defendant-appellee Ford Motor Co., the car's manufacturer. Plaintiff claims that the representations made to him indicated that the car had a shatter-proof glass windshield which would not shatter, break or fly. Defendant Ford's catalogues and printed matter, given to plaintiff by St. John prior to sale, also represented that the car had a shatter-proof glass windshield. Plaintiff was injured while driving his Model A when a pebble struck and shattered the window, causing glass to fly into plaintiff's eyes. Plaintiff lost sight in his left eye, and his right eye. The trial court refused to admit evidence of Ford's printed warranty and court entered judgment for both Defendants; plaintiff appealed.

 Can liability attach to a defendant in a tort action for a breach of an implied or express warranty without privity of contract between the party offering the warranty and the injured party?

 If an injured purchaser of ordinary experience and reasonable prudence could not have discovered the defect, a breach of an express warranty is actionable in tort, even without privity of contract.

 If an injured purchaser of ordinary experience and reasonable prudence could not have discovered the defect, a breach of an express warranty is actionable in tort, even without privity of contract. Plaintiff reasonably relied upon Ford's printed warranty; he was an ordinary person unable to discover a defect by the usual customary examination of the automobile whether glass which would not fly or shatter was used in the windshield. In *Mazetti v. Armour & Co.*, we held that a restaurant keeper could recover damage to his business when a customer was served defective canned food manufactured by the defendant. The analogy to the instant case is clear. This rule and those of companion cases do not rest upon contractual obligations, but rather on the principle that the original act of delivering the product is wrong when, because a product lacks certain qualities that the manufacturer represented it as having, the absence of which could not be readily detected by the consumer, the article is not safe for ordinary use for which the customer would ordinary use it. We note that the traditional doctrine of caveat emptor ["let the buyer beware"] does not apply here, since it would be unjust to apply the doctrine to permit manufacturers to create a demand for their products by making false representations about the qualities which they did not possess and allow then allow the manufacturers to escape liability because there is no privity of contract. In sum, we hold that Ford's printed material was improperly excluded from evidence - it was for the jury to determine whether Ford's failure to properly outfit the windshield was the proximate cause of plaintiff's injury.

 Reversed with respect to Defendant Ford; affirmed as to Defendant St. John.

Henningsen v. Bloomfield Motors Inc.

Supreme Court of New Jersey, 161 A.2d 69 (1960)

FACTS

Mr. Henningsen purchased a car from Defendant Bloomfield Motors Inc., a retail car dealer, who in turn received it from Defendant Chrysler Corporation, the car's manufacturer. Mr. Henningsen gave the car to his wife for Christmas. Plaintiff Mrs. Henningsen suffered severe injuries a few years later when the steering mechanism failed and the car crashed into a wall. When he purchased the car, Mr. Henningsen signed a contract without reading the 8½ inches of fine print. This fine print contained a "warranty" clause which disclaimed all implied warranties and which granted an express warranty for all defects within 90 days or 4,000 miles, whichever came first. Plaintiff sued both defendants; the trail court dismissed the negligence counts but ruled for plaintiff based on the implied warranty of merchantability. Both defendants appealed, and the appeal was certified directly to the Supreme Court of New Jersey.

Does an adhesion contract take priority over or superior to a statutory implied warranty of merchantability?

An adhesion contract does not take precedence over a statutory implied warranty of merchantability.

In order to ameliorate the harsh effects of the doctrine of caveat emptor, many jurisdictions have imposed an implied warranty of merchantability on the sales of all goods. This warranty states, in essence, that the goods sold must be reasonably fit for the general purpose for which they were manufactured and sold and that it [the warranty] extends to *all* foreseeable users of the product. In an effort to circumvent these requirements, many manufacturers, including Chrysler, include an express warranty provision which disclaims all statutory implied warranties. We are thus called upon to address the effect of an express warranty provision and what weight, if any, to give it. Traditional contract principles allow parties the freedom of contract, and the law recognizes and permits parties to contract away their mutual obligations. However, with respect to auto sales, the disclaimer of implied warranties is considered an adhesion contract - a contract whereby weaker party [usually the buyer] is subject to the terms dictated by the stronger party [usually the seller]. The purchaser has no opportunity to bargain for different terms. Ultimately, he must either take it or leave it. Since the buyer and seller occupy grossly unequal bargaining positions, we feel that in the interests of fairness and justice, an implied warranty of merchantability must take precedence over an adhesion contract. That is, that fairness and justice must take priority over the principle of freedom of contract. Here, Chrysler's attempted disclaimer of an implied warranty of merchantability is so detrimental to public policy and the public good so as to mandate its invalidity by this court.

Affirmed.

Greenman v. Yuba Power Products Inc.

Supreme Court of California, 377 P.2d 897 (1963)

FACTS

Plaintiff Greenman brought a suit based on a breach of implied and express warranty and in negligence against Defendant-manufacturer Yuba Power Products Inc. and the retailer of a Shopsmith, a combination power tool that could be used as a saw, drill and lathe. Plaintiff's wife gave him the Shopsmith for Christmas and while he was properly using it to lathe a piece of wood, he was injured when the wood flew out of the machine and struck him. At trial, the evidence showed that the Shopsmith was defectively designed and constructed. The jury returned a verdict in favor of the retailer but against Yuba Power based on a negligence and/or breach of express warranty theory. Yuba Power's motion for a new trial was denied by the court and a judgment on the verdict was entered. Yuba Power appealed.

Is a manufacturer strictly liable when he places an article in the stream of commerce that proves defective and causes injury?

Manufacturers are strictly liable for injuries caused by defective products provided that the user is unaware of the defect.

Yuba Power contends that plaintiff is barred from recovery for breach of warranty because he did not provide notice of the defect to Yuba Power within a reasonable time after the injury, as required by §1769 of the Civil Code. Like other provisions of the U.C.C., §1769 does not apply to actions by injured consumers against manufacturers which arise independently of a contract of sale between the parties. Therefore, plaintiff's action for breach of the express warranties contained in the brochure is not barred. Moreover, to impose strict liability on the manufacturer, as we see here, the plaintiff was not required to establish that Yuba Power even made an express warranty since this action is not governed by the contract law of express warranties. Under a strict liability theory, Yuba Power would be liable if the Shopsmith caused injury and if Yuba Power knew that the Shopsmith was to be used without inspection for defects - nothing more is required. Plaintiff provided ample evidence to show that 2) he was injured while using the Shopsmith in a way it was intended to be used; 2) as a result of a defect in design and manufacture; 3) he was not aware of the defect; and 4) the defect made the Shopsmith unsafe for its intended use.

The judgment is therefore affirmed.

Rix v. General Motors Corp.

Supreme Court of Montana, 723 P.2d 195 (1986)

FACTS

Plaintiff Michael Rix was injured when his pickup was rear-ended by a new G.M. two-ton truck, manufactured by Defendant General Motors Corporation, which had been equipped with a water tank after sale. Plaintiff sued defendant on a theory of strict liability and the parties stipulated that the accident occurred because of brake failure caused by a brake tube coming free from the top of a Hydrovac, the truck's brake booster unit. Plaintiff argued that the brake failure occurred as the result of a manufacturing defect in the tube during the truck's assembly at the G.M. manufacturing plant and that the brake system was defectively designed. In support of his defective design argument, plaintiff reasoned that a truck of its size should have been equipped with a dual braking system in order to provide extra braking power. Defendant, on the other hand, argued that the tube was defective because it had been altered after it left its assembly line and further maintained that the single braking system was not unreasonably dangerous and that the accident would have occurred even if a dual braking system was present. A jury verdict was entered in favor of the defendant and plaintiff appealed arguing that the jury was erroneously instructed with respect to the manufacturing defect issue.

 Is a manufacturer strictly liable if it sells a product manufactured in defective condition which is unreasonably dangerous and causes injury to another, direct consumer or otherwise?

 A manufacturer who places a product in the stream of commerce is strictly liable for manufacturing defects of that product that reach the consumer without substantial change in the defective condition and whose defective condition proximately caused injury to the plaintiff.

 A manufacturer who places a product in the stream of commerce is strictly liable for manufacturing defects of that product that reach the consumer without substantial change in the defective condition and whose defective condition proximately caused injury to the plaintiff. A manufacturing defect is an imperfection(s) that inevitably occurs in a small percentage of products of a given design as a natural result of the failure of the manufacturing process. Whether the intended design was safe or not does not affect a *manufacturing* defect claim, though it might impact a claim for injuries relating to a defective *design* of a product. Therefore, provided that the forgoing criteria are met, a manufacturer is strictly liable. The jury was properly instructed regarding manufacturing defects.

 Reversed and remanded.

Prentis v. Yale Mfg. Co.
Supreme Court of Michigan, 365 N.W.2d 176 (1984)

FACTS

Plaintiff John Prentis was employed as a foreman in an automobile dealership's parts department. In April of 1970, he was using a battery-powered forklift to lift an engine into a truck's cargo bed. The forklift was a stand-up or walking type, rather than a riding machine with a seat, and it was operated by lifting its handle up and down, much lie the handle of a wagon. When the machine experienced a power surge, plaintiff lost his footing and fell to the ground. The force of the fall caused multiple fractures to his hip, and it is believed that his injuries resulted from the fall alone. Consequently, plaintiff sued for an alleged design defect, arguing that defendant should have provided a seat or platform for the operator of the forklift. The trial judge refused to instruct the jury on breach of warranty and instead instructed the jury on a single theory of negligent design. The Court of Appeal reversed, holding that both instructions should have been given. An appeal was made to the Supreme Court of Michigan.

 Should a risk-utility balancing test [referred to in the case as a negligence test] apply to products liability actions predicated upon defective design?

 Design defect cases should be judged under a risk-utility balancing test which weighs the risks of injury against the costs of safer design.

 Design defect cases should be judged under a risk-utility balancing test which weighs the risks of injury against the costs of safer design. In manufacturing defect cases, a determination as to whether a product is defective if fairly straightforward since the condition of the product is evaluated only against the manufacturer's own production standards. Whether a product's design is "defective," however, is not so clear-cut. This is because only in design defect cases is a court called upon to supply the standard for defectiveness. To that end, it is condition of the product rather than on the manufacturer's conduct to which the trier of fact must garner attention. Such a task is complex, and there is no simple test. To alleviate this condition, we adopt a pure negligence, risk-utility test in products liability cases predicated upon defective design which tracks the Model Uniform Product Liability Act (UPLA). The approach of the ULPA has been approved by several commentators whose analysis is instructive. First, unlike manufacturing defects, design defects result from deliberate decisions on the part of manufacturers, and plaintiffs should be able to learn about these facts through liberalized modern discovery rules. Second, a negligence standard would encourage the design of safer products by rewarding careful manufacturers and penalizing the careless ones. Third, a high threshold of fault is required in design defect cases, since a verdict for the plaintiff is a determination that the entire product line is defective. The traditional tort law of negligence serves this purpose better. Fourth, the negligence standard promotes a greater intrinsic fairness since a careful manufacturer should not bear the burden of paying for losses caused by a negligent seller. Hence, we find the formula adopted by the ULPA on the question of defective design to have the merit of being clear an understandable. We therefore hold that in this products

Prentis v. Yale Mfg. Co.
Supreme Court of Michigan, 365 N.W.2d 176 (1984)

liability action against a manufacturer for an alleged defect of design, where the jury was properly instructed on the theory of negligent design, the trial judge's refusal to instruct on breach of warranty was not reversible error.

The judgment of the Court of Appeals is reversed and the judgment of the trial court is reinstated.

O'Brien v. Muskin Corp.
Supreme Court of New Jersey, 463 A.2d 298 (1983)

FACTS

Plaintiff Gary O'Brien, then 23 yards of age, was injured after he arrived at his neighbor's home uninvited and dove head-first into an above-ground swimming pool. The swimming pool had four foot walls and was filled with water of about 3 ½ feet deep; the outer wall of the pool bore a decal that warned "DO NOT DIVE" roughly one-half inch high letters. Plaintiff dove either from a platform by the pool or from the roof of an adjacent eight-foot high garage. When plaintiff's outstretched hands hit the bottom of the pool and made contact with the vinyl bottom, his hands slid apart and his head struck the bottom. Plaintiff sued Defendant Muskin Corp., the pool's manufacturer, for a design defect [i.e., the slippery vinyl surface] and for inadequate warnings. The trial court did not allow the jury to consider whether manufacturing the pool with a vinyl liner constituted a design defect; only the adequacy of the decal warning. The appellate division reversed a judgment for defendant and plaintiff appealed.

 Does a plaintiff bear the burden of proving a design defect?

 A plaintiff must make a prima facie showing that the product at issue is defective based on the risk-utility analysis.

 There are a number of tests which can be used for determining whether a product is defective. One test, the consumer expectations test, recognizes that the failure of a product to perform safely may be viewed as a violation of the reasonable expectations of a consumer. This standard does not apply to the instant action, however, because the pool fulfilled its function as a place to swim. However, another test, the risk-utility analysis, is more suitable to the case at bar. Factors relevant to the risk-utility analysis include: the usefulness and desirability of the product; the likelihood that the product will cause injury; the availability of a safer substitute product; the manufacturer's ability to eliminate the unsafe character of the product, and the associated costs; the user's ability to avoid danger by the exercise of reasonable care; the user's anticipated awareness of the inherent dangers and their avoidability; and the feasibility of spreading the loss by price-setting or through liability insurance. However, the plaintiff must establish a prima facie case of defect with reference to the above, and the defendant is free to offer any proof, as part of a viable defense, including "state-of-the-art" evidence. Evidence that the manufacturer designed the product with state-of-the-art technology and materials, together with other evidence relevant to the risk-utility analysis, may constitute a viable defense, though not an absolute defense, supporting a judgment in favor of the defendant. Here, the trial court should have permitted the jury to consider whether the risks of injury so outweighed the utility of the product as to constitute a defect given the dimensions of the pool and the slipperiness of its bottom.

 Affirmed and remanded.

Anderson v. Owens-Corning Fiberglass Corp.

Supreme Court of California, 810 P.2d 549 (1991)

FACTS

Plaintiff Carl Anderson contracted asbestosis and other lung ailments through exposure to asbestos products while working as an electrician at a naval shipyard from 1941 to 1976. Plaintiff encountered the asbestos while working in the vicinity of others who were removing and installing asbestos products aboard ships. Plaintiff sued Defendant Owens-Corning Fiberglas Corp. under a products liability theory, based upon defendant's failure to warn of the risk of harm from asbestos exposure. The trial court allowed state-of-the-art evidence of the known and knowable risks of asbestos at the time defendant distributed their insulation products. The trial court granted a new trial following a verdict for defendant. On appeal, the parties argued the admissibility of state-of-the-art evidence in a failure to warn case.

In an action based upon a warnings defect, is "state-of-the-art" evidence admissible?

In a warnings defect case, evidence of the "state of the art" is admissible in an action based upon an alleged failure to warn; however, evidence that a particular risk was not known or knowable by the defendant at the time of manufacture and/or distribution provides a valid defense.

Knowledge or knowability must be an element of a cause of action for failure to warn in a products liability action. Without it, a manufacturer would become the insurer of the safety of the product's user. Strict liability was never intended to impose absolute liability upon manufacturers in such a way. We reject plaintiff's argument that the requirements of knowledge and knowability together with the admission of state-of-the-art evidence inappropriately introduce negligence concepts into strict liability cases directing the trier of fact's attention to the conduct of the manufacturer rather than to the condition of the product itself. This is permissible. We find support in the fact that many prior decisions have incorporated negligence principles into the strict liability analysis. Moreover, warnings defects necessarily relate to a failure unrelated to the product itself. Thus, while a manufacturing or design defect can be evaluated without reference to the conduct of the manufacturer, a failure to warn can not. Failure to warn in strict liability differs prominently from failure to warn in negligence. Strict liability imposes a much lower burden for plaintiffs - they must prove only that the manufacturer ignored what was generally known or knowable in the scientific community about a product. In a negligence case, however, all the elements must be proven – this includes a showing that the manufacturer was unreasonable, a requirement that does not exist in strict liability.

Affirmed.

Friedman v. General Motors Corp.
Supreme Court of Ohio, 331 N.E.2d 702 (1975)

FACTS

Plaintiff Morton Friedman alleged that when he turned the ignition key on his 17-month-old 1966 Oldsmobile Toronado while the gearshift was in the "drive" position, the vehicle to started, leaped forward, startled him and caused him to lose control, injuring himself and his family. Plaintiff sued Defendant General Motors Corp., the manufacturer, for the alleged defect. At the close of his case, the trial court granted defendant's motion for directed verdict on the ground that plaintiff had not proved that the vehicle was defective. The Court of Appeals reversed the judge's decision, ruling that reasonable minds could differ on the evidence presented and the Ohio Supreme Court granted review.

Was the plaintiff's evidence of sufficient quality to overcome the defendant's motion for a directed verdict; specifically, may a plaintiff utilize circumstantial evidence in order to make a prima facie case of a defective product?

A defect may be proven by circumstantial evidence, where a preponderance of that evidence establishes that the accident was caused by a defect and not other possibilities, although not all possibilities need be eliminated.

In this case, plaintiff was required to prove that the Oldsmobile was defective; that the defect existed at the time the car left the factory; and that the defect was the proximate cause of the accident and injury. The defect may be proven by circumstantial evidence, where a preponderance of that evidence establishes that the accident was caused by a defect and not other possibilities, although not all possibilities need be eliminated. Here, plaintiff did make a prima facie case based on circumstantial evidence. A jury could have found that the transmission linkages and adjustments were original, factory-set, adjustments and the defective condition, if established, was a defect created by the manufacturer and not by some 3rd party after delivery [the car dealership, for example]. Alternatively, the jury might have inferred that the car always started in "Park" or that when the gear shift indicator registered "Drive" after the accident, it accurately reflected the position of the indicator. Finally, the record clearly established that the Oldsmobile could not have started unless the contacts in the neutral start switch were in the Neutral or Park position. Even though the transmission gears and gear shift indicator were in Drive, if the contacts in the neutral start switch were in Neutral or Park, the ignition key would start the car and the front wheels would rotate immediately. Viewing the evidence in a light most favorable to plaintiff, we rule that a reasonable jury could have concluded that defendant was guilty of manufacturing a defective automobile.

Affirmed.

Daly v. General Motors Corp.
Supreme Court of California, 575 P.2d 1162 (1978)

FACTS

The decedent was driving his Opel, a car manufactured by Defendant General Motors, between 50 and 70 miles per hour when he struck a highway divider. The car spun around, and the decedent was thrown from the vehicle and suffered fatal head injuries. The plaintiffs claimed that the door lock was defectively designed because of its exposed push button which, they claim, was forced open during the original collision. Over plaintiffs' objections, the defendants introduced evidence that the vehicle was equipped with a seat belt shoulder harness system and a door lock, either of which if used, would have prevented the deceased from being thrown from the car. The deceased was not wearing his seatbelt, nor were his doors locked, despite the fact that the owner's manual contained warnings to that effect. Moreover, the deceased was intoxicated, which the jury was advised was admitted for the limited purpose of determining whether Daly used the vehicle's safety equipment. The jury returned a verdict for all defendants.

Under California law, should damages be mitigated to reflect the amount the plaintiff's negligent conduct contributed to the injury in a strict liability action involving an alleged product defect?

Where a plaintiff's negligent conduct contributed to his injury, his damages will reduced, if at all, to the extent that his negligent conduct contributed to his injury.

While a defendant's liability for injuries caused by a defective product governed by the law of strict liability, his *damages* for the injuries he sustained will be reduced in proportion to his own negligent conduct. Strict products liability places the burden of loss on manufacturers, rather than on the victims of product defects. Comparative negligence principles are not in opposition to nor frustrated by the policy goals of strict liability law. This is because product liability retains the strict liability doctrine: plaintiffs are still relieved from the burden of proving negligence by the manufacturer or distributor of defective products. The cost of compensating victims of defective products remains on the manufacturer, though proportionately reduced, and will, through him, be "spread among society." And there is no policy reason why such damages, caused by the plaintiff's own negligent conduct, should not be borne, at least in part, by him. Such a policy is consistent with promoting the equitable allocation of loss among all parties in proportion to their fault. Under our present law, assumption of risk by a consumer is a complete defense to a strict liability action for a product defect. Were the same plaintiff to sue under a negligence theory, his own negligence would reduce, but not eliminate, his recovery in proportion to that negligence. Thus, by extending comparative principles to strict liability actions, as we do now, we are in the majority of jurisdictions that have done so.

Reserved.

Ford Motor Co. v. Matthews
Supreme Court of Mississippi, 291 So.2d 169 (1974)

FACTS

Earnest Matthews was killed as a result of being run over by his tractor and dragged underneath a disc attachment. It was alleged that plaintiff was standing beside his tractor when he started it and the tractor was in gear at the time, even though the tractor was equipped with a starter safety switch designed to prevent the tractor from being started in gear. Plaintiff-appellee, the administratrix of Matthews' estate, sued under a strict product liability theory, arguing that a plunger connected to the safety switch was defective and allowed the tractor to be started in gear. The trial court, sitting without a jury, found for the plaintiff-administratrix and entered a judgment against Defendant-appellant Ford Motor Co. for $74,272.65; defendant appealed.

Can a manufacturer be held liable for those injuries caused by the reasonably foreseeable uses of its products?

Manufacturers will be held strictly liable for the reasonably foreseeable uses of their products, including the abnormal, unintended or misuse of the product [if such misuse is also reasonably foreseeable].

A manufacturer will be held strictly liable for injuries caused by reasonably foreseeable uses of its products. Although misuse of a product that causes injury is normally a bar to strict liability, a manufacturer will be held liable if such misuse was reasonably foreseeable. Here, defendant relies on a comment to the Restatement (Second) of Torts section 402A, which states that sellers are not liable for injuries resulting from abnormal handling of a product. However, the cases cited by defendant are ones in which there was no defect, and even if there was a defect, it [the defect] played no part in the causation of the accident. In this case, the failure of the safety switch to prevent the tractor from starting in gear was a cause of the accident. There was no misuse of the product as to relieve defendant from liability. As we have already stated, manufacturers are not liable for injuries resulting from abnormal use of a product if such use was *not* reasonably foreseeable. This was not the case here. Defendant could be foreseen by defendant that a tractor operator might carelessly start a tractor without first making sure that it was not in gear. Thus, even if Matthews was negligent, such negligence was reasonably foreseeable and will not a bar to an action based on strict liability resulting from the defective condition of the tractor.

Affirmed.

Medtronic Inc. v. Lohr

U.S. Supreme Court, 518 U.S. 470 (1996)

FACTS

In response to the mounting consumer and regulatory concern, Congress enacted the statute at issue here: the Medical Device Amendments of 1976 (MDA), 90 Stat. 539. The Act classifies medical devices in three categories based on the risk that they pose to the public. Devices that present no unreasonable risk of illness or injury are designated Class I and are subject only to minimal regulation by "general controls." Devices that are potentially more harmful are designated Class II; although they may be marketed without advance approval, manufacturers of such devices must comply with federal performance regulations known as "special controls." Finally, devices that either "present a potential unreasonable risk of illness or injury," or which are "purported or represented to be for a use in supporting or sustaining human life or for a use which is of substantial importance in preventing impairment of human health," are designated Class III. Pacemakers are Class III devices. Before a new Class III device may be introduced to the market, the manufacturer must provide the FDA with a "reasonable assurance" that the device is both safe and effective. Despite its relatively innocuous phrasing, the process of establishing this "reasonable assurance," which is known as the "premarket approval," or "PMA" process, is a rigorous one. Manufacturers must submit detailed information regarding the safety and efficacy of their devices, which the FDA then reviews, spending an average of 1,200 hours on each submission. Not all, nor even most, Class III devices on the market today have received premarket approval because of two important exceptions to the PMA requirement. First, Congress realized that existing medical devices could not be withdrawn from the market while the FDA completed its PMA analysis for those devices. The statute therefore includes a "grandfathering" provision which allows pre-1976 devices to remain on the market without FDA approval until such time as the FDA initiates and completes the requisite PMA. Second, to prevent manufacturers of grandfathered devices from monopolizing the market while new devices clear the PMA hurdle, and to ensure that improvements to existing devices can be rapidly introduced into the market, the Act also permits devices that are "substantially equivalent" to pre-existing devices to avoid the PMA process. Although "substantially equivalent" Class III devices may be marketed without the rigorous PMA review, such new devices are subject to the requirements of §360(k). That section imposes a limited form of review on every manufacturer intending to market a new device by requiring it to submit a "premarket notification" to the FDA (the process is also known as a "§510(k) process"). If the FDA concludes on the basis of the §510(k) notification that the device is "substantially equivalent" to a pre-existing device, it can be marketed without further regulatory analysis. As a result, the §510(k) premarket notification process became the means by which most new medical devices - including Class III devices - were approved for the market. As have so many other medical device manufacturers, Defendant-petitioner Medtronic Inc. took advantage of §510(k)'s expedited process in October of 1982, when it notified FDA that it intended to market its Model 4011 pacemaker lead as a device that was "substantially equivalent" to devices already on the market. Defendant-Cross petitioner Lora Lohr was dependent on pacemaker technology for the proper functioning of her heart. In 1987 she was implanted with a Medtronic Model 4011 pacemaker. On December 30, 1990, the pacemaker failed, allegedly resulting in a "complete heart block" that required emergency surgery. According to her physician, a defect in the device was the likely cause of the failure. In 1993 Lohr and her husband filed this action alleging negligence and strict liability. The negligence count alleged a breach of Medtronic's "duty

Medtronic Inc. v. Lohr

U.S. Supreme Court, 518 U.S. 470 (1996)

to use reasonable care in the design, manufacture, assembly, and sale of the subject pacemaker." The strict liability count alleged that the device was in a defective condition and unreasonably dangerous to foreseeable users at the time of its sale. A third count alleging breach of warranty was dismissed for failure to state a claim under Florida law. Medtronic removed the case to Federal District Court, where it filed a motion for summary judgment arguing that both the negligence and strict liability claims were pre-empted by 21 U.S.C. §360k(a). The District Court initially denied Medtronic's motion, finding nothing in the statute to support the company's argument. The Court of Appeals reversed in part and affirmed in part - rejecting the Lohrs' broadest submission, it first decided that "common law actions are state requirements within the meaning of §360k(a)," but then held that pre-emption could not be avoided by Medtronic by merely alleging that the negligence flowed from a violation of federal standards and concluded that the Lohrs' negligent design claims were not pre-empted. It rejected Medtronic's argument that the FDA's finding of "substantial equivalence" had any significance with respect to the pacemaker's safety. Medtronic filed a petition for certiorari seeking review of the Court of Appeals' decision in the U.S. Supreme Court insofar as it affirmed the District Court and the Lohrs filed a cross petition seeking review of the judgment insofar as it upheld the pre-emption defense.

 Is a state common-law negligence action against a medical device manufacturer of an allegedly defective apparatus preempted by the Medical Device Amendments of 1976 [a federal statute]?

 The Medical Device Amendments of 1976 does not preempt a state common-law negligence action against a medical manufacturer of an allegedly defective apparatus.

 We turn first to a consideration of petitioner Medtronic's claim that the Court of Appeals should have found the entire action pre-empted and then to the merits of the Lohrs' cross petition. In its petition, Medtronic argues that the Court of Appeals erred by concluding that the Lohrs' claims alleging negligent design were not pre-empted by 21 U.S.C. § 360k(a). That section provides that "no State or political subdivision of a State may establish or continue in effect with respect to a device intended for human use any requirement (1) which is different from, or in addition to, any requirement applicable under this chapter to the device, and (2) which relates to the safety or effectiveness of the device or to any other matter included in a requirement applicable to the device under this chapter." Medtronic suggests that any common law cause of action is a "requirement" which alters incentives and imposes duties "different from, or in addition to" the generic federal standards that the FDA has promulgated in response to mandates under the MDA. In essence, the company argues that the plain language of the statute pre-empts any and all common law claims brought by an injured plaintiff against a manufacturer of medical devices. Medtronic's argument is not only unpersuasive, it is implausible. Under Medtronic's view of the statute, Congress effectively precluded state courts from affording state consumers any protection from injuries resulting from a defective medical device. Moreover, because there is no

Medtronic Inc. v. Lohr
U.S. Supreme Court, 518 U.S. 470 (1996)

explicit private cause of action against manufacturers contained in the MDA, and no suggestion that the Act created an implied private right of action, Congress would have barred most, if not all, relief for persons injured by defective medical devices. Medtronic's construction of §360k would therefore have the perverse effect of granting complete immunity from design defect liability to an entire industry that, in the judgment of Congress, needed more stringent regulation in order "to provide for the safety and effectiveness of medical devices intended for human use," 90 Stat. 539 (preamble to Act). It is, to say the least, "difficult to believe that Congress would, without comment, remove all means of judicial recourse for those injured by illegal conduct," *Silkwood* v. *Kerr McGee Corp.*, and it would take language much plainer than the text of §360k to convince us that Congress intended that result. Furthermore, if Congress intended to preclude all common law causes of action, it chose a singularly odd word with which to do it. The statute would have achieved an identical result, for instance, if it had precluded any "remedy" under state law relating to medical devices. "Requirement" appears to presume that the State is imposing a specific duty upon the manufacturer, and although we have on prior occasions concluded that a statute pre-empting certain state "requirements" could also pre-empt common law damages claims, that statute did not sweep nearly as broadly as Medtronic would have us believe that this statute does. As in *Cipollone v. Liggett Group Inc.,* we are presented with the task of interpreting a statutory provision that expressly pre-empts state law. However, the pre-emptive statute in *Cipollone* was targeted at a limited set of state requirements - those "based on smoking and health" - and then only at a limited subset of the possible applications of those requirements - those involving the "advertising or promotion of any cigarettes the packages of which are labeled in conformity with the provisions of" the federal statute. In that context, giving the term "requirement" its widest reasonable meaning did not have nearly the pre-emptive scope nor the effect on potential remedies that Medtronic's broad reading of the term would have in this case. The Court in *Cipollone* held that the petitioner in that case was able to maintain some common law actions using theories of the case that did not run afoul of the pre-emption statute. Here, however, Medtronic's sweeping interpretation of the statute would require far greater interference with state legal remedies, producing a serious intrusion into state sovereignty while simultaneously wiping out the possibility of remedy for the Lohrs' alleged injuries. Given the ambiguities in the statute and the scope of the preclusion that would occur otherwise, we cannot accept Medtronic's argument that by using the term-requirement," Congress clearly signaled its intent to deprive States of any role in protecting consumers from the dangers inherent in many medical devices. Other differences between this statute and the one in *Cipollone* further convince us that when Congress enacted §360k, it was primarily concerned with the problem of specific, conflicting State statutes and regulations rather than the general duties enforced by common law actions. Unlike the statute at issue in *Cipollone*, §360k refers to "requirements" many times throughout its text. In each instance, the word is linked with language suggesting that its focus is device specific enactments of positive law by legislative or administrative bodies, not the application of general rules of common law by judges and juries. For instance, subsections (a)(2) and (b) of the statute also refer to "requirements"--but those "requirements" refer only to statutory and regulatory law that exists pursuant to the MDA itself, suggesting that the pre-empted "requirements" established or continued by States also refer primarily to positive enactments of state law. Moreover, in subsection (b) the FDA is given authority to exclude certain "requirements" from the scope of the pre-emption statute. Of the limited number of "exemptions" from pre-emption that the FDA has granted, none even remotely resemble common law claims. An examination of the basic purpose of the legislation as well as its history entirely supports our rejection of Medtronic's extreme position. The MDA was enacted "to provide for the safety and effectiveness of medical devices intended for human use." Medtronic asserts that the Act was also intended, however, to-protect innovations in device technology from being `stifled by unnecessary restrictions,' and that this interest extended to the pre-emption of common law claims. While the Act certainly reflects some of these concerns, the legislative history indicates that any fears regarding regulatory burdens were related more to the risk of *additional* federal and state regulation rather than the danger of preexisting duties under common law. Indeed, nowhere in the materials relating to the Act's history have we discovered a reference to a fear that product liability actions would hamper the development of medical devices. To the extent that Congress was concerned about protecting the industry, that intent was manifested primarily through fewer substantive requirements under the Act, not the pre-emption provision; furthermore, any such concern was far outweighed by concerns about the primary issue motivating the MDA's enactment: the safety of those who use medical devices. The legislative history also confirms our understanding that §360(k) simply was not intended to pre-empt most, let alone all, general common law duties enforced by damages actions. There is, to the best of our knowledge, nothing in the hearings, the committee reports, or the debates suggesting that any proponent of the legislation intended a sweeping pre-emption of traditional common law remedies against manufacturers and distributors of defective devices. If Congress intended such a result, its failure even to hint at it is spectacularly odd, particularly since Members of both Houses were acutely aware of ongoing product liability litigation. Along with the less than precise language of §360k(a), that silence surely indicates that at least some common law claims against medical device manufacturers may be maintained after the enactment of the MDA. Accordingly, the judgment of the Court of Appeals is reversed insofar as it held that any of the claims were preempted and affirmed insofar as it rejected the preemption defense.

 The cases are remanded for further proceedings.

Peterson v Lou Bachrodt Chevrolet Co.
Supreme Court of Illinois, 329 N.E.2d 785 (1975)

FACTS

Two young siblings, Maradean and Mark Peterson, aged 11 and 8, respectively, were struck by a 1965 Chevrolet on September 3, 1971. Maradean died on the day of the accident, and one of Mark's legs had to be amputated. Plaintiff James Peterson, the children's father, sued the driver of the used car, its owners, and the used car dealer, Defendant Lou Bachrodt Chevrolet Company for the wrongful death of his daughter and in strict liability. Plaintiff alleged that defendant sold the used car on June 11, 1971 in a defective condition; that the car was not reasonably safe for driving because the braking system was missing several essential pieces. Defendant defended on the ground that it was not liable under a strict products liability theory. The circuit court dismissed the products liability count, the appellate court reversed, and the Illinois Supreme Court granted review.

 Can a second-hand retailer, who is outside of the original manufacturing-retaining-marketing chain of the allegedly product, be held liable under a strict products liability theory?

 A second-hand retailer, who is outside of the original manufacturing-retaining-marketing chain of the allegedly defective product, is not subject to strict products liability.

 A second-hand retailer, who is outside of the original manufacturing-retaining-marketing chain of the allegedly defective product, is not subject to strict products liability. The basic premise of strict liability is that losses should be borne by those who have created the risk and reaped the profit by placing the product in the stream of commerce. While we have previously imposed strict products liability upon wholesalers through whose warehouse a packaged product passed unopened. That imposition of liability, and that imposed on some retailers, was justified because their position in the marketing process enabled them to exert pressure on the manufacturer to enhance the safety of the product. Hence, a wholesaler or retailer who neither creates nor assumes the risk is entitled to indemnity from the party who is ultimately responsible - the manufacturer. In this case, however, there is no evidence that the defect [in the braking system] existed when the product [the car] left the control of the manufacturer. Nor is there any evidence that the defect was created by the second-hand retailer itself – i.e., the used car dealer. Hence, we decline to make used car dealers the insurer against defects which come into existence *after* the chain of distribution was completed.

 Judgment of the Appellate Court is reversed and the circuit court is affirmed.

Hector v. Cedars-Sinai Medical Center
Court of California, 225 Cal.Rptr. 595 (1986)

FACTS

Plaintiff Frances Hector was implanted with a defective pacemaker at Defendant Cedars-Sinai Medical Center which was manufactured by American Technology Inc. Plaintiff sued defendant for negligence, strict liability and breach of warranty; the latter moved for partial summary judgment on the strict liability and breach of warranty claims alleging as a matter of law that there were no triable issues of fact because it was not a part of the production and marketing endeavor, thus barring any liability on its part. Defendant maintained that it simply provided medical services to plaintiff. The trial court granted the defendant's motion and the plaintiff appealed, arguing the court erred in finding the defendant exempt from the application of the strict products liability doctrine.

Is a provider of medical services subject to strict products liability?

Providers of medical services are not subject to strict products liability.

A provider of medical services is not subject to strict products liability. Strict liability has been extended to retailers who are engaged in the business of distributing goods to the public, but only where they play an integral and vital part in the overall production and marketing enterprise. Courts have declined to apply strict liability to those who are "outside of the chain;" that is, those entities who are not involved in the manufacture, wholesale, retail or marketing system. In this case, defendant does not manufacture pacemakers or routinely stock pacemakers. Nor is it in the business of recommending, selling, distributing or testing pacemakers. Defendant simply provides professional medical services. This is the essence of the relationship between it and the plaintiff. Therefore, it is not subject to strict liability. The rational behind the imposition of strict liability is to insure that the costs of injuries are borne by the manufacturers rather than powerless consumers. In this case, defendant is in no position to pressure the manufacturer of the pacemaker to make a safer product. If liability were imposed upon defendant, it would have to distribute the risks and costs among the public, resulting in higher costs for health care. This is not sound public policy. In light of the above, we conclude that the trial court did not err in granting the motion for partial summary judgment.

The order is affirmed.

Philadelphia Electric Co. v. Hercules Inc.
United States Court of Appeals, 762 F.2d 303 (3rd Cir. 1985)

FACTS

Property originally owned by the Pennsylvania Industrial Chemical Corporation ("PICCO"), "the Chester site," was sold to Gould in 1971 and then resold to Plaintiff Philadelphia Electric Co. ("PECO") in 1974. PICCO operated a hydrocarbon resin manufacturing plant at the site. Several years later, the Pennsylvania Department of Environmental Resources, a state agency, discovered that toxic materials similar to those once produced by PICCO were seeping out of the property and into the Delaware River. Plaintiff, the present owner, was forced to cleanup the pollution at a cost of almost $400,000. Thereafter, plaintiff sued Defendant Hercules, Inc, the successor-in-interest to PICCO, to recover the damages and to enjoin any further pollution. As PICCO's successor, defendant expressly agreed to assume all debts, obligations and liabilities of PICCO. Plaintiff's suit was premised on public and private nuisance claims. The district court awarded damages and an injunction in favor of plaintiff and the defendant appealed.

 Can a purchaser of real property recover from a seller under a *private nuisance* theory for conditions existing on the actual land transferred, thereby circumventing vendor liability inherent in the rule of *caveat emptor* ["let the buyer beware"]?

 Does a plaintiff have standing to bring an action for *public nuisance* when he/it suffers no "particular damage" and whose specific rights have not been disturbed in the exercise of a right common to the general public?

 An action for *private nuisance* can generally be brought only by neighboring landowners and requires an invasion of another's interest in the private use and enjoyment of land; actions for *public nuisance* exist where there is an unreasonable interference with a right common to the general public and can be brought by members of the public whose general rights have been interfered with and who have suffered "particular damage" as a result.

 A seller of real property is not liable to a purchaser of the property for private nuisance. A private nuisance is the non-trespassory invasion of another's interest in the private use and enjoyment of his land. In this case, defendant did not interfere with plaintiff's use and enjoyment of the land as the doctrine of *caveat emptor* ("let the buyer beware") applies. *Caveat emptor* thus shifts the risks of the sale from the seller to the buyer. Here, the plaintiff-buyer had a full opportunity to inspect the condition of the land prior to purchase, and we must assume that the price of the land was appropriately discounted to reflect the toxic condition. Although defendant could be liable for private nuisance to *neighboring land owners*, defendant is not liable to plaintiff who was a remote purchaser of the land. Turning to the second issue at bar, we hold that a party has no standing to bring a claim for public nuisance when the party suffers no particular damage in the exercise of a right common to the general public. An action for public nuisance is a low-grade criminal offense, in which a party interfering with a public right may be liable. To recover for a public nuisance, a party must suffer a kind of harm different from that suffered by other members of the general public. Here, the plaintiff suffered no such harm, since the right

Philadelphia Electric Co. v. Hercules Inc.

United States Court of Appeals, 762 F.2d 303 (3rd Cir. 1985)

interfered with by defendant actions was the right to "pure water." Plaintiff did not allege that it used the waters in the Delaware River itself, or that it was directly harmed in any way by the pollution of those waters. Thus, as the purchaser of PICCO's land, plaintiff had no cause of action against PICCO's successor, the defendant, for private or public nuisance.

The injunction is accordingly vacated and the judgment for damages is reversed.

Morgan v. High Pen Oil Co.
Supreme Court of North Carolina, 77 S.E.2d 682 (1953)

FACTS

Plaintiff Morgan owned a tract of land on which he had a dwelling, a restaurant, and accommodations for 32 trailers. Defendant High Penn Oil Co. owned an adjoining tract on which it operated an oil refinery at a distance of about 1,000 feet from plaintiff's dwelling. Plaintiff complained that on several occasions the refinery emitted nauseating gases which invaded his land and rendered persons of ordinary sensitiveness uncomfortable and sick. Defendant failed to put an end to its atmospheric pollution after notice and demand from the plaintiff. Thereafter, plaintiff then sued to recover damages and to obtain an injunction. The trial court, finding that there was a private nuisance, entered a judgment in favor of plaintiff for $2,500 and enjoined defendant from continuing the nuisance. Defendant appealed.

Must private nuisances classified as nuisance *per accidens* or in fact be operated negligently in order to establish a cause of action for private nuisance?

An intentional interference which interferes with another's use and enjoyment of his land is an nuisance which is actionable at law, even if the offending party does not do so in a negligent manner.

Negligence is not required to establish a cause of action for private nuisance. There are two types of private nuisance - nuisances *per se*, or at law, and *per accidens*, or in fact. Nuisances *per se* are acts, occupations or structures that are at all times and under any circumstances nuisances, regardless of location or surroundings. In this case, defendant's oil refinery is a lawful enterprise, so it cannot constitute negligence *per se*. Nuisances *per accidens* become nuisances by reason of their location or the manner in which they are operated. Defendant incorrectly asserts that its refinery cannot become a nuisance *per accidens* unless it is constructed or operated in a negligent manner. An invasion of another's interest in the use and enjoyment of land is intentional when the person causing the nuisance acts for the purpose of causing it, or knows that it is resulting from his conduct, or knows that it is substantially certain to result from his conduct. Negligence plays no part here; it is not an element of liability. In this case, defendant intentionally and unreasonably caused noxious gases and odors to escape onto plaintiff property. This pollution substantially impaired the plaintiff's use and enjoyment of his land. Thus, defendant is liable for intentional private nuisance *per accidens*, and an injunction and damages is appropriate. New trial ordered, however, because of an error in the jury instructions.

New trial ordered.

Carpenter v. The Double R Cattle Company Inc.

Supreme Court of Idaho, 701 P.2d 222 (1985)

FACTS

Plaintiff-appellant Carpenter was a homeowner in Idaho living near a cattle feedlot operated by Defendant-appellee The Double R Cattle Company, Inc. Plaintiff alleged that defendant's feedlot, which had been expanded to accommodate the feeding of approximately 9,000 cattle, caused noxious odors, the pollution of river and ground water, insect infection, birds, dust and noise. The trial court found that the feedlot did not constitute a nuisance. Plaintiff appealed, and the Court of Appeals reversed on the ground that the trial court failed to give a jury instruction that the injured party could be compensated even though the gravity of harm is outweighed by the utility of conduct if the harm is "serious" and the payment of damages is "feasible" without forcing the business to discontinue. The Idaho Supreme Court granted defendant's petition for review.

In Idaho, should the interests of the community, which includes the utility of the conduct at issue, be considered in determining the existence of a nuisance?

In Idaho, should compensation be given to persons suffering from a continuing nuisance, while allowing the nuisance to continue?

In Idaho, the interests of the community, which includes the utility of the conduct at issue, should be considered in determining the existence of a nuisance and where a serious nuisance is allowed to continue, the injured party need not be compensated for the interference.

The interests of the community, which include the utility of the conduct, should be considered in determining the existence of a nuisance. Our state is sparsely populated and its economy depends largely upon the benefits of agriculture, lumber, mining and industry. To refuse to consider the utility of certain agricultural conduct when ruling on nuisance liability would place an unreasonable burden on the agriculture industry upon which our state depends. With regard to the compensation issue, we hold that compensation need not be given to persons suffering from a continuing nuisance. While §826(b) of the Restatement (Second) of Torts allows for the finding of a continuing nuisance and for the payment of compensation to the injured parties, we feel that this would unreasonably burden the person causing the nuisance. Thus, defendant need not compensate plaintiff and the cattle feedlot can continue to operate. In sum, we find that the trial court did not err in refusing to give an instruction based on Section 826 (b) of the Restatement, which does not represent the law of our state.

Affirmed.

Winget v. Win-Dixie Stores Inc.

Supreme Court of South Carolina, 130 S.E.2d 363 (1963)

FACTS

Plaintiff Winget brought an action for damages and a permanent injunction against Defendant Winn-Dixie Stores, Inc., alleging that its newly constructed retail grocery store in Sumter, South Carolina constituted a nuisance both because of its proximity in relation to plaintiff's property and the manner of its operation. Plaintiff alleged that the store attracted crowds of people and automobiles which caused traffic and fumes; that defendant erected fans which blew against the trees on plaintiff's property; that floodlights from the store cast a bright glare over his property, and that noxious odors, paper and trash from the store encroached on his land. At the close of trial, defendant moved for a directed verdict and the trial court held that the evidence was lacking to sustain the plaintiff's allegations. Nevertheless, the trial court submitted the issue of nuisance [with respect to the operation of the store] to the jury. The jury awarded $5,000 of damages to plaintiff, but the judge denied injunctive relief. Defendant appealed.

 Can the operation of a lawful business in an area lawfully zoned constitute a nuisance because of its location?

 Do interfering acts by the defendant which are not normal or necessary incidents of the operation of the nuisance-causing business give rise to damages which are actionable?

 The operation of a lawful business in an area lawfully zoned does not constitute a nuisance because of its location; however, even a lawfully zoned business may be a nuisance if it is operated so as to unreasonably interfere with the health of its neighbors, or their use or enjoyment of their land.

 The operation of a lawful business in a properly zoned area does not constitute a nuisance by reason of its location. In this case, defendant properly located its store in an area zoned for retail business, and the mere location does not constitute a nuisance. Turning to the second issue, we hold that interfering acts by the defendant which are not normal or necessary incidents of the operation of the nuisance-causing business can give rise to damages which are actionable. Lawfully zoned businesses may not unreasonably interfere with the health or comfort of their neighbors. Here, the crowds of customers, automobile traffic, trash trucks and street sweepers do not support a cause of action for nuisance because all are natural consequences of the operation of the grocery store itself. On the other hand, the wind from the fans, the floodlights, the noxious odors, and the trash, all give rise to a reasonable inference that such acts are not the normal incidents of the operation of the business. Thus, the trial judge properly denied defendant's motion for directed verdict and properly allowed the determination to be made by the jury. That said, defendant's motion for a new trial should be granted because the trial court erred in admitting testimonial evidence of depreciation in market value of the property. Damages were improperly calculated because the *location* of the supermarket did not, in itself, constitute a nuisance. Therefore, the amount of the judgment awarded in favor of the plaintiffs for the diminution in property value, was erroneous. Only damages that may have resulted from defendant's *operation* of the supermarket should have been considered. The failure to strike the testimony was prejudicial.

Reversed and remanded.

Boomer v. Atlantic Cement Co. Inc.

Court of Appeals of New York, 309 N.Y.S2d 312 (1970)

FACTS

Defendant Atlantic Cement Company operated a large cement plant near Albany, New York. Neighboring land owners, including Plaintiff Boomer and others, brought suit against the defendant for nuisance claiming that the dirt, smoke, and vibration emanating from the plant caused injury to their properties. The trial court found that a nuisance existed; allowed temporary damages but denied the requested injunction.

 Should the court resolve the litigation between the parties as equitably as possible or should it channel private litigation into broad public objectives seeking the promotion of the general public welfare?

 A court may grant injunctive relief to the plaintiff *conditioned on* the payment of permanent damages by the defendant to the plaintiff; an act which would compensate the latter for the total economic loss to their property, present and future, caused by the defendant's operations, and preclude future recovery by them or their grantees, upon proof that the defendant maintained a nuisance that caused damage to the plaintiffs' property.

 A court may grant an injunction that is conditioned on the defendant's payment of permanent damages to the plaintiff. New York has abandoned the rule which mandates an injunction upon a finding of a nuisance. In its place, a court may grant an injunction which would have the effect of halting all of the defendant's operations, but then lift that injunction once the defendant pays the plaintiff permanent damages. The theory of damage is the "servitude on land" of plaintiffs imposed by defendant's nuisance. The judgment, by allowance of permanent damages imposing a servitude on the land, which is the basis of the actions, has the effect of precluding future recovery by plaintiffs or their grantees. Moreover, the payment of permanent damages to the plaintiff seems the more equitable and fair solution: It compensates the plaintiff for his total economic loss to property but does not destroy the defendant's business because it does not shut down the defendant's business operations. An alternative approach and solution which grants injunctive relief conditioned on the defendant's eliminating the nuisance by a certain future date seems both legally and technologically unworkable. We have no way of knowing how quickly, if at all, technology will progress to allow the defendant to improve its operations and eliminate the nuisance; and a defendant has no control over the rate of such research. Moreover, added court supervision over the projected time period would stymie the our judicial system.

 Reversed.

Spur Industries, Inc. v. Del E. Webb Development Co.

Supreme Court of Arizona, 494 P.2d 700 (1972)

FACTS

The area located along Grand Avenue; roughly 15 mi. west of the urban center of Phoenix was first put into agricultural use in 1911 and was used primarily for farm-related activities until the late 1950s. Four years later, the retirement community of Youngtown was established in the region for senior citizens. By 1956, feedlots were developed about 2 ½ miles south of Grand Avenue and by mid 1959, between 7,500 and 8,500 head of cattle were being fed there. In May 1959, Plaintiff Del E. Webb Development Co. (Webb) commenced development on a residential community known as Sun City using 20,000 acres of farmland it previously purchased; land that was less expensive than the land closer to Phoenix. One year later, Defendant Spur Industries Inc. (Spur) bought the feedlots and began an operational and geographic expansion program. In early 1960, Webb offered these newly built homes for sale, situated just 2 ½ miles north of the Spur lots. Four months later, roughly 500 houses were either completed or in the process of being built. Ironically, at this juncture, Plaintiff Webb did not consider the smells emanating from defendant's feedlots to be problematic and continued its expansion south of Grand Avenue. By 1962, the feedlots grew to 114 acres from 35. By December 1967, defendant's lots were within 500 ft. of Webb's property. Only Plaintiff Webb filed an action to enjoin defendant's operation of the feedlots, arguing it was public nuisance; the citizens of Sun City and Youngtown did not. At the time of the complaint, 20,000 to 30,000 head of cattle were being fed producing over 1,000,000 lbs. of manure per day. Although the defendant employed suitable housekeeping practices with regard to the lots, the odor and flies nonetheless created an annoying, if not unhealthy situation. The citizens of Sun City eventually complained about the situation and Webb faced sales resistance with regard to selling new homes in the area.

(1) Can a lawful activity become a nuisance because others have moved into the area <u>after</u> the commencement of the activity and thus be subject to the nuisance? (2) Assuming such an activity can be enjoined, should the injunction-requesting party be required to provide compensation for the cost of ending the activity?

A lawful activity can become a nuisance and thus be enjoined if others thereafter entered the zone of activity; however, if the party requesting the injunction created the need for the injunction, that party can be required to provide compensation for relocating or halting the nuisance-causing activity.

(1) Yes. A lawful activity can become a nuisance and thus be enjoined if others thereafter entered the zone of activity. A public nuisance is one that affects the rights enjoyed by the general public. In the instant case, we are persuaded that the feedlots constituted both a public and private nuisance to the extent that the Sun City residents were involved. Arizona State law §36-601 codifies public nuisances as including "any conditional place in populous areas which constitutes a breeding place for flies, which are capable of carrying and transmitting disease-causing organisms to any person or persons." Accordingly, Sun City fulfills the "populous area" element of the law. Additionally, we note that the plaintiff lost sales, a real and apparent injury, such that it had standing to bring this action. (2) Yes. The complaining party can be required to provide recompense to the nuisance-causing party for the cost of relocating

Spur Industries Inc. v. Del E. Webb Development Co.

Supreme Court of Arizona, 494 P.2d 700 (1972)

or ceasing the activity. It is important to note that a court of equity is charged with the protection of all parties' interests, not just the public's interest. As such, the interests of a lawful business operation whose activities thereafter become a nuisance because of the encroachment of others must also be protected. In these so called "coming to the nuisance" cases, the law has held the complaining party may not obtain relief if it came to an area with knowledge that the area was used or to be used for industrial or agricultural development. But the law is flexible to advance what is fair and practical under a given set of facts. In the instant case, the evidence shows that Spur Industries and its predecessors in title were unaware at the time their feedlot operation commenced that an entire city would be built around them forcing them to move and defendant must move its operations because it is in the public's interest to do so. Similarly, plaintiff is entitled to relief because of the damage caused by the defendant's feedlot activities upon the Sun City residents. However, it would be inequitable to allow Webb, a real estate developer, who has already received the benefit of low rural land prices to build a city and then use the existence of that city as a tool to neutralize a nuisance without paying the offender. We stress, however, that this type of relief is narrowly drawn and applied to specific causes of action where a developer has brought in those very residents which cause the once lawful activity to become a nuisance. Thus, having brought people to the nuisance to the foreseeable detriment of Spur, Webb must indemnify Spur for a reasonable amount of the cost of moving or shutting down.

A lawful activity can become a nuisance and thus be enjoined if others thereafter entered the zone of activity; however, if the party requesting the injunction created the need for the injunction, that party can be required to provide compensation for relocating or halting the nuisance-causing activity. Judgment affirmed in part, reversed in part, and remanded.

Belli v. Orlando Daily Newspapers Inc.

U.S. Court of Appeals, 389 F.2d 579 (5th Cir. 1967)

FACTS

In 1955, Plaintiff-attorney Melvin Belli, a lawyer of national prominence, agreed to serve as a member on one of the panels at the Florida Bar Association's annual convention in Miami. Plaintiff served on the panel with the understanding that the Florida Bar would pay his and his wife's hotel bill. Nine years later, Miss. Jean Yothers, a columnist, published an article in the Orlando Evening Star, recounting a story that she had been told by another attorney, one Leon Handley, which stated, in effect, that plaintiff had charged hundreds of dollars of clothing to his hotel room and then left Florida, "taking" the Florida bar and leaving them to pay the entire tab. That this was his "plan" all along. The story was admittedly false. Plaintiff sued Defendant Orlando Daily Newspapers, Inc., owner of the Orlando Evening Star, for damages resulting from the libelous article and slanderous [oral] story. The district court dismissed plaintiff's complaint holding [erroneously] that whether a statement is defamatory *per se* is for the court to decide. Plaintiff appealed arguing that whether the publication was capable of having a defamatory interpretation is for a jury to determine, not the court.

 If a publication is capable of being interpreted or construed in two different ways; one defamatory and one not, who determines whether the defamatory interpretation should govern?

 Where the character of statement is ambiguous, the trier of fact, and not the court, must determine whether it constitutes a defamatory publication.

 Where the character of statement is open to more than one interpretation, the trier of fact, and not the court, must determine whether it constitutes a defamatory publication. In Florida, a written statement constitutes libel per se if it is: a) false, b) unprivileged, and c) exposes a person to distrust, hatred, contempt, ridicule, or obloquy, or d) has the tendency to injure a person in his personal, social, official, or business relations or life. In Florida, the court must initially determine whether the words at issue are capable of more than one meaning. If so, then the jury must determine whether the statement was in fact defamatory. On the other hand, if only meaning can be construed and the statement is *not* considered ambiguous, then the *court* may declare the statement defamatory or not. Here, Yothers' statement was capable of being interpreted as conveying that plaintiff tricked and deceived the Florida Bar out of hundreds of dollars. We think that the statement does carry a defamatory meaning. In contrast, the defendant has shown that the article may be reasonably interpreted as non-defamatory. Thus, it is for the jury to determine whether plaintiff has, in fact, been defamed.

 Reversed and remanded.

Grant v. Reader's Digest Association

U.S. Court of Appeals, 151 F.2d 733 (2nd Cir. 1945)

FACTS

Defendant Reader's Digest Association, a New York Corporation, published in its periodical read by the general public, a false statement that Plaintiff Sidney S. Grant was a representative of the Communist Party. Plaintiff -attorney, a Massachusetts lawyer sued defendant for libel. The district court dismissed the complaint for insufficiency in law upon its face [failure to state a claim]. Plaintiff appealed.

Should the defamatory nature of a statement be determined in reference to how "right minded" people [the majority norm of the general public] would understand the statement?

A statement may be defamatory if it injures a person's reputation in the minds of some people, without reference whether these people are "right minded," the majority, the so-called "norm" of society, or "wrong minded," the so-called minority viewpoint of society.

A statement may be defamatory provided that there are *some* people in whom the statement would arouse hatred, contempt, scorn and the like. Whether or not this statement damaged the reputation of the plaintiff to a degree necessary to be considered libelous is for the jury to decide. In making their determination, they are not limited to determining how "right-minded" people would feel about the statement so long as there are some people who might find the statement libelous. The district court erred in imposing the "right-minded" standard.

Judgment reversed and the cause remanded.

Kilian v. Doubleday & Co. Inc.
Supreme Court of Pennsylvania, 79 A.2d 657 (1951)

FACTS

Joseph O'Connell was a soldier and disabled veteran of World War II. He and other disabled veterans were students in an English class at the American University in Washington. The course consisted, in part, of the writing by the students of essays or stories about their personal experiences in the war. Each student in the class, 53 in all, wrote an account. O'Connell wrote about the incidents that allegedly occurred at the Lichfield Camp in England. His story and several other essays from the students in the class were published in a book by Defendant Doubleday & Co., Inc. O'Connell's essay narrated incidents said to have occurred at Lichfield and were described to him by those who allegedly had actually witnessed them. However, O'Connell wrote in the first person, and the essay read as if he was actually at Lichfield and had actually witnessed and experienced the events he wrote about. Several accounts in his story involved Plaintiff Colonel James A. Kilian, the commanding officer at Lichfield at the time, who was described as a dictator and who was described as often imposing cruel and unusual punishment on the soldiers. These events were laid out in graphic detail. At the end of the article, O'Connell's English professor, Dr. Wolf, appended a footnote which stated that plaintiff was convicted of permitting cruel and unusual punishment. What the story failed to mention, however, was that plaintiff was acquitted of any and all of the foregoing charges. At trial, defendant asserted that the story was a true and accurate account, an affirmative defense to the plaintiff's charge of libel. Yet no witnesses at trial could substantiate the truthfulness of the story. The trial court charged the jury that if they found the defendant's account to be substantially true, then a judgment would be rendered in his favor [he would be held not liable]. The jury rendered a verdict for defendant. Plaintiff challenged the jury instruction and appeals the refusal of the trial court to grant a new trial.

 Should a court instruct the jury that if they find the defendant's account to be substantially true, such a finding serves as an absolute defense to defamation charge when the evidence does not support the charge of deformation?

 The court should not *instruct* the jury as to the defense of "substantial truth" if no evidence is presented in support of the charge, even though substantial truth is a valid absolute defense.

 The court should not instruct the jury as to the defense of "substantial truth" if no evidence is presented in support of the charge, even though substantial truth is a valid absolute defense. If O'Connell's account of the events at Lichfield were even substantially true, then defendant could not be held liable for its publication. This is because truth is an absolute defense to defamation. However, this was not the case here. O'Connell was not an eyewitness to any of the accounts in his story and none of the witnesses at trial could substantiate the specific defamatory accounts made about plaintiff while at Lichfield. Moreover, while it was true that plaintiff had been charged of aiding and abetting the imposition of cruel and unusual punishment, the footnote recounted his conviction without stating that he had been acquitted. The implication here was that plaintiff was actually guilty of the charge and that defendant was essentially corroborating the accounts of cruel punishment. In light of

Kilian v. Doubleday & Co. Inc.
Supreme Court of Pennsylvania, 79 A.2d 657 (1951)

---

the above, the court should not have submitted to the jury the question whether the publication was substantially true.

Reversed and new trial awarded.

Neiman-Marcus v. Lait

U.S District Court, Southern Dist. Of New York, 13 F.R.D. 311 (1952)

FACTS

Defendant Lait and others authored a book entitled "U.S.A. Confidential" that contained several defamatory references to employees of Plaintiff Neiman-Marcus Co, a Texas corporation operating a department store in Dallas. Specifically, the book stated that several of plaintiff's models were call girls; that the plaintiff's salesgirls were also call girls who were more fun, were not at "snooty" as the models and who charged substantially for their "services;" that many of the plaintiff's designers were "faggots" and that most of the salesmen were "fairies." The class of plaintiffs consisted of 9 individual models suing together as a group, 15 of 25 salesmen, 30 of 382 saleswomen, and the Neiman-Marcus Corporation itself. Defendant brought a motion to dismiss the claims of each group of plaintiffs.

Where a publication libels some or less than all of a designated small group, does a cause of action exist for each individual member of the group?

Where a publication libels some but not all of the persons in a designated small group, a cause of action exists in individual members of the group.

Where a publication libels some but not all people in a designated small group, a cause of action exists in individual members of the group. Where the group or class libeled is large, no member can sue even though the language used includes all members. On the other hand, where the group or class libeled is small, and each and every member of the class is referred to, then any individual member can sue. These are widely accepted prepositions. However, conflict arises when the publication libels some or less than all of a designated small group. Some courts say no cause of action exists in any individual of the group; other courts allow such an action. Here, we find that the plaintiff salesmen do have a cause of action. This is because of the language used to defame, namely that "most . . . are fairies." It is fairly specific. Accordingly, defendant's motion to dismiss the salesmen for failure to state a claim upon which relief can be granted is denied. However, the plaintiff saleswomen do not have a cause of action. The alleged defamatory statements in defendants' book speak of the saleswomen *generally;* the statement does not refer to some specific ascertained member of the class. Moreover, the group of saleswomen is large, consisting of 382 members and no reasonable person would conclude that defendant was actually referring to any specific, individual saleswoman. Thus, the 30 saleswomen fail to allege that any of them specifically were defamed. Accordingly, defendant's motion to dismiss their cause of action is granted. The entire complaint is dismissed with leave to file separate complaints as to the salesmen, models, and the corporation.

See Rule above.

Bindrim v. Mitchell

Court of Appeal of California, Second Dist., 92 Cal.App.3d 155 (1979)

FACTS

Plaintiff Paul Bindrim, a Ph.D. and licensed psychologist, conducted "nude marathon" in group therapy to help people overcome their inhibitions via the removal of their clothes. Defendant Gwen Davis Mitchell, a successful novelist, attended plaintiff's nude-therapy weekend. Defendant signed a contract promising not to write anything regarding the workshop or take any photographs of the event. Nevertheless, shortly thereafter, defendant contracted with Doubleday (co-defendant), a publishing house, and published a novel called *Touching* based on the nude-therapy technique she observed. The novel was critical of nude therapy and included Dr. Simon Herford, a fictional psychiatrist and lead character who conducted nude therapy in the same manner as plaintiff. Plaintiff sued both defendants for libel; the jury awarded substantial damages to the former. The court granted a new trial conditioned on plaintiff's acceptance of a remittitur and all parties to this action appealed.

 Can a fictional story be considered defamatory if reasonable readers could reasonably construe the account to be about the plaintiff?

 A fictional story can be considered libelous if sensible readers could reasonably construe the account to be about or represent the plaintiff.

 A fictional story can be considered libelous if sensible readers could reasonably construe the account to be about or represent the plaintiff. Both defendants contend on appeal that plaintiff failed to show that he [plaintiff] was identified as the fictional character, Dr. Herford, in the book. In support of their contention, both defendants cite *Wheeler v. Dell Publishing Co.*, which involved an alleged libel caused by a fictional account of an actual murder. In *Wheeler*, a reasonable person who was in the position to identify the real person with the fictional character in the account would not have reasonably identified and equated the two - the character in *Wheeler* was very different from the real-life individual. This is in contrast to the instant facts where several witnesses who read defendant's novel identified plaintiff as the actual fictional character. Although Dr. Herford [the fictional character in the book] had a different physical description than plaintiff, the Herford practiced nearly identical nude therapy as the plaintiff such that a reasonable person reading *Touching* would understand that Herford was, in actual fact, the plaintiff. Judgment is affirmed, although it is modified as to damages.

 Affirmed.

Shor v. Billingsley
Supreme Court, New York County, Special Term, 158 N.Y.S.2d 476 (1956)

FACTS

On a nationwide television show, one person ad-libbed the remark: "Want to know something? I wish I had as much money as [plaintiff] owes . . . [to] everybody . . ." [We assume that the defendant, Billingsley was sued by Plaintiff Shor for libel.] Defendant brought a motion to dismiss on the ground that the remark was spoken, and thus could not form the basis for a cause of action for libel.

Can a defamatory remark, not read from a script but [ad-libbed] from a telecast, and broadcasted on a nationwide televised program constitute libel?

A defamatory remark broadcasted on a nationwide televised program, not read from a script but ad-libbed, constitutes libel.

A defamatory remark broadcasted on a nationwide televised program constitutes libel. The appellate courts in our jurisdiction have held that the utterance of defamatory remarks, *read from a script* into a microphone and broadcast, constitute the publication of libel. However, the fact that defendant's comments were *ad-libbed*, and not read from a script, does not alter the analysis or its conclusion – it is libel. Radio reaches a vast audience, and the broadcast of scandalous utterances is in general as potentially harmful as a publication by writing. This is true even though radio broadcasts lack the same durability as written libel. It still has the equal capacity to damage a reputation. Because damage is the basis for common-law defamation, defamation by radio should be actionable *per se* as libel. Accordingly, no special damages need to be proven.

The motion to dismiss is denied.

Terwilliger v Wands

Court of Appeals of New York, 17 N.Y. 54 (1858)

FACTS

Defendant Terwilliger made several disparaging statements to a third party regarding Plaintiff Wands. Specifically, defendant stated, among other comments and upon asking some questions, that plaintiff went to Mrs. Fuller's house in order to have intercourse with Mrs. Fuller, and that plaintiff did all that he could to keep Mrs. Fuller's husband in the penitentiary so he could have free access to her. Plaintiff sued defendant for slander. The only damages proven were that plaintiff became ill and was unable to work after hearing the reports circulated by defendant. Defendant moved for nonsuit and the court sustained the motion.

Must the plaintiff prove special damages that were the natural, immediate and legal consequence of the words spoken when bringing an action for slander against a defendant?

In an action for slander, the plaintiff must prove special damages that were the immediate consequence of the words spoken.

In an action for slander, the plaintiff must prove special damages that were the natural, immediate and legal consequence of the words spoken. The only exception to this rule is in cases of slander *per se,* where no special damages need be proven. The defamation in the instant action can not be considered slander *per se*. Hence, plaintiff must state some particular damage to his reputation, and he must prove that he was prevented by the slander from receiving that which would otherwise be conferred upon him. In this case, the plaintiff provided evidence of his physical sickness but did not prove that anybody who heard the remarks actually treated plaintiff differently or that the statement had even the slightest influence upon the listeners' opinion of him after it was heard. Thus, plaintiff's sickness must be ascribed to his own personal *apprehension* of a perceived loss of his character by others, rather than any *actual* loss of reputation, since there was no evidence offered of any *actual* harm. Consequently, plaintiff cannot recover for slander.

Judgment affirmed.

Economopoulos v. A.G. Pollard Co.
Supreme Judicial Court of Massachusetts, 218 Mass. 294 (1914)

FACTS

Plaintiff George Economopoulos was shopping at a retail store owned by Defendant A.G. Pollard Company when a clerk working for defendant accused the plaintiff of stealing a handkerchief. The statement made by the clerk to the plaintiff was in English and the evidence showed that no other persons heard *this* statement. Thereafter, another clerk, one Miralos, who was Greek, repeated the allegedly defamatory statement in Greek. The evidence showed that while the Greek statement was heard by others, there was no evidence that anyone understood it but the plaintiff. Plaintiff sued for the allegedly defamatory statements. The trial court entered a verdict for defendant and plaintiff brings exceptions.

Must a false statement be heard <u>and</u> understood by a 3rd party in order to be considered defamatory?

In order to be considered defamatory, a false statement must be published [other elements of the tort must also be present], which means that it must have been communicated to someone other than the person defamed.

In order to be considered defamatory, a false statement must be heard and understood by a 3rd party. Here, there was no evidence that anyone other than plaintiff was present when the English-speaking clerk accused plaintiff of the theft in English. Therefore, no one *heard* this statement. Moreover, there was no evidence that anyone besides plaintiff *understood* the words communicated by the Greek speaking clerk in Greek. Therefore the element of publication was lacking.

Exceptions overruled.

Carafano v. Metrosplash.Com Inc.
U.S. Court of Appeals, 339 F.3d 1119 (9th Cir. 2003)

FACTS

Matchmaker.com is a commercial internet dating service and site owned and operated by Defendant Metrosplash.com Inc. For a fee, members post anonymous profiles and then may view profiles of other members in their area contacting them by email sent through the matchmaker.com server. On October 23, 1999, an unknown person using a computer in Berlin posted a "trial" personal profile of Plaintiff Christianne Carafano in the L.A. section of the site. Carafano, known by her stage name as Chase Masterson, is a well-known film and television actress. The false and unsolicited profile contained several sexually suggestive responses to questions about the actress. The profile, however, did not include a last name for Chase or indicate Carafano's real name, but it did list two of her movies and included pictures of her, her house address and her email address. Unaware of the false posting, Carafano soon began receiving messages responding to the profile. Numerous mailing, postings, emails and voicemail messages soon followed. Thereafter, Siouxzan Perry, who maintained Carafano's professional and authorized website learned of the false posting. Plaintiff filed suit against Matchmaker and its corporate successors, alleging invasion of privacy, misappropriation of the right to publicity, deformation and negligence. The district Court granted the defendants' motion for summary judgment. Plaintiff appealed.

Are plaintiff's claims barred by 47 U.S.C. $230(c)(1)$ ["no provider or user of an interactive computer service shall be treated as the publisher or speaker of any information provided by another information content provider"]? Or, stated another way: Can a provider or user of an interactive computer service be held liable for deformation [libel or slander] as a publisher or speaker of false information about another provided to it by a third party?

A provider or user of an interactive computer service will not be held liable for deformation [libel or slander] as a publisher or speaker of false information about another when such information is provided to it by a third party.

Plaintiff's claims are barred by 47 U.S.C. $230(c)(1)$, which provide that "no provider or user of an interactive computer service shall be treated as the publisher or speaker of any information provided by another information content provider." Accordingly, a provider or user of an interactive computer service will not be held liable for deformation [libel or slander] as a publisher or speaker of false information about another when such information is provided to it by a third party. Through this provision, Congress granted most Internet Service Providers (ISPs) immunity from liability so long as the information was provided by another party. As a result, internet publishers are treated differently from corresponding publishers in print, television and radio. In the instant case, the fact that some of the content was formulated in response to Matchmaker's questionnaire does not alter this conclusion. Defendant was not responsible, even in part, for associating certain multiple choice responses with a set of physical characteristics, a group of essay answers and a photograph. Here, critical information about plaintiff's home address, movie credits, email address and home phone number were transmitted unaltered to profile viewers. Thus, defendant did not play a significant role in creating, creating, developing or "transforming" the relevant content.

Carafano v. Metrosplash.Com Inc.

U.S. Court of Appeals, 339 F.3d 1119 (9th Cir. 2003)

Although utterly deplorable, we conclude that Congress intended service providers such as the defendant to be afforded immunity from suit.

 Judgment of the District Court is affirmed.

Ogden v. Association of the United States Army

U.S. District Court, District of Columbia, 177 F.Supp 498 (1959)

FACTS

It can be inferred that Defendant Association of the United States Army published a defamatory statement regarding Plaintiff Ogden in a book published in November, 1955. However, plaintiff filed suit almost 4 years later, after the one-year statute of limitations for defamation had run in the District of Columbia, the relevant jurisdiction for purposes of this action. Plaintiff alleged that the subsequent sales of the book constituted separate "publications" thus raising separate causes of action with respect to the statute of limitations [the statute of limitations would start, over and again, after *each* consecutive book was published]. Defendant moved for summary judgment based on the statute of limitations.

 Does every sale of an allegedly defamatory book constitute a distinct "publication" and create a separate cause of action for libel or should the so-called modern "single publication rule" be the law in the District of Columbia?

 The publication of a book gives rise to only one cause of action for libel, which accrues at the time of the *original* publication [called the "single publication rule"].

 Separate causes of action for libel are not created via the multiple publication of the same book within which the alleged defamatory statement exists. Therefore, every sale of an allegedly defamatory book does not constitute a separate and actionable "publication" and create a discrete cause of action for libel. Today, we adopt the modern "single publication rule" which has been adopted by most jurisdictions; that the publication of a book gives rise to only one cause of action for libel, which accrues at the time of the original publication. As such, we reject the plaintiff's position, which is not unlike the English common law rule, where every sale or delivery of a libelous matter constituted a new publication, and therefore a new cause of action accrued on each occasion. Such a rule would create havoc in our courts by creating a multiplicity of suits and undermining the underlying principle supporting the statute of limitations. While the number of copies and rate of recurrence of the defamatory publication is a factor to be considered in determining the amount of damages to be awarded, it has no impact on the cause of action or the statute of limitations.

 Defendant's motion for summary judgment is granted.

New York Times v. Sullivan
U.S. Supreme Court, 376 U.S. 254 (1964)

FACTS

Plaintiff-respondent L.B. Sullivan, an elected official in Montgomery, Alabama, brought suit in a state court alleging that he had been libeled by an advertisement in corporate Defendant-petitioner's newspaper, The New York Times, the text of which appeared over the names of the four individual petitioners and many others. The advertisement included statements, some of which were false, about police action allegedly directed against students who participated in a civil rights demonstration and against a leader of the civil rights movement; respondent claimed the statements referred to him because his duties included supervision of the police department. The trial judge instructed the jury that such statements were "libelous per se," legal injury being implied without proof of actual damages, and that for the purpose of compensatory damages malice was presumed, so that such damages could be awarded against petitioners if the statements were found to have been published by them and to have related to respondent. As to punitive damages, the judge instructed that mere negligence was not evidence of actual malice and would not justify an award of punitive damages; he refused to instruct that actual intent to harm or recklessness had to be found before punitive damages could be awarded, or that a verdict for respondent should differentiate between compensatory and punitive damages. An Alabama state court jury awarded Sullivan damages of $500,000, finding the ad libelous per se, and actionable without proof of malice or special damages. The award was affirmed by the Alabama Supreme Court. The U.S. Supreme Court granted certiorari.

Does the United States Constitution limit a state's power to award damages in a libel action brought by public official against critics of his official conduct?

The First Amendment delimits a State's power to award damages for libel actions brought by public figure against critics of their official conduct such that a showing of actual malice is required to create liability for such criticism.

We hold that a State cannot under the First and Fourteenth Amendments award damages to a public official for defamatory falsehood relating to his official conduct unless he proves "actual malice" - that the statement was made with knowledge of its falsity or with reckless disregard of whether it was true or false. Application by state courts of a rule of law, whether statutory or not, to award a judgment in a civil action, is "state action" under the Fourteenth Amendment. Expression does not lose constitutional protection to which it would otherwise be entitled because it appears in the form of a paid advertisement. Factual error, content defamatory of official reputation, or both, are insufficient to warrant an award of damages for false statements unless "actual malice" - knowledge that statements are false or in reckless disregard of the truth - is alleged and proved. State court judgment entered upon a general verdict which does not differentiate between punitive damages, as to which under state law actual malice must be proved, and general damages, as to which it is "presumed," precludes any determination as to the basis of the verdict and requires reversal, where presumption of malice is inconsistent with federal constitutional requirements. The evidence was constitutionally insufficient to support the judgment for respondent, since it

New York Times v. Sullivan

U.S. Supreme Court, 376 U.S. 254 (1964)

failed to support a finding that the statements were made with actual malice or that they related to respondent. Accordingly, the judgment of the Alabama Supreme Court is reversed and the case is remanded for further action not inconsistent with the opinion.

 Judgment reversed and remanded.

St. Amant v. Thompson
U.S. Supreme Court, 390 U.S. 727 (1968)

FACTS

Plaintiff-respondent, Thompson, a deputy sheriff and elected official in Montgomery, Alabama, brought suit in state court alleging that he had been libeled by an advertisement in corporate Defendant-petitioner's newspaper, the text of which appeared over the names of the four individual petitioners and many others. The advertisement included statements, some of which were false, about police action allegedly directed against students who participated in a civil rights demonstration and against a leader of the civil rights movement; respondent claimed the statements referred to him because his duties included supervision of the police department. The trial judge instructed the jury that such statements were "libelous per se," legal injury being implied without proof of actual damages, and that for the purpose of compensatory damages malice was presumed, so that such damages could be awarded against petitioners if the statements were found to have been published by them and to have related to respondent. As to punitive damages, the judge instructed that mere negligence was not evidence of actual malice and would not justify an award of punitive damages; he refused to instruct that actual intent to harm or recklessness had to be found before punitive damages could be awarded, or that a verdict for respondent should differentiate between compensatory and punitive damages. The jury found for respondent and the State Supreme Court affirmed. The United States Supreme Court granted certiorari.

Should a "reasonably prudent person" standard be utilized in cases of deformation where actual malice exists?

For purposes of actual malice, the "reasonably prudent person" standard should not be utilized because reckless disregard [for purposes of the actual malice standard] requires a high degree of actual awareness of the probable falsity of a statement.

The "reasonably prudent person" standard has no place in deformation cases which involve actual malice and therefore should not be employed. This is because a reckless disregard requires a higher degree of actual awareness of the probable falsity of a statement than that afforded by the "reasonably prudent person" standard. Specifically, reckless conduct is not measured by a negligence benchmark; that is, whether a reasonably prudent man would have published the statement. Rather, the standard is whether the publisher of the statement did in fact act recklessly. Consequently, we hold that a State cannot, under the First and Fourteenth Amendments, award damages to a public official for defamatory falsehood relating to his official conduct unless he proves "actual malice" - that the statement was made with knowledge of its falsity or with reckless disregard of whether it was true or false. Application by state courts of a rule of law, whether statutory or not, to award a judgment in a civil action, is "state action" under the Fourteenth Amendment. Expression does not lose constitutional protection to which it would otherwise be entitled because it appears in the form of a paid advertisement. Factual error, content defamatory of official reputation, or both, are insufficient to warrant an award of damages for false statements unless "actual malice" - knowledge that statements are false or in reckless disregard of

St. Amant v. Thompson

U.S. Supreme Court, 390 U.S. 727 (1968)

the truth - is alleged and proved. State court judgment entered upon a general verdict which does not differentiate between punitive damages, as to which under state law actual malice must be proved, and general damages, as to which it is "presumed," precludes any determination as to the basis of the verdict and requires reversal, where presumption of malice is inconsistent with federal constitutional requirements. The evidence was constitutionally insufficient to support the judgment for respondent, since it failed to support a finding that the statements were made with actual malice or that they related to respondent.

 Reversed and remanded.

Harte-Hanks Communications Inc. v. Connaughton

U.S. Supreme Court, 491 U.S. 657 (1989)

FACTS

Plaintiff-respondent Daniel Connaughton was the unsuccessful challenger for the position of Municipal Judge of Hamilton, Ohio, in an election conducted on November 8, 1983. A local newspaper, the Journal News, published by petitioner supported the reelection of the incumbent. A little over a month before the election, the incumbent's Director of Court Services resigned and was arrested on bribery charges, and a grand jury investigation of those charges was in progress on November 1, 1983. On that day, the Journal News owned by Defendant-petitioner Harte-Hanks Communications Inc., ran a front-page story quoting a grand jury witness (Thompson) as stating that respondent had used "dirty tricks" and offered her and her sister jobs and a trip to Florida "in appreciation" for their help in the investigation. Respondent filed a diversity action against petitioner for libel in Federal District Court, alleging that the story was false, had damaged his personal and professional reputation, and had been published with actual malice. After listening to six days of testimony and three taped interviews - one conducted by respondent and two by Journal News reporters - and reviewing the contents of 56 exhibits, the jury was given instructions defining the elements of public figure libel and directed to answer three special verdicts. It found by a preponderance of the evidence that the story in question was defamatory and false, and by clear and convincing proof that the story was published with actual malice, and awarded respondent $5,000 in compensatory damages and $195,000 in punitive damages. The Court of Appeals affirmed. It separately considered the evidence supporting each of the jury's special verdicts, concluding that neither the finding that the story was defamatory nor the finding that it was false was clearly erroneous. In considering the actual malice issue, but without attempting to make an independent evaluation of the credibility of conflicting oral testimony concerning the subsidiary facts underlying the jury's finding of actual malice, the court identified 11 subsidiary facts that the jury "could have" found and held that such findings would not have been clearly erroneous, and, based on its independent review, that when considered cumulatively they provided clear and convincing evidence of actual malice. The case now comes before the U.S. Supreme Court for review.

 May a public figure recover damages for a defamatory falsehood without presenting clear and convincing evidence that the defendant published the false and defamatory material with actual malice, i.e., with knowledge of falsity or with a reckless disregard for the truth?

 A plaintiff [public figure] must prove by clear and convincing evidence that the defendant published the false and defamatory material with actual malice, i.e., with knowledge of falsity or with a reckless disregard for the truth.

 A showing of "highly unreasonable conduct constituting an extreme departure from the standards of investigation and reporting ordinarily adhered to by responsible publishers" cannot alone support a verdict in favor of a public figure plaintiff in a libel action. Rather, such a plaintiff must prove by clear and convincing evidence that the defendant published the false and defamatory material with actual malice, i.e., with knowledge of falsity or with a reckless disregard for the truth. Although there is language in the Court of Appeals' opinion

---

Harte-Hanks Communications Inc. v. Connaughton

U.S. Supreme Court, 491 U.S. 657 (1989)

suggesting that it applied the less severe professional standards rule, when read as a whole, it is clear that this language is merely supportive of the court's ultimate conclusion that the Journal News acted with actual malice. A reviewing court in a public figure libel case must "exercise independent judgment and determine whether the record establishes actual malice with convincing clarity" to ensure that the verdict is consistent with the constitutional standard set out in *New York Times Co. v. Sullivan*, and subsequent decisions. Based on this Court's review of the entire record, the Court of Appeals properly held that the evidence did in fact support a finding of actual malice, but it should have taken a somewhat different approach in reaching that result. While the jury may have found each of the 11 subsidiary facts, the case should have been decided on a less speculative ground. Given the trial court's instructions, the jury's answers to the three special interrogatories, and an understanding of those facts not in dispute, it is evident that the jury must have rejected (1) the testimony of petitioner's witnesses that Thompson's sister, the most important witness to the bribery charges against the Director of Court Services, was not contacted simply because respondent failed to place her in touch with the newspaper; (2) the testimony of the editorial director of the Journal News that he did not listen to the taped interviews simply because he thought that they would provide him with no new information; and (3) the testimony of Journal News employees who asserted that they believed Thompson's allegations were substantially true. When those findings are considered alongside the undisputed evidence, the conclusion that the newspaper acted with actual malice inexorably follows. The evidence in the record in this case, when reviewed in its entirety, is "unmistakably" sufficient to support a finding of actual malice.

Affirmed.

Gertz v. Robert Welch Inc.
U.S. Supreme Court, 418 U.S. 323 (1974)

FACTS

A Chicago policeman named Richard Nuccio was convicted of murder. The victim's family retained Plaintiff-petitioner Elmer, a reputable attorney, to represent them in civil litigation against Nuccio. Defendant-respondent Robert Welch, Inc. published an article that purported to show that Nuccio was innocent, that the prosecution of Nuccio was part of a Communist conspiracy to discredit the local police, and it falsely stated that petitioner had arranged Nuccio's "frame-up," implied that petitioner had a criminal record, and labeled him a "Communist-fronter." Petitioner brought this diversity libel action against respondent. After the jury returned a verdict for petitioner, the District Court decided that the standard enunciated in *New York Times Co. v. Sullivan*, which bars media liability for defamation of a public official absent proof that the defamatory statements were published with knowledge of their falsity or in reckless disregard of the truth, should apply to this suit. The court concluded that that standard protects media discussion of a public issue without regard to whether the person defamed is a public official as in *New York Times* or a public figure, as in *Curtis Publishing Co. v. Butts*. The court found that petitioner had failed to prove knowledge of falsity or reckless disregard for the truth and therefore entered a j.n.o.v. (the reversal of a jury's verdict by a judge when the judge believes that there were insufficient facts upon which to base the jury's verdict or that the verdict did not correctly apply the law) for respondent. The Court of Appeals affirmed.

In defamation action, is the criticism of *private* persons entitled to *any* constitutional protection?

Individual states may impose liability for defamation against a private person based on negligence under the First Amendment, but may not award punitive damages without a showing of actual malice.

A publisher or broadcaster of defamatory falsehoods about an individual who is neither a public official nor a public figure may not claim the New York Times protection against liability for defamation on the ground that the defamatory statements concern an issue of public or general interest. Because private individuals characteristically have less effective opportunities for rebuttal than do public officials and public figures, they are more vulnerable to injury from defamation. Because they have not voluntarily exposed themselves to increased risk of injury from defamatory falsehoods, they are also more deserving of recovery. The state interest in compensating injury to the reputation of private individuals is therefore greater than for public officials and public figures. To extend the New York Times standard to media defamation of private persons whenever an issue of general or public interest is involved would abridge to an unacceptable degree the legitimate state interest in compensating private individuals for injury to reputation and would occasion the additional difficulty of forcing courts to decide on an ad hoc basis which publications and broadcasts address issues of general or public interest and which do not. So long as they do not impose liability without fault, the States may define for themselves the appropriate

Gertz v. Robert Welch Inc.

U.S. Supreme Court, 418 U.S. 323 (1974)

---

standard of liability for a publisher or broadcaster of defamatory falsehood which injures a private individual and whose substance makes substantial danger to reputation apparent. The States, however, may not permit recovery of presumed or punitive damages when liability is not based on knowledge of falsity or reckless disregard for the truth, and the private defamation plaintiff who establishes liability under a less demanding standard than the New York Times test may recover compensation only for actual injury. Petitioner was neither a public official nor a public figure. Neither petitioner's past service on certain city committees nor his appearance as an attorney at the coroner's inquest into the death of the murder victim made him a public official. Petitioner was also not a public figure. Absent clear evidence of general fame or notoriety in the community and pervasive involvement in ordering the affairs of society, an individual should not be deemed a public figure for all aspects of his life. Rather, the public-figure question should be determined by reference to the individual's participation in the particular controversy giving rise to the defamation. Petitioner's role in the Nuccio affair did not make him a public figure.

Reversed and remanded.

Dun & Bradstreet Inc. v. Greenmoss Builders Inc.

U.S. Supreme Court, 472 U.S. 749 (1985)

FACTS

Defendant-petitioner Dun & Bradstreet, a credit reporting agency, sent a report to five subscribers indicating that Plaintiff-respondent Greenmoss Builders inc., a construction contractor, had filed a voluntary petition for bankruptcy. The report was false and grossly misrepresented respondent's assets and liabilities. Thereafter, petitioner issued a corrective notice, but respondent was dissatisfied with this notice and brought a defamation action in Vermont state court, alleging that the false report had injured its reputation and seeking damages. After trial, the jury returned a verdict in respondent's favor and awarded both compensatory or presumed damages and punitive damages. But the trial court believed that *Gertz v. Robert Welch, Inc.* controlled, and granted petitioner's motion for a new trial on the ground that the instructions to the jury permitted it to award damages on a lesser showing than "actual malice." The Vermont Supreme Court reversed, holding that *Gertz* was inapplicable to non-media defamation actions. The U.S. Supreme Court granted certiorari.

In order to recover punitive damages in defamation actions involving private matters, must proof of actual malice be shown?

Defamatory statements regarding matters which are purely private, as opposed to matters of public concern, subject the publisher to punitive damages without requiring the plaintiff [the person against whom the defamatory statements are directed] to prove actual malice.

The fact that the jury instructions in question referred to "malice," "lack of good faith," and "actual malice," did not require the jury to find "actual malice," as respondent contends, where the instructions failed to define any of these terms. Consequently, the trial court correctly concluded that the instructions did not satisfy *Gertz*. Permitting recovery of presumed and punitive damages in defamation cases, absent a showing of "actual malice," do not violate the First Amendment when the defamatory statements do not involve matters of public concern. In light of the reduced constitutional value of speech on matters of purely private concern, as opposed to speech on matters of public concern, the state interest in compensating private individuals for injury to their reputation adequately supports awards of presumed and punitive damages - even absent a showing of "actual malice." *Gertz* does not apply to this case. Petitioner's credit report concerned no public issue but was speech solely in the individual interest of the speaker and its specific business audience. This particular interest warranted no special protection when it was wholly false and damaging to the victim's business reputation. Moreover, since the credit report was made available to only five subscribers, who, under the subscription agreement, could not disseminate it further, it cannot be said that the report involved any strong interest in the free flow of commercial information. And the speech here, like advertising, being solely motivated by a desire for profit, is hardy and unlikely to be deterred by incidental state regulation. In any event, the market provides a powerful incentive to a credit reporting agency to be accurate, since false reporting is of no use to creditors. THE CHIEF JUSTICE concluded

Dun & Bradstreet Inc. v. Greenmoss Builders Inc.

U.S. Supreme Court, 472 U.S. 749 (1985)

that *Gertz* is inapplicable to this case, because the allegedly defamatory expression involved did not relate to a matter of public concern, and that no other reason was needed to dispose of the case. JUSTICE WHITE concluded that *Gertz* should not be applied to this case either because *Gertz* should be overruled or because the defamatory publication in question did not deal with a matter of public importance.

 The judgment is affirmed.

Philadelphia Newspapers Inc. v. Hepps

U.S. Supreme Court, 475 U.S. 767 (1986)

FACTS

Plaintiff-appellee Hepps is the principal stockholder of Defendant-appellee Philadelphia Newspapers Corporation that franchises a chain of stores selling beer, soft drinks, and snacks. Appellant owner published a series of articles in its Philadelphia newspaper whose general theme was that Hepps, the franchisor corporation, and its franchisees (also appellees) had links to organized crime and used some of those links to influence the State's governmental processes. Appellees then brought a defamation suit in a Pennsylvania state court against the newspaper owner and the authors (also appellants) of the articles in question. Concluding that the Pennsylvania statute giving the defendant the burden of proving the truth of allegedly defamatory statements violated the Federal Constitution, the trial court instructed the jury that the plaintiff bore the burden of proving falsity. The jury ruled for appellants and therefore awarded no damages to appellees. The Pennsylvania Supreme Court, concluding that a showing of fault did not require a showing of falsity, held that to place the burden of showing truth on the defendant did not unconstitutionally inhibit free debate, and remanded the case for a new trial. Defendant-appellee Philadelphia Newspapers sought review by the U.S. Supreme Court.

Under the First Amendment, who bears the burden of proof, if at all, on the issue of the falsity of the defamatory statement in a defamation action against a newspaper brought by the plaintiff who is a private individual?

In a defamation action by a private individual against a newspaper, the plaintiff–complainant has the burden of proof that the defamatory statement is false.

In a case such as this one, where a newspaper publishes speech of public concern about a private figure, the private-figure plaintiff cannot recover damages without also showing that the statements at issue are false. Because in such a case the scales are in an uncertain balance as to whether the statements are true or false, the Constitution requires that the scales be tipped in favor of protecting true speech. To ensure that true speech on matters of public concern is not deterred, the common-law presumption that defamatory speech is false cannot stand. While Pennsylvania's "shield law," which allows employees of the media to refuse to divulge their sources, places a heavier burden on appellees, the precise scope of that law is unclear and, under these circumstances, it does not appear that such law requires a different constitutional standard than would prevail in the absence of such law.

Reversed and remanded.

Milkovich v. Lorain Journal Co.

U.S. Supreme Court, 497 U.S. 1 (1990)

FACTS

While Plaintiff-petitioner Milkovich was a high school wrestling coach, his team was involved in an altercation at a match with another high school's team. Both he and School Superintendent Scott testified at an investigatory hearing before the Ohio High School Athletic Association (OHSAA), which placed the team on probation. They testified again during a suit by several parents, in which a county court overturned OHSAA's ruling. The day after the court's decision, Defendant-respondent Lorain Journal Company's newspaper published a column authored by respondent Theodore Diadiun, which implied that Milkovich lied under oath in the judicial proceeding. Milkovich commenced a defamation action against respondents in the county court, alleging that the column accused him of committing the crime of perjury, damaged him in his occupation of teacher and coach, and constituted libel per se. Ultimately, the trial court granted summary judgment for respondents. The Ohio Court of Appeals affirmed, considering itself bound by the State Supreme Court's determination in Superintendent Scott's separate action against respondents that, as a matter law, the article was constitutionally protected opinion. The U.S. Supreme Court granted certiorari.

Do statements of opinion enjoy special constitutional protections and immunity from liability for defamation?

Statements of opinion do not enjoy special constitutional protections and immunity from liability for defamation such that liability may be imposed where a statement of opinion reasonably implies false and defamatory facts.

The First Amendment does not require a separate "opinion" privilege limiting the application of state defamation laws. Statements of opinion do not enjoy special constitutional protections and immunity from liability for defamation. Rather, statements of opinion are treated as any other statement for purposes of defamation actions. While the Amendment does limit such application, *New York Times Co. v. Sullivan*, provides the breathing space that freedoms of expression require to survive is adequately secured by existing constitutional doctrine. Foremost, where a media defendant is involved, a statement on matters of public concern must be provable as false before liability can be assessed, *Philadelphia Newspapers, Inc. v. Hepps*, thus ensuring full constitutional protection for a statement of opinion having no provably false factual connotation. Next, statements that cannot reasonably be interpreted as stating actual facts about an individual are protected, thus assuring that public debate will not suffer for lack of "imaginative expression" or the "rhetorical hyperbole" which has traditionally added much to the discourse of this Nation. The reference to "opinion" in dictum in *Gertz v. Robert Welch, Inc.*, was not intended to create a wholesale defamation exemption for "opinion." Read in context, the Gertz dictum is merely a reiteration of Justice Holmes' "marketplace of ideas" concept. Simply couching a statement - "Jones is a liar" - in terms of opinion - "In my opinion, Jones is a liar" - does not dispel the factual implications contained in the statement. A reasonable factfinder

Milkovich v. Lorain Journal Co.

U.S. Supreme Court, 497 U.S. 1 (1990)

could conclude that the statements in the Diadiun column imply an assertion that Milkovich perjured himself in a judicial proceeding. The article did not use the sort of loose, figurative, or hyperbolic language that would negate the impression that Diadiun was seriously maintaining Milkovich committed perjury. Nor does the article's general tenor negate this impression. In addition, the connotation that Milkovich committed perjury is sufficiently factual that it is susceptible of being proved true or false by comparing, *inter alia*, his testimony before the OHSAA board with his subsequent testimony before the trial court. This decision balances the First Amendment's vital guarantee of free and uninhibited discussion of public issues with the important social values that underlie defamation law and society's pervasive and strong interest in preventing and redressing attacks upon reputation.

 Reversed and remanded.

Sindorf v. Jacron Sales Co. Inc.

Court of Special Appeals of Maryland, 341 A.2d 856 (1975)

FACTS

Plaintiff-appellant Sindorf worked as a salesman for the Pennsylvania division of Defendant-appellee Jacron Sales Co but then resigned 18 months later amidst a dispute with the company over his sales practices. Specifically, defendant claimed that plaintiff was selling to people without adequately checking their credit ratings. Defendant allegedly withheld some of his commissions until they [defendant] received payment for all of the sales. In response, plaintiff kept some of defendant's inventory as partial payment for commissions owed to him. Not long after he left defendant's employ, plaintiff then went to work for Tool Box Corporation. Bob Fridkis, the vice president of the Virginia branch of the defendant corporation, called the president of Tool Box, William Brose, a competitor and friend, to inquire whether plaintiff had commenced working for Tool Box before leaving his company. In the call, Fridkis told Brose that plaintiff had been fired and that "a few cash sales and quite a lot of merchandise was not accounted for" and well as making other disparaging remarks concerning the plaintiff. Plaintiff sued for defamation but the trial court held that Fridkis conversation was constitutionally privileged and not made with malice. The trial court then granted defendant's motion for directed verdict and the plaintiff appealed.

Is there a qualified privilege which protects communications made by a past employer about a past employee to a new employer; and, if so, must the communications be published in a reasonable manner and for a proper purpose in order for it to serve as a defense to defamation?

Qualified privileges protect persons speaking in their own self-interest such as communications made by a past employer about a past employee to a new or prospective employer; and for the qualified privilege to serve as a defense to defamation cause of action the communications must be published in a reasonable manner and for a proper purpose.

The law in our state [Maryland common law] holds that a defamatory publication is conditionally privileged where the communicating party and the recipient have a mutual interest in the subject matter, or some duty with respect thereto. As a result, a conditional privilege occurs where a former employer communicates with a new or prospective employer about a former employee. Hence, a qualified privilege exists which protects communications made by a former employer about a former employee to a new employer and the trial court did not err in holding as a matter of law that defendant had a conditional privilege to communicate defamatory statements about plaintiff to Tool Box via William Brose. Turning to the next issue, we hold that in order for qualified privileges to serve as defenses to defamation, the communications must be published in a reasonable manner and for a proper purpose. The [privileged] statements must not be disseminated to any 3rd party other than those interested parties and the conveyer of the communication must establish the reasonableness of the publication and its proper purpose. These include the conveyer's reasonable belief in the truth of his own statements, the nature of the language used, whether the statements were unsolicited or compelled and whether the statement were made to an appropriate person(s). Here, the statements made to the president of Tool

Box, William Brose, were volunteered. A publisher's motive will be more carefully scrutinized if his statements were volunteered as opposed to being compelled to speak. Moreover, Fridkis incorrectly told Tool Box that plaintiff had been fired, when in fact he had resigned. This was a complete fabrication. We think that a reasonable person could conclude that Fridkis' statement was an effort to pressure plaintiff into returning the inventory which he was holding. Considering all of the evidence and inferences in a light most favorable to the defendant, we believe that reasonable minds could not differ in finding that defendant, through Fridkis, did in fact abuse the privilege to defame by excessive publication or by use of occasion for an improper purpose. Therefore, the question of malice should have gone to the jury with instructions and the trial judge erred in granting the motion for directed verdict.

Reversed and remanded.

Joe Dickerson & Assoc. LLC v. Dittmar

Supreme Court of Colorado, 34 P.3d 995 (2001)

FACTS

Defendant Joe Dickerson & Associates LLC and Joe Dickerson were hired during a custody dispute to investigate Plaintiff Rosanne Marie Dittmar. During the course of their investigation, defendant noticed inconsistencies in the way plaintiff came to possess certain bear bonds. He reposted the results of his investigation to authorities. Thereafter plaintiff was charged and convicted of felony theft of these bonds. Dickerson publishes a newsletter called "The Dickerson Report," which is sent free of charge to law enforcement agencies, financial institutions, law firms and others. In it, recounted his investigation of Dittmar; including the fact that the jury convicted her of theft, how the court ordered her to pay restitution to the theft victim, and mentioned her by name and photograph. Plaintiff sued defendant for deformation, outrageous conduct and invasion of privacy by appropriation of another's name and likeness. The trial court granted summary judgment for defendants on all claims. With respect to plaintiff's claim for invasion of privacy by appropriation of another's name or likeness [the only claim relevant on appeal], the trial court noted that Colorado has not explicitly recognized this tort. The court of appeals reversed. Defendant appealed.

 Can a defendant be held liable for appropriating another's name and likeness in Colorado?

 The tort of invasion of privacy appropriation of another's name and likeness is cognizable under Colorado law and consists of the following elements: 1) the defendant must have used the plaintiff's name or likeness; 2) the defendant used the plaintiff's name or likeness for the use of his own purpose or benefit, commercially or otherwise; 3) the plaintiff must have suffered damages; and 4) the defendant caused the damages incurred.

 According to the Restatement (Second) of Torts 652C, appropriation requires more than just a mere publication of the plaintiff's name or likeness; or by reference to it in connection with legitimate mention of his public activities; nor is the value of his likeness appropriated when it is published for purposes other than taking advantage of his reputation, prestige, or other value associated with him for the purposes of publicity – something more is required. The tort of invasion of privacy appropriation of another's name and likeness requires the following: 1) the defendant must have used the plaintiff's name or likeness; 2) the defendant used the plaintiff's name or likeness for the use of his own purpose or benefit, commercially or otherwise; 3) the plaintiff must have suffered damages; and 4) the defendant caused the damages incurred. Applying these elements to the case at bar, we conclude that plaintiff Dittmar alleged sufficient facts to satisfy each of the required elements. We do not require the plaintiff to prove the value of her identity. Thus we hold that the trial court erred in granting summary judgment to the defendants on the grounds that the plaintiff failed to provide evidence of the *value* of her name and likeness. However, our inquiry does not end here. Having defined the elements of the tort of invasion of privacy by appropriation of name or likeness, we now consider the defendant's argument that he trial court properly granted him summary judgment because

Joe Dickerson & Assoc. LLC v. Dittmar

Supreme Court of Colorado, 34 P.3d 995 (2001)

his publication of the plaintiff's name and picture was constitutionally protected speech as a matter of law. We note that our review is de novo because this is a question of law. To be actionable, we must determine whether the defendant's use of the plaintiff's name and picture was for commercial or non-commercial purposes. Courts have repeatedly held that, in order to be actionable, the use of the plaintiff's identity must be more directly commercial than simply being printed in a periodical that operates for profit. Applying the forgoing rule, we conclude that defendant's publication was primarily non-commercial because it related to a matter of public concern, namely the facts of the plaintiff's crime and felony conviction.

 Judgment of the court of appeals is reversed and re remand to that court with instructions to reinstate the trial court's order granting summary judgment to the defendant.

Sanders v. American Broadcasting Co. Inc., et. al.

Supreme Court of California, 978 P.2d 67 (1999)

FACTS

Defendant Stacy Lescht, a reporter employed by Defendant American Broadcasting Company (ABC), obtained employment as a "telepsychic" with the Psychic Marketing Group (PMG), which also employed Plaintiff Mark Sanders in the same capacity. While Lescht worked in PMG's L.A. office, she secretly videotaped her conversations with several coworkers, including plaintiff. Plaintiff sued both defendants, among other causes of action, for invasion of privacy by intrusion. The jury found for plaintiff, but the court of appeal reversed the resulting judgment in his favor on the ground that the jury finding for the defense on another cause of action, violation of Penal Code 632, established that plaintiff could have had no reasonable expectation of privacy in his workplace because such conversations could be overheard by others in the shared office. The Supreme Court of California granted review.

 Do office co-workers, for the purposes of the tort of intrusion, have a complete expectation of privacy in their office conversations against covert videotaping by another [the "intruder"] even though such interactions and conversations can be seen and overheard by other co-workers?

 Office workers, for the purposes of the tort of intrusion, do not have a *complete* expectation of privacy in their office conversations; however, they may nevertheless have a claim for invasion of privacy by intrusion based on a television reporter's covert videotaping of that conversation.

 Whether a reasonable expectation of privacy is violated depends on the exact nature of the conduct and the surrounding circumstances. In addition, liability under the tort of intrusion requires the invasion to be highly offensive to a reasonable person, considering, among other factors, the motives of the alleged intruder. The scope of our review does not include any question regarding the offensiveness or inoffensiveness of defendants' conduct. We hold only that, where the other elements of the intrusion tort are proven, the cause of action is not defeated as a matter of law simply because the elements or conversations upon which the defendant allegedly intruded were not completely private. Defendants claim that a "complete expectation of privacy" is necessary to recover for intrusion. We disagree. This claim is inconsistent with case law as well as with the common understanding of privacy; and defendants offer no case law which suggests otherwise. We thus conclude that in the workplace, as elsewhere, the reasonableness of a person's expectation of visual and audible privacy depends not only on who might have been able to observe the subject interaction, but on the identity of the claimed intruder and the means of intrusion. Therefore, a person who lacks a reasonable expectation of complete privacy in a conversation, because it could be seen and overheard by coworkers (but not the general public), may nevertheless have a claim for invasion of privacy by intrusion based on a television reporter's covert videotaping of that conversation.

 Judgment of the Court of Appeal is reversed, and the cause is remanded to that court for further proceedings not inconsistent with our opinion.

Hall v. Post

Supreme Court of North Carolina, 372 S.E.2d 711 (1988)

FACTS

Plaintiffs Susie Hall and her adoptive mother, Mary Hall, brought separate claims for tortious invasion of privacy based upon two articles printed in *The Salisbury Post* and written by special assignment reporter, Defendant Rose Post. The fist article concerned a search by Lee and Aledith Gottschalk for Aledith's daughter by a previous marriage, who she and her former husband abandoned some 17 years prior. The article indicated that her former husband had made arrangements 17 years ago for a babysitter named Mary Hall [plaintiff] to keep the child for a few weeks; he later told Aledith after the two left that he had signed papers authorizing the bay's adoption. The article ended with a public plea to anyone reading to contact the couple if they knew the whereabouts of the baby. Shortly after the article was published the Gottschalks were contacted and informed of the child's identity and location. A second article was then printed which reported that the couple had located the "lost" "child" and identified the child as Susie Hall and her adoptive mother as Mary Hall. The article also provided details regarding a telephone encounter between Mary Hall and the Gottschalks. The plaintiffs alleged that they had to fee their homes because of the public attention the two articles aroused. The trial court found for the plaintiffs and the Court of Appeals affirmed. An appeal was made to the Supreme Court of North Carolina.

 Is the public disclosure of truthful "private" facts about the plaintiff by the defendant actionable at law as an invasion of privacy tort?

 The public disclosure of truthful "private" facts about the plaintiff by the defendant is not actionable at law as an invasion of privacy tort

 The public disclosure of truthful "private" facts about the plaintiff by the defendant is not actionable at law as an invasion of privacy tort. Under the definition of private facts tort set out in the Restatement (Second) of Torts, liability will be imposed for publication of "private" facts when the matter publicized is of a kind that (a) would be highly offensive to a reasonable person, and (b) is not of legitimate concern to the public. While element (b) may be true, plaintiff's have not proven element (a) adequately applies to their situation - that the two publications would be highly offensive to a reasonable person. At any rate, even in light of the above, we are persuaded not to adopt for two primary reasons: First, decisions by the U.S. Supreme Court, scholarly articles and the restatement make it clear that the private facts branch of the invasion of privacy tort is, at the very least, constitutionally suspect. Second, the constitutionally suspect private facts branch of the invasion of privacy tort will almost never provide a plaintiff with any advantage not duplicated or overlapped by the tort of intentional infliction of emotional distress and possibly by other torts such as trespass or intrusive invasion of privacy. With that said, we conclude that any possible benefits which might accrue to plaintiffs are entirely insufficient to justify adoption of the constitutionally suspect private facts invasion of privacy tort which punishes defendants for the typically American act of broadly proclaiming the truth by speech or writing.

Hall v. Post

Supreme Court of North Carolina, 372 S.E.2d 711 (1988)

Accordingly, we reject the notion or claim for invasion of privacy by public disclosure of true but "private" facts. In light of the foregoing, the decision of the Court of Appeals is reversed.

Decision of the Court of Appeals is reversed.

Cantrell v. Forest City Publishing Co.

U.S. Supreme Court, 419 U.S. 245 (1974)

FACTS

Plaintiff Petitioners, Margaret Cantrell and her son, brought a diversity action against Defendant-respondents Forest City Publishing Co., a newspaper publisher and a reporter, for invasion of privacy based on a feature story in the newspaper discussing the impact upon petitioners' family of the death of the father, Melvin Cantrell, who was one of 43 people who died when a bridge collapsed. The story concededly contained a number of inaccuracies and false statements about the family. The District Judge struck the claims for punitive damages for lack of evidence of malice "within the legal definition of that term," but allowed the case to go to the jury on the "false light" theory of invasion of privacy, after instructing the jurors that liability could be imposed only if they found that the false statements were published with knowledge of their falsity or in reckless disregard of the truth, and the jury returned a verdict for compensatory damages. The Court of Appeals for the 6th Circuit reversed, holding that the District Judge should have directed a verdict for respondents, since his finding of no malice in striking the punitive damages claims was based on the definition of "actual malice" established in *New York Times Co. v. Sullivan*, and thus was a determination that there was no evidence of the knowing falsity or reckless disregard of the truth required for liability. The U.S. Supreme Court granted certiorari.

Must knowledge of falsity or reckless disregard of the truth be proven in order to recover for the tort of "false light" ["False light" is a claim that publicity invades a person's privacy by a false statement or representation that would be highly offensive to a reasonable person]?

Knowledge of falsity or reckless disregard of the truth need not be proven in order to recover for the tort of "false light;" however, actual malice must be proven in order to recover.

The Court of Appeals erred in setting aside the jury's verdict. The record discloses that the District Judge, when he dismissed the punitive damages claims, was not referring to the *New York Times* "actual malice" standard but to the common law standard of malice that is generally required under state tort law to support an award of punitive damages. In a "false light" case, the focus is on the defendant's attitude toward the plaintiff's privacy and not on the truth or falsity of the material published. Specifically, in order to recover for "false light," the *New York Times* malice standard must be applied: knowledge of falsity or reckless disregard of the truth -- must be proven. Therefore, the judge was not actually determining that petitioners failed to introduce evidence of knowing falsity or reckless disregard of the truth. Moreover, the evidence was sufficient to support jury findings that respondents had published knowing or reckless falsehoods about petitioners, particularly with respect to "calculated falsehoods" about petitioner mother's being present when the story was being prepared, and that respondent reporter's writing of the story was within the scope of his employment at the newspaper so as to render respondent publisher vicariously liable under *respondeat superior* for the knowing falsehoods in the story. Applying the foregoing to the instant case, we hold that in order to recover punitive damages, plaintiffs would have to show some personal ill-will or wanton disregard of their rights. This malice standard would focus on defendant's attitude toward their privacy, not towards the

Cantrell v. Forest City Publishing Co.

U.S. Supreme Court, 419 U.S. 245 (1974)

truth or falsity of the material it published. The wrong standard was applied. We thus conclude that the District Judge was referring to the punitive standard of malice, not the actual malice standard of *New York Times*.

 Judgment of the Court of Appeals is reversed and remanded.

Hustler Magazine v. Falwell
U.S. Supreme Court, 485 U.S. 46 (1988)

FACTS

Plaintiff-respondent the Reverend Jerry Falwell, a nationally known minister and commentator on politics and public affairs, filed a diversity action in Federal District Court against Defendant-petitioners, Hustler Magazine, a nationally circulated magazine and its publisher, Larry Flynt, to recover damages for, *inter alia*, libel and intentional infliction of emotional distress arising from the publication of an advertisement "parody" which, among other things, portrayed respondent as having engaged in a drunken incestuous rendezvous with his mother in an outhouse. The jury found against respondent on the libel claim, specifically finding that the parody could not "reasonably be understood as describing actual facts . . . or events," but ruled in his favor on the emotional distress claim, stating that he should be awarded compensatory and punitive damages. The Court of Appeals affirmed, rejecting petitioners' contention that the "actual malice" standard of *New York Times Co. v. Sullivan* must be met before respondent can recover for emotional distress. Rejecting as irrelevant the contention that, because the jury found that the parody did not describe actual facts, the ad was an opinion protected by the First Amendment to the Federal Constitution, the court ruled that the issue was whether the ad's publication was sufficiently outrageous to constitute intentional infliction of emotional distress. The U.S. Supreme Court granted certiorari.

In order for a plaintiff-public figure to recover for intentional infliction of emotional distress must he prove actual malice on the part of the defendant?

Public figures who are suing as plaintiffs for intentional infliction of emotional distress must show that the false statement of fact was made with actual malice by the defendant.

In order to protect the free flow of ideas and opinions on matters of public interest and concern, the First and Fourteenth Amendments prohibit public figures and public officials from recovering damages for the tort of intentional infliction of emotional distress by reason of the publication of a caricature such as the ad parody at issue without showing in addition that the publication contains a false statement of fact which was made with "actual malice," i.e., with knowledge that the statement was false or with reckless disregard as to whether or not it was true. The State's interest in protecting public figures from emotional distress is not sufficient to deny First Amendment protection to speech that is patently offensive and is intended to inflict emotional injury when that speech could not reasonably have been interpreted as stating actual facts about the public figure involved. Here, respondent is clearly a "public figure" for First Amendment purposes, and the lower courts' finding that the ad parody was not reasonably believable must be accepted. "Outrageousness" in the area of political and social discourse has an inherent subjectiveness about it which would allow a jury to impose liability on the basis of the jurors' tastes or views, or perhaps on the basis of their dislike of a particular expression, and cannot, consistently with the First Amendment, form a basis for the award of damages for conduct such as that involved

Hustler Magazine v. Falwell

U.S. Supreme Court, 485 U.S. 46 (1988)

here. Here, plaintiff was a public figure. The jury already found that the caricature did not contain a statement of fact. Thus, plaintiff cannot recover.

 Reversed.

Ashby v. White
Court of King's Bench, 1 Eng.Rep. 417 (1703)

FACTS

Plaintiff Ashby, a free burgess of a corporation, had the right to vote in a Parliamentary election which was blocked by an election official. As a result, plaintiff did not to vote. The candidate for whom plaintiff desired to vote was elected even though Ashby was not able to cast his ballot. Thereafter, plaintiff sued for infringement of his right to vote.

Can a person sue for a violation of his civil right(s) when no pecuniary or other material injury results?

A person sue for a violation of his civil right(s), even when no financial or other material injury results.

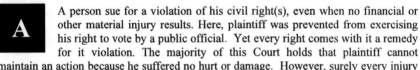

A person sue for a violation of his civil right(s), even when no financial or other material injury results. Here, plaintiff was prevented from exercising his right to vote by a public official. Yet every right comes with it a remedy for it violation. The majority of this Court holds that plaintiff cannot maintain an action because he suffered no hurt or damage. However, surely every injury to a right creates an injury, pecuniary or not. Even though this may increase the numbers of lawsuits, it is necessary in order to protect individual rights. In my opinion, the judgment should be for plaintiff.

Judgment for plaintiff.

Camp v. Gregory

U.S. Court of Appeals, 67 F.3d 1286 (7th Cir. 1995)

FACTS

Anthony Young was shot and killed two blocks from his aunt's home. At the time of his death, he was sixteen years old and a ward of the Department of Children and Family Services (DCFS). Plaintiff Elnora Camp, Anthony's aunt, was originally his guardian, but felt she was unable to provide the type of highly structured and nurturing environment necessary to ensure Anthony's well-being. For this reason, she sought the appointment of another guardian. DCFS was appointed as Anthony's guardian by the state court, and Defendant Gregory was assigned to be his caseworker. A DCFS referral form recommended a highly structured environment for Anthony; however, defendant chose to return Anthony to plaintiff's care. Thereafter, defendant failed to make any referrals or applications for appropriate educational or guidance programs, despite numerous requests from plaintiff. Defendant was informed by plaintiff that Anthony was placing himself in dangerous situations and jeopardizing his education and physical well-being, and reiterated that she [plaintiff] could not ensure his safety. Three months later, Anthony died while still under his plaintiff's care as the result of a gang-related incident, though the evidence is unclear. Plaintiff claims that defendant denied Anthony's substantive due process by failing to ensure that he was placed in a safe living environment. The district court dismissed the suit, believing that the U.S. Supreme Court's decision in *DeShaney v. Winnebago County Dept. of Social Services* shielded defendant from liability for his decision where to place Anthony. Plaintiff appeals to the U.S. Court of Appeals, 7th Circuit.

 If a child is a ward of the State, can a government official be held liable for his death?

 A public official who has deprived someone of his constitutional rights may nonetheless enjoy immunity from an action for civil damages if his actions were objectively reasonable.

 A public official who has deprived someone of his constitutional rights may be held liable, but may nonetheless enjoy immunity from an action of civil damages if his actions were objectively reasonable. In this case, plaintiff maintains that her nephew's (Anthony's) death resulted directly from defendant's failure to arrange for him to be placed in an appropriate environment as his duly appointed guardian. On the other hand, defendant argues that under *DeShaney v. Winnebago County Dep't of Social Services*, controls. In *DeShaney*, the Court held that due process did not require the state to protect a child from the abuse he suffered at the hands of his father. Thus, defendant argues that neither he nor the State bore any duty to protect Anthony from a danger. However, *DeShaney* does not preclude liability when the state, as guardian of the child, places that child in an environment where harm results. A child has a due process right not to be placed with a custodian who the state knows will fail to exercise the necessary degree of supervision and care due him. Thus, if a DCFS caseworker places a child in a foster home where he knows the child will likely suffer abuse, he can be held liable. On the other hand, whether the defendant's duty extended to dangers outside of the household to which he had returned Anthony is not so clear-cut. It would be a great burden to place on the caseworker a duty to evaluate and protect a child from dangers outside of the household. With that said, parents are not the insurers of their children's conduct, but they can be held liable for their omissions when they fail to exercise a reasonable degree of supervision. Along with the parental obligation to supervise a child's activities outside the home is a duty on the part of the state not to place a child in its care with an adult that it knows will not or cannot exercise that degree of care required for the child's welfare. Thus, we believe that when a DCFS caseworker places a child in a home knowing that his caretaker cannot provide reasonable supervision, and the failure to provide that degree of supervision and care results in injury to the child outside of the home, the caseworker may be held liable for a deprivation of liberty *if* the injury suffered by the child is reasonably foreseeable to the official *and* a sufficient causal link between the failure to provide reasonable supervision and the injury exists. Even so, a public official who has deprived someone of his constitutional rights may nonetheless enjoy immunity from an action for civil damages if his actions were objectively reasonable. What we mean by "objectively reasonable" is that "his conduct does not violate clearly established statutory or constitutional right of which a reasonable person would have known." Although we believe that plaintiff's complaint alleged facts sufficient to state a claim for the deprivation of Anthony's liberty in violation of his Fourteenth Amendment right to substantive due process, we also conclude that defendant is entitled to qualified immunity.

 Affirmed.

Memphis Comm. School Dist. v. Stachura

U.S. Supreme Court, 477 U.S. 299 (1986)

FACTS

Plaintiff-respondent Stachura, a tenured teacher in the Memphis, Michigan, public school system was suspended following some parents' complaints about his teaching methods in a seventh-grade life science course that included the showing of allegedly sexually explicit pictures and films. Before being reinstated, brought suit in Federal District Court under 42 U.S.C. §1983 against Defendant-petitioner the Memphis Community School District, Board of Education, Board Members, school administrators, and parents alleging that his suspension deprived him of liberty and property without due process of law and violated his First Amendment right to academic freedom. He sought both compensatory and punitive damages. The District Court instructed the jury on the standard elements of compensatory and punitive damages and also charged the jury that additional compensatory damages could be awarded based on the value or importance of the constitutional rights that were violated. The jury found petitioners liable, awarding both compensatory and punitive damages. The Court of Appeals affirmed. The U.S. Supreme Court granted certiorari.

Can §1983 damages be measured by the jury's determination of the abstract "value" or "importance" of the constitutional right infringed?

Damages based on the abstract "value" or "importance" of constitutional rights are not a permissible element of compensatory damages in 1983 cases.

Damages based on the abstract "value" or "importance" of constitutional rights are not a permissible element of compensatory damages in §1983 cases. The basic purpose of §1983 damages is "to compensate persons for injuries that are caused by the deprivation of constitutional rights." The instructions at issue cannot be squared with *Carey v. Piphus* [the basic purpose of § 1983 damages is to compensate persons for injuries that are caused by the deprivation of constitutional rights], or with the principles of tort damages on which *Carey* and 1983 are grounded. Damages measured by the jury's perception of the abstract "importance" of a constitutional right are not necessary to vindicate the constitutional rights that §1983 protects, and moreover are an unwieldy tool for ensuring compliance with the Constitution. Since such damages are wholly divorced from any compensatory purpose, they cannot be justified as presumed damages, which are a substitute for ordinary compensatory damages, not a supplement for an award that fully compensates the alleged injury. The erroneous instructions were not harmless error where the verdict did not specify how much of the compensatory damages were designed to compensate respondent for his injury and how much reflected the jury's estimation of the value of the constitutional rights that were infringed.

Reversed and remanded.

Texas Skaggs Inc. v. Graves
Court of Appeals of Texas, 582 S.W.2d 863 (1979)

FACTS

Plaintiff-appellee Sharon Graves, a former checker for Defendant Texas Skaggs, Inc., wrote two checks totaling $34.70 to purchase groceries at one of the defendant's stores. Although she did not know it at the time, her husband had withdrawn all of the funds from her account after the two had separated. Thus, plaintiff's checking account had insufficient funds to cover the checks written for the groceries. As soon as she found out that the checks had bounced, plaintiff immediately purchased a money order and mailed it to defendant. Nevertheless, a manager employed by the defendant filed an affidavit for a warrant for plaintiff's arrest under the Arkansas Hot Check Law. A week later, plaintiff was arrest by the police. Plaintiff was later released and the checks were returned to her because the checks had, in fact, been paid. However, defendant's employee wanted her prosecuted anyway and so forced the action. A municipal judge dismissed the criminal proceeding when the "hot checks" could not be produced. Plaintiff filed an action for malicious prosecution, and the jury awarded $20,000 in damages to her. Defendant appealed.

 Can a plaintiff bring a suit for malicious prosecution be maintained when the criminal proceeding against her ended with a dismissal rather than an acquittal?

 In order to be held liable for malicious prosecution, the following elements must be present there must be: 1) a criminal prosecution instituted or continued by the defendant against the plaintiff; 2) a termination of the prosecution in favor of the accused; 3) an absence of probable cause for the proceeding; 4) malice; and 5) damages.

 A plaintiff may still bring a suit for malicious prosecution when the criminal proceeding against her ended with a dismissal rather than an acquittal. In order to be held liable for malicious prosecution, the following elements must be present there must be: 1) a criminal prosecution instituted or continued by the defendant against the plaintiff; 2) a termination of the prosecution in favor of the accused; 3) an absence of probable cause for the proceeding; 4) malice; and 5) damages. In this case, all of the foregoing elements were met: a criminal prosecution was initiated by the defendant; the evidence shows that defendant lacked probable cause to continue the prosecution [a lack of probable cause exists when a man of ordinary caution and prudence "the reasonable person standard" does not believe that the accused is guilty of the crime alleged *or* when those with special knowledge of the facts actually knew that the accused was not guilty] since the defendant knew, or should have known, that plaintiff did not write the checks with the intent to defraud as evidenced by her immediate purchase of a money order and subsequent mailing to the defendant to cover the overdraft after learning that the checks had bounced; malice existed on behalf of defendant [lack of probable cause itself gives rise to an inference of malice] as evidenced by its continued prosecution after it learned of the corrected payment; plaintiff was positively damaged - she was both publicly humiliated and shunned by several prospective employers because of her arrest record; and finally, we find that the criminal

Texas Skaggs Inc. v. Graves
Court of Appeals of Texas, 582 S.W.2d 863 (1979)

proceedings terminated in favor of plaintiff. Although the case was dismissed, we conclude that had the matter been pressed to its conclusion, she would likely have secured an acquittal. In addition, we and Prosser are in accord with the rule established by the Restatement (Second) of Torts §§ 658, 659 which states that an abandonment of proceedings where the prosecution has become impossible constitutes a termination in favor of the accused.

 Affirmed.

Friedman v. Dozorc
Supreme Court of Michigan, 312 N.W.2d 585 (1981)

FACTS

In 1970, Leona Serafin entered Outer Drive Hospital for the treatment of a gynecological problem. While there, Plaintiff Dr. Friedman recommended the surgical removal of a kidney stone. During the surgery, she began to ooze blood uncontrollably. Five days later, she died from a rare blood disease, the cause and cure of which remain unknown. The administrator of Ms. Serafin's estate filed a malpractice action against Dr. Friedman, the hospital, and other doctors though its lawyers, attorneys Dozorc (defendant) and Golden. After receiving a directed verdict of no cause of action in his favor, the plaintiff-physician commenced this suit for negligence, abuse of process and malicious prosecution against defendant-attorney Dozorc. Plaintiff argues that an attorney owes a present or prospective adverse party a duty of care to conduct a reasonable investigation and have a good-faith basis for asserting the action against his adversary, the breach of which will give rise to a cause of action in negligence. Defendant argues that no such actionable duty to an adverse party exists. The trial court granted summary judgment for defendants, finding that no such duty exists. The Court of Appeals affirmed in part and reversed in part: it affirmed the dismissal of the negligence and abuse of process claims, but reversed the dismissal of plaintiff's cause of action for malicious prosecution. Both parties appealed; plaintiff appeals the dismissal of his cause of action for malicious prosecution, while defendant cross-appeals the reversal of the dismissal of plaintiff's cause of action for malicious prosecution.

 Does an attorney owe a present or prospective adverse party a duty of care to conduct a reasonable investigation and have a good-faith basis for asserting the action against his adversary, the breach of which will give rise to a cause of action in negligence?

 With regard to the cause of action for malicious prosecution of civil proceedings, must a plaintiff prove a special injury?

 An attorney does not owe an actionable duty to conduct a reasonable investigation nor must he have a good-faith basis for asserting the action against his adversary; however, the attorney may be held liable for malicious prosecution of civil proceedings if, in addition to a special injury, the adversary can prove 1) the prior proceedings terminated in favor of the present plaintiff; 2) the absence of probable cause for those proceedings; and 3) "malice," a/k/a "a purpose other than that of securing the proper adjudication of the claim in which the proceedings are based."

 An attorney does not owe an actionable duty to conduct a reasonable investigation nor must he have a good-faith basis for asserting the action against his adversary. While an attorney may have such a duty to his client, we decline to extend the duty to protect his client's adversary, because such a duty would be inconsistent with the basic precepts of the adversary system. With respect to plaintiff's abuse of process claim, we note that he must plead and prove 1) an

Friedman v. Dozorc

Supreme Court of Michigan, 312 N.W.2d 585 (1981)

ulterior purpose and 2) an act in the use of process which is improper. Plaintiff failed to allege the second element, and thus summary judgment is proper and this claim was correctly dismissed. With regard to the tort cause of action for malicious prosecution of civil proceedings, we hold that in addition to a special injury, the adversary can prove 1) the prior proceedings terminated in favor of the present plaintiff; 2) the absence of probable cause for those proceedings; and 3) "malice," a/k/a "a purpose other than that of securing the proper adjudication of the claim in which the proceedings are based." Because plaintiff failed to allege any special injury, we reverse the decision of the Court of Appeals and affirm the trial court's grant of summary judgment in favor of defendant.

 Affirmed in part; reversed in part.

Grainger v. Hill
Court of Common Pleas, 132 Eng.Rep 769 (1838)

FACTS

Plaintiff Grainger was the owner of a ship which he mortgaged to Defendant Hill and others for 80£, with a covenant for repayment in September 1837. Under this agreement, plaintiff was allowed to retain command of the ship and conduct voyages for his own profit. Sometime later, defendant, through duress, tried to force plaintiff into relinquishing control of the ship by threatening to arrest him unless he paid the mortgage immediately. This attempt by the defendant was rebuffed by the plaintiff and plaintiff refused to pay since the mortgage was not yet due. Nevertheless, defendant instituted legal proceedings against plaintiff, knowing that plaintiff could not provide bail. Plaintiff was kept imprisoned until he finally relinquished the vessel. Plaintiff brought an action for abuse of process. Defendant filed a motion for nonsuit, alleging that the suit commenced by defendant had not terminated, therefore he [plaintiff] was not entitled to bring an abuse of process cause of action.

 Must a legal proceeding have concluded in order for the accused to sue for abuse of process?

 Former proceedings need not be terminated, nor founded upon reasonable and probable cause, in order to bring action for abuse of process.

 A legal proceeding need not have been concluded in order for the accused to sue for abuse of process. Defendant claims that it is necessary to show that a previous proceeding has terminated, and that there was no probable cause for the previous proceeding. That would be true were this an action for malicious prosecution. It is not. This action by plaintiff is for abuse of process. In this case, plaintiff claims that this action was created and brought by the defendant to extort property from him. In such as case, the action does not require the termination of previous proceedings or a lack of probable cause in order to be brought.

 Judgment for plaintiff; nonsuit denied.

Swinton v. Whitinsville Savings Bank

Supreme Judicial Court of Mass., 42 N.E.2d 808 (1942)

FACTS

Plaintiff Swinton purchased a house in Newton, Massachusetts, from Defendant Whitinsville Savings Bank (Bank). Approximately two years after the purchase, Swinton learned that the house was infested with termites so he sued the Bank, claiming that it knew the house was infested with termites, that it falsely and fraudulently concealed this fact from him and that he could not have readily observed this condition upon inspection. As a result, Swinton claimed to have been put to great expense to repair and prevent the house from being further destroyed by the termites.

 Is the failure to disclose a defect actionable as a misrepresentation?

 The failure of a seller to disclose a defect is not a misrepresentation that will support an action for fraud, absent a special duty or relationship.

 The failure of a seller to disclose a defect is not a misrepresentation that will support an action for fraud, absent a special duty or relationship. In the instant case, the Bank did not actively represent that there was no termite infestation and there was no special relationship or duty between the parties which would mandate such a disclosure. Lastly, there was no proof offered to show that the bank prevented Swinton from making an inspection of the house on his own or through an agent hired by him. The sale of the house was made simply at "arm's length."

 Judgment affirmed.

Griffith v. Byers Constr. Co. of Kansas Inc.

Supreme Court of Kansas, 510 P.2d 198 (1973)

FACTS

Plaintiff Griffith and others purchased homes in the City of Wichita, Kansas. The land, however, was once part of an abandoned oil field and the soil contained high concentrations of saline. Defendant Byers Construction Company developed this property and had knowledge of the soil conditions, but did not disclose those conditions to plaintiff and the other home buyers. Consequently, plaintiff and the others sued defendant for 1) breach of the implied warranty of fitness and 2) fraudulent concealment. Plaintiff alleged that defendant graded and developed the area in such a manner that it became impossible for plaintiff to discover the presence of the saline in the soil. Defendant defended on the ground that, as a matter of law, no claims for fraud could be maintained because no privity existed between it, as the defendant-developer, and the home buyers. Summary judgment was granted in favor of the defendant and the plaintiff appealed.

Can a developer be liable for concealing facts from a home buyer regarding the integrity of the soil when such defects do not affect the structural qualities of the homes themselves when the home buyer has acted in reliance thereupon?

In the real estate context, one who makes a fraudulent misrepresentation or concealment is subject to liability for pecuniary loss to person or class of persons whom he intends or has reason to expect to act or to refrain from action in reliance upon the misrepresentation or concealment.

Usually, the party with knowledge has a duty to disclose when a legally actionable relationship exists between the parties or when custom in the trade so dictates. Where the relationship involves the building/sale of real estate, the rule stated in *Jenkins v. McCormick* is applicable. In *Jenkins,* the court held that where a vendor has knowledge of a latent defect, failure to disclose the defect constitutes actionable fraud. In this case, the defendant was not a seller of the property at issue [defendant was the developer/builder]. As such, defendant was not in direct privity with the plaintiff-buyers. Nevertheless, plaintiff and the other purchasers were within the "class of persons" whom the defendant intended and had reason to expect would purchase and build their homes. Thus, the failure of defendant to disclose the *material* defects in the soil to the plaintiff could constitute actionable fraudulent concealment. We note that for the fraudulent concealment to be actionable, it must also be material to the transaction. Here, the concealment was material since a buyer of a residential home would surely attach importance to a soil condition whose defects would affect the present and future value of the home. However, with respect to the claim of breach of implied warranty, we arrive at a different conclusion. A real estate developer by subdividing and offering lots for sale as a choice of residential home sites does not by implication warrant the fertility of the soil. Thus, liability based on an implied warranty of soil cannot reasonably be imposed upon the real estate developer in this case.

The order of summary judgment is affirmed as to those claims based on implied warranty but reversed as to the claims based on fraud.

Derry v. Peek

House of Lords, 14 App.Cass. 337 (1889)

FACTS

Plaintiff Sir Henry William Peek purchased shares of stock in the Plymouth, Devonport and District Tramways Company. In making his investment in the company, plaintiff relied on a prospectus that stated that the company could legally use steam or mechanical power, instead of horses, in operating its tram and that such an alternate power source would result in cost savings and increased profits for the company and its shareholders. The company proceeded to construct its tramways and thereafter, the Board of Trade allowed the company to use steam or mechanical power, but only on limited portions of the line. The directors of the Company refused to consent to the company opening the completed part of their lines until the uncompleted portioned were completely constructed and ready for use. In consequence, the company was wound up [to reduce the resources and activities of a business or enterprise with the intent of eventually ceasing all operations as a going concern]. Plaintiff sued Defendant William Derry, the company's chairman and four of its directors for deceit. The action was dismissed on the ground that that the defendants' honestly believed it had those rights stated in the prospectus and that their conduct was not reckless. On appeal, the dismissal was reversed on the ground that the statements in the prospectus were made without any reasonable grounds for believing them. Defendant and the others appeal to the House of Lords.

In a suit for deceit, is proof that the statement was made negligently, without more, sufficient to sustain the cause of action?

In order to sustain an action for deceit, there must be proof of fraud; fraud is proved when it is shown that the false representation has been made 1) knowingly, or 2) without belief in its truth, or 3) recklessly, careless whether it is true or false.

In a suit for deceit, proof that the statement was made negligently, without more, is not sufficient to sustain the cause of action. Therefore, one who honestly believes his statement to be true, even if such a belief is made negligently or unreasonably, will not be held liable for misrepresentation. In order to sustain an action for deceit, there must be proof of fraud; fraud is proved when it is shown that the false representation has been made 1) knowingly, or 2) without belief in its truth, or 3) recklessly, careless whether it is true or false. Hence, one who knowingly or recklessly makes a false can entertain no honest belief in its truth. Once more, the motive behind the statement is immaterial. Consequently, only if the person has an honest belief in the truth of the statement will liability **not** attach. However, to unravel what the speaker actually believed is no easy task. Thus, courts must judge the speaker's actual belief by an objective standard: Would a reasonable man, similarly situated, believe what was stated?

Order of the Court of Appeals is reversed.

International Products Co. v. Erie R.R. Co.
Court of Appeals of New York, 244 N.Y. 331 (1927)

FACTS

Plaintiff International Products Co. was expecting a valuable consignment of goods to be delivered and stored at a dock until they could be reshipped. The shipment was covered by insurance until it reached the site of storage. Wanting to insure the goods after that time, plaintiff asked Defendant Erie R.R. Co. where the goods would be stored. Defendant informed plaintiff that the goods were stored at Dock F. Believing the goods had already arrived at that specific dock, plaintiff obtained insurance in reliance thereupon. However, the goods later arrived and were sent to and stored at Dock D. After the consignment was destroyed by a fire, plaintiff attempted to collect on the policy. However, the insurance company refused to pay, as the description of the storage site of the goods was different from the actual site of the loss. Thereafter, plaintiff sued defendant to recover its damages. The trial court directed a verdict for plaintiff, and the Appellate Division affirmed. Defendant appealed.

May liability be imposed on a defendant for its negligently false statements when such statements were relied upon by the plaintiff?

Based on a case-by-case basis, the American Rule imposes liability for false statements made negligently that induce reliance in another.

The English Rule of *Derry v. Peek*, where negligence is not a sufficient ground for imposing liability for deceit, has not been adopted in our country. In England, the rule is fixed: Generally speaking, there is no duty to use any care whatever in making statements and no such thing as liability in negligence in words as distinguished from acts. However, American courts have imposed liability not on any and all negligent statements, but rather only on those which give rise to a duty legally recognized. Thus, based on a case-by-case basis, the American Rule imposes liability for false statements made negligently that induce reliance in another. Liability in such cases only arises when there is a duty, if there is one at all, to give the correct information and requires the following: 1) knowledge that the information is required for a serious purpose; 2) knowledge that the listener intends to rely upon the statement; and 3) an injury occurring because of the reliance. Each case must be decided on the peculiar facts presented. Here, the defendant had a duty to speak with care, which it did not. Defendant negligently answered the plaintiff's question knowing that it was to become the bailee of its goods, knowing that the plaintiff was to obtain insurance for those goods, realizing that its response would be relied upon by the plaintiff. Plaintiff, on the other hand, made an inquiry that was in the usual course of business and consistent with such practices, received a response by the defendant which it relied upon to its detriment, and suffered a resulting proximate loss. The fact that the statement was not made to further defendant's own purposes is immaterial.

Affirmed.

Winter v. G.P. Putnam's Sons

U.S. Court of Appeals, 938 F.2d 1033 (9th Cir. 1991)

FACTS

Plaintiff Winter bought a book written by two British authors and originally published by a British publishing company. The book, entitled "The Encyclopedia of Mushrooms," was a reference guide which contained information on the habitat, collection, and cooking of mushrooms. This book was published by Defendant G.P. Putnam's Sons, an American book publisher, which purchased copies of the book from the British publisher and distributed the finished product in the United States. Defendant neither wrote nor edited the book. Plaintiff relied on descriptions in the book in determining which mushrooms were safe to eat. After cooking and eating the harvest, plaintiff became critically ill and required liver transplants [only Plaintiff Winter is referenced here, not the other plaintiff]. Plaintiff brought suit in strict liability and under other theories of liability. He alleged that the book contained erroneous and misleading information concerning the identification of the most deadly species of mushrooms. Defendant moved for summary judgment based upon 1) the information in the book does not provide the proper basis for imposing strict liability; and 2) the defendant is not liable under any remaining theories of liability because a publisher does not have a duty to investigate the accuracy of the text it publishes. The district court granted defendant's motion for summary judgment. Plaintiff appealed.

I^1 For the purposes of products liability law, are the ideas and expressions included in a book considered a "product"?

I^2 Can a publisher be held liable for failure to investigate the accuracy of the contents of the books it publishes?

R Products liability law does not encompass those ideas and expressions contained in a book; and a publisher is not under a legal duty to investigate the accuracy of the contents of the books it publishes.

A Products liability law does not encompass those ideas and expressions contained in a book; and a publisher is not under a legal duty to investigate the accuracy of the contents of the books it publishes. The language of products liability law focuses on tangible items and does not take into consideration the unique characteristics of ideas and expression. We place a high priority on the unhindered fee exchange of ideas and expression. To hold the doctrine applicable to such intangibles, in the absence of fault or a special undertaking or responsibility, would seriously inhibit and adversely impact those who wish to share new thoughts and theories with others. As a result, we decline to expand products liability law to embrace the ideas and expressions in a book. Turning to the second issue, we conclude that defendant has no duty to investigate the accuracy of the books it publishes. A publisher may, of course, assume such a burden, but no such a duty should be imposed legally on publishers. In light of inevitable First Amendment implications and the social costs that would flow from a holding to the contrary, we decline defendant's invitation to impose such a duty on the defendant-publisher. We also reject plaintiff's request to hold a publisher liable for not giving a warning that 1) the information in the book is not complete and that a consumer may not fully rely on it; or 2) the publisher has not investigated the text and cannot guarantee its accuracy. With respect to the first, a publisher would not know what, if any, warnings were required without engaging in a detailed analysis of the factual contents of the book. This would force a publisher to do exactly what we have said it has no duty to do. With respect to the second, such a warning is unnecessary given that no publisher has a duty to act as a guarantor. Hence, the decision of the district court is affirmed.

Decision of the district court is affirmed.

Hanberry v. Hearst Corp.
Court of Appeal of California, 81 Cal.Rptr. 519 (1969)

FACTS

Plaintiff-appellant Hanberry purchased a pair of shoes form Defendant Akron, which were manufactured by Defendant Handal. Plaintiff suffered severe physical injuries when she wore the shoes on the vinyl flooring of her kitchen, slipped and fell. Plaintiff sued both defendants for the allegedly defective shoes and also sued Defendant-appellee Hearst Corporation, publisher of *Good Housekeeping* magazine, for negligently reviewing and giving a *Good Housekeeping Consumers' Guaranty Seal* of approval to the shoes. *Good Housekeeping* guaranteed the truthfulness of the claims made in the magazine and the quality of any goods to which it granted a seal of approval. Plaintiff alleged that defendant was careless and negligent in reviewing the shoes, and that she purchased the shoes without testing them because she relied on the *Good Housekeeping* approval and guarantee. Defendant demurred to the actions against it and the court dismissed the claims against defendant. Plaintiff appealed.

Can a publisher be held liable to the buyer of a product if the former endorsed the product and the latter bought the product in reliance thereupon?

A publisher may be held liable to a buyer for endorsing a product which the latter purchased in reliance upon the former's endorsement, which causes an injury to the latter and which proves to be defective.

A publisher may be held liable to a buyer for endorsing a product which the latter purchased in reliance upon the former's endorsement, which causes an injury to the latter and which proves to be defective. Defendant first argues that the review was merely a statement of opinion and, therefore, not actionable. However, since the very purpose of the seal and it certification was to induce and encourage the public to buy the shoes, defendant's argument that its endorsement cannot be considered a legally inducing factor is weak. Defendant stood in a far superior position to plaintiff, holding itself out as a disinterested 3rd party; neither a manufacturer nor seller of the goods. Defendant represented to the public that it possessed superior knowledge and special information concerning the shoes, and under such circumstances defendant may be liable for negligent representation of either fact or opinion. Defendant next argues that it is common knowledge that the slippery nature of the shoes was a matter of common knowledge. This may be true, however, it is a question to be determined by the trier of fact at trial, not for the court via the granting of a dismissal in favor of the defendant. We are not prepared at this stage to hold that, *as a matter of law*, liability will not attach under *any* circumstances based upon a defectively designed shoe.

Judgment of dismissal is reversed.

Richard v. A. Waldman and Sons Inc.

Supreme Court of Connecticut, 232 A.2d 307 (1967)

FACTS

Plaintiff Richard purchased a house from Defendant A. Waldman and Sons, Inc. and relied on a plot plan prepared by a registered engineer and land surveyor. About four months after the delivery of the deed to the plaintiff, defendant discovered that the southeast corner of the house was only 1.8 foot from the boundary of the lot. As a result, plaintiff was actually trespassing on his neighbor's lot every time he left his back door and stoop. A certificate of occupancy was thus erroneously issued based on the survey submitted by the defendant and indicated that the house complied with zoning regulations. Thus, the house failed to comply with zoning regulations. Prior to this discovery, both parties were unaware of the violations. Plaintiff sued for misrepresentation; and defendant argued that at most there was an innocent misrepresentation of fact on its part. The trial court disagreed with the defendant and the plaintiff obtained a judgment for damages; defendant appealed.

 May an innocent misrepresentation be actionable if the declarant has the means of knowing, ought to know, or has the duty of knowing the truth?

 An innocent misrepresentation be actionable if the declarant has the means of knowing, ought to know, or has the duty of knowing the truth.

 An innocent misrepresentation be actionable if the declarant has the means of knowing, ought to know, or has the duty of knowing the truth. Defendant, as developer of residential real estate, had special means of knowledge [regarding the zoning law]; a matter particularly relating to its business and matter upon which plaintiff was entitled to rely. It is not necessary for the plaintiff to prove that defendant *actually knew* that the representations were false; nor must the plaintiff allege fraud or bad faith. Defendant had special knowledge, was commercially involved in and responsible for the preliminary and final plan for the building and locating the structure was then built on the lot. He has alleged all the material facts to support his claim and demand for damages. The plan was in the nature of a warranty, and plaintiff can recover damages for the difference between the actual value of the property and the value of the property had it been as represented. There was no error.

 Affirmed.

Credit Alliance Corp. v. Arthur Andersen & Co.
Court of Appeals of New York, 65 N.Y.2d 536 (1985)

FACTS

In this opinion, the Court of Appeals of New York addresses two appeals with a critical issue in common: the liability of an CPA firm which prepared financial statements to a contracting party, upon which a 3rd party lender relied in providing credit. In the first appeal, *Credit Alliance Corp. v. Anderson & Co.*, Defendant Arthur Andersen, an accounting firm, provided audited financial statements pursuant to a contract it had with L.B. Smith, Inc. L.B. Smith used the prepared statements to obtain credit from Plaintiff Credit Alliance. Plaintiff sued defendant for damages sustained in reliance on the statements, alleging that the statements were inaccurate because of the defendant's failure to use the proper auditing standards. The trial court denied defendant's motion to dismiss, and the appellate court affirmed. Defendant appealed.

In the other appeal, *European Am. Bank & Trust Co. v. Strahs & Kaye*, the defendant, Strahs & Kaye, a CPA firm, provided audited financial statements under a contract with Majestic Electro. A 3rd party, Plaintiff European American Bank, not in privity to the contract, relied on the statements and provided loans to Majestic in reliance thereupon. Plaintiff sued defendant for seriously inflated Majestic's assets, resulting in injury to the plaintiff when Majestic went bankrupt. The trial court granted defendant's motion to dismiss, the appellate division reversed, and the defendant appealed.

Can a CPA firm [accountant] be held liable to a 3rd party who relies upon financial reports which were prepared negligently?

CPA firms and accountants may be held liable to 3rd parties who rely on omissions/ misrepresentations/exaggerations when contractual privity or its equivalent exists and the following prerequisites exist: 1) the accountants were aware of the purposes the statements would be used for; 2) a known third party was intended to rely on the statements; and 3) there was some conduct on the part of the accountants linking them to the 3rd party.

Our holding with regard to both appeals is based on the holdings of *Ultramares Corp. v. Touche*, where an accounting firm not liable to a 3rd party having no contractual privity with accountants for misrepresentations in financial statement, and *Glanzer v. Shepard*, where liability may attach in the absence of contractual privity when information is directly transferred to the non-contracting 3rd party who relies thereon. In *Ultramares*, the accountants prepared financial statements solely for **their** client, and the client gave one of the statements to a lender who relied on the information contained in the statement. In *Glanzer*, the declarant furnished one copy of a weight certificate to the contracting party, the seller of goods, and another copy directly to the non-contracting buyer. In that case, we allowed an action for negligence against the defendants, despite the absence of a contract between the parties, because the plaintiff's intended reliance on the information directly transmitted by the defendants, created a bond so closely approaching privity that it was, in practical effect, virtually indistinguishable therefrom. In light of the above, we announce the following rule: Accountants may be held liable to non-contracting parties

Credit Alliance Corp. v. Arthur Andersen & Co.
Court of Appeals of New York, 65 N.Y.2d 536 (1985)

who rely to their detriment on inaccurate financial reports if: 1) the accountants were aware of the purposes the statements would be used for; 2) a known third party was intended to rely on the statements; and 3) there was some conduct on the part of the accountants linking them to the third party. Turning to the two appeals before us, we note the following: In *Credit Alliance*, there was no privity nor any equivalent relationship sufficient to impose liability on the defendant because no adequate allegation existed to show that the defendant was hired to prepare reports with the specific purpose of helping a 3rd party, here L.B. Smith, obtain credit. Accordingly, the *Credit Alliance* causes of action are dismissed and the appellate division's order is reversed. We now address the second appeal. Conversely, in *European American*, Defendant S & K was well aware that the goal of the audits it prepared of the Majestic Electro Company was to provide Plaintiff EAB with financial information; information it relied upon in provided loans to Majestic. Thus, the order of the appellate division in *European American* is affirmed.

Order affirmed.

Citizens State Bank v. Timm, Schmidt & Co.

Supreme Court of Wisconsin, 335 N.W.2d 361 (1983)

FACTS

Defendant Timm, Schmidt & Co., an accounting firm, prepared financial statements for Clintonville Fire Apparatus, Inc ("CFA"). Relying on these statements, Plaintiff Citizens State Bank loaned $380,000 to CFA. Defendant subsequently discovered mistakes in its statements totaling over $400,000, and thereafter called all of CFA's loans due. CFA went into receivership and was dissolved, and plaintiff was paid for all but $150,000 of the loans it lent CFA. Plaintiff sued defendant for the amount unpaid and unrecovered – $150,000. Defendant moved for summary judgment, arguing and submitted affidavits that it had no knowledge that CFA intended to obtain loans from plaintiff or any other lender. The trial court granted defendant's motion, the appellate court affirmed and the plaintiff appealed.

 May CPA firms and accountants be held liable for the negligent preparation of financial reports [statements of financial condition, retained income and earnings and changes in financial condition – in essence, an audit] to a 3rd parties not in privity with it but who rely on the report?

 CPA firms and accountants can be held liable for the negligent preparation of financial reports to 3rd parties, even if privity is lacking.

 Accounts have long been held not liable for their negligence to relying 3rd parties not in privity under the rule set forth in *Ultramares Corp. v. Touche.* Today we depart from that rule and hold that in this state, privity is not required for liability, nor may an accountant escape liability by claiming that he had no actual knowledge that the person/entity who/which relied upon the financial statement was using it to evaluate whether it should make a loan to another party. Our holding is consistent with general negligence law, in which a tortfeasor is liable for all foreseeable consequences of his act except as those consequences are limited by policy factors. We have previously set out a number of public policy reasons for not imposing liability despite a finding of negligence. The include: 1) the fact that the jury is too remote from the negligence; 2) the injury is wholly out of proportion to the culpability of the defendant; 3) that in retrospect, it appears too highly extraordinary that he negligence should have brought about the harm; 4) that allowance of recovery would place an unreasonable burden on the tortfeasor; or 5) would open the way for fraudulent claims. In this case, these public policy exceptions should be applied at trial after the facts of the case have been fully explored, such that a motion for summary judgment is improper. Lastly, we note that defendant failed to establish that it was entitled to summary judgment as a matter of law. Defendant's submitted affidavits do not dispose of the issue that it was foreseeable that a negligently prepared financial statement could cause harm to plaintiff.

 Reversed and remanded.

Ultramares Corp. v. Touche, Niven & Co.

Court of Appeals of New York, 170 N.E. 441 (1931)

FACTS

In 1924, Defendant Touche, a CPA firm, prepared and certified a balance sheet for its client, Fred Stern & Co. evidencing the latter's condition of its business; that it was solvent and had a net worth of over $1 million. The truth, however, was that Stern was actually insolvent, and its balance sheet made up of false statements of income and expenses prepared by Stern executives. Defendant prepared the balance sheet knowing that it would be shown to banks, creditors, stockholders, purchasers or sellers but it did not know that the balance sheet would be shown specifically to Plaintiff Ultramares Corp., a company doing business with Stern as a factor (one who transacts business for another; an agent; a substitute; especially, a mercantile agent who buys and sells goods and transacts business for others in commission; a commission merchant or consignee). In reliance on the balance sheet, Ultramares advanced money to Stern, but lost it when Stern went bankrupt.

Can an action for misrepresentation be brought against a 3rd party based on its negligent misstatement when there is no privity of contract or prior relationship between the 3rd party and the plaintiff?

If there is privity of contract or a prior contractual relationship between the party making the negligent statement and the party to whom the statement is made, an action for misrepresentation may be sustained.

If there is privity of contract or a prior contractual relationship between the party making the negligent statement and the party to whom the statement is made, an action for misrepresentation may be sustained. Negligent misrepresentation is not the same as fraud. We note the distinction: fraud requires intent to deceive while negligent misrepresentation does not require the maker of the misrepresentation to know that the representation is false. Thus, the field of liability should not be enlarged to cover everyone those who might be injured by a negligent misstatement.

Plaintiff's cause of action for negligent misrepresentation dismissed and a new trial granted with respect to the negligence cause of action.

Williams v. Rank & Son Buick Inc.

Supreme Court of Wisconsin, 170 N.W.2d 807 (1969)

FACTS

Plaintiff Williams went to Defendant Rank & Son Buick, Inc. and looked at a used Chrysler automobile to buy. He alleged that defendant's salesman fraudulently told him that the car had air conditioning and that it had been described in an advertisement upon which he relied. Although he took it for a test drive for 1 ½ hours before he purchased it, he claims not to have realized, until several days later that it did not, in fact, have air conditioning. Thereafter, he sued defendant for damages. The trial court granted a judgment for $150 in favor of plaintiff; defendant appealed.

 Can a plaintiff recover for damages when he relied on a statement which was obviously false?

 A person cannot recover for an obviously false misrepresentation; the obviousness of which should be judged by the intelligence and experience of the misled person and the relationship between the parties.

 A person cannot recover for an obviously false misrepresentation; the obviousness of which should be judged by the intelligence and experience of the misled person and the relationship between the parties. Here, plaintiff had ample opportunity to inspect the obviousness of the statement's truth or falsity, and there were no barriers or impediments to his inquiry - defendant made no effort to interfere with the plaintiff's examination of the car. And while defendant's salesman did make a false statement, plaintiff was intelligent enough to have tested the air condition system of the automobile prior to purchase for himself. Indeed, he took the car, unaccompanied by the salesman, for a test drive for 1½ hours. We are reminded that no fiduciary relationship existed between the parties. Had plaintiff reasonably inspected the car, by a mere flip of a knob, he would have found out that the car did not have air conditioning. Thus, as a matter of law, plaintiff was not justified in relying on the oral representations of the salesman.

 Reversed.

Saxby v. Southern Land Co.

Supreme Court of Appeals of Virginia, 63 S.E. 423 (1909)

FACTS

Defendant Southern Land Co. represented that a farm, known as Winslow, contained at least 150 acres of pine lumber of which about 20 acres had been burned over and contained about 120 acres of timber, about 60 acres of which had been burned over. In reality, the land contained only 60 acres of non-burned timber. Defendant also misrepresented that the timber would sell for $4 per cord, and that the land would yield 100 bushels of potatoes per acre. Plaintiff Saxby, the buyer, sued for these misrepresentations. Defendant demurred to the complaint, contending that the representations were merely statements of opinion. The trial court sustained the demurrer, and the plaintiff appealed.

Can a defendant be held liable for the tort of misrepresentation when he makes a misstatement of opinion to a plaintiff?

Statements of opinion do not give rise to liability for misrepresentation.

A misrepresentation, the falsity of which will afford ground for an action for damages, must be of an existing fact, and not the mere expression of an opinion. Thus, a misstatement of opinion, however strong or forceful, does not give rise to liability for misrepresentation and an individual is not justified in relying on mere opinions. With respect to the inst case, the facts indicate that defendant was not asserting a fact in stating the number of acres of pine; the statements were sufficiently indefinite to have required plaintiff to probe deeper. Moreover, the predictions about the selling price of wood and the likely potato crop were not assertions of fact, since the production of land in the future and the price of cordwood in the future are dependent upon so many conditions that no assertion of an existing fact could be made with respect thereto. Thus, all of the statements relied on by the plaintiff were merely "trade talk" of the defendant.

The order sustaining the demurrer must be affirmed.

Vulcan Metals Co. v. Simmons Mfg. Co.

U.S. Court of Appeals, 248 Fed. 853 (2nd Cir. 1918)

FACTS

Defendant-respondent Simmons Manufacturing Co. sold all of its patents to some vacuum cleaners, along with all of its tools, dies and equipment for the manufacture the cleaners, together will all machines and parts on hand, to Plaintiff-appellant Vulcan Metals Co. Prior to the sale, during negotiations, a Simmons agent told Vulcan that its vacuum cleaner was a superior mode, very easy to operate and that no one outside the company knew the machines were not on the market. After the sale, however, Vulcan learned that the machines did not work as claimed, were unmarketable and that Simmons had engaged in previous marketing efforts resulting in the sale of only 60 or so machines. Consequently, Vulcan sued Simmons for deceit, claiming that its purchase of the machines, patents and related materials was based on Simmons's false representations with respect to the product. Simmons counterclaimed on the (promissory) notes Vulcan signed for part of the purchase price. The district court entered directed verdicts for Simmons on both the original action and on Simmons's counterclaim, finding that Vulcan had not proved any actionable fraud. An appeal was made to the 2nd Circuit.

 Can an action for deceit be sustained by the false statements of a seller as to the quality of goods sold by him?

 An action for deceit cannot be sustained by the false statements of a seller as to the quality of goods sold by him because reasonable people do not rely on the seller's statements with respect to such representations.

 An action for deceit cannot be sustained by the false statements of a seller as to the quality of goods sold by him because reasonable people do not rely on the seller's statements with respect to such representations - Vulcan had ample opportunity to inspect the goods before purchasing them. Such statements are regarded as "puffing" or "dealer's talk." However, with respect to Simmons's declaration that the vacuum had not been marketed, an action for deceit may be sustained because such a statement does not relate to the quality of the goods and because it may have been material to and reasonably have been relied upon by Vulcan in making the decision to purchase. Next, we address whether any such misrepresentation claimed by Vulcan was cured by the recital in the sales contract (the so-called "retraction" or "recital") – thereby quashing liability on the part of Simmons. An adequate retraction of the false statement before the execution of the contract would provide a valid defense; however, that was not the case here. The recital contained with the sales contract (which recited the fact that both parties were engaged in the sale and that the first party has been engaged in the manufacture of vacuum cleaners) and signed by both parties was not placed in the contract in a way certain "to catch the eye of the reader" and so cannot operate as a retraction of any false statement.

 Judgment for Simmons in the action for deceit reversed; judgment for Simmons on its counterclaim on the promissory note affirmed.

Sorenson v. Gardner

Supreme Court of Oregon, 334 P.2d 471 (1959)

FACTS

Plaintiff-buyer Sorenson sued Defendant-seller Gardner for deceit, alleging that defendant falsely represented that the house he bought from the latter was constructed in a workmanlike manner and met all code requirements, particularly with respect to the electric wiring, plumbing, and the septic tank and sewage disposal systems. At trial, plaintiff produced evidence showing that certain code requirements were not met. The trial court granted a judgment for $2,000 for plaintiff; defendant appealed.

Can a defendant be held liable for fraud predicated on misrepresentations of law or misrepresentations as to matters of law?

If the representation by the seller-speaker to the buyer-recipient concerns the legal effect of facts not disclosed or otherwise known to the recipient, liability may be imposed for a false representation as to a matter of law in a business transaction may be imposed; however, if all the facts believed by the seller-speaker are conveyed to the buyer-recipient, then such representation is an expression of opinion and is not actionable.

If the representation by the seller-speaker to the buyer-recipient concerns the legal effect of facts not disclosed or otherwise known to the recipient, liability may be imposed for a false representation as to a matter of law in a business transaction may be imposed. If, however, all the facts believed by the seller-speaker are conveyed to the buyer-recipient, then such representation is an expression of opinion and is not actionable. Here, defendant represented that the house complied with the minimum code requirements. There was evidence that plaintiff was ignorant of the facts regarding code compliance. Thus, defendant is not entitled to a directed verdict. Reversed, however, and new trial ordered on the grounds of error in instructing the jury as to the measure of damages.

Reversed and new trial ordered.

McElrath v. Electric Investment Co.

Supreme Court of Minnesota, 131 N.W. 380 (1911)

FACTS

Defendant Electric Investment Co. was the owner of some summer hotel property in Antlers Park, Minnesota, which it leased to Plaintiff McElrath. Plaintiff intended to operate the property as a summer resort. Plaintiff claims that defendant falsely represented that an electric railroad would soon be completed by a 3rd party that would run electric cars to Antlers Park during the summer, making the Park an important summer resort for people living in the surrounding area and that plaintiff would make not less than $1,500 per year running the hotel after expenses. Plaintiff sued, claiming false representation. Defendant demurred to the complaint arguing that the false representations were not actionable because there were merely predictions of future intentions. The trial court overruled the general demurrer, and defendant appealed.

 Can a defendant be held liable for misrepresentation for predictions of future intentions, made to the plaintiff-recipient, which creates in him the belief that the predictions are fact?

 A defendant-speaker will not be held liable for predictions of future events unless the defendant-speaker knows of an existing fact(s) which would thwart the future event from occurring.

 A defendant-speaker will not be held liable for predictions of future events unless the defendant-speaker knows of an existing fact(s) which would thwart the future event from occurring. In this case, defendant intended to create in plaintiff the belief that a railroad would be built which would actually service the surrounding area and stop at Antlers Park. Consequently, plaintiff was justified in relying on these representations which, if proven false, are actionable and would allow the plaintiff to recover damages for defendant's fraud. Turning to the other two representations, however, we find that plaintiff did not state facts sufficient to constitute an action for misrepresentation. The statements regarding the popularity of the summer resort as an attraction for the people of Minneapolis and the forecast of future income of not less than $1,500, was grounded entirely in conjecture and speculation. Whether the "facts" of two statements could have actually come true would depend on a number of uncertain factors, all of which were out of the control of defendant.

 Affirmed.

Burgdorfer v. Thielemann

Supreme Court of Oregon, 55 P.2d 1122 (1936)

FACTS

Plaintiff Charles Burgdorfer brought suit against Defendant Carl Thielemann for deceit claiming that the latter fraudulently induced him [plaintiff] to exchange a total of $2,323 in notes and a mortgage for two lots by falsely promising that he [defendant] would pay a $500 mortgage on one of the two lots. It is alleged by the plaintiff that he relied to his detriment on the defendant's statement but that defendant never really intended to pay the $500 mortgage. The trial court rendered a judgment for plaintiff and the defendant appealed, arguing that 1) the trial court committed error by permitting plaintiff to testify as to the defendant's alleged promise to pay off the mortgage; and 2) the statute of frauds prohibits such testimony, since the oral promise to pay the $500 mortgage could not be performed within one year. To be enforceable, it must have been reduced to a writing and signed by the party sought to be charged.

Can a defendant be held liable for deceit [fraudulent misrepresentation] when he professes an intent to do or not to do something but he really intends to do the contrary?

A defendant can be held liable for deceit [fraudulent misrepresentation] when he professes an intent to do or not to do something but he really intends to do the contrary.

A defendant can be held liable for deceit [fraudulent misrepresentation] when he professes an intent to do or not to do something but he really intends to do the contrary – it is a clear case of fraud. The state of a person's mind, and his future intentions, is a fact. A misrepresentation as to the state of the person's mind is, therefore, a misstatement of fact. Here, it is our opinion that defendant never intended to pay the $500 mortgage, such that plaintiff was justified in relying on his statement to the contrary and was damaged as a consequence thereof. With regard to defendant's claim that the statue of frauds provides a valid defense; we find defendant's argument flawed, and plaintiff may testify as to the statement. This is because the purpose of the testimony was to prove fraud and not to establish the agreement. Therefore, the statute of frauds is not applicable.

Affirmed.

Hinkle v. Rockville Motor Co. Inc.

Court of Appeals of Maryland, 278 A.2d 42 (1971)

FACTS

In January of 1970, Plaintiff Donald Hinkle purchased a 1969 Ford Galaxie automobile from Defendant Rockville Motor Company, Inc. Plaintiff alleged that defendant represented to him that the car was new, however, plaintiff subsequently discovered that the car had over 2,000 miles; had been involved in an accident, and that the front and rear portions had been welded together after being severed in the accident. Plaintiff brought the mileage issue to defendant's attention and was compensated in the amount of $109.86, the amount of his first payment to the defendant, in exchange for a release from any and all future claims against it. It was not until, April 1970, some four months later, that plaintiff claims to have found out about the accident history of the car. Alleging that defendant fraudulently concealed the true state of the car, plaintiff sought $100,000 in damages for the deceit. At the close of trial, defendant moved for a directed verdict on grounds that plaintiff failed to produce evidence of the actual value of the automobile. The trial court granted defendant's motion even though plaintiff had produced expert testimony that the effects of the accident could be remedied and the car could be returned to new condition for $800. Plaintiff appealed.

 May a plaintiff recover "benefit of the bargain" in an action for misrepresentation a/k/a deceit?

 In Maryland, an injured plaintiff may recover either "benefit of the bargain" or "out of pocket" expenses as a measure of damages for misrepresentation depending on the facts and circumstances of the case at hand.

 In Maryland, an injured plaintiff may recover either "benefit of the bargain" or "out of pocket" expenses as a measure of damages for misrepresentation depending on the facts and circumstances of the case at hand. The benefit of the bargain theory allows a party to be compensated based on the difference between the value of property as represented and the actual value of the property. By contrast, an "out of pocket" measure of damages allows a party to recover only that which he actually paid for to remedy the injury he sustained. A review of several cases, texts and commentators reveals on the subject suggests that either the benefit of the bargain or the out-of-pocket theory may be applied to actions for deceit. In this case, plaintiff provided expert testimony regarding the cost of necessary repairs thus demonstrating the existence of damages and provided an adequate measure upon which they could be predicated. Thus, the trial court erred in directing a verdict against plaintiff for failing to produce evidence upon which damages could be awarded.

 Reversed and remanded.

Ratcliffe v. Evans
Court of Appeal, 2 Q.B. 524 (1892)

FACTS

Plaintiff Ratcliffe and his father conducted business as an engineer and boiler maker under the name Ratcliffe & Sons. After the father died, plaintiff continued the business. However, Defendant Evans, the publisher of the Country Herald, published a statement in its newspaper to the effect that plaintiff had ceased to carry on business and that the firm no longer existed. Plaintiff sued defendant for the allegedly false and malicious publication. The jury entered a verdict for plaintiff, finding that the writing was a false statement intentionally made to cause damage to plaintiff. At trial, the only proof of damages was that of a general loss of business without proof of any loss of particular customers or orders. Defendant appealed, arguing that plaintiff was required to prove specific damages rather than general damages.

With regard to the tort of "injurious falsehood," is evidence of general damages sufficient to sustain the cause of action?

With regard to the tort of "injurious falsehood," evidence of general damages, such as a general decline in business, may be sufficient to sustain the cause of action.

With regard to the tort of "injurious falsehood," evidence of general damages, such as a general decline in business, may be sufficient to sustain the cause of action. The action for written or oral falsehoods, not actionable per se or defamatory, which is maliciously published to cause damage and which actually does so is analogous to an action for slander of title. To support the cause of action, actual damage must be shown. By contrast, general damages are presumed with respect to a cause of action for personal libel. In the case before us, a falsehood was openly disseminated through the press, read and probably acted on by persons who the plaintiff never heard of. Thus, to refuse to admit this evidence would involve an absolute denial of justice and of redress for the intentionally false and injurious statements. Specific damages need not be proven.

Appeal dismissed.

Horning v. Hardy

Court of Special Appeals of Maryland, 373 A.2d 1273 (1977)

FACTS

Plaintiffs (the "Hardys") sued defendants (the "Hornings") for trespass and ejectment, alleging that the latter were developing property that the plaintiffs owned without their permission. Defendants developed one house and were in the process of closing the sale, but on the morning of the closing date, the plaintiffs' attorney told the buyers that the plaintiffs were the actual owners of the property. The buyers rescinded the sale, and the house went unsold. In reaction thereto, defendants filed a counterclaim for slander of title and interference with contract. The trial court ruled against both the plaintiffs' initial suit and the defendants' counterclaim, holding that the plaintiffs failed to establish that they owned the property through deed or adverse possession and that the plaintiffs were privileged to state that they actually owned the property to the buyers, respectively.

Does a qualified privilege exist and serve as a defense to the tort action for injurious falsehood or disparagement [sometimes referred to as "disparagement of property," "slander of goods," or "trade libel"]?

A qualified privilege exists to protect claimed interests in property, even if a false statement is published which causes an injury to the recipient.

A qualified privilege exists to protect claimed interests in property, even if a false statement is published which causes an injury to the recipient. Injurious falsehood may consist of the publication of a statement derogatory to plaintiff's title to property, or to his business in general, or his personal affairs, of a kind calculated to prevent others from dealing with him [the property owner] and made with malice. With respect to the instant case, an injurious falsehood was made by the plaintiff, since they were not actually the owners of the property but claimed to the defendants' potential buyer that they were. Nevertheless, a qualified privilege precludes liability for this tort which may be raised by the plaintiffs absent actual malice. That is, if evidence of actual malice is proffered, the purported owner may forfeit use of the qualified privilege. In this case, however, the simple failure on the part of the plaintiffs to probe and confirm the true ownership of the land does not constitute actual malice on their part and thus does not cause them to forfeit the qualified privilege. Thus, we hold that the plaintiff did not abuse their conditional privilege.

Affirmed.

Testing Systems Inc. v. Magnaflux Corp.

U.S. District Court, Eastern Dist. of New York, 251 F.Supp 286 (1966)

FACTS

Plaintiff Testing Systems, Inc. and Defendant Magnaflux Corp. were competitors engaged in the manufacture of equipment, devices and systems to test industrial and commercial materials. Plaintiff claimed that defendant allegedly circulated a false report to plaintiff's customers which stated that the U.S. government had tested plaintiff's product and found it to be only 40% as effective as defendant's testing systems. Plaintiff's complaint also alleged that at a manufacturer's convention, defendant's agent stated to plaintiff's customers "in a loud voice" that plaintiff's devices were "no good" and that the "government is throwing them out." As a consequence, plaintiff sued for trade libel, and defendant moved to dismiss the action, on the ground that such unfavorable comparisons are protected from liability for injurious falsehood.

 Does an absolute privilege exist to protect a defendant-declarant from unfavorable comparisons of fact made by it regarding a plaintiff-competitor's product?

 A competitor is not absolutely privileged to make false assertions of fact which unfavorably compare its products to a competitor's product.

 A defendant-declarant [competitor] is not absolutely privileged to make false assertions of fact which unfavorably compare its products to a competitor's product. The general rule is that no liability will be imposed for statements which adversely compare a competitor's product to the product of the declarant. The motivation for this general rule is grounded in the importance of protecting a tradesman's right of free speech and the necessity of allowing the public to learn the relative merits of particular products, however disseminated. On the other hand, *false assertions of fact* made in an unfavorable comparison may be actionable. Here, if defendant indeed made a false factual statement by declaring that the U.S. government had found defendant's products to be 40% as effective as its own, then defendant will be held liable. By invoking the reputation of a 3rd party, the U.S. Government, the defendant gave added authenticity to its statements. Hence, it is the judgment of this court that the defendant's assertions are actionable.

 The claim should not be dismissed.

Lumley v. Gye

Queen's Bench, 118 Eng.Rep. 749 (1853)

FACTS

Plaintiff Lumley, the lessee and manager of the Queen's Theatre, hired performer Johanna Wagner for a number of exclusive performances. The contract provided that Wagner would not sing nor use her talents elsewhere with plaintiff's express permission during the term of the contract. Defendant Gye induced Wagner not to perform at Lumley's theater. He both knew about the terms of her contact with plaintiff and did so intending to cause harm to him.

Can liability be cast upon a 3rd party who induces another to breach an employment contract with his/her employer?

A 3rd party who induces another to breach an employment contract with his/her employer either wrongfully or maliciously will be held liable to the employee's ex-employer.

A 3rd party who induces another to breach an employment contract with his/her employer either wrongfully or maliciously will be held liable to the employee's ex-employer. When the party inducing the breach knew about the contract, or intended to do some harm to the non-breaching party malice is present. Here, it is no defense to liability that Wagner had not yet begun to sing at plaintiff's theater, because the law does not recognize a distinction between the wrong done in inducing a breach before an employee who has started to work, and the wrong done by inducing an employee to stop working after the performance has commenced.

Judgment for the plaintiff.

Bacon v. St. Paul Union Stockyards Co.

Supreme Court of Minnesota, 201 N.W. 326 (1924)

FACTS

Plaintiff Bacon, an employee of the Drover Livestock Commission Co., was engaged in the buying and selling livestock in Defendant St. Paul Union Stockyards Co.'s stockyards. Plaintiff sued for the tort of wrongful interference with contract alleging that defendant prevented him from carrying on his occupation by excluding him from the stockyards and by forbidding any person or corporation from dealing with him in or around the stockyards. Defendant demurred to the complaint, and the trial court sustained the demurrer. Plaintiff appealed.

Can a defendant be held liable for interfering with the plaintiff's employment contract with a 3rd party?

Liability will attach to the wrongful interference with a party's ability to carry out a contract with a 3rd party.

Liability will attach to the wrongful interference with a party's ability to carry out a contract with a 3rd party. It appears from the complaint that plaintiff had steady employment and that the defendant wrongfully, willfully, and unlawfully prevented him from continuing in that employment, causing him to breach his employment contract. We feel that such interference constitutes a violation of plaintiff's rights and embodies the tort of wrongful interference. While defendant may have had valid reasons for its actions, such reasons do not appear on the face of the complaint. Therefore, the granting of the defendant's demurrer must be reversed.

Granting of the defendant's demurrer must be reversed..

Della Penna v. Toyota Motor Sales U.S.A. Inc.

Supreme Court of California, 902 P.2d 740 1995)

FACTS

Plaintiff Della Penna, an automobile wholesaler doing business as Pacific Motors, was in the "resale" business of buying Lexus automobiles at near retail price and then exporting them to Japan for resale. Concerned that the re-export market for Lexus models would put at risk its newly developed network of Lexus dealerships in the American market, since both production and availability of the Lexus in America is limited, Defendant Toyota Motor Sales, U.S.A., Inc. inserted in its dealership agreements a "no export" clause which provided that the dealers were authorized to sell the Lexus only to customers in the United States, and not for resale or use outside the United States. Moreover, defendant compiled a list of "offenders" which included suspected dealers and others believed to be involved with the Lexus foreign resale market. It distributed this list to American Lexus dealers who were additionally warned that doing business with the "offenders" could lead to sanctions. Sanctions included the possible reduction of a dealer's allocation of stock and/or possible reassessment of the dealer's franchise agreement. The resulting policy caused plaintiff to loose business until eventually all his sources declined to sell any Lexus cars to him. As a consequence, plaintiff sued defendant alleging state antitrust claims and interference with his economic relationship with Lexus retail dealers, a tort action. The trial court granted defendant's motion to dismiss with respect to the antitrust claim, but the tort claim went to the jury. At the request of the defendant and over the objection of the plaintiff, the trial court modified the standard jury instructions to require that the defendant's interference be proven to have been "wrongful" by the plaintiff. The jury returned a verdict for defendant. The Court of Appeals reversed, holding that the modified jury instruction was erroneous, and ordered a new trial. The Supreme Court of California granted defendant's petition for review.

 Must a plaintiff who alleges an interference with economic relations by a defendant prove "wrongfulness" as an element of the prima facie case?

 In order to recover for an alleged interference with economic relations, a plaintiff must plead and prove, as part of its case-in-chief, that the defendant 1) knowingly interfered with the plaintiff's expectancy; *and* 2) engaged in conduct that was wrongful by some legal measure other than the fact of interference itself.

 In order to recover for an alleged interference with economic relations, a plaintiff must plead and prove, as part of its case-in-chief, that the defendant 1) knowingly interfered with the plaintiff's expectancy; *and* 2) engaged in conduct that was wrongful by some legal measure other than the fact of interference itself. In *Top Service Body Shop, Inc. v. Allstate Ins. Co.*, the Oregon Supreme Court held that a claim of interference with economic relations is made out when interference resulting in injury to another is wrongful by some measure beyond the interference itself. Over the past decade or so, close to a majority of the high courts of American jurisdictions have imported into the economic relations tort variations on the *Top Service* line of reasoning, explicitly approving a rule that requires the plaintiff in such a suit to plead and prove the alleged interference was either "wrongful," "improper,"

Della Penna v. Toyota Motor Sales U.S.A. Inc.

Supreme Court of California, 902 P.2d 740 1995)

"illegal," "independently tortious" or some variant on these formulations. In searching for a means to recast the elements of the economic relations tort and allocate the associated burdens of proof, we are guided by an overmastering concern articulated by high courts of other jurisdictions and legal commentators: the need to draw and enforce a sharpened distinction between claims for the tortious disruption of an existing contract and claims that a prospective contractual or economic relationship has been interfered with by the defendant. Thus, it is incumbent on us to firmly distinguish the two kinds of business contexts, bringing a greater attentiveness to those relationships that have ripened into agreements, while recognizing that relationships which have not exist in a zone where the rewards and risks of competition take precedence. Beyond that, we need not tread today. Thus, it is sufficient to dispose of the issue before us today by holding that a plaintiff seeking to recover for an alleged interference with economic relations has the burden of pleading and proving that the defendant's interference was wrongful by some legal measure beyond the fact of interference itself. It follows that the trial court did not err in modifying the jury charge to include the "wrongful conduct" definition and requirement. Hence, the judgment of the Court of Appeal is reversed and the cause is remanded with directions to affirm the judgment of the trail court.

Judgment of the Court of Appeal is reversed and the cause is remanded.

Adler, Barish, Daniels, Levin and Creskoff v. Epstein

Supreme Court of Pennsylvania, 393 A.2d 1175 (1978)

FACTS

Defendant-appellee Alan Epstein was an associate at Plaintiff-appellant-law firm Adler, Barish, Daniels, Levin and Creskoff. After defendant's employment relationship there terminated, he sought to lure away clients from plaintiff to his new law firm. Defendant called the clients, met them in person, and sent them form letters which the clients could use to discharge plaintiff as their counsel. All the clients had to do was sign this discharge form, and mail it back to defendant in a pre-addressed stamped envelope, which he provided. The Court of Common Pleas granted defendant relief by enjoining defendant's campaign to obtain plaintiff's clients, and a final decree was entered which enjoined defendants from communicating with plaintiff's clients which had active legal matters until a certain date. However, those clients were not prevented voluntarily discharging plaintiff as counsel. The Superior Court reversed, and the Supreme Court of Pennsylvania allowed an appeal.

 Can a state constitutionally impose the tort of interference with contractual relations on an attorney who encourages clients to move from his former law firm to his current law firm?

 A state can constitutionally impose the tort of interference with contractual relations on an defendant-attorney who encourages clients to move from his former law firm to his current law firm if he does anything more than notify the clients that he has formed [moved to] a new law practice.

 In *Virginia Pharmacy Board v. Virginia Consumer Council*, the Supreme Court held that speech which does no more than propose a commercial transaction is protected by the First and Fourteen Amendments. Thus, under *Virginia Pharmacy*, a state could not impose a blanket prohibition against truthful advertising of routine legal advertisements. After *Ohralik v. Ohio State Bar Association*, however, states were allowed to regulate the commercial transactions that attorneys engage in with clients via the tort of interference with contractual relations, for example. Thus, to determine whether an actor's conduct in intentionally interfering with an existing contract or prospective contractual relation of another was improper or not, we consider 1) the nature of the actor's conduct; 2) the actor's motive; 3) the interests of the other with which the actor's conduct interferes; 4) the interests sought to be advanced by the actor; 5) the social interests in protecting the freedom of action of the actor and the contractual interests of the others; 6) the proximity and remoteness of the actor's conduct to the interference; and 7) the relations between the parties. Here, defendant's intentional interference was improper because it violated recognized ethical codes of conduct for attorneys in this state with regard to the solicitation of prospective clients; it had the potential to unduly influence plaintiff's clients and impact active and ongoing cases by adversely affecting the informed and reliable decisionmaking ability of the clients with regard to those cases; it had an immediate impact on plaintiff's revenue as plaintiff's fee arrangements with clients were a source of income protected from outside interference; the circumstances surrounding defendant's departure unduly suggested a course of action [leave plaintiff] that unfairly prejudiced plaintiff; and because defendant took advantage of his access to plaintiff's private information [client lists], no public interest is served in

Adler, Barish, Daniels, Levin and Creskoff v. Epstein
Supreme Court of Pennsylvania, 393 A.2d 1175 (1978)

condoning the use of confidential information which has these effects.

 Judgment reversed.

Brimelow v. Casson

Chancery Division, 1 Ch. 302 (1923)

FACTS

Jack Arnold managed a traveling burlesque group known as the "King Wu Tut Tut Revue," but he paid the chorus girls very poorly. Because of their exceptionally low wages, the girls were very poor and were forced into prostitution. Appalled by this, one Lugg, who was secretary of the Actor's Association, on behalf of the girls, persuaded the owners of the theaters with which Arnold had contracts to cancel the contract and not to enter into future contracts until higher wages were paid to the female employees. It is presumed that Plaintiff Brimelow was a representative of the owners of the burlesque group and defendant Casson was a member of the Actor's Association.

 Can interference with contractual relations be actionable if it is done in the public interest?

 Interference with contractual relations is not improper if it is done in the public interest.

 We clearly acknowledge that an intentional interference with the current and future contractual relations was committed against the defendant's interest by the former. Accordingly, we today must decide whether this conduct was improper. We conclude that was not since a privilege existed – a duty owed to the girls and done in the public interest and for its benefit.

 Action dismissed.

Harmon v Harmon

Supreme Judicial Court of Maine, 404 A.2d 1020 (1979)

FACTS

Plaintiff Richard Harmon was to inherit some property from his mother, J.F. Harmon, upon her death. In an effort to get this property before she died and before plaintiff received it, Defendants H.C. Harmon and V.S. Harmon, plaintiff's brother and sister-in-law, employed fraud and undue influence to induce the mother, who was in ill health and old age, to transfer this property to them while she was still alive [inter vivos]. By her 1976 will and her more recent will and statements, the mother made it clear that she originally intended at least half of this property to go to plaintiff. The Superior Court dismissed the action upon defendants' motion on grounds that 1) the complaint failed to state a claim upon which relief could be granted; and 2) the plaintiff lacked standing to proceed against the defendants. Plaintiff appealed to the Supreme Judicial Court of Main from that order of dismissal.

Can one be held liable for interfering with another's possible inheritance by unduly influencing the testatrix to transfer property to a third person prior to her death?

One can be held liable for interfering with another's likely inheritance by unduly influencing the testatrix to transfer property to a third person prior to her death?

In *Cyr v. Cote,* we recognized that even a mere *expectancy* of an inheritance is something that the law will protect. In that case, we specifically addressed the issue of whether it is tortious to effectively disinherit legatee by inducing legatee to make inter vivos transfer. Thus, we will protect this expectancy interest even though it is possible that the testator might change her will even without any undue influence exerted by a third party. We find support for this position in the law of contracts, where the law protects *prospective* and *future* economic relations, in the writings of Prosser and in the Restatement. We therefore conclude that when a person interferes with a gift or transfer that would have likely been received by another, a tort has been committed for which redress may be sought. In this case, we go a step further than we did in *Cyr* and allow a plaintiff to proceed to enforce this liability, as a cause of action in tort, before the testatrix dies, as we have seen in a case involving a victim of a tortious interference with a contract of employment or where a life insurance policy has been permitted to proceed.

Judgment reversed.

Neibuhr v. Gage

Supreme Court of Minnesota, 108 N.W. 884 (1906)

FACTS

Plaintiff Neibuhr possessed 91 shares of stock in the corporation, Gage, Hayden & Co. having a face value of $9,100. Defendant Gage threatened that he would falsely tell the police that plaintiff was guilty of grand larceny unless plaintiff transferred his shares of the stock to defendant. Although plaintiff alleged that he was innocent of grand larceny, he claimed that defendant threatened to produce false testimony against him, thus insuring his arrest. Consequently, plaintiff transferred the shares of stock. Plaintiff brought this action for duress to recover damages he claimed he suffered by reason of being compelled while under duress to transfer his shares to the defendant. Plaintiff recovered a verdict of $8,478 in his favor; and the trial court denied the defendant's motion for j.n.o.v. [judgment notwithstanding the verdict, a/k/a reversal of the jury's verdict], but granted a new trial. Both parties appealed.

Is duress based on misrepresentation actionable as a tort cause of action?

Duress based on misrepresentation is actionable as a tort cause of action.

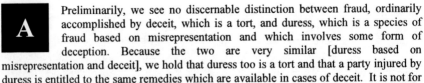

Preliminarily, we see no discernable distinction between fraud, ordinarily accomplished by deceit, which is a tort, and duress, which is a species of fraud based on misrepresentation and which involves some form of deception. Because the two are very similar [duress based on misrepresentation and deceit], we hold that duress too is a tort and that a party injured by duress is entitled to the same remedies which are available in cases of deceit. It is not for the defendant to determine the choice of remedy for the injured party. Here, defendant threatened to falsely tell the police that plaintiff was guilty of grand larceny. Under threat of immediate arrest, plaintiff transferred the shares of stock to the defendant. Thus, defendant committed the tort of duress based on misrepresentation.

Judgment reversed.

Freeman & Mills Inc. v. Belcher Oil Company

Supreme Court of California, 900 P.2d 669 (1995)

FACTS

Defendant Belcher Oil Company hired a law firm, Morgan, Lewis & Bockius (Morgan), to represent it in a lawsuit. Defendant's general counsel, William Dunker, signed a letter of understanding with a Morgan partner, Donald Smaltz, stating that defendant would pay all costs incurred on its behalf, including fees for accountants. Smaltz then hired Plaintiff Freeman & Mills to provide a financial analysis and litigation support for defendant in its lawsuit. About one month later, Dunker left defendant's employ and was replaced by Neil Bowman. The next month, Bowman became dissatisfied with Morgan's efforts and the law firm was discharged. Bowman asked Morgan for a summary of all work performed by plaintiff, and, at the same time, directed Smaltz to have plaintiff stop their work for defendant. This was done, and plaintiff's total bill amounted to $77.538.13. Payment was never made, so plaintiff then billed defendant directly. Defendant complained that it had not been consulted about the extent of plaintiff's services, and suggested that plaintiff look to Morgan for any payment due. Ultimately, plaintiff sued defendant, alleging breach of contract, "bad faith denial of contract," and quantum meruit. At trial, plaintiff was awarded $25,000 in compensatory damages, and $477,538.13 in punitive damages, and the judgment was entered accordingly. In three post-trial motions filed by the plaintiff, a "corrected" judgment of $131,614.93 in compensatory damages was entered instead of $25,000, and $400,000 in punitive damages [reduced from $477.538.13]. Defendant appealed from the "corrected" judgment and plaintiff cross-appealed. The Court of Appeals found there was no justification for a tort theory of recovery under *Seaman's Direct Buying Service, Inc. v. Standard Oil Co*, and as such reversed the judgment of the trial court and remanded the case for retrial limited to the issue of damages under plaintiff's breach of contract cause of action.

 Can a plaintiff recover damages when, in addition to breaching the contract, the defendant seeks to shield itself from liability by denying, in bad faith and without probable cause, that the contract exists?

 A plaintiff cannot recover damages when the defendant denies, in bad faith and without probable cause, that the contract exists because there is no tort cause of action based on a defendant's bad faith denial of the existence of a contract between the parties.

A We granted review in this case to resolve some of the widespread confusion that has arisen regarding the application of our opinion in *Seaman's Direct Buying Service, Inc. v. Standard Oil Co.* We held in that case that a tort cause of action might lie "when, in addition to breaching the contract, [defendant] seeks to shield itself from liability by denying, in bad faith and without probable cause, that the contract exists." *Seaman's* incorrectly recognized a tort cause of action based on the defendant's bad faith denial of the existence of a contract between the parties were none existed and, as such, should be overruled. We find justification for this decision today in many of the pertinent Court of Appeal decisions which recognize compelling policy reasons supporting the preclusion of tort remedies for contractual breaches outside the insurance context. These reasons, as set forth in *Harris v. Atlantic*

Freeman & Mills Inc. v. Belcher Oil Company

Supreme Court of California, 900 P.2d 669 (1995)

Richfield Co., include 1) the different objectives underlying the remedies for tort and contract breach, 2) the importance of predictability in assuring commercial stability in contractual dealings, 3) the potential for converting every contract breach into a tort, with accompanying punitive damage recovery, and 4) the preference for legislative action in affording appropriate remedies. The foregoing policy considerations fully support our decision to overrule *Seaman's* rather than attempt to clarify its uncertain boundaries. Moreover, it seems anomalous to characterize as "tortious" the bad faith denial of the existence of a contract, while treating as "contractual" the bad faith denial of liability or responsibility under an acknowledged contract. Were we to include bad faith denials of liability within *Seaman's* scope, every contract breach could potentially be converted into a tort. Thus, we overrule *Seaman's* and hold that the judgment of the Court of Appeal, reversing the trial court's judgment in plaintiff's favor and remanding the case for a retrial limited to the issue of damages under plaintiff's breach of contract cause of action, and for judgment in favor of defendant on plaintiff's bad faith denial of contract cause of action, is affirmed.

Affirmed.

Nash v. Baker

Court of Appeals of Oklahoma, 522 P.2d 1335 (1974)

FACTS

Plaintiff-appellant Marian Nash brings suit against Defendant-appellee Baker, a wealthy widow, for interference with and loss of paternal relations and for loss of affection, on her behalf and on behalf of her children, the minor-plaintiffs. Marian Nash was married to James Nash, and they had five children. Defendant-appellee, it was alleged, lured away James Nash with the promise of a finer home, sexual charms, and other inducements. The jury found for defendant on this action and dismissed the complaint for loss of paternal relations; plaintiff appealed.

 Does Oklahoma recognize the tort of intentional interference with paternal relations; and, if so, does a minor child have a common law right to sue a 3rd person whose luring away of his/her father breaks up the parents' marriage and deprives the child of his father's society and guidance?

 The claim of "intentional interference with paternal relations" is not considered a tort such that a minor does not have any right to sue a 3rd party for luring away of his/her father.

 At common law, spouses had a cause of action for loss of affection but their children did not have the right to sue for loss of *paternal* affections. As no such right exists today, we are not inclined to create one for the benefit of such children since the modern trend is towards divorce based "no fault" and that the fault leading up to the breakup of the marriage may not be so readily determinable in court, and that what caused the person to be "lured away" was not the emotional/economic magnetism of the 3rd party but rather the vacuum that existed in the home irrespective of the existence of that 3rd party. Therefore, plaintiffs have no cause of action against defendant.

 Judgment affirmed.

Burnette v. Wahl

Supreme Court of Oregon, 588 P.2d 1105 (1978)

FACTS

Three identical cases have been consolidated for appeal. Defendant Wahl failed to support, nurture and care for her five children, the minor plaintiffs, (hereinafter "Burnette"); left them unattended for long periods of time, and refused to financially support them children before finally abandoning them as they now are wards of the state. These acts caused emotional and psychological injury to the plaintiffs, although they suffered no physical harm.

Can a parent be held liable in tort for failing to support, nurture and care for her children?

In Oregon, liability does not attach to a parent *in tort* who fails to support, nurture and care for her children.

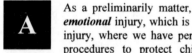

As a preliminarily matter, we note that the claim before us is based on *emotional* injury, which is unlike claims against a parent based on *physical* injury, where we have permitted recovery. Oregon statutes provide broad procedures to protect children, such as support actions and criminal sanctions; however, they do not establish a tort action for damages for emotional injury - and there is no such action at common law. Thus, in order for this action is to exist, if at all, we must create it. Before we tread into this area, however, we must confirm that such an act would not interfere with the total legislative scheme. Upon closer analysis, we feel that it would. In this case, it is possible that the creation of an action against parents for emotional injury due to neglect would conflict with the policy of reuniting abandoned children with their parents or with those policies encompassing as state actions whose goal it is to permanently divest parents of custody. Lastly, as a matter of social concern, the legislature is simply better equipped, institutionally speaking, to address this issue. Plaintiffs argue that we should create an action created here because defendant intentionally abandoned her children. As we have already said, were we to do so, it would obstruct with other policy goals of the legislature and additionally interfere in other areas that we do not allow recovery for. Children of divorced parents would almost always have an action for emotional injury against their divorced parents, for example. Plaintiffs next argue that the common law tort of alienation of affection is applicable because such a cause of action is intended to compensate one spouse for the intentional alienation of the other spouse's affection. The statement of the argument is its refutation - the tort is only available for one *spouse* against another. At any rate, this tort has been abolished by the Oregon Legislature. Consequently, the plaintiffs fail to state a cause of action.

Judgment affirmed.

Nearing v. Weaver
Supreme Court of Oregon, 670 P.2d 137 (1983)

FACTS

Plaintiff Henrietta Nearing was separated from her husband, Robert Nearing, Sr., in November 1979. On April 16, 1980, he entered plaintiff's home without permission and assaulted her. Plaintiff called the police and Defendant-Police Officer Martin Weaver responded with other police officers (defendants). The husband was arrested, charged with assault, and a restraining order was issued against him with a copy of the order and proof of service sent to the police department. On May 12 and 13, the husband twice again entered her home without permission, first damaging the promises, and thereafter attempting to remove the children. Plaintiff again called Officer Weaver (defendant), and asked him to arrest her husband for violating the restraining order. No arrest warrant was issued. The husband returned to plaintiff's home three more times that month and on the last occasion assaulted plaintiff's friend and damaged his van. Defendant told plaintiff that her husband would be arrested as this was "his second offense;" however, no action was ever taken. Two days later, he threatened to kill plaintiff's friend, and a few days after that he again assaulted plaintiff's friend outside his home. Plaintiff claimed that, as a result of the defendants' failure to enforce the restraining order, she and her children suffered severe emotional distress, physical injuries and psychological impairment. Defendants denied the allegations and pleaded the affirmative defenses of immunity and discretion. The circuit court granted summary judgment for the defendants, and the Court of Appeals affirmed. The case now comes before the Oregon Supreme Court.

 Can defendant-police officers who knowingly fail to enforce a judicial retraining order be held liable to a plaintiff-victim for the emotional and physical harm that results from that failure?

 Defendant-police officers who knowingly fail to enforce a judicial retraining order can be held liable to a plaintiff-victim, the intended beneficiary of the order, for the emotional and physical harm that results from that failure if there exists a legal right arising independently of the ordinary tort elements of a negligence action; if so, defendants are precluded from raising the affirmative defenses of official discretion and official immunity in relation thereto.

 Defendant first argues that the law does not allow recovery on the theory of negligent infliction of emotional distress. Yet the law does allow recovery when the defendant's conduct infringes some legal right of the plaintiff, ***independent*** of an ordinary tort claim for negligence and the duty defendant is alleged to have neglected was not simply an ordinary, common law duty of due care to avoid predictable harm to another, it is a specific duty imposed by statute for the benefit of individuals identified by a judicial order. Thus, a duty clearly existed on the part of defendant toward plaintiff. Defendant next contends that the police officers are immune from liability since they were engaged in a discretionary function or duty. However, discretion exists only insofar as an officer has been delegated responsibility for value judgments and policy choices among competing goals and priorities. No discretion of that kind in enforcing restraining orders exists here, as judicial decrees are not open to value judgments or interpretation by those charged with enforcing them. As such, the circuit court erred in denying plaintiff's motion to strike this defense. Defendant also claims

Nearing v. Weaver
Supreme Court of Oregon, 670 P.2d 137 (1983)

---

official immunity under the Oregon statutes. That section, however, provides immunity for making good faith arrests, not for failing to do so. To hold otherwise would undermine the legislative purpose of the statute, thus this affirmative defense raised by defendant should also have been stricken. This disposes of the issues actually raised by the parties; however, the dissent raises several issues which we must also address. First, the dissent asserts that we "overrule" two cases in which the court declined to find defendants liable for injury resulting from conduct contrary to statutes. Yet neither case was cited by defendant and neither case holds that statutory duties never give rise to civil liability unless the legislature makes that intention explicit in the text or accompanying explanations. That conclusion must be reached for different statutes on a case-by-case basis. Second, the dissent states that this decision creates "strict" liability. We have, however, made it clear that the liability is not absolute; there may be defenses. Next, the dissent asserts that the plaintiffs did not make a claim based on the statute. This is not entirely true since plaintiff's argument to the circuit did indeed cover both a common law and a statutory theory. Finally, the dissent simply opposes tort liability for injuries caused by disregard of the statute on policy grounds, because it may cost local governments money. To that there are two answers. The first, the same argument can be made against all claims under the Tort Claims Act, yet the act was nevertheless enacted. This is a claim under The Torts Claim Act; and the Act makes a public defendant liable in the same manner as the hard caused by a private defendant. That policy decision was made by the legislature; it is not a new policy choice to be made in this case. Second, there is no liability if the statute is actually followed. When compliance with the statute, unless prevented by good cause, will avoid exposure to liability, the argument that there should be no liability because of the potential expense actually is an argument for a privilege not to comply with the statute. But that policy choice, like the policy of the Tort Claims Act, also has been settled by the legislature. Here, there was a specific duty toward the plaintiff's, thus the decision of the court of Appeals affirming the summary judgment must be reversed and the case remanded to the circuit court for further proceedings.

 Reversed and remanded.

Bivens v. Six Unknown Named Agents of Federal Bureau of Narcotics

U.S. Supreme Court, 403 U.S. 388 (1971)

FACTS

Plaintiff-petitioner Bivens' complaint alleged that Defendant-respondents, agents of the Federal Bureau of Narcotics acting under color of federal authority, made a warrantless entry of his apartment, searched the apartment, and arrested him on narcotics charges. All of the acts were alleged to have been done without probable cause. Petitioner's suit to recover damages from the agents was dismissed by the District Court on the alternative grounds (1) that it failed to state a federal cause of action and (2) that respondents were immune from suit by virtue of their official position. The Court of Appeals affirmed on the first ground alone. The U.S. Supreme Court granted certiorari.

 Does a federal cause of action exist under the Fourth Amendment for which damages are recoverable upon proof of injuries resulting from federal agents' violation of that Amendment?

 A federal cause of action does exist under the Fourth Amendment for which damages are recoverable upon proof of injuries resulting from federal agents' violation of that Amendment.

 Plaintiff-petitioner's complaint states a federal cause of action under the Fourth Amendment for which damages are recoverable upon proof of injuries resulting from the federal agents' violation of that Amendment. The Fourth Amendment provides that: "The right of the people to be secure in their persons, houses, papers, and effects, against unreasonable searches and seizures, shall not be violated . . . ." In *Bell v. Hood*, we reserved the question whether violation of that command by a federal agent acting under color of his authority gives rise to a cause of action for damages consequent upon his unconstitutional conduct. Today we hold that it does. Respondents do not argue that petitioner should be entirely without remedy. In respondents' view, however, the rights that petitioner asserts - primarily rights of privacy - are creations of state and not of federal law. Accordingly, they argue, petitioner may obtain money damages to redress invasion of these rights only by an action in tort, under state law, in state court. We reject this argument because the common law state actions applicable here were created to protect one private citizen from another, and do not effectively deal with the unique problem of a government official searching the home of a private citizen in violation of the Fourth Amendment. An agent acting in the name of the United States possesses a far greater capacity for harm than an individual trespasser exercising no authority other than his own. A homeowner may feel compelled to consent even though he doesn't want to, because the officer appears to have authority. Here, plaintiff-petitioner has alleged that the defendant-respondents searched his home in violation of the Fourth Amendment. This is sufficient to survive a demurrer.

 Judgment reversed.

Alexander v. Sandoval

U.S. Supreme Court, 532 U.S. 275 (2001)

FACTS

As a recipient of federal financial assistance, the Alabama Department of Public Safety (Department), of which petitioner Alexander is the Director, is subject to Title VI of the Civil Rights Act of 1964. Section 601 of that Title prohibits discrimination based on race, color, or national origin in covered programs and activities. Section 602 authorizes federal agencies to effectuate §601 by issuing regulations, and the Department of Justice (DOJ) in an exercise of this authority promulgated a regulation forbidding funding recipients to utilize criteria or administrative methods having the effect of subjecting individuals to discrimination based on the prohibited grounds. Respondent Sandoval brought this class action to enjoin the Department's decision to administer state driver's license examinations only in English, arguing that it violated the DOJ regulation because it had the effect of subjecting non-English speakers to discrimination based on their national origin. Agreeing, the District Court enjoined the policy and ordered the Department to accommodate non-English speakers. The Eleventh Circuit affirmed. Both courts rejected petitioners' argument that Title VI did not provide respondents a cause of action to enforce the regulation. The U.S. Supreme Court granted certiorari.

Can private individuals sue to enforce disparate-impact regulations promulgated under Title IV of the Civil Rights Act of 1964?

There is no private right of action to enforce disparate-impact regulations promulgated under Title VI.

There is no private right of action to enforce disparate-impact regulations promulgated under Title VI. Three aspects of Title VI must be taken as given. First, private individuals may sue to enforce §601. Second, §601 prohibits only intentional discrimination. Third, it must be assumed for purposes of deciding this case that regulations promulgated under §602 may validly proscribe activities that have a disparate impact on racial groups, even though such activities are permissible under §601. This Court has not, however, held that Title VI disparate-impact regulations may be enforced through a private right of action. *Cannon* was decided on the assumption that the respondent there had intentionally discriminated against the petitioner. In *Guardians Assn. v. Civil Service Commission of New York City,* we held that private individuals could not recover compensatory damages under Title VI except for intentional discrimination. Of the five Justices who also voted to uphold disparate-impact regulations, three expressly reserved the question of a direct private right of action to enforce them. Nor does it follow from the three points taken as given that Congress must have intended such a private right of action. There is no doubt that regulations applying §601's ban on intentional discrimination are covered by the cause of action to enforce that section. But the disparate-impact regulations do not simply apply §601 - since they forbid conduct that §601 permits - and thus the private right of action to enforce §601 does not include a private right to enforce these regulations. That right must come, if at all, from the independent force of §602. Like substantive federal law itself,

---

private rights of action to enforce federal law must be created by Congress. This Court will not revert to the understanding of private causes of action, represented by *J. I. Case Co. v. Borak,* that held sway when Title VI was enacted. That understanding was abandoned in *Cort v. Ash.* Nor does the Court agree with the Government's contention that cases interpreting statutes enacted prior to *Cort v. Ash* have given dispositive weight to the expectations that the enacting Congress had formed in light of the contemporary legal context. The search for Congress's intent in this case begins and ends with Title VI's text and structure. The "rights-creating" language so critical to *Cannon*'s §601 analysis is completely absent from §602. Whereas §601 decrees that "[n]o person ... shall ... be subjected to discrimination," §602 limits federal agencies to "effectuat[ing]" rights created by §601. And §602 focuses neither on the individuals protected nor even on the funding recipients being regulated, but on the regulating agencies. Hence, there is far less reason to infer a private remedy in favor of individual persons. The methods §602 expressly provides for enforcing its regulations, which place elaborate restrictions on agency enforcement, also suggest a congressional intent not to create a private remedy through §602. We reject arguments that the regulations at issue contain rights-creating language and so must be privately enforceable; that amendments to Title VI in §1003 of the Rehabilitation Act Amendments of 1986 and §6 of the Civil Rights Restoration Act of 1987 "ratified" decisions finding an implied private right of action to enforce the regulations; and that the congressional intent to create a right of action must be inferred.

Reversed.

De Falso v. Bernas

U.S. Court of Appeals, 244 F.3d 286 (2nd Cir. 2001)

FACTS

Plaintiffs bought and proposed to develop land in the Township of Delaware, Sullivan County, New York. Named defendants were an assortment of public officials and private individuals who were apart of, or influenced, the local government of the Township. After plaintiffs purchased the property, the defendants, including Defendant William Dirie, a supervisor of the Town of Delaware and firewood salesman, engaged in a number of threats and intimidation to force plaintiffs to give over the property and employ individuals under threat that development approvals would be withheld. Plaintiffs brought an action under 18 U.S.C. 1962(c) of the Racketeer Influence and Corrupt Organizations Act (RICO) claiming that plaintiffs' real estate activities were impeded as a result of defendants' operation of the Town of Delaware, as a RICO enterprise. Plaintiffs claimed that the action arose out of a conspiracy, plan or scheme among the defendants to use the Township as a racketeering enterprise to extort money, real property and personal property through the misuse of certain public offices. A jury awarded the plaintiffs a verdict of $1.6 million. The District Court vacated the award and the defendants appealed to the Court of Appeals, 2nd Circuit.

 Where a group's real estate activities to develop land in a Township have been impeded by public and private individuals who were apart of, or influenced, the local government of the Township by threats of intimidation, may the RICO Act be used to exact liability on the offending group?

 In order to establish a violation of 18 U.S.C. 1962(c), a plaintiff must show 1) conduct 2) of an enterprise 3) through a pattern 4) of racketeering activity, and that sufficient proximate causation exists between the defendants' acts and the injury sustained by the plaintiffs.

 Where a group's real estate activities to develop land in a Township have been impeded by public and private individuals who were apart of, or influenced, the local government of the Township by threats of intimidation, the RICO Act be used to exact liability on the offending group providing that all the RICO elements are met and sufficient proximate causation exists between the defendants' acts and the injury sustained by the plaintiffs. We hold that this latter requirement, that of proximate causation, has not been met in the instant case. In order to establish a violation of 18 U.S.C. 1962(c), a plaintiff must show 1) conduct 2) of an enterprise 3) through a pattern 4) of racketeering activity, where the term "enterprise" is defined in the statute as including any individual, partnership, corporation, association, or other legal entity, and any group or union of individuals associated in fact though not a legal entity; and the term "racketeering activity" is defined broadly to encompass a variety of state and federal offenses including, *inter alia*, murder, kidnapping, gambling, arson, bribery, bribery, and extortion. In this case, we address each of the RICO elements in turn. **The "enterprise" element:** In *United States v. Angelilli,* the Court concluded that "on its face the definition of an enterprise to include *any* legal entity," that the wording is ***unambiguously broad.*** The *Angelilli* analysis applies with equal force in this case. Throughout this action, the only enterprise alleged by the plaintiffs was the Town of Delaware, and the jury specifically found it to be a RICO enterprise. We agree. **The "conduct" element:** The jury specifically found that the named defendants each "conducted or participated in the conduct of the affairs of the Town of Delaware through a pattern of racketeering activity," and the record here contains ample evidence from with a reasonable jury could have found that defendants each had a part in directing the Town's affairs. **The Predicate acts, i.e., the "pattern" of "racketeering activity":** Defendants argue that plaintiffs failed to establish a pattern of racketeering activity since RICO defines a patter as "at least two acts of racketeering activity." There is sufficient evidence from which a reasonable jury could conclude that the escalating nature of the defendants' demands – such as their demanding an increasing interest in the gravel pit – indicated that they had no intention of stopping once they met some immediate goal. Based on this evidence, the jury could reasonably conclude that the defendants would have continued to extort the plaintiffs in the future. **Proximate causation:** To prove proximate causation, the plaintiff would have had to offer evidence that they were otherwise entitled to approval of Phase II construction and that no independent, intervening factors affected their ability to sell the lots. This they failed to do. The causal link between the plaintiffs' evidence and the inability to sell the Phase II lots is too weak to satisfy the proximate causation requirement. Hence, the District Court was correct in vacating the $1.6 million award. We vacate the $1,000 award against Defendant Dirie for the truck wheels and tires extorted for the benefit of his son but affirm the judgments of the District Court in all other respects.

Affirmed in part.

Pulliam v. Coastal Emergency Svcs.

Supreme Court of Virginia, 509 S.E.2d 307 (1999)

FACTS

In the early morning hours of December 15, 1995, Mrs. Pullman arrived at the emergency room of Southside Hospital complaining that her legs were "aching." She was examined and prescribed a muscle relaxant and sent home. She returned to the emergency room later that morning complaining of general weakness, particularly in her lower extremities. She was started on intravenous fluid and subjected to a CT scan and lumbar puncture. Thereafter her condition worsened and she was transferred to the ICU. By that night, she was pronounced dead. A medical malpractice action was brought against the doctor who treated her, for whom Defendant Coastal Emergency Services was vicariously liable, by her plaintiffs, her husband [the executor of her estate] and son. The jury returned a verdict of $2,045,000. Pursuant to Virginia Statute, Code §8.01-581.15, the trial judge reduced the verdict to one million dollars. This appeal followed.

Is the medical malpractice cap, embodied by Virginia Statute Code §8.01-581.15, constitutional?

The medical malpractice cap embodied by Virginia Statute Code §8.01-581.15 does not violate any constitutional guarantees.

In *Etheridge v. Medical Center Hospitals*, we rejected challenges to the constitutionality of the medical malpractice cap based upon contentions the cap "violates the Virginia Constitution's due process guarantee, jury trial guarantee, separation of powers doctrine, prohibitions against special legislation, and equal protection guarantee, as well as certain parallel provisions of the Federal Constitution." It is clear that we cannot grant the plaintiff relief without overruling *Etheridge,* therefore, the doctrine of stare decisis ["a thing already decided"] is implicated. In Virginia, the doctrine is more than a mere cliché, it plays a significant role in the orderly administration of justice by assuring consistent, predictable and balanced application of legal principles. In the absence of flagrant error or mistake, we will not disturb precedent. In this case, we find none of plaintiff's arguments persuasive. Plaintiff relies on two cases, *Hertzel v. Prince William City* and *Feltner v. Columbia Pictures Television*, to support his conclusion that the cap violates the right to a jury trial. Plaintiff first attempts to equate remittitur with the medical malpractice cap. They are not the same. Remittitur is used only after a court has determined a party has not received a fair and proper jury trial; the cap is applied only after a plaintiff has had the benefit of a proper jury trial. In the latter situation, there is no right to a new trial. Plaintiff next argues that the cap is a taking under the 5th Amendment of the Constitution of the United States. We disagree. It is only when a right has accrued or a claim has arisen that it is subject to the protection of the due process clause. The plaintiff's cause of action for wrongful death has not accrued at the time the cap was imposed upon recoveries in medical malpractice cases. Thus, one cannot obtain a property interest in a cause of action that has not accrued, and there is nothing to prevent the General Assembly from limiting the remedy, so far as unaccrued causes of action are concerned. Accordingly, no

Pulliam v. Coastal Emergency Svcs.

Supreme Court of Virginia, 509 S.E.2d 307 (1999)

violation of the "taking" clauses has occurred here. There is also no violation of the Equal Protection since the *Etheridge* court enunciated the correct level of scrutiny and that the rational basis test continues to provide the proper standard for determining whether there has been a denial of due process or equal protection in a case such as this. Lastly, plaintiff argues that the cap violates the separation of powers doctrine and invades the province of the judiciary. We again disagree. Under Art. VI , §14 of the Virginia Constitution, the General Assembly's authority extends "to all subjects of legislation not herein restricted or forbidden," and that the common law is one are where its authority has not been restricted. Accordingly, the legislature has the power to provide, modify, or repeal a remedy. We there reaffirm *Etheridge* today and hold that the medical malpractice cap embodied by Virginia Statute Code §8.01-581.15 does not violate any constitutional guarantees.

Affirmed.

Blankenship v. Cincinnati Milacron Chemicals Inc.

Supreme Court of Ohio, 433 N.E.2d 572 (1982)

FACTS

Plaintiff Blankenship, along with several other employees, was injured when exposed to chemicals while working at Defendant Cincinnati Milacron Chemicals facility, alleging that the fumes of certain chemicals rendered them sick, poisoned and permanently disabled. Plaintiff and the other employees alleged that defendant knew the conditions existed, knew the conditions caused injury, failed to warn the employees, failed provide medical examinations as required by law, and failed to notify the appropriate state and federal agencies, also required by law. As a consequence, plaintiff and the others brought suit alleging that defendant's omissions were intentional, willful and malicious and that they were due compensation for the injury they sustained as a result. The trial court dismissed the action on grounds that the action was barred by relevant sections of the Ohio constitution, including Section 35, Article II, and Ohio's Workers' Compensation Act.

 Under Ohio law, can an employee maintain an action at law against his employer for an intentional tort?

 Under Ohio law, an employee may maintain an action at law against his employer for an intentional tort.

 The primary focus of the dispute between the parties centers upon the question of whether the Workers' Compensation Act is intended to cover an intentional tort committed by employers against their employees. We hold that it does not. The Ohio legislature has authority to provide for a system of workers' compensation pursuant to the powers granted to it by Ohio's Constitution. The scheme of workers' compensation compels employers to contribute to a collective fund which is used to pay for injuries sustained by their employees while on the job. In return for their contributions into this pool, employers are protected from any employee suit for an injury arising out of the employee's employment. However, employers are not immune from suit in cases involving *intentional* torts because such [intentional] torts are not considered to "arise out" of employment. Moreover, if we bar suit for an intentional tort, as an employer could commit an intentional tort with impunity with the knowledge that, at the very most, his workers' compensation premiums may rise slightly, which in turn will make the workplace less safe, thus undermining the policy goals behind the system. Here, plaintiff and the employees have made allegations of an intentional tort. They should be allowed to prove these allegations.

 Judgment reversed.

Mclaren Legal Publishers LLC

For a full catalog of our books,
please visit our website
www.mclarenpublishing.com